LOVE,

and gender

in the world religions

THE LIBRARY OF GLOBAL ETHICS AND RELIGION

General Editors: Joseph Runzo and Nancy M. Martin

Volume I, *The Meaning of Life in the World Religions*, ISBN 1–85168–200–7
Volume II, *Love, Sex, and Gender in the World Religions*, ISBN 1–85168–223–6
Volume III, *Ethics in the World Religions*, ISBN 1–85168–247–3

RELATED TITLES PUBLISHED BY ONEWORLD

Avatar and Incarnation, Geoffrey Parrinder, ISBN 1–85168–130–2
Believing – An Historical Perspective, Wilfred Cantwell Smith, ISBN 1–85168–166–3
Celebrate, Margo Westrheim, ISBN 1–85168–199–X
Concepts of God, Keith Ward, ISBN 1–85168–064–0
Faith and Belief: The Difference Between Them, Wilfred Cantwell Smith,
    ISBN 1–85168–165–5
The Fifth Dimension, John Hick, ISBN 1–85168–191–3
God and the Universe of Faiths, John Hick, ISBN 1–85168–071–3
God, Chance and Necessity, Keith Ward, ISBN 1–85168–116–7
God, Faith and the New Millennium, Keith Ward, ISBN 1–85168–155–8
In Defence of the Soul, Keith Ward, ISBN 1–85168–040–3
Jesus and the Muslim, Kenneth Cragg, ISBN 1–85168–180–9
Life After Death, Farnáz Ma'sumián, ISBN 1–85168–074–8
Muhammad and the Christian, Kenneth Cragg, ISBN 1–85168–179–5
Muslims and Christians Face to Face, Kate Zebiri, ISBN 1–85168–133–7
Patterns of Faith Around the World, Wilfred Cantwell Smith, ISBN 1–85168–164–7
The Phenomenon of Religion, Moojan Momen, ISBN 1–85168–161–2
Religious Truth for our Time, William Montgomery Watt, ISBN 1–85168–102–7
The Sense of God, John Bowker, ISBN 1–85168–093–4
Sexual Morality in the World's Religions, Geoffrey Parrinder, ISBN 1–85168–108–6
Ultimate Visions, edited by Martin Forward, ISBN 1–85168–100–0
The Universe Within, Anjam Kursheed, ISBN 1–85168–075–6
A Wider Vision, Marcus Braybrooke, ISBN 1–85168–119–1

LOVE, SEX

and gender

in the world religions

EDITED BY

Joseph Runzo and Nancy M. Martin

Volume II
in
The Library of Global Ethics and Religion
General Editors: Joseph Runzo and Nancy M. Martin

ONEWORLD

OXFORD

LOVE, SEX AND GENDER IN THE WORLD RELIGIONS

Oneworld Publications
(Sales and Editorial)
185 Banbury Road
Oxford OX2 7AR
England
http://www.oneworld-publications.com

Oneworld Publications
(US Marketing Office)
160 N. Washington St.
4th floor, Boston
MA 02114
USA

© Joseph Runzo and Nancy M. Martin 2000

ISBN 1–85168–223–6

Cover design by Design Deluxe
Typeset by Saxon Graphics, Derby, UK
Printed and bound in England by Clays Ltd, St Ives plc

This volume is dedicated to

JULIUS LIPNER AND ARVIND SHARMA

Friends and Fellow Bhaktas

Just before dawn, lover and beloved awake ...
She asks, "Do you love me or yourself more?
Really, tell the absolute truth."
He says, "There's nothing left of *me*.
I'm like a ruby held up to the sunrise.
Is it still a stone, or a world
made of redness? It has no resistance
to sunlight."
This is how Hallaj said, *I am God*,
and told the truth!

Rumi (1207–1273)[†]

[†]Trans. Coleman Barks, *The Essential Rumi* (San Francisco: HarperSanFrancisco, 1995), pp. 100–101.

CONTENTS

ILLUSTRATIONS

Photographs: Joseph Runzo, Nancy M. Martin, Ann D. Martin, and Chantal Regnault

CONTRIBUTORS

CLARE B. FISCHER is Aurelia Henry Reinhardt Professor of Religion and Culture at Starr King School within the Graduate Theological Union. She is a leading feminist theological scholar and recognized authority on Simone Weil, with research interests in ethics, sociology of religion, feminist theory, comparative myth, and ritual (including fieldwork in Indonesia). Among her published works are *Breaking Through: Bibliography of Women and Religion* and *Of Spirituality: A Feminist Perspective*.

CHARLOTTE FONROBERT is an Assistant Professor of Talmud at the University of Judaism in Los Angeles. Her research focuses on feminist interpretations of Rabbinic texts and the relationship between the religious cultures of Rabbinic Judaism and early Christianity, especially concerning gender issues. She has just completed a book entitled *Menstruation and the Construction of Gender in Talmudic Culture*, with Stanford University Press.

JOHN STRATTON HAWLEY is Professor of Religion at Barnard College, Columbia University. A renowned scholar of Hinduism, he has published ten books, including four on Krishna and the devotional culture of North India, and six edited volumes on a wide range of comparative and indologic subjects, including *Devi: Goddesses of India; Sati, The Blessing and the Curse*; and *Fundamentalism and Gender*. He is currently completing work on the translation of a critical edition of the poetry of Surdas.

CARTER HEYWARD is Howard Chandler Robbins Professor of Theology at Episcopal Divinity School, an ordained Episcopal priest, and a leading feminist theologian. Among her ten books are *Our Passion for Justice: Images of Power, Sexuality, and Liberation*; *Staying Power: Reflections on Gender, Justice, and Compassion*; and *Touching our Strength: The Erotic as Power and the Love of God*. Her current research focuses on christology; the connections and tensions of gender/sex, race, and power; and racism as a theological problem.

P. JEFFREY HOPKINS is Professor of Indo-Tibetan Buddhist Studies at the University of Virginia. Acknowledged as one of the foremost experts on Tibetan Buddhism, his extensive list of publications includes the editing and translation of numerous Tibetan texts as well as writings of the Fourteenth Dalai Lama. His research focuses on Buddhist philosophy, tantric doctrines and practices, oral traditions of Tibetan philosophy and practice, and Tibetan language. Among his books are *The Tantric Distinction: A Buddhist's Reflection on Compassion and Emptiness* and *Sex, Orgasm, and the Mind of Clear Light*.

ZAYN KASSAM is Assistant Professor of Religion at Pomona College. She is an historian of religion with expertise in Islam and Hinduism and secondary specializations in Buddhism and Judaism. Her primary areas of research include gender issues, especially related to women in Islam, and comparative philosophy and mysticism. She is currently working on a book on divine-human configurations in Hinduism and Islam.

WILLIAM R. LaFLEUR is E. Dale Saunders Professor in Japanese Studies and Professor of Religious Studies at the University of Pennsylvania. He has published eight books on Buddhism and Japanese culture including *The Karma of Words: Buddhism & the Literary Arts in Medieval Japan*; *Liquid Life: Abortion and Buddhism in Japan*; and *Freaks and Philosophers: Minding the Body in Medieval Japan*. He is now completing a book on Japanese attitudes toward organ transplantation.

KAREN LEBACQZ is Robert Gordon Sproul Professor of Theological Ethics at Pacific School of Religion within the Graduate Theological Union. A foremost religious ethicist, she has written extensively on professional ethics, theories of justice, and bioethics. Her seven books include *Sex in the Parish*; *Justice in an Unjust World*; *Six Theories of Justice*; *Professional Ethics: Power and Paradox*; and *Word, Worship, World and Wonder: Reflections on Christian Living*.

JULIUS LIPNER is a distinguished member of the faculty of Divinity at Cambridge University and was the first director of the Dharam Hinduja

Institute of Indic Research. Working in the field of the comparative study of religion, he has special interests in Buddhist, Hindu and Christian traditions. Among his books are *The Face of Truth* (on Ramanuja); *Hindu Ethics: Purity, Abortion and Euthanasia;* and *Hindus: Their Religious Beliefs and Practices.* He is currently working on a book on God and love.

ELIZABETH McALISTER is Assistant Professor of Religion at Wesleyan University. With expertise in religion in America and African religious traditions, she has published numerous articles on Haitian Vodou, both in its original Haitian context and as it has been transformed in its movement to the United States. An authority on the role of music in Vodou rituals, she has also produced a number of compact discs on Haitian sacred music.

VIVIAN-LEE NYITRAY is Associate Professor of Religious Studies at the University of California, Riverside. She is the author of *Mirror of Virtue,* a study of four Han dynasty biographies, and co-editor of *The Life of Chinese Religion.* Her current research focuses on the confrontation between Confucianism and feminist discourse.

ARVIND SHARMA is a renowned scholar of Hinduism and of issues concerning women and religion. Having taught at the University of Queensland and the University of Sydney in Australia, he is now the Birks Professor of Comparative Religion at McGill University in Canada. Among the more than thirty books he has published are *Our Religions; Women in World Religions; Religion and Women; Today's Women in World Religions;* and *Feminism and World Religions,* and he is the co-editor of *The Annual Review of Women in the World Religions.*

KAREN JO TORJESEN is Margo L. Goldsmith Professor of Women's Studies in Religion, co-director of the Institute for Antiquity and Christianity and director of the Women's Studies of Religion program at Claremont Graduate University. As an authority on women and religion, her research interests include constructions of gender and sexuality in early Christianity, authority and institutionalization in the early churches, and the comparative study of Greek and Latin patristic traditions. Her most recent book is entitled *When Women Were Priests: Women's Leadership in the Early Church and the Scandal of their Subordination in the Rise of Christianity.*

The Editors

NANCY M. MARTIN received her M.A. from the University of Chicago Divinity School and her Ph.D. from the Graduate Theological Union, Berkeley. An Assistant Professor of Religious Studies at Chapman University, she is an historian of religion with expertise in Asian religions, gender issues, and comparative mysticism. Involved in extensive fieldwork in Rajasthan, her research focuses on devotional Hinduism, women's religious lives, and the religious traditions of low-caste groups in India. She is the recipient of a Graves Award for the Humanities. She is co-editor of *The Meaning of Life in the World Religions* and is currently completing a book on the sixteenth-century saint Mirabai, entitled *Mirabai Manifest: The Many Faces of a Woman Poet-Saint in India.*

JOSEPH RUNZO received his M.A. and Ph.D. in philosophy from the University of Michigan and M.T.S. in philosophical theology from Harvard Divinity School. He is Professor of Philosophy and Religious Studies at Chapman University and Life Fellow at Clare Hall, Cambridge University. He is the recipient of five National Endowment for the Humanities Fellowships and Awards. Working in the fields of philosophy of religion, epistemology, and ethics, he has published six books: *Reason, Relativism, and God; Religious Experience and Religious Belief; Is God Real?; Ethics, Religion and the Good Society; World Views and Perceiving God;* and (co-editor with Nancy M. Martin) *The Meaning of Life in the World Religions.* He has just completed *Global Philosophy of Religion: A Short Introduction* and is currently working on a book entitled *Religion, Sex and Love: Reflections of the Divine.*

ACKNOWLEDGMENTS

This volume is the second in a series offering a pluralistic and global perspective on questions of religion and ethics. The editors wish to thank Novin Doostdar and Juliet Mabey of Oneworld for their invaluable support for The Library of Global Ethics and Religion. We also wish to thank Helen Coward, Victoria Warner, and Rebecca Clare for their superb and tenacious editorial work on the manuscript. The present volume has benefitted from the pluralistic vision of the importance of issues of gender and love in the world religions of Arvind Sharma and Julius Lipner, to whom the volume is dedicated, as well as from the work of all the contributors to this volume who share this vision. The groundwork for this volume was begun at a conference held at Chapman University in 1998 which was made possible by the Huntington and Griset Lectureship funds. We wish to acknowledge all those who participated in those initial conversations, including not only a number of contributors to this volume but also Linda Hess, Mark Juergensmeyer, Christopher Key Chapple, Cynthia Humes, Frances Adeney, Jennifer Rycenga, Daniel Campana, Kathryn Poethig, Miranda Shaw, Kevin O'Brien, Marvin Meyer, June O'Conner, Matthew Schneider, Elizabeth Say, Jody Myers, Nayereh Tohidi, Craig Ihara, Dale Wright, Phyllis Herman, and Rita DasGupta Sherma.

We are grateful to Dr. Russell Martin and Ann D. Martin for their generosity and support of this project, and also to our friend Yukihiro Aizawa. We would also like to thank a number of our students: Joie Karnes, Jason Bricker, Kass Holmstrom, and especially Beverly Worden, for the help with the conference that first brought a number of the contributors together. We owe a special debt of gratitude to Jessie Stevens whose dedication, hard work, and good cheer made the completion of this manuscript an especially enjoyable experience.

Finally, this book benefitted from the co-operative efforts of the Global Ethics and Religion Forum, a new society of scholars in Europe, Canada, India, and the United States, dedicated to promoting a wider understanding both of religious pluralism and of ethical issues among the world religions in a global context. We wish to thank our friends in the Forum, some of whom have essays in the present volume, for their steadfast support.

INTRODUCTION

Two forces which gathered strength in the last half of the twentieth century now dominate the world religions at the beginning of the twenty-first century. The first is the globalization of religions and their resulting encounter with each other, and the second is the need to redefine attitudes toward gender as women have stepped forward to insist that their full humanity be acknowledged in the religious as well as the social realm.

In a process begun in the nineteenth century and accelerated in the twentieth, the great religions of the world became truly global in the geographic distribution of their adherents and so began to impact and influence each other's adherents in new ways. From Asia, Buddhism and Hinduism began seriously to influence the West for the first time in the twentieth century, in part spurred by the first meeting of the Parliament of the World Religions in Chicago in 1893. And while the proselytizing traditions of Christianity and Islam had already become prominent as they spread globally from their inception, after the 1940s the Holocaust and the eventual establishment of a Jewish state brought new worldwide attention and increased global acceptance of Judaism. Many of these great religions had come in contact before this time and even grown up side by side, but a truly global presence of each and the accompanying growth of understanding leading to a deeper appreciation of alternate traditions is a twentieth-century phenomenon.

Among the official decrees of Vatican II, the watershed Roman Catholic Council of 1963–65, was *Nostra Aetate*, the Dogmatic Constitution on "The Relationship of the Church to Non-Christian Religions." In *Nostre Aetate* the world's largest organized religious tradition, which has one billion adherents today and represents fully half of world Christendom, declared that "all peoples comprise a single community" and that

> From ancient times down to the present, there has existed among diverse peoples a certain perception of that hidden power which hovers over the course of things and over the events of human life ... such a perception and such a recognition instill the lives of these peoples with a profound religious sense. Religions bound up with cultural advancement have struggled to reply to these same questions with more refined concepts and in more highly developed language.
>
> Thus in Hinduism men contemplate the divine mystery and express it through an unspent fruitfulness of myths and through searching philosophical inquiry. They seek release from the anguish of our condition through ascetical practices or deep meditation or a loving, trusting flight toward God.
>
> Buddhism in its multiple forms acknowledges the radical insufficiency of this shifting world. It teaches a path by which men, in a devout and confident spirit, can either reach a state of absolute freedom or obtain supreme enlightenment by their own efforts or by higher assistance.
>
> Likewise, other religions to be found everywhere [the footnote in the text indicates that this is meant to apply in part to African traditions] strive variously to answer the restless searchings of the human heart by proposing "ways," which consist of teachings, rules of life, and sacred ceremonies.
>
> The Catholic Church rejects nothing which is true and holy in these religions.[1]

Nostre Aetate goes on to address Islam – "Upon the Moslems, too, the Church looks with esteem" – and Judaism and "the spiritual bond linking the people of the New Covenant with Abraham's stock," in later sections.

Moving into the latter third of the century, the World Council of Churches extended the inclusive and/or pluralistic tendencies of Christendom. Islam became a rapidly growing presence in the United States and other developed nations. Shinto/Buddhist Japan became an economic superpower and – just as happened with the Islamic states of the Oil Cartel – this brought their religion to the world stage. The plight of Tibetan Buddhism and the flight of the Fourteenth Dalai Lama to India and then the West were well publicized. The Anglican Bishop Desmond Tutu was internationally prominent in the struggle against apartheid in South Africa, even as the Hindu Mahatma Gandhi had been at the beginning of the century in South Africa and then in the Indian independence struggle, and so on. World religions became part of the social-political-economic global fabric in a way that now has made it increasingly hard to practice religion in isolation from global concerns, and even intellectually dishonest to do so without some global perspective and without taking other religious traditions into account.

The second great force at the turn of the century is itself global: the emergence of women in the public sphere, including the public face of religion. This is in part a function of women's growing economic and political power, but also a result of religion itself coming into the public sphere in new ways. Many aspects of religion have long been considered private and relegated largely to the context of home and family, where women have often been the primary practitioners, though men might dominate in institutional leadership positions. As both religion and women move out of the private into the public sphere, new challenges arise. For example, central facets of family and home – particularly love and sex – which have more traditionally been the purview of women and of religion have entered the realm of public discussion around the globe.

The present volume deals with the unique historical intersection of these issues at the close of the twentieth century and the beginning of the twenty-first, examining aspects of love, sex, and gender in the global context of the world religions. It is the second volume in the "Library of Global Ethics and Religions" which explores contemporary ethical questions in a global religious context and strives to present the work of prominent scholars and the diverse viewpoints of the world religions in an accessible manner. As did the first volume in the series, entitled *The Meaning of Life in the World Religions*, the present volume brings classic sources of text and tradition, philosophy and practice together with innovative ideas and proposed trajectories of change emerging out of classic traditions, to address important ethical issues, in this case relating to love, sexuality, and gender.

The discussion of these topics within the chapters of the volume is wide ranging, from the exploration of love and relationality as the fundamental defining element of religiosity and the wholly appropriate use of the language of sexuality to articulate the relationship of human and divine, to religious ways of defining gender roles and the role of religion in sexual ethics. In a sense this volume, like the previous one, is also about the meaning of life, for how religions conceive of what it is to be truly human, as well as life's meaning, is reflected in each religion's models and mandates for human love and sexuality and for the understanding of gender. Hence, our exploration of love, sex, and gender within a given religious tradition allows us to wrestle with the very heart of that tradition – its fundamental understanding of the nature of human beings; of relationships between humans, the world, and the Divine; of embodiment; and of the spiritual journey and life's meaning. So while the world religions illuminate our understandings of love, gender, and sexuality, our understanding of the world religions is, in turn, illumined by their views on love, sex, and gender.

The parameters of our discussion are set out in the first two chapters of the volume. Joseph Runzo begins by noting the widespread use of an "erotic aesthetic" to describe and articulate the relationship between human and Divine, offering us examples from across the world religions of the varied but extensive use of sexual and gendered imagery to describe religious experience. Such widespread use suggests that sexual symbolism is appropriate, and Runzo argues that it can only be so if humans have the capacity to experience the Transcendent in personal relational terms. Then erotic love becomes a symbol for divine–human encounter because that encounter shares a recognizable commonality with human-human love. Indeed Runzo argues that the highest human as well as divine love – which he calls "seraphic love" – includes traditional notions both of *agape* and of *eros*, the latter characterized by relationality, vulnerability, surrender, integration, union, and equality. The "erotic aesthetic" of religious representation points to the dimensions of *eros* in the love that flows from the Transcendent and is the ideal for human love as well, including but by no means limited to love expressed in sexual terms.

However, if we move beyond the assertion that the symbolism of erotic love is an appropriate way to describe the experience of divine love to the assertion that the way of love is the highest way to the Transcendent, we are on much shakier ground. William LaFleur introduces a Zen Buddhist "irritant" into our discussion of the place of both the "erotic aesthetic" and sexuality in the pursuit of religious transformation. Zen challenges Western assumptions of the primacy of romantic love and sexuality, suggesting that these may be very positive aspects of our lives, but spiritual transformation (for the Zen practitioner achieved at least in part through meditation) is far more important, and the relationship between spiritual teacher and disciple far more intimate. Ordinary human relations, including sexual ones, then become a field of practice, a locus for developing much deeper compassion and for coming up against those aspects of ourselves that still require change. But these ordinary relations are not the highest goal in themselves. LaFleur cautions against employing the "hermeneutic of suspicion" indiscriminately with respect to issues of love, sex, gender, and religion, suggesting that we seriously examine such phenomena as single-gender monasteries and the non-sexualized intimacy in teacher-disciple relations, not in reductionistic terms as necessarily reflective of sexual repression and sublimation but rather as potentially valuable facets of the journey toward religious transformation. With these caveats in mind, we move more deeply into the subject matter.

LOVE AND RELIGION

Julius Lipner begins this section of the book by proposing that perhaps "love" would be a uniquely appropriate choice of themes for the comparative study of religions and a good case study for a "humanistic" (as opposed to "scientific") method of examining religious phenomena – one which honors the wholistic experience of human beings and notions of truth other than those objectively provable. Acknowledging and then setting aside objections to comparative study generally, Lipner points to the open-endedness of religious traditions' self-understandings and affirms the need to listen to multiple voices within each to move toward a general understanding of any one tradition as well as for comparative analysis. The comparison he then develops is between Christian *agape* and *prema* in devotional Hinduism, exploring in rich detail the nature of the love advocated by each. Love is absolutely foundational to both traditions, with the Divine encountered in deeply personal terms as the God of Love who loves human beings, and with humans being called into a life of love for God and for their fellow human beings. Lipner demonstrates convincingly both the centrality of love in understanding these traditions and the fundamental tie between this theological understanding and ethical action in the world.

In the chapter that follows, Nancy Martin picks up the thread of Hindu devotion, exploring the place of gender in the language and experience of love for the Divine, particularly when the Ultimate is encountered as the Great Goddess, Mahadevi. When human relations serve as models and emotional training ground for human–divine relations, gender necessarily enters in, because human beings experience such relations as gendered embodied beings. Martin explores how this gendering plays out in the experience and understanding of the Divine, particularly in the context of loving the Goddess. Finally she suggests that gender distinctions are seemingly so fundamental to human experience that they become emblematic of duality and manifestation itself in Hindu traditions. As such they may reinforce in us a deluded dualistic and hierarchical understanding of reality paralleling socially constructed gender relations, but, particularly in the transformative context of loving the Goddess, they may also offer us a way into an appreciation of embodied existence and an affirmation of difference *without* hierarchy or "othering" – a spiritual goal of both devotional and tantric strands of Hinduism alike.

While Martin develops the theme of love in terms of the human–divine relationship, in the next chapter Charlotte Fonrobert turns to the other thread of Lipner's discussion – love in relation to one's fellow human beings. Fonrobert takes up the specific issue of love and sexuality within the Jewish tradition, noting the affirmation of the goodness of sexuality and the imbuing of the sex act with a mystical understanding of participating in God's ongoing creation of the world. Yet unregulated sexual desire is recognized as dangerous, and she identifies taming strategies within Judaism for containing this desire, foremost of which is the celebration of sexuality and desire only within the bounds of marriage.

The second taming strategy is more subtle. The language of passionate erotic love, Fonrobert suggests, is reserved for the human–divine relationship, for love of God and God's love for the individual and for Israel, thus moving it out of the more dangerous realm of human relations. Here a religious "erotic aesthetic" (to use Runzo's term) displaces the language of erotic love away from human sexual relations into a more strictly religious and allegorical context. The study of Torah is described as a relationship of lovers in which the Torah is feminine, and a clear competition is articulated between love of God expressed in erotic terms and devotion to family and the sexual love of the marriage bed. Fonrobert, a professor of Talmud, is actively struggling with her tradition's ways of gendering theological discourse and desire and its objectification of women in both contexts. The texts of the past are thoroughly androcentric. Only when women become the subjects of both theological discourse and desire, she suggests, will radical change come – when men and women who love the Torah (and God whose mind is revealed therein) rethink these relationships in newly gendered terms.

In the next chapter Elizabeth McAlister explores understandings of love in a radically different tradition, that of Haitian Vodou, with its deep African roots and Catholic Christian veneer. African religions, too, became global in recent centuries in part through the violent diaspora of the slave trade. This tradition acknowledges the presence of a high God, but concerns related to love, sexuality, and gender belong to the more immediate realm of the spirits, encountered directly through possessed priests and priestesses. The distinctive personalities and narrative biographies of the spirits reflect multiple dimensions of the experiences and social constructs of gender, love, and sexuality that shape the lives of those who "serve" them, and in possession encounters these spirits offer insight and healing to individuals and ways of making right relationships among community members. Romantic erotic love is desirable (and indeed one may marry a spirit), but it is also recognized as hopelessly idealistic and inherently unstable in the severe economic conditions under which many of those who serve the spirits live. Sexually explicit and obscene language in this context can also become a language of parody, humor, and resistance to both stereotypes of Haitians and oppressive authority figures. It may be the only real language available for this purpose, and the spirits use it as well, not only for resistance but also to get people to laugh at themselves.

Gendered constructs of romantic erotic love, and the struggle to move away from the objectification of women in this context, are also the subject of Clare Fischer's analysis of the work of the poet Hilda Doolittle (H.D.). Even as later writers on feminist spirituality would do, H.D. left the religious tradition of her childhood (though her Moravian Christian upbringing continued to have a strong influence on her subsequent spiritual journey) and looked to the past to recover women's voices and spiritual foremothers. However, she did not, like some later writers, seek to escape an objectifying understanding of women in heterosexual erotic love through an emphasis on maternal love (the dangers of such a move are made clear by Fischer and are also apparent in Martin's discussion of Hindu goddesses). Instead, H.D. chose to explore and depict woman as embodied desiring subject through an exploration of the figure of Helen (of Troy but also Egypt). Fischer's study of H.D.'s work and life offers us a portrait of an individual woman's spiritual journey, but one which is emblematic of women's journeys both within and outside of the world religions, as they seek to reshape understandings and experiences of erotic love *and* paths to religious transformation which, rather than denigrate, affirm women and embodied existence.

GENDER AND RELIGION

In the next section of the volume we turn more explicitly to issues of gender and religion, and particularly to women and religion. Arvind Sharma begins the section with a discussion of theoretic approaches to the topic, suggesting that this subject must be approached from multiple directions. He points out that our study of religion and its oppression of women is largely a secular and sociological study, while religions themselves understand their purpose not as the reinforcement of social structures (although they may do this) but as the salvation or liberation of human beings. We must distinguish between intent and impact, he suggests. In a similar way we must be attentive both to women as women and to women as human beings as we approach the study of women and religion.

What is needed, then, is a theory both of "religion and women" and of "women and religion." With regard to the former, Sharma posits that although most religions assert a salvation or liberation that is open to all without consideration of gender and an understanding of ultimate reality as beyond gender distinctions, in the everyday world ultimate reality is often imaged in gendered terms, and this imaging as well as other social factors affects the liberative or salvific possibilities of religion for women (and others less privileged such as those of low caste in the Indian context). With regard to "women and religion," he acknowledges that the position of women in religion is related directly to their social and political positioning which indeed may be reinforced by religious authority and language. But even so, he suggests that women's religious affiliation may be based not simply on such factors but on a real experience of the salvific or liberative power of the tradition for them as human beings, even though they may be simultaneously oppressed as women. Like LaFleur and Lipner in different ways, he asks us to take religion and women's religiosity seriously and not to reduce religion merely to an agent of gender oppression.

The essays that follow in this section explore dimensions of gender and religion in particular traditions, addressing both "women and religion" in Sharma's terms and "religion and women." Vivian-Lee Nyitray takes us into the world of Confucianism, primarily in the Chinese context, suggesting that in the contemporary world Confucianism is faced, as are the other religious traditions of the world, with complex questions of love, sexuality, and gendered human relations and its "real trouble" is that it has yet to come to terms with them. Women remain subordinate in this fundamentally hierarchical understanding of social relations, though as Nyitray carefully details, their complementary role has been variously defined across the centuries, and Buddhism and Taoism have offered alternative constructions of gender. Nyitray suggests that if Confucianism is to adapt to the challenges of sexuality and gender in today's world, then change must come at the level of family relations where the subordination of women is inscribed and might be facilitated by bringing to the fore the religious value of human-heartedness (ren), the highest Confucian virtue which calls for a deep respect and reverence for others and a deep sense of mutual responsibility – what we might characterize as an agapeistic love, to borrow Lipner's term.

In the next chapter Karen Jo Torjesen turns to early Christianity to explore the ways in which gendered imagery, shaped by understandings of gender in the Roman world in which Christianity emerged, colored understandings of salvation. Gender difference was defined in terms of a single sex – the male – with females as inferior or defective males. Maleness was the measure of perfected humanness and reflective of the true "image of God," and femaleness was seen as an aberration and an inferior state. This inherently inferior nature had implications for women's status and behavior in early Christian communities, though because these groups met in homes (the acceptable realm of women), women were able to hold leadership positions.

Such an understanding of gender difference also had implications in early theologies of salvation which used gendered imagery. Torjesen finds examples of gender crossing in the extracanonical gospels: Jesus assures the disciples in the Gospel of Thomas that he will make Mary Magdalene male so that she too may enter the kingdom of heaven. (Similar debates over whether one must be male to reach enlightenment are found in Jainism and Buddhism, but there one has the possibility of rebirth as a different gender, though within each tradition arguments were made both for and against the possibility of liberation in a woman's body.) A second model affirms the restoration of an androgynous wholeness, which preceded the fall into sexual difference. Still another possibility is put forward by the woman theologian Philoumene who asserted that souls themselves are gendered and remain so as they were originally created. She was in effect putting forward a two-sex theory of gender difference and an affirmation of that difference without a hierarchical relation between the two. Torjesen's work clearly demonstrates the impact of constructions of gender on understandings of salvation.

In the chapter that follows, Zayn Kassam focuses on Islam, pointing to the highly politicized nature of the discussions of women's position and gender issues, since criticism of the treatment of women within Islamic cultures was a primary element in the rhetoric of colonialism, used to justify domination. Any critique from within the tradition may be consequently viewed as tantamount to betrayal, either as siding with the colonizers or advocating "Westernization." So it is a delicate balance that must be maintained by a scholar such as herself who loves both Islam and women and by those who work for reform within Islamic communities.

Kassam traces traditional sources for Islamic views of gender and women's status and explores changing interpretations across the centuries.

In the final essay in this section, John Stratton Hawley takes up the language of Hindu devotion to Krishna and explores the gendered nature of longing in *bhakti* traditions. The intense longing of lover for divine Beloved is portrayed as a feminine prerogative and a disease where God as male is largely indifferent. But what kind of "woman" is this, who longs so excruciatingly for the male God? Exploring this imagery in depth, Hawley posits a male psychological displacement of fear of the diseases of the hot season and the monsoon (which is also recognized as the season of most intense love longing) – diseases which are seen as the both the grace and the curse of goddesses – and a transference of the childhood anxiety of the male child's separation from the mother onto a female figure who now must suffer separation from the male god who is the cause of her disease. Looking to Indian medical texts and understandings of the female body even as Torjesen has in the Christian context, Hawley finds further support for how males play at the emotions and experiences of women while disempowering and subordinating women, making them object rather than active subject of their bodily experiences. This gendered language of longing thus reflects human gender relations, inverting them and cloaking them in the "vestments of religion." This is not the last word on this complex phenomenon, however, for such imagery may also prove to be expressive of a genuine deep and passionate love of God.

SEXUAL LOVE AND RELIGION

The final section of the volume explores issues of sexual ethics and contemporary understandings of sexual difference. Karen Lebacqz leads off the section with a discussion of the need to take discussions of sexuality and sexual ethics out of the private realm and to explore the public and political dimensions of sexuality. Drawing on the works of Lisa Cahill and Marvin Ellison, Lebacqz seeks to construct a sexual ethics that takes embodiment seriously, without falling into essentialist traps, and that takes seriously the socially constructed nature of sexuality, without falling into a post-modern relativism which offers no basis to challenge oppression. Though she admires Cahill's attempt to find a firm ground for sexual ethics, in the end she cannot accept her conclusion that heterosexual marriage best promotes the goods of embodied sexuality – private pleasure, interpersonal intimacy, and social reproduction or kinship. She rejects Cahill's underlying assumption that because sex can produce children, it ought to lead to this outcome. Though Lebacqz does not want to essential-ize the body as a basis for defining sexual behavior, she does take seriously the possible role that biology might play in sexual ethics. She also respects Ellison's emphasis on the socially constructed nature of sexuality and understandings of the body and his call for a sexual ethics of justice and lib-eration (although she suggests that he relies on unacknowledged Christian understandings of justice to identify oppression and injustice). In shaping a Christian sexual ethics for the twenty-first century, Lebacqz suggests that: (1) the public dimensions of sexuality (both its socially constructed nature and its effects on the bearing of children) must be taken into account; (2) fidelity and stability of context are key; and (3) a non-oppressive context for both men and women is essential. Indeed Lebacqz suggests that a truly global sexual ethics that might be affirmed by multiple religious traditions would likely be one grounded in justice.

The final two essays deal with sexual ethics and the roots of sexual oppression and violence, while at the same time exploring the positive reli-gious role of sexuality. Jeffrey Hopkins argues that sexual violence directed at women and gay men is rooted in the bifurcation of reason and sexual pleasure. Tibetan Buddhism offers a method of spiritual transformation and unification, facilitated by the orgasmic bliss of sexual intercourse which leads to a realization of the fundamentally non-dual and empty nature of the reality underlying appearances. Sexual pleasure (engaged in in the appropriate context and in the appropriate way) opens the practi-tioner to the highest level of consciousness, while reason, though affirmed as on a continuum with the highest level, is recognized as a lower level of consciousness.

Though this practice is articulated in heterosexual terms, Hopkins believes that this is not essential – blissful orgasmic experience is the key. Similarly in his opening essay, Runzo notes the predominance of hetero-sexual imagery in the "erotic aesthetic," but he suggests that while this is largely reflective of the social marginalization of the relatively small per-centage of homosexuals in comparison to heterosexuals, homosexuality does enter religious discourse in social contexts where it is more acceptable and even flourishes. Hopkins further suggests that homophobia and the need to exert sexual dominance may reflect a fear of losing one's sense of self in orgasmic bliss (although from a Buddhist perspective that lower and false self needs to be shed to reach these higher levels of consciousness). Sex thus becomes both religious practice and the ground of religious experi-ence and transformation.

In the final essay in the volume, the Christian feminist theologian Carter Heyward offers a strong affirmation of sexual pleasure and erotic love as both sacred and an avenue into the experience of God. Even as Hopkins suggests a split between reason and sexual pleasure at the root of relational and sexual violence, so Heyward points to the split between love and justice, the former relegated to the private realm, the latter to the public. Like Lebacqz, Cahill and Ellison, she calls for the movement of love and sexuality into the public realm but also for the movement of justice into both the religious and the formerly private arena of sex and human relations. She advocates a justice-love or "right relation" in a mutuality that calls those in relation into the fullness of love of God, world, and one another with all the struggle that deepening love and intimacy requires. For this we must transform our justice system away from adversarial litigation and toward mutuality and relation – with room for accountability but also for serious apology and for forgiveness. The sacred power which fuels mutual relation, justice-making and love-making, Heyward names "erotic power." This "erotic power" is our longing for connectedness and relationality that images the love of God, a positive creative force for healing, that we know and experience with our whole bodies. Heyward draws together the threads of discussion interwoven through the volume when she suggests that *eros* and love are the life-force of religion and the manifestation of divine love, inseparable from gendered embodiment and the pursuit of justice.

NOTES

1. *Nostre Aetate* in *The Documents of Vatican II* (America Press, 1966), Walter M. Abbott, S.J., general editor and Very Rev. Msgr. Joseph Gallagher, translation editor, pp. 660–62.

Part I

LOVE AND SEX IN THE CONTEXT OF RELIGION

Plate 1 Bas relief of the ithyphallic Egyptian god Min at the Temple of Amun, built in the fourteenth century BCE under Amanofis III at Luxor. The facing Greek relief of Alexander the Great making offerings to derive power symbolically from this oldest of the Egyptian deities was added ten centuries later. Photo: *Joseph Runzo.*

1

THE SYMBOLISM OF SEX *and the* REALITY OF GOD

Joseph Runzo

Observed from the outside, it is easy to overlook the Cornaro Chapel in Rome. But inside, this modest church contains one of the most extraordinary and erotic sculptures in all religious art: Gianlorenzo Bernini's *The Ecstasy of St. Theresa*. Intimate and transcendent, earthly and other worldly, erotic and eternal, human and divine, the marble renders St. Theresa of Avila's renowned experience of God in the swooning form of this sixteenth-century Spanish nun, while above, the figure of an angel is poised with arrow in hand to strike her breast, the two bathed with the golden rays of heaven's light. The angel draws St. Theresa's clothes back to expose her breast, Theresa's ecstasy is transparently physical, and the arrow is a traditional phallic symbol.

In contrast, it is impossible to miss the open and public impact of the huge, soaring, exterior walls of the Kandariya Mahadeva temple, in Khajuraho, Madhya Pradesh, India (see a comparable example in plate 14). Here there is a celebratory cornucopia of entwined, human sexual couplings, rising up, level upon level, toward the sky and the pinnacles of the gods. Yet while intentionally arresting, these exterior erotic temple sculptures are not intended ultimately to distract the devotee from the quietude of the deepest recesses of the innermost sanctum and place of deity – the *garbhagriha*, literally the "womb-chamber" of the Hindu temple.

Bernini's sculpture, like Western religious art in general, represents an historical event, a precise moment in time when the divine and the human meet in *ekstasis*. On the other hand, the nameless Hindu temple sculptors of the eleventh century CE, whose legacy we see at Khajuraho, carved representations of eternal moments of Brahman's plentitudinous manifestation in the *lila* of Kama – that is, in the serendipitous playfulness of love for the world, and love in the world. Whether public or private, eternal or temporal, Hindu or Christian, these inspired, erotic representations comingle the profane and the sacred. As we shall see, sexual symbolism is appropriate to represent the relation between the human and the divine. The two issues I want to address here are *how* religions use sexual symbolism to refer to the Transcendent and, more important, *why* this is appropriate symbolism.

THE USE OF SEXUAL IMAGERY

The enormous variation in the use of sexual imagery within each religious tradition must be acknowledged. Even more so I do not mean to imply that among the different world religions sexual symbolism is used in the same way. Thus, in Hinduism and Christianity sexual imagery serves as a "pointer" to a higher reality, in Buddhism it can be a device for emptying the mind to attain *nirvana*, or the fullness of emptiness. And one striking feature of Asian traditions is the prominent place given to the female divine, perhaps in part because Indic religion arises within agrarian-based cultures more oriented toward women. This contrasts with the herdsman-based cultures of the Middle East, within which the great male-oriented monotheisms of the West arose, where the model of the male as herdsman/shepherd predominates.[1] However, despite this acknowledged diversity, there is a natural so to say "erotic aesthetic" in the human use of myth and symbol, dance and music, story and theology, and painting and sculpture to refer to the divine.

Let us begin in the West by considering St. Theresa's own account of her experience of God:

> I saw an angel close by me, on my left side, in bodily form. He was not large, but small of stature, and most beautiful … I saw in his hand a long spear of gold, and at the iron's point there seemed to be a little fire. He appeared to me to be thrusting it at times into my heart, and to pierce my very entrails; when he drew it out, he seemed to draw them out also, and to leave me all on fire with a great love of God. The pain was so great, that it made me moan; yet so surpassing was the sweetness of this excessive pain, that I could not wish to be rid of it. The soul is satisfied now with nothing less than God.[2]

Theresa is representative of the "bride mystics" in the Christian tradition who express profound encounter with the Divine in sexual symbolism. Another figure in this tradition, the Blessed Angelo da Foligno, writing some 250 years earlier than St. Theresa, says:

> I prayed God that He would give me something of Himself ... Then were the eyes of my soul opened and I beheld love advancing gently toward me ... This love came toward me after the manner of a sickle ... when it first appeared unto me it did not give itself unto me in such abundance as I expected, but part of it was withdrawn ... I was filled with love and inestimable satiety; but although it did well satisfy me, it did generate within me so great an hunger that all my members were loosened and my soul fainted with longing to attain unto the remainder.[3]

We should not be misled into supposing that these experiences could be dismissed as some sort of "female" mysticism. One of the greatest of all bride mystics is the Spanish saint, San Juan de la Cruz (John of the Cross), who wrote such mystical classics as *Dark Night of the Soul* and *Living Flame of Love*.

Going back in the West to the earlier Jewish tradition, we find the passionate eroticism of the *Song of Songs* which later served as an instructional text for many classical Christian mystics as they sought a deeper understanding of the divine–human relationship:

> My beloved is to me a bag of myrrh,
> that lies between my breasts ...
>
> My beloved is mine and I am his.[4]

This sexual imagery became transmuted in the Christian monastics, but also in the hasidic strands of Judaism, into an erotic representation of the divine–human encounter. Within the Jewish kabbalistic tradition, while sexual imagery is not directly used to represent divine–human encounter, as the eminent Jewish scholar Gershom Scholem points out, God is seen as the locus of sexuality: "in God there is a union of the active and the passive, procreation and conception, from which all mundane life and bliss is derived."[5] In the Islamic tradition, we find a similar erotic aesthetic in Rumi, the greatest of all Persian mystic poets:

> For God hath mingled in the dusty earth
>   A draught of Beauty from his choicest cup.
> 'Tis *that*, fond lover – not these lips of clay –
>   Thou art kissing with a hundred ecstasies ...[6]

Finally, another Western monotheistic way to understand divine–human relationship in erotic terms is found in the famous Jewish kabbalistic mystical text the *Zohar* or *The Book of Splendor*. While not directly eroticizing divine–human relationality, it does so indirectly by portraying the Torah itself as lover to the devoted reader of Torah:

> What a multitude of humans there are who dwell in confusion, failing to perceive the way of truth that abides in Torah, and the Torah, in love, summons them day by day to her, but woe, they do not so much as turn their heads ...

> She may be compared to a beautiful and stately maiden, who is secluded in an isolated chamber of a palace, and has a lover of whose existence she alone knows. For love of her he passes by her gate unceasingly, and turns his eyes in all directions to discover her ... She thrusts open a small door in her secret chamber, for a moment reveals her face to her lover, then quickly withdraws it. He alone, none else, notices it; but he is aware it is from love of him that she has revealed herself to him for a moment, and his heart and his soul and everything within him are drawn to her.[7]

If we turn now to the Asian traditions, we find both copious and salient uses of sexual imagery. In the Hindu tradition, Parvati, the divine female consort of the great god Shiva, pursues him relentlessly, first outdoing Shiva in meditative practice to get his attention and then making endless love to win the Dark Lord. Shiva is an ascetic, a warrior, a father, and also a great lover (in the same vein, Michelangelo's stunning Florentine statue of David expresses the erotic power of this paradigmatic Western man of God). Parvati is a mother and also a lover, and their relationship of love is mirrored in the world.

Interestingly, parallels to the Indic gendered eroticism of deity can be found in the earliest strands of pharaonic Egypt which shares with Hinduism an organic worldview of interconnectedness, with an emphasis on both relationality and the female divine. In the Egyptian conception, the eternal cycle of the universe is bounded by the male earth (Geb) and the female sky (Nut). While Christianity and Islam have typically understood God in Godself in non-sexual terms, not surprisingly a better comparison within monotheism to Hinduism is found in Jewish Kabbalism. Gershom Scholem points out that,

> Non-Jewish [Western] mysticism, which glorified and propagated asceticism, ended sometimes by transplanting eroticism into the relation of man to God. Kabbalism, on the other hand, was tempted to discover the mystery

of sex within God himself … every true marriage is a symbolical realization of the union of God and the Shekhinah [the glory of God as it appears].[8]

This tendency to locate the locus of sexuality in the Divine raises interesting questions about the comparisons and contrasts between gendered divine representation in Christian, Islamic, and traditional Hebrew views, on the one hand, and in Asian views on the other hand.

THE VARIETIES OF GENDER

In opposition to the received Western conception, in the Asian traditions females and thus the Devi are seen as active, immanent, and accessible, while male deities tend to be passive and (as they are also in the West) transcendent and not readily accessible. Thus the salient iconographic form for Hinduism is the Shaivite *linga/yoni*, either in its partially iconic form with a face on the linga, or in its purely geometric aniconic form as symbolically infinite. Significantly, in this erotic aesthetic the *linga* rises *up* from the *yoni*, emphasizing a deeper generative symbolism within the sexual symbolism, and illustrating the paramount doctrine of Hinduism that all power is female – i.e. *shakti* – and hence that male energy is not only inchoate *in* but constantly reinitiated *by* female energy (see plates 4 and 8).

Again comparing this with the West, one of the earliest Nile Valley gods is the ithyphallic Min,[9] whose statues at Coptos predate the unification of Egypt in 3000 BCE, and who later would be merged with the great god Amun as the Amun-Min of the monumental temples of Karnac and Luxor (see plate 1). However, much like the indigenous Indian tradition, the early Egyptian pantheon also includes goddesses, eminent among them Hathor, the goddess of sexuality who finds a later parallel in the Greek Aphrodite. As the Egyptologist Alison Roberts says, "Hathor is the dynamic partner … without Hathor, quite simply, there would not be any movement of the sun; like Shiva without shakti, the sun king simply would not stir."[10] Likewise, in the ancient Mesopotamian cosmology, the female divine figures prominently: Nammu is the mother who gave birth to Ansar (the male heaven) and Kisar (the female earth); later gods are produced through sexual intercourse among the gods; and the most important female deity of all periods of ancient Mesopotamia is Inanna or Ishtar, the goddess of love and sexual behavior (and also of war, "the playground of Ishtar"). Yet the female divine did not carry over into the monotheisms of the West even as female divinity not only lived on but retained a prominent place in the developed Asian traditions.

The Indic view of energy as female and the female as more accessible undergirds the development of the *tantras* during the middle of the first millennium CE. The ensuing tantric traditions in both Hinduism and Buddhism are an attempt to cut through Brahmanic ritual and hierarchy and calcifying conception and reach *moksha/nirvana* in this lifetime – and for this, maleness needs the complementarity of female *shakti* as a necessary gateway. Thus arose the Vajrayana, or "thunderbolt way," a term appropriately derived from the *vajra* or thunderbolt of the Indian god Indra, capable of blasting away illusion and bringing enlightenment. A central iconographic representation in Tibetan Buddhism is the *yab-yum* – i.e. father/mother – imagery of sexual union. In one variation, the fierce Vajrapani – the bodhisattva who is literally "*vajra*-in-hand" and is compassion as skillful means – is united sexually and spiritually with the female figure of wisdom.

The Chinese traditions share a similar erotic aesthetic of the complementarity of male and female principles – of yin and yang. Important in this view is that all yin has some yang in it and vice versa. Thus, yin and yang are actually *inter*dependent, and the ideal is to avoid opposition and to achieve a balance between them.[11] We find this parallel in Hinduism in the words of the tenth-century Shiva devotee Devara Dasimayya:

> Suppose you cut a tall bamboo in two;
> make the bottom piece a woman,
> the headpiece a man;
> rub them together
> till they kindle:
>   tell me now,
> the fire that is born,
> is it male or female?[12]

In the Chinese traditions, Taoism also adds the idea of a Great Mother and that of the female as having an inexhaustible life force that she can give to the male in union. In the *Tao Te Ching*, composed some twenty-three hundred years ago, we read:

> The Valley Spirit never dies.
> It is named the Mysterious Female.
> And the Doorway of the Mysterious Female
> Is the Base from which Heaven and Earth sprang.[13]

Visually, one is reminded of Gustave Courbet's powerful 1866 painting of the genital region of a quietly reclining female torso entitled *The Origin of the World*, or the naked dancing female figure of Auguste Rodin's 1890 sculpture *Iris, God's Messenger*, which portend the public emergence of female erotic power in the West from the *fin de siècle* into the twentieth century.

However, we have to be careful here not to treat categories of difference in sex and gender as if they were either absolutes or necessarily transhistorical. Devara Dasimayya's image of the "male" and "female" bamboo merging in the fire serves as a warning. And we need to take into account the occurrence of the *inversion* of male/female metaphors, such as we find in this passage from St. Francis de Sales in his 1616 treatise *On the Love of God:*

> Have you noticed ... the ardor with which little children often cling to the mother's breast when they are hungry? ... It is the same with the soul that is in repose and quiet before God ... It uses the will as a mouth whereby the insensible delight and satiety it takes in enjoying God's presence find entrance.[14]

Michael Fishbane observes about Judaism that "the legal category of *person* in Jewish law is a male construct, so that women (and minors and so forth) are, in effect, conceived of as incomplete males. The category of *woman* is a mirror category, a negative requiring a positive for self-definition."[15] This Jewish conception – at least the legal conception – is the obverse of the Hindu metaphysics of maleness coming from the femaleness of *shakti*, and very unlike the Taoist conception of the essential complementarity of male and female. Or just considering the West in itself, Thomas Laqueur's brilliant study *Making Sex: Body and Gender from the Greeks to Freud* demonstrates the social and historical development of the notion of two biological sexes from the long accepted one-sex conception in the West, under which females were simply less developed or undeveloped biological males, to the point that it can be said that "sometime in the eighteenth century, sex as we know it was invented."[16] Still, while we keep in mind potential differences in usage and meaning transhistorically within as well as among the world religions, we can now turn to the question of why gendered sexual symbolism and metaphor has offered appropriate and rich resources for understanding the divine–human encounter.

THE PROBLEM OF REFERENCE AND REPRESENTATION

Though fraught with problems and potential pitfalls, there is a profound epistemological value to religious sexual symbolism. To see this, let us turn once again to the ecstasy of St. Theresa of Avila. St. Theresa felt she encountered the Transcendent. The problem is, how can she, and in turn Bernini, express this encounter? This is just one instance of a far-reaching problem.

Human ideas and means of expression come from the natural order. However, there is no one-to-one correspondence between the natural and the supernatural. So on the one hand, we cannot make *univocal* reference to the Transcendent – e.g. we cannot use terms for God in the same sense that we use them to refer to natural things. And yet, on the other hand, we will be rendered mute if every attempt to communicate about the Divine is a mere equivocation. So as Thomas Aquinas pointed out, our attempts to refer to the Transcendent must fall in between these extremes; they must be *analogical*. That is, we can only refer to the Transcendent by analogy with things in this world.[17] In order to express successfully ideas about the Transcendent, we must use elements of the natural order which have a *partial* likeness – for they cannot have a full likeness – to the Transcendent.

Of course sexual symbolism, because it is so powerful, is sometimes used in a religious context for political or social reasons rather than to refer directly, and so in part literally, to the Transcendent. Sexual symbolism can be used to protest the established religious order, to break calcified religious conventions, or to critique an unfair social order built on religious misperceptions. So for example, the sixteenth-century Indian saint Mirabai breaks her marriage vows and devotes herself entirely to Krishna as his "lover," overthrowing the established hierarchy (see plate 12), and Vodou practitioners use sexual reference to controvert the ruling Western Christian church with its negative views of African culture.[18] However, these sociopolitical "protest" uses of sexual imagery are effective only because they are parasitic on more established uses of sexuality in religious language. And it is those more established, foundational uses of sexual imagery which are intended as direct and thus in part literal references to the Transcendent.

Whether we can ever be successful in making reference to the Transcendent, much less know that our references are successful, is a complex epistemological question which I have addressed elsewhere.[19] What we are addressing here is why sexual symbolism in particular would be appropriate, if successful. And first, why is the direct use of sexual symbolism for referring to the divine virtually universal? Three observations are in order.

Firstly, sexual symbolism will be appropriate to divine–human encounter just in so far as personhood can be attributed to the Transcendent. In this vein, I am using the descriptor "God" to designate a personal being. Thus, the "Reality of God" in the title of this chapter refers to the God who is "Abba" to Jesus,[20] the God of "Abraham, Isaac and Jacob," as well as the God of Ishmael – or as the Qur'an begins "Allah, Lord of the Worlds, the Beneficent, the Merciful" – as well as, for example, the God of the great Hindu philosopher–theologian Ramanuja. In sum, I am using "God" to refer broadly to the Transcendent conceived as entering into *personal* relationships. While Paul Tillich is right to say that for the theist "God is the fundamental symbol for what concerns us ultimately," the "Ground of Being" (as Tillich designates the Transcendent), or the non-personal Transcendent of Plotinus, or of Spinoza, or of contemporary process theology, or Shankara's advaita vedantic Hinduism, or Theravada Buddhism, are not the conceptions I am addressing here. I am addressing the view that, in the words of the Christian theologian Sallie McFague, "the universe is neither indifferent nor malevolent but that there is a power (and a *personal* power at that) which is on the side of life and its fulfillment." [21]

Secondly, for those who do believe in a God who has indeed manifest Godself in the universe, it is expectable that the divine relationality would be present in the experience of humans within *all* the great religious traditions. As the Christian writer St. Paul says, momentarily overlooking the human capacity for self-deception and hubris, "ever since the creation of the world (God's) invisible nature ... has been clearly perceived in the things that have been made."[22] If God is omnipresent and sexual symbolism appropriate to the divine–human encounter, the universality of sexual symbolism would be a natural consequence.

Lastly, without endorsing a fully Jungian analysis of symbols, Carl Jung's foundational proposal that humans share archetypes helps explain this universality of sexual imagery for personalistic conception of the Transcendent: "like the instincts, the collective thought patterns of the human mind are innate and inherited. They function, when the occasion arises, in more or less the same way in all of us."[23] It is a common human frustration that the manifestation of God is more subtle than overt.[24] But if the Transcendent *is* personal, we would expect the hard-wiring of the brain, as passed on from past human experience, to include dispositions to detect the personal Transcendent. As Jung says, "just as the human body represents a whole museum of organs, each with a long evolutionary history behind it, so we should expect to find that the mind is organized in a similar way."[25] The archetypes of sexual symbolism may be just such genetically based dispositions to express divine–human encounter. Thus, via the hard-wiring of the brain, humans would not just culturally, but perhaps even genetically, carry on the capacity to detect a relational, personal Transcendent.

Having said all this, even if the unconscious is guided by archetypal inherited sexual symbolism, should not the mystic and the religiously devout make a *conscious* effort to turn away from the profane? After all, Hinduism reveres the *sannyasin* or renouncer ascetic, Buddhism enjoins non-attachment, and Roman Catholicism is committed to a celibate priesthood. As St. Francis de Sales, in support of celibacy, says:

> human bodies are like glass vessels that cannot be carried about while touching one another without risk of breakage … No matter how fresh the water within a vessel may be, once it has been touched by any beast of earth, it cannot keep its freshness for long.[26]

But sexual symbolism is appropriate for divine–human encounter because, even more fundamentally, sexual symbolism is appropriate for expressing the divine reality itself. As Robert Nozick notes "in sex one can also engage in metaphysical exploration, knowing the body and person of another as a map or microcosm of the very deepest reality, a clue to its nature and purpose."[27] Transferring this to the divine–human encounter, there is, so to speak, at the deepest level a "divine metaphysics of love." For as the Christian book of I John succinctly puts it in a sentiment shared by the *bhakti* Hindu tradition, "God is love, and he who abides in love abides in God, and God in him."[28]

SYMBOLS AND SEX

The use of sexual symbolism does not imply that God is physical – that would be the mistake of univocal predication. But to avoid equivocation there must be *some* literal meaning to the symbolism. Since sexual symbolism is both inextricably relational and inextricably gendered, the use of sexual symbolism implies that God *literally* can be conceived of as both personal and gendered. As already observed regarding the latter, it is important to keep in mind that gender is a fluid notion. Hence appropriately, symbolic representations of the Divine often include a co-mingling of gender: androgenous representations of Shiva; the *yab-yum* of Tibetan

Buddhism; the Chinese yin and yang; the transformed indic male bodhisattva of compassion, Avalokiteshvara, who becomes first the Chinese female bodhisattva Kuan-Yin and then the Japanese female bodhisattva Kannon (see plate 9).

To see better how symbols function in religion, consider Paul Tillich's suggestion that symbols have six characteristics: (1) symbols point beyond themselves; (2) they participate in that to which they point; (3) they open up new levels of reality; (4) symbols unlock dimensions of our spirits (Tillich uses the more Western term "souls") which correspond to the new levels of reality disclosed; (5) they cannot be produced intentionally; and (6) they live and die according to the situation in which they arise.[29] While I do not endorse every aspect of Tillich's analysis, it will be helpful to consider each of these points in turn.

Taking points (1) and (3) together, symbols point beyond themselves and open up new levels of reality which could not otherwise be accessed.[30] Not only are our finitely limited concepts unable fully to express the transcendent and infinite, we also want to be able to express the non-intellectual *affective* aspects of encountering the Divine. Hence, we need the emotive as well as the analogical power of symbols, whether in language, action or art, to enhance and expand our sensitivity to the Transcendent.

Sexual symbols open humans to the divine metaphysics of love. In the West, the symbolism of God as bridegroom, the bride mystical tradition in general, and Bernini's *Ecstasy of St. Theresa* in particular clearly function this way. Likewise, Mahadeviyakka, the Hindu *bhakti* saint of the twelfth century, sings of her love for Shiva, using the complete abandonment of sexual ecstasy as an analogy to the utter commitment of faith:

> He bartered my heart,
>   looted my flesh
>   claimed as tribute
>   my pleasure,
>   took over
>   all of me.[31]

In the Vaishnava tradition, Krishna, eighth avatar of Vishnu, is the dark-skinned lover, playing his flute to entice devotees, who encircle him in the *rasamandala,* each facing inward toward Krishna and each convinced that Lord Krishna loves him or her specially, while he loves all (see plate 3).

Now, perhaps one could excise all sexual symbolism in religion and replace it with another sort of symbolism, but the replacement symbolism could no more completely capture the divine–human encounter than does sexual symbolism. The use of sexual symbolism to convey a glimpse of the Transcendent is no different in kind from any other representation of divine–human encounter: expressing the Divine is, so to speak, *symbols all the way down.* (This does not mean that the Transcendent must itself be just symbols. Sometimes symbols do not point to anything beyond themselves – and this is the risk of using symbols – but symbols can sometimes successfully point beyond themselves. The ancient Israelites claimed that the golden calf failed, where the Ten Commandments succeeded, in pointing to the truly Transcendent.)

Consider characteristics (2) and (4) of symbols: they participate in that to which they point, and they unlock dimensions of our spirits which correspond to the new dimensions of reality disclosed. Sexual symbolism is fundamentally relational. The erotic aesthetic of the experience of the Divine fundamentally both reflects and enables humans *to participate in* the Divine love. The deepest relation between humans and the Divine is a love relationship. Even as the expression "God is mind" falls stillborn from philosophical–theological texts, "God is love" springs forth in relational promise, an intimation of the divine metaphysics of love.

Finally, consider characteristics (5) and (6): the idea that symbols cannot be produced intentionally and that they live and die in the situation within which they are formed. Here I would disagree with Tillich – and incidentally Jung – because sexual symbols, like all aesthetic symbols, can be produced intentionally. On this score, a better analysis is offered by Sallie McFague's notion of theology as constructive, as modeling God through the use of metaphor.

Metaphors are constructed symbols. As McFague notes, the use of metaphor in theology "encourages ... novel ways of expressing the relation between God and the world," for they are "imaginative leaps across a distance – the best metaphors always give both a shock and a shock of recognition."[32] Sexual symbolism provides both a shock – suddenly seeing the Divine in blatantly erotic terms – and more importantly a shock of recognition. For those who experience the passion of faith, encountering the Divine is so profound – the devout feels so vulnerable and yet so integrated, so desirous to be one with the beloved – that only the archetype of sexual experience seems to compare. This is beyond the merely rational, beyond the belief or even the knowledge that one ought to pattern one's will after God's will. This is affective and intuitional. As the twelfth-century *bhakti* saint Basavanna says of Shiva:

When
like a hailstone crystal
like a waxwork image
the flesh melts in pleasure
  how can I tell you? ...

I touched and joined
my lord of the meeting rivers.
How can I talk to anyone
of that?[33]

However, McFague misconstrues the nature of metaphor when she says that a "metaphor is a word or phrase used inappropriately" and that "God-language can refer only through the detour of a description that properly belongs elsewhere."[34] McFague is mistaken because a metaphor can only be used successfully if there are certain features which the new referent and the normal referent of the metaphor have in common. That is, metaphors are, in part, literal predications. As we say, Richard is "lion-hearted" or "life is a stage" because the members of each pair – Richard and a lion; life and a theater – have certain characteristics in common. So too, God is bride or bridegroom to the devout because God shares some characteristics of earthly lovers. And so too, sexual union is a symbol for union with the Divine because they have common features.

SERAPHIC LOVE

Symbols point. What the sexual symbolism of religion points to is not physical. It points to the divine love, to the desire for concurrence of wills. The divine love in turn informs human love and the physical. This is clear in such notions as the Jewish idea of the sacredness of sex. As the Jewish kabbalistic text the *Zohar* says, "The Divine Presence rests on the marital bed when both male and female are united in love and holiness."[35]

Further, the metaphysics of love in human–divine encounter is not only relational – it is *transformative*. In the trenchant words of the ninth-century Vaishnava saint, Nammalvar:

he who devoured the seven worlds
made me his own cool place
  in heaven
and thought of me
  what I thought of him
and became my own thoughts.[36]

In the divine metaphysics of love, human love transforms us because it participates in God's transforming love: "we love because God first loved us."[37] Appropriately in this erotic aesthetic, the symbol that is *eros* participates in the Reality that is God.

I have suggested elsewhere that this highest transforming love is "seraphic love," a love which has two poles – *agape* and *eros*.[38] *Eros* is an insuperable dimension of seraphic love, God's love is seraphic, and so human love which properly reflects God's love has the dimensionality of *eros*. For *eros*, as an inextricable part of the highest love, is not only the desire to be with the beloved – it is in a sense a desire to *be* the beloved, for it is the desire to be of one will with the beloved. In divine–human encounter, this is the desire, the *eros*, to have concurrence of will with God.

HETEROSEXUAL AND HOMOSEXUAL LOVE

The erotic aesthetic of most religious language is heterosexual, principally modeled after heterosexual marriage. But this heterosexual emphasis does not in itself preclude the religious acceptability of homosexual love, nor does it preclude the possibility of the inclusion of homosexual love in the religious erotic aesthetic. So why isn't homosexual love typically included as a positive model in traditional religious language?

The world religions are not, as is commonly assumed, simply consistently anti-homosexual. But homosexual love is generally marginalized in human society, and therefore marginalized in religion, which is a social construction. One obvious reason for this societal marginalization is that the disposition to homosexuality is expressed in a relatively small portion of the population, and social structures, including religious structures, normally focus on the concerns of the clearly predominant – for it is usually also the dominant – majority population. However, these forces can operate in reverse. When a minority of the population assumes dominance, or when the minority wants to confront the prejudices of the majority, or when the majority sets out to protect the interests of a minority, this transference (or attempted transference) of social power will lead to a greater *religious* visibility for a minority such as the homosexual population.

Here are some of the variant religious attitudes toward homosexuality: in opposition to standard Western views, the *Laws of Manu* of classical Hinduism condemns female homosexuality more harshly than male homosexuality. However, by the time of the pluralistic medieval period of Hinduism some writers indicate that homosexuality is not uncommon, and not a perversion.[39] Similarly, homosexuality flourished in medieval China. This was largely due to the strong presence of homosexuality in the imperial court. But this was also grounded in Taoist conceptions of yin–yang: for males, homosexuality can be acceptable because two yang elements do not lose vital force through intimate contact – male yang is only quenched by excessive contact with female yin – and for females, homosexuality is acceptable because the loss of vital force is not even an issue. A third major Asian tradition, Buddhism, begins as an ascetic way of life in the *sangha* with strong sexual proscriptions. But again by the Middle Ages, homosexuality becomes more prevalent within the then large, extended and insular monastic communities.

Japanese Buddhism makes a particularly interesting study because four elements lead to the rise of *nanshoku* or "forbidden colors," the prevalent male–male homosexuality of Tokugawa Japan,[40] the important 250 year period from 1603 to 1868 which saw the development of the great city of Edo, that is, present-day Tokyo. Those four conjoining elements were: (1) the monastic life of Zen Buddhism with its roots in Taoist Chinese notions of yin–yang; (2) the all male samurai traditions of the Tokugawa Shogunate; (3) the rise of a large bourgeois leisure class; and underlying this, (4) the rise of a large urban population. The samurai traditions in Kamakura, the previous capital, had been hospitable to the arrival of Ch'an Buddhism from China, supporting its spread throughout Japan as "Zen" Buddhism, and thus supplanting the older Mahayana traditions which had arrived earlier. The close interplay of Zen monastic life and samurai warrior codes, coupled with urbanization, gave homosexuality a prominent place in official (including religious) Japanese culture. Indeed, looking for an individual to credit, it is said without disapproval that Kukai himself, the famous founder of Shingon Buddhism, brought *nanshoku* back from China in 806 CE.

The phenomenon of homosexuality as a latent force in religious society which only comes to public expression with social acceptance can also be seen in the history of the Western monotheisms. The priestly code in the Hebrew scriptures condemns male homosexuality outright: "their blood shall be upon them" (Leviticus 20:13). But lesbianism is ignored, most likely because, not unlike Taoism, the principle concern was loss of the man's vital "seed." (It is worth noting that the infamous "sin" of the people of Sodom and Gomorrah was not homosexuality as is commonly thought, but avarice: they had "surfeit of food, and prosperous ease, but did not aid the poor and needy" [Ezekiel 16:49].) The strong sexual proscriptions of the Islamic tradition, one of the two most populous faiths which are founded in the Hebrew scriptures, includes the express rejection of homosexuality in the Qur'an, a view which is emulated for example in the teachings of Baha'u'llah, the Iranian founder of the Baha'i faith. The strong social control of Islamic faith obviates public support for homosexuality in predominantly Islamic countries.

Turning to the most populous tradition today, Christianity, we find St. Paul, writing in the context of the overtly licentious and Dionysian world of the Romans, condemning both male and female homosexuality, though this pales in comparison with his main concern, which is idol worship – turning away from God – and, echoing Ezekiel, the bad character traits that result: "Full of envy, murder, strife, deceit, malignity, they are gossips, slanderers, haters of God, insolent, haughty, boastful, inventors of evil, disobedient to parents, foolish, faithless, heartless, ruthless" (Romans 1:26). In the medieval church, female homosexuality was mainly ignored, while male homosexuality was strongly condemned, even as Augustine uncomfortably accepted prostitution as a necessary "lawful immorality," and St. Thomas Aquinas picked up the refrain with the declaration "take away the sewer and you will fill the palace with pollution ... take away prostitutes from the world and you will fill it with sodomy," a decidedly misogynist conclusion based on the perceived importance of combating homosexuality. But some strands of the modern Christian church, confronted with the fact of social tolerance for homosexuals in, for example, the U.S. and Britain, have come to officially tolerate and even sometimes embrace sincere homosexual love, like heterosexual love, as a gift from God. As the moderate Anglican theologian Brian Hebblethwaite says:

> It is widely believed that homosexual orientation is in many human beings a natural – in the sense of genetically based – condition. In these circumstances, it may be argued, a committed and faithful homosexual relationship is a moral good, and not to be condemned as if it were on a level with sexual promiscuity. When the singer Peter Pears refers to his life with [the British composer] Benjamin Britten as a "gift from God" beyond desert, not only the creativity but also the moral goodness of that relationship should be apparent to the Christian as to any moralist.[41]

Thus, the inclusion of homosexual love within the religious understanding of genuine love sometimes comes with a broader social acceptance of homosexual love. But the language of homosexual love can also be employed religiously as a social/religious protest. This is powerfully presented by Elizabeth McAlister in her analysis of love, sex and gender in Haitian Vodou,[42] where homosexual jibes are employed by Haitian Vodou priests and spirits as a way of critiquing the conventional religious structure in which "elite" Catholicism is superior to "base" African traditions with their life-affirming embrace of sexuality within religion.

However, putting aside such socio-political critiques, two rather different questions about the religious meaning of homosexual love can be raised: (1) is homosexuality *per se* immoral in a particular strand of a tradition, for if so, homosexual love obviously will have no positive religious value in that strand of the tradition; and (2) if homosexuality is not regarded as immoral (e.g. because it is regarded as genetically based) in a particular strand of a tradition, then the question arises as to what might be its positive symbolism for divine relationality. Regarding the second question, the Roman Catholic thinker Jack Dominick has argued that while sex should be reserved for the constancy of a married relationship, the value of sex is "to be found in its ability to maintain ... relationship" through "personal and sexual affirmation, reconciliation, hope and thanksgiving."[43] These characteristics could of course be found in, to quote Hebblethwaite again, "a committed and faithful homosexual relationship."

COOL HEART

Let me end with an observation about Buddhism, a tradition which might least well fit this analysis of the religious significance of sexual imagery. Buddhism enjoins non-attachment – which is often understood as "a cool heart" (see plate 2). This seems *prima facie* to preclude the passion of seraphic love, much less allow for the personal divine–human encounter I have been describing. But consider Thich Nhat Hanh, a Vietnamese Mahayana Buddhist monk, who uses the symbol of his lifelong love of a woman – a love never physically consummated – as a skillful means to explain the practice of cultivating *bodhichitta* – i.e. of "cultivating the mind of love" – in his book by that name. His love for her is transformed into a love for all. And tantric forms of Buddhism, such as present-day Tibetan Buddhism, directly employ the imagery and practice of erotic love as a skillful means toward enlightenment.[44] I will leave to others the question of whether the language of erotic love fits additional forms of Buddhism.

NOTES

1. Still, we find the Middle Eastern Sufi poet Rumi saying:
    Woman is a ray of God: she is not the earthly beloved.
    She is creative: you might say she is not created.
    Jalalu'l-Din Rumi in *Rumi: Poet and Mystic,* trans. Reynold A. Nicholson
    (Oxford: Oneworld, 1995), p. 44 (*Math* I, 2431).
2. St. Theresa of Avila, *Autobiography* (New York: Columbia Press, 1911),
    trans. E. Allison Peers, chapter 29, p. 215. This experience occurred in
    1559.
3. Angela da Foligno, *The Divine Consolation of the Blessed Angela da Foligno*
    (New York: Cooper Square, 1966), trans. Mary G. Steegmann, pp. 178–79.
4. Song of Solomon 1:13 and 2:16 (RSV).
5. Gershom G. Scholem, *Major Trends in Jewish Mysticism* (New York:
    Schocken, 1954), p. 227.
6. Rumi, *Rumi: Poet and Mystic,* p. 45 (*Math* V, 372).
7. *Zohar: The Book of Splendor,* ed. Gershom G. Scholem (New York:
    Schocken, 1949), p. 89. See also Charlotte Fonrobert "To Increase Torah
    is to Increase Life," in *The Meaning of Life in the World Religions,* ed.
    Runzo and Martin (Oxford: Oneworld, 1999), p. 81.
8. Scholem, *Major Trends in Jewish Mysticism,* p. 235.
9. This is like the earliest strands of indigenous Indian tradition about the
    ithyphallic Shiva, which later reasserted itself over the imported Vedic
    gods of the Indo-Aryans.
10. Alison Roberts, *Hathor Rising: The Power of the Goddess in Ancient Egypt*
    (Vermont: Inter Traditions International, 1997), pp. 66–67.
11. In the seventh century CE, Tung-hsuan sagely wrote in his *Art of Love* that:
    Of all the ten thousand things created by Heaven, man is the most precious.
    Of all the things that make man prosper none can be compared to sexual
    intercourse. It is modeled on Heaven and takes its pattern by Earth. It
    regulates Yin and rules Yang. Those who understand its significance can
    nurture their nature and prolong their years; those who miss its true nature
    will harm themselves and die before their time.
12. Devara Dasimayya in *Speaking of Śiva* (New York: Penguin, 1973), trans.
    A. K. Ramanujan, p. 110.
13. Geoffrey Parrinder, *Sex in the World Religions* (New York: Oxford Press,
    1980), p. 78.
14. St. Francis de Sales, *On the Love of God* (New York: Image Books, 1963),
    trans. John K. Ryan, p. 292.
15. Michael Fishbane, "The Image of the Human and the Rights of the Indi-
    vidual in Jewish Tradition" in *Human Rights and the World's Religions,* ed.
    Leroy S. Rouner (Notre Dame: Notre Dame University Press, 1988), p. 27.
16. Thomas Laqueur, *Making Sex: Body and Gender from the Greeks to Freud*
    (Cambridge, Mass.: Harvard University Press, 1990), p. 149.

17. See Thomas Aquinas, *Summa Theologica* Pt. I, Q 13, Art. 5.
18. See Elizabeth McAlister, "Love, Sex and Gender Embodied: The Spirits of Haitian Vodou," chapter 6 of this volume.
19. See Runzo, *Reason, Relativism and God* (London: Macmillan Press; New York: St. Martin's, 1986), especially chapter 8; and *World Views and Perceiving God* (London: Macmillan Press; New York: St. Martin's, 1994).
20. Mark 14:36, Rom. 8:15 and Gal. 4:6.
21. Sallie McFague, *Models of God* (Philadelphia: Fortress Press, 1987), p. x.
22. Rom. 1:20.
23. Carl G. Jung, *Man and His Symbols* (London: Penguin, 1990), p. 75. He says "the unconscious seems to be guided ... chiefly by instinctive trends, represented by corresponding thought forms – that is, by the archetypes." On p.78, unlike Freud, Jung thinks religion is valuable for modern persons, but he is, even so, a non-realist about the Transcendent. A similar sort of position has more recently been set forth by Don Cupitt.
24. On the positive side it can be argued that this epistemic distance between humans and God actually preserves human free will from what would otherwise be the constant overwhelming presence of God.
25. Jung, *Man and His Symbols,* p. 67.
26. St. Francis de Sales, *Introduction to the Devout Life* (New York: Image Books, 1950), trans. John K. Ryan, p. 159. Martin Buber, while admitting in *I and Thou* that the "passion of erotic fulfillment" can serve as a metaphor for the dissolution of barriers between persons in the "I-thou" encounter, cautions about sexual ecstasy that the actuality of every hour is of greater importance than such "enigmatic webs at the *margins* of being."
27. Robert Nozick, *The Examined Life* (New York: Simon and Schuster, 1989), p. 67.
28. I John 4:16 (RSV).
29. Paul Tillich, *The Dynamics of Faith* (New York: Harper and Row, 1957), pp. 41–43.
30. For Tillich faith is our ultimate directedness toward that which transcends finite reality. This is why as Tillich says, "the language of faith is the language of symbols." Tillich, *The Dynamics of Faith*, p. 45.
31. Mahadeviyakka, *Speaking of Śiva*, p. 125.
32. McFague, *Models of God*, p. 35.
33. Basavanna in *Speaking of Śiva*, p. 89.
34. McFague, *Models of God,* pp. 33–34.
35. Cited in *Heavenly Sex: Sexuality in the Jewish Tradition* by Dr. Ruth Westheimer and Jonathan Mark (New York: Continuum, 1993) p. 5.
36. Nammalvar, *Hymns for the Drowning* (London: Penguin, 1993), trans. A. K. Ramanujan, p. 50.
37. I John 4:19.

38. See "Meaning and Eros in Life and Religion" in *The Meaning of Life in the World Religions,* ed. Joseph Runzo and Nancy M. Martin, pp. 187–201.

39. See Geoffrey Parrinder, *Sexual Morality in the World Religions* (Oxford: Oneworld, 1996), pp. 20–21.

40. I owe this discussion of Tokugawa Japan to the superb study of this interplay of monastic Buddhism and homosexuality in Gary P. Leupp's *Male Colors* (Berkeley: University of California Press, 1995).

41. Brian Hebblethwaite, "The Varieties of Goodness," in *Ethics, Religion and the Good Society* (Louisville: Westminster Press, 1992), p. 8.

42. See chapter 6 of this volume.

43. Jack Dominick, "Sex Within Marriage," in *Sexuality and the Sacred: Sources for Theological Reflection*, ed. James B. Nelson and Sandra P. Longfellow (Louisville: Westminster Press, 1994), pp. 264 and 270.

44. See Jeffrey Hopkins, "Reason and Orgasm in Tibetan Buddhism," chapter 14 of this volume.

Plate 2 Leading Zen master of the Rinzai School of Buddhism in Japan, founded by Eisai (1141–1215), which teaches the possibility of instantaneous enlightenment (*satori*) through vigorous meditation (*zazen*) and the use of *koans* under the strict supervision of a Zen master. Kencho-ji Temple, Kamakura, Japan. Photo: *Joseph Runzo.*

2

LOVE'S INSUFFICIENCY: ZEN *as* IRRITANT

William R. LaFleur

Love is important, but compassion is deeper. We must solve this deeply. To have compassion is to have the same mind as the other. Understand?

Taisen Deshimaru[1]

Don't just do something. Sit there, stupid!

·American Zen quip

Zen has been the subject of a fair amount of Western scholarship, and the more specific topic of Zen and gender has been taken up in some fine studies.[2] Zen and love, however, at least to my knowledge, has not been given scholarly attention. Western scholars have ignored this topic, but as a matter of fact, some people both in America and Europe involved in the practice of Zen have been unusually curious about it. This is simply because of the truly radical institutional change that has accompanied the transplantation of Japanese Zen into Western societies. The nub of this change has been that for the first time in Zen's history it has become commonplace to have both male and female practitioners in the same physical location for meditation, instruction, and daily living. In the Asian past there were instances of males and females doing meditation in one place, but these were rare and certainly not extended into the whole routine of diurnal and nocturnal life together. In America the greatest growth of interest in Zen practice took place during the 1960s and 1970s, a period during which the single-gender college and the gender-differentiated dormitory were becoming nearly passé. Why, many assumed, should the location for meditation, living, and sleeping be any different? So, in contrast to its Asian background, Zen in the West went "co-ed" with extraordinary speed.

To go from a tradition of separately gendered monastic traditions to halls of meditation filled with persons of both genders has been a change that gave many involved in it a fairly rough ride. The various Zen teachers in both America and Europe had to face – with virtually no precedents or guidelines in the traditional materials – the difficulty of having to give direction to eager students who also were quite happy to be sexually active and ready to make the most of the fact that on a daily basis they were in physical proximity to one another. In America many entered the path of Zen while at the same time being very interested in having sexual relations and even in finding mates – preferably from within the pool of fellow practitioners. To Zen teachers from Asia not trained to deal with such questions, these Westerners posed questions about what Zen might do for their "relationships." And since the questioners were Americans rather than Japanese, when they used the word "relationship," they definitely did *not* mean something between themselves and their parents![3]

It may still be an open question whether or not this "co-ed" development in Western Zen will, over the long run, work. Students here obviously have pushed the question of "Zen and relationships" far up on the list of questions they habitually addressed to their teachers. And their teachers have had the daunting task of trying to articulate a position on these questions out of traditional materials packed with nothing so obvious as a sustained silence on them. Robert Aitken, a highly-respected American Zen master who taught for many years in Hawaii and someone who had spent much time in Japan, admits to having confronted something of a dilemma when, in the course of giving a series of lectures on ethics to his assembled students in Hawaii, he came to the Buddhist precept which enjoins sexual purity. He writes of finding virtually no materials on the topic. He checked the elaborate subject index of the *Kosoku zenshû zenmon kôan taikan*, a directory of some 5,500 Zen koans, and found there no entry for sex. Therefore, to his students, who almost certainly were expecting otherwise, he said:

> After a careful search of the literature you can find cautions by Dogen Zenji to avoid sexual gossip, but that is about all, except for this precept and its brief commentaries. In the Zen monastery food, sleep, zazen, work, and even going to the toilet are organized and scheduled, but it is as though sex does not exist. I am not so naive as to suppose that this could be possible, but I must say that the mildest kind of homosexual fooling around among

young monks was all the sex I ever observed in several months of residence in a Japanese Zen monastery.[4]

This was probably not, we may assume, a very welcome word to what was probably a gathering of primarily heterosexual, hormone-influenced, twenty- and thirty-year-old Americans trying to be practitioners of Zen in close proximity to the erotically charged beach cultures of Hawaii.

The reasons for this thunderous silence in the Asian tradition are multiple and would include, I suspect, some degree of "repression" of what is biological in our sexual make-up as humans. It needs to be noted, however, that the Zen tradition (perhaps in contrast to the tantric one in this) had no reason to elevate amorous relationships as having transcendent significance. The contrast between this and what we know of the West's traditions, both Jewish and Christian, is fairly sharp. Halberthal and Margalit, two Israeli scholars, convincingly show the degree to which the ancient Jews modeled their own one-on-one relationship to God on the intimacy and exclusivity of the monogamous marriage.[5] And, as is well known, in Christianity the relationship between Christ and the church is constructed by a similar simile of fidelity. Although the complicated connections between *agape* and *eros* as terms for "love" in that tradition cannot be easily summarized, the net effect has been to privilege as central what comes translated as the word "love."[6] Among precious things "the greatest of these is love" became the way in which I Corinthians 13 has over time been seen to privilege love in Western civilization. (It may be worth noting that in Japan many non-Christians contemplating marriage will opt for a church wedding – along with a Bible, a cross, and a vested clergyman – in part because the churches there have long referred to their deity as the "God of Love" and weddings, these people assume, are the right time to place emphasis on love.)

Buddhist temples and even Shinto shrines cannot compete with Christianity in the language and rituals of love. And this suggests, at least in part, why Robert Aitken found no reference to these things in the books he consulted. The Zen tradition had seen love neither as a signifier of the Transcendent nor as something to be privileged. And within East Asia if any human relationship were to be seen as special, it historically tended to be that between parents and children. My suggestion is that this helps us understand why there was a considerable gap experienced by Western persons, steeped in the West's expectations, when they began to practice Zen and discovered that the teachers of the Asian tradition stumbled and mumbled when asked about these things. "What," these Americans and Europeans asked, "does Zen have to say about relationships?"

Charlotte Joko Beck of San Diego, a senior and highly respected Zen teacher, has, I think, been unusually lucid in her address to this question. She writes in a way that deflates the term "relationship" as usually used by Americans. In response to inquiries about how Zen might enhance amorous relationship, she answers in a way that pulls down one thing and raises others:

> Every moment in our life is relationship. There is nothing except relation-
> ship. At this moment my relationship is to the rug, to the room, to my own
> body, to the sound of my voice. There is nothing except my being in rela-
> tionship at each second.[7]

Noting that "love is a word not often mentioned in Buddhist texts," Beck has stressed the value of what she calls "practicing with relationships."

Practicing *with* relationships? This is not unlike, I suggest, something known in physical exercise. The person developing the strength of his or her abdominal muscles through sit-ups, for instance, may at some point add metal weights to the part of the body being lifted – so as to increase the stress and the effect. This is somewhat analogous to what is meant by Zen practice here. And relationships can be used to make the practice toward perfection more difficult – virtually the opposite of the more common notion that they are like a soft, comfortable corner into which our small egos can retreat so as to be reinflated when hurt. Beck writes:

> Why are relationships such excellent practice? Why do they help us go into
> what we might call the slow death of the ego? Because, aside from our
> formal sitting, there is no way that is superior to relationships in helping us
> see where we're stuck and what we're holding on to. As long as our buttons
> are pushed, we have a great chance to learn and grow. So a relationship is a
> great gift, not because it makes us happy – it often doesn't – but because any
> intimate relationship, if we view it as practice, is the clearest mirror we can
> find.[8]

Beck inverts things. People ask: "What can Zen do for my relationship?" and she asks them to ask themselves: "What can a relationship do for my practice of Zen?"

The historian within me is interested in how this position both differs and is like the more traditional view within East Asian Zen. On one level it differs inasmuch as the masters of China, Korea, and Japan did not, to my knowledge, conceive of enlisting what we today call "relationships" into service within the context of the range of disciplines and austerities that constituted Zen practice. In that sense this is a real innovation and one that is probably directly due both to the "co-ed" nature of Zen practices in the West and to the fact that female teachers such as Beck have for the most part faced this question much more courageously and openly than have their male counterparts.

On another level, however, the principles articulated by Beck would seem to be consistent with the Asian tradition. When in her writings one finds the rare reference to the word "love," this comes forward accompanied by the linguistic equivalent of flashing lights at a railroad crossing. When that word is there, it is time to be on guard. Beck writes: " … 'romantic' love…has little to do with love. It is good to investigate what love is and how it is connected to practice, since the two fruits of our practice are wisdom and compassion."[9] This is to say that wisdom and compassion are, ultimately, the more important goals and values.

I call attention to another place where things are put in order of importance, one that comes in an easily overlooked phrase in Beck's discourse, something that shows up when she writes: *"Aside from our formal sitting,* there is no way that is superior to relationships in helping us see where we're stuck and what we're holding on to." Relationships here, if grasped as tools for the clarification of life, are seen as having marvelous potential, but even then such potential is not quite equivalent to that of "our formal sitting." The language here, while probably a bit obscure to others, is perfectly straightforward to persons who are somewhat involved in Zen training. They know that the term "formal sitting" refers to the regimen they have adopted for themselves, one that involves dedicated periods of time spent in meditation, preferably on a cushion with the body in either the classic "lotus" position or a near approximation thereof. Also some ongoing and active relationship to an experienced teacher who will guide the practitioner in these things is a clear desideratum. The point I am making here is that in Beck's discussions what is called "our formal sitting" remains the still unparalleled context for all the goals she has in mind. Relationships can only come second.

This is profoundly important. Ours is, I would argue, a society which, at least for the most part, implicitly embraces a sequence of preferences. Love retains, even in its secularized forms, the aura of that which many would identify as the highest of values. But since love in its most concrete forms is, most feel, far preferable to its expression in the abstract, intimacy has become the operative word with special resonance. To so stress love as intimate is on one level to affirm, rightly I think, that love without vulnerability is vapid and that vulnerability is more likely to be present in intimate contexts. However, because the term "intimacy" also tends to suggest – at least today – the notion of a relationship that has likely become sexual, it is, in fact, the sexual union that has become the *de facto* template of love in contemporary society. "The greatest of these is love" has in the secularized West become, for all practical purposes "the greatest of these is sex."

Our problem today, I think, is that of trying to figure out how to back away from that conclusion (one that both feeds and is fed by our industries of entertainment) while at the same time refusing to cast sex once again as defiling or even to deny that, just as being "married" will in no way guarantee that a married couple's erotic relationship will be a "good" in their lives, so too the unmarried state does not foreclose the possibility of sex being a true "good" in life. This is our dilemma.

Although it does not solve all these problems, useful tools can be plucked out of Beck's statement that "Aside from our formal sitting, relationships [are unparalleled] in helping us see where we're stuck and what we're holding on to." Here is a wisdom drawn not from a divine authority but from a long tradition of sustained observation, primarily by the person engaged in meditation, on experience. It is on that basis that the value hierarchy is redrawn: to say that sex can clearly be a good in our lives as human beings is not the same as saying it will always and everywhere be what is the best within them. To go back to the terminology of Zen, the priorities would be "sitting" first, "relationships" second.

Therefore, I think we have gained much by the way in which Beck and others have directly faced and examined the connections between love and wisdom or, alternatively, those between "relationships" and what in Zen is called "practice." These were examinations that the separated and cloistered monks and nuns of traditional Zen avoided – either because these were not pressing problems or because they were repressed ones.

Still the privileging of "practice" is traditional. And I think this can be demonstrated by a passage from the writings of Dogen (1200–1253), the medieval Japanese Zen master whose works have greatly interested certain philosophers and religious thinkers in the West. Here I translate this bit of text because it provides Dogen's answer to a question which could be: "What is the locus of the highest intimacy?" This is the question to which, as suggested above, we already know the likely response of contemporary society.

So what would Dogen have seen as the unparalleled locus of intimacy?

The answer to that – and I think it would be one shared with virtually every other Zen teacher in the East Asian tradition – would be that the most intimate of human relationships is that between a Zen master and the person who is training under his or her tutelage. And the elegant and definitive model for this both in Dogen and others is the relationship between the persons whose status we, with terminology that is in many ways unfortunate, have come to designate as the "patriarchs" of Zen. The assumption in virtually the whole Zen tradition is that the nexus between these persons is that of a deep, life-and-death emotional bond, one that surpasses every other kind of relationship either known or imaginable. The relationship between Zen teacher and student is understood to be emotional and existential; it is also physical even though not sexual. When compared to it, all other kinds of human relationships – even if erotic, sexual, and relatively uninhibited – are on a lesser level.

An essay of Dogen probably composed in 1243 and entitled "Menjû" demonstrates the core of what I take to be his thinking about intimacy. The two Chinese ideographs of the term *menjû* mean "face-reception" and in the vocabulary of Zen refer to the idea that the transmission of the Dharma was understood to be not via scriptures but in contexts of a series of face-to-face interrogations and communications between master and disciple.

At least as I read the texts of Dogen, there is in them a fair amount of very concrete bodily imagery.[10] In fact, at times Dogen appears to employ what his audience or readership knew of erotic experience and then turns that knowledge to other ends. I think that is what happens in what follows, and in my translation I flag such diction with italics. Dogen writes:

> Persons who rightly transfer the clear-visioned eye, an eye that at this very moment and without obstruction has Shakyamuni Buddha himself in view, are persons who are *more intimate* with Shakyamuni than Shakyamuni [is with himself]. Such persons are about to make Shakyamuni Buddhas of both the past and the future visually present before their own eyes – even more distinctly than whatever [ordinary] object of sight might be there right now. Thus if you wish to prize Shakyamuni Buddha and if you wish to be *enamoured with* Shakyamuni, you ought deeply to reverence this face-to-face transmission, and you ought to prostrate yourself before someone who is so invaluable and is so extraordinarily difficult to link up with in life. This is to prostrate yourself before the Tathagata and to have face-to-face interaction with the Tathagata. When you worship the unchangeability that is inherent in the practicing of a transmission which is face-to-face and Tathagata-to-Tathagata, you may begin to wonder who the "self" might

have become and who the "other" might have become in such a context. [But] what you must do is simply pour your most *tenacious love* and your most *protective possessiveness* into this activity.[11]

It is not, I think, to push the textual evidence too far to say that Dogen here employs what most humans already know about sexual love and even about the temporary sense of a lost self-identity that occurs within sexual "climax." He does this, however, to make a point about enlightenment as a permanent and far deeper erasure of self.

We may be misled by our own language habits of thinking about time if we assume that here Dogen is referring to the transmission of the Dharma down a simple historical trajectory, always from a "patriarch" in a superior position to someone in an inferior, strictly receptive one. The focus in the above passage seems quite different – namely, that at the level of intimacy envisioned here the ordinary hierarchy of superior and inferior drops away. He refers to a union of Tathagata and Tathagata. "Self" and "other" become relativized, not ultimately meaningful. And this, I suggest, is compatible with the well-known statement of Dogen in his "Genjô kôan" essay: "To study the Buddha way is to study the self. To study the self is to forget the self. To forget the self is to be actualized by myriad things."[12]

This is to privilege "practice" and its ultimate goals over "relationships" and their penultimate ones. And Dogen, to a degree not yet sufficiently recognized, was not averse to introducing playfulness, even a playfulness based on knowledge of sex, into what is the panoply of linguistic tools used by him to convey his central points. These are part of what Hee-Jin Kim referred to as Dogen's "deliberate, often brilliant 'misinterpretations' of certain notions and passages of Buddhism."[13] And one of these, I suggest, is his use of vocabulary about love, sex, and passion in his presentation of just how face-to-face the transmission of the Dharma might get. He invites his hearer/reader to bring to mind the experience of sexual climax in order to say: "Ah ha, what you think of as climax is only *ante*-climax. I tell you here about the climax that climaxes all supposed climaxes!" Is it not appropriate for us to imagine that the large assembly of tonsured monks, persons we should not assume to be without sexual experience, would have been smiling or sniggering during this portion of their master's lecture, a lecture which in its *double entendre* and utter playfulness was humorously serious? We need to note the terms: "more intimate," "enamoured with," "tenacious love," and "protective possessiveness." And all of this, after all, is in an essay with a title that could be rendered "Passing [something] from one face directly into another face." The image is powerful if used to communicate the conventional ideas of a master-to-student or even a person-to-person transmission – of information, of wisdom, or whatever. It becomes, however, significantly more powerful when it is recognized that Dogen is depicting a mode of interaction in which *on the deepest level possible* the boundaries of "self" and of self-enclosure have been dissolved.

I wish to draw out a few observations based on the above. The first is that, while the more open discussions of these things in Western Zen is an apt way of meeting the condition of practice contexts that are not segregated by gender, it would probably be wise to refrain from celebrating this as some kind of *improvement* brought to Zen by persons in the West. Zen gone co-ed is not necessarily a Zen with a moral edge over its Asian parent. It is still possible to make a strong case for providing the option of monastic communities within contemporary society. As the important research by Paula Arai, arising out of her Harvard dissertation, suggests, it is very often mature women who in Japan have recently been finding special value in taking the tonsure and going off to live in nunneries – especially those of the Soto denomination founded by Dogen. Finding that the motivation of these women for entering such a life is generally both different and more commendable than that of their male counterparts, Arai writes:

> Now the world of the nuns is a harbor for the traditional values and lifestyle of Zen. They generally continue the rhythm of life they learned at the nunnery, they remain celibate, and they do not have access to opportunities for making any sizeable amount of money.[14]

This forcefully reminds us that some individuals even today clearly find their life fulfillment in relationships that are *not* lived in a one-to-one, eroticized intimacy with a member of the opposite sex. In fact, it may be that one result of the new pragmatism advocated by Richard Rorty might be that, especially for some women, the choice to live in separate communities is preferable. "That is to say, self-selected groups of women could retreat into private communities long enough to develop new and autonomous vocabularies."[15] Perhaps the future of Zen and similar movements lies in having concurrent modes – one for persons who want to incorporate erotic relationships into their practice and another facilitating more monastic lifestyles. Such might be one application of Rorty's depiction of emerging society as "a bazaar surrounded by lots and lots of private clubs."[16]

Secondly, a society with the intellectual and religious latitude to see both of these modes as equally viable would probably have to be one for which reductive theories about religion have become less determinative than they have tended to be in the recent past. That is, we will have to gain distance from what has been our fascination with the toolbox full of intellectual wrenches and screwdrivers fashioned in the West during the past two centuries. We will, at least, need to show greater caution when using the heavy machinery of what Ricoeur called the "hermeneutics of suspicion."[17]

Concretely, we will have to question the adequacy of our usual questions – interpretative patterns that resisted complexity in favor of single-factor explanations. Is the relationship between Zen master and disciple really one of a merely disguised homoerotic sexual interest, something simply repressed and kept from moving to the point where, if honest, the persons involved really would like it to move? Do notions of sadism and masochism really tell us what is the essence of what is going on in the imposed discomforts, even pain, of the Zen monastic life? And is the whole monastic institution deliberately organized as a hierarchical structure only so that it and its abbot might most effectively wield power or, at least, hope to wield political power in the larger society and to garner vast amounts of patronage? And is this whole thing nothing more than a conservative political ideology masquerading as religious truth? We will, I suggest, have to feel less easy with assuming that just even to raise such suspicions is to debunk the phenomenon in view.

Thirdly, I suggest we might take advantage of how eccentric to our own culture a thinker such as Dogen might be – especially as in this new century we may need to rethink our views of love and intimacy. I have claimed that at present the sexual relationship between consenting adults, especially if it is more-or-less long-term, seems to have become *the* template for intimacy in our society. This is why, as noted, the practitioners of Zen in America and Europe are having so much difficulty with this question. The weight of our own immediate culture is extraordinarily heavy, so that some within Western Zen communities want a Zen unlike that of Dogen, one with a more "modern" and more "positive" approach to sex. I am, in a word, much less certain that we need to move quickly to "correct" or "improve" the Asian tradition, to turn something we view as "negative" into its opposite.

Taisen Deshimaru, a Japanese Soto master based in France, was someone who, although himself controversial in some ways, at least showed a positive unwillingness to accept the simple assumption that the West will simply have to correct the received Asian tradition on this point. To him that assumption seemed a bit too easy, too ready to congratulate rather than question our own modern and Western cultural mode. I suggest we might do ourselves and our society a favor by positing and practicing the viability of another, an alternative, template for real intimacy. Within the Zen tradition purity is a value, but an obsession with the notion of purity is not. And since the tradition comes fitted out with elements of humor, this point is made in a rather well-known story about Tanzan and Ekido. I use it here both to bring my discussion to a close and because the story seems to transfer into the domain of sex Dogen's dictum that "flowers fall when we cling to them."

> [Two monks] Tanzan and Ekido were once traveling together down a muddy road. A heavy rain was falling. Coming around a bend, they met a lovely girl in silk kimono and sash, unable to cross the inter-section. "Come on, girl," said Tanzan at once. Lifting her in his arms, he carried her over the mud. Ekido did not speak again until that night when they reached a lodging temple. Then he could no longer restrain himself. "We monks don't go near females," he told Tanzan, "especially not young and lovely ones. It is dangerous. Why did you do that?" "I left the girl there," said Tanzan. "Are you still carrying her?"[18]

NOTES

1. Philippe Coupey, ed. *Sit: Zen Teachings of Master Taisen Deshimaru* (Prescott, AZ: Hohm Press, no date), p. 45.

2. See Miriam Levering, "Lin-chi (Rinzai) Ch'an and Gender: The Rhetoric of Equality and the Rhetoric of Heroism," in *Buddhism, Sexuality, and Gender*, ed. José Ignacio Cabezón (Albany: SUNY Press, 1985), pp. 137–156 and Paula K. R. Arai, "Sôtô Zen Nuns in Modern Japan: Keeping and Creating Tradition," as republished in *Religion and Society in Modern Japan*, Mark R. Mullins, et. al. (Berkeley: Asian Humanities Press, 1993), pp. 203–218. Writing on gender in other forms of Buddhism is, of course, much more extensive. See especially Miranda Shaw, *Passionate Enlightenment: Women in Tantric Buddhism* (Princeton: Princeton University Press, 1994) and, in Japanese, Minamoto Junko, *Bukkyô to sei* [Buddhism and Sex] (Tokyo: San'ichi shobô, 1996) and the Jan. 1995 [No.30] issue of the journal *Bukkyô*.

3. In his *Chûsei no ai to jûzoku: emaki no naka no nikutai* [Love and Dependency in Medieval (Japan): Bodies in the Picture-scrolls], Hotate Michihisa demonstrates that what he calls the "structure of love" [*ai no katachi*] in that period is most clearly shown in the way parents carry the children to safety on their backs [*onbu*] and that religious value is often

graphically articulated by showing persons of religious importance doing the same for others. (Tokyo: Heibonsha, 1986, pp. 132–154.)

4. Robert Aitken, *The Mind of Clover: Essays in Zen Buddhist Ethics* (San Francisco: North Point Press, 1984), p. 38.

5. Moshe Halberthal and Avishai Margalit, *Idolatry*, trans. Naomi Goldblum (Cambridge: Harvard University Press, 1992), pp. 9–36.

6. For a discussion of the place of *eros* and *agape* in Christian understandings of love, see Joseph Runzo, "Eros and Meaning in Life and Religion" in *The Meaning of Life in the World Religions*, ed. Joseph Runzo and Nancy M. Martin (Oxford: Oneworld, 1999).

7. Charlotte Joko Beck, *Everyday Zen: Love and Work* (San Francisco: Harper San Francisco, 1989), p. 77.

8. Ibid., pp. 88–89.

9. Ibid., p. 71.

10. Translations of Zen texts have not been protected from an impulse often felt by translators of "religious" texts – that is the temptation to "elevate" them by playing down the role and import of bodily imagery in them. See my entry "Body" in *Critical Terms for Religious Study*, ed. Mark C. Taylor (Chicago: University of Chicago Press, 1998), pp. 36–54.

11. The original I have used is in ed. *Dôgen*, Terada Tôru and Mizuno Yaoko, [Part I] in *Nihon shisô taikei* vol. 13 (Tokyo: Iwanami shoten, 1972), p. 112. A translation of this entire essay can be found in *Moon in a Dewdrop: Writings of Zen Master Dôgen*, ed. Kazuaki Tanahashi (San Francisco: North Point Press, 1985), pp. 175–183.

12. Tanahashi, ibid., p. 70.

13. Hee-Jin Kim, "The Reason of Words and Letters: Dôgen and Kôan Language," in *Dôgen Studies*, ed. William R. LaFleur (Honolulu: University of Hawaii Press, 1985), p. 60.

14. Arai, "Sôtô Zen Nuns," p. 214.

15. David L. Hall, *Richard Rorty: Prophet and Poet of the New Pragmatism* (Albany: State University of New York Press, 1994), p. 195.

16. Ibid.

17. This point is in intended agreement with that of Arvind Sharma in his chapter in this volume.

18. As in *Zen Flesh, Zen Bones: A Collection of Zen and Pre-Zen Writings*, ed. Paul Reps (New York: Doubleday, 1989), p. 18.

Part II

LOVE AND RELIGION

Plate 3 Towering several stories high, this contemporary wall mural of Krishna shows the amorous god playing the lilting notes on his flute, a sound which no devotee can resist. Jawar Kala Kendra, Jaipur, India. Photo: *Nancy M. Martin*

3

THE GOD OF LOVE *and the* LOVE OF GOD *in* CHRISTIAN AND HINDU TRADITIONS[1]

Julius J. Lipner

A QUESTION OF METHOD

When two different cultures confront each other amid life's complexities, what might one expect in the minds and hearts of those who make the encounter? Puzzlement, incomprehension, fear, wonder, repulsion, a quickening of interest, a desire to explore, understand, assimilate, to change and be changed? These reactions are all possibilities, and two or more may co-exist variously, depending on circumstance. Each of us has probably been in this situation many times in today's multifariously interactive world – at least in the world in which the reader of this chapter would live.

To appreciate the issues I wish to raise here, let us first fix our attention on an intercultural encounter that was to be of momentous significance. When Jesus, the Palestinian Jew, declared to Pilate, the Roman governor, that fateful morning in the Praetorium (John 18:33f.) that he had come into the world to bear witness to the truth, and Pilate answered, "What is truth?", in what language did they converse? Aramaic? Hebrew? Latin? Greek? Did they speak through an interpreter? We do not know. The scholars tell us that Pilate had already been in Palestine for about four years, so he knew something about the culture, and presumably the language, of the people he governed.[2] We also do not know what lay behind Pilate's enigmatic question (*ti estin aletheia* in the Greek text).[3] Could the "truth" of which Jesus spoke be grasped by his foreign listener – still more or less a stranger not only to Jesus' culture, but also perhaps to the religious message that Jesus intended to convey? For the purposes of the Gospel text, it seems that Jesus thought that understanding was not beyond Pilate, else he would not have spoken to him as he did.

And what might Pilate have said, I wonder, if Jesus had declared instead that it was to bear witness to the love (*agape*) of his heavenly Father that he had come into the world? Would this have made a more poignant impact, and significantly changed the course of events?[4] I do not wish to engage in idle speculation. I am trying to point out that we react differently to different words and their contexts, and – their cognitive content apart – the emotional freight of words for "love" seems to differ profoundly from the emotional freight of words for "truth," notwithstanding the philosophical and experiential connections often perceived to exist between these words. To make use of a distinction drawn by the comparative religionist, Raimon Panikkar, between "terms" and "words" – the former, emotionless technical tools of the scientific approach, the latter, "historico-cultural crystallizations of human experience," pregnant with possibilities and meaning[5] – are there not grounds for thinking *prima facie* that words for "love" with their evocations of human outreach and solidarity would be more effective at communicating across gender and cultural boundaries than the seemingly more abstract words for "truth," "goodness" and so on? Are not barriers of "otherness" more porous when it comes to words of love, pain, joy, sorrow – so experientially direct and humanly evocative – in contrast to apparently more abstract or theoretical expressions? "Love" then seems to be a better starting-point as purveyor of interreligious and cross-cultural understanding than a number of possible rivals.

This does not mean that cultures have not sought to refine, even stylize, their understanding of love in poetry, art, and music, of course. But these elegances are aesthetically successful only in so far as they do not destroy the living freshness of the experience they seek to convey. Thus "love" seems to speak more directly, in contexts of greater human solidarity and transformative response, than many other words. It is important to keep this in mind during the course of this chapter. I am advocating and attempting a human dialogue, rather than a cerebral one. Perhaps what has been wrong so far with conventional attempts at interreligious understanding has been their generally bloodless, abstract character. What is needed more than anything else when trying to build cultural and gender bridges in an age more conscious than ever of various forms of human fragmentation is a new wholistic methodology. I am trying both to implement such a method as well as to contribute to conceptual understanding on my topic. In such discourse not only the literal proposition, but also analogy, narrative, myth, metaphor and other tropes must combine to play their part. The result will be a *cumulative* effect, a wholistic picture that will function at different levels of our awareness – rational, affective, imaginative, evaluative – and induce a form of understanding that will be more comprehensive, engaging and transformative than has generally been the case hitherto. This will be a "comparative" understanding in a more rounded sense of the word. In this chapter I can but introduce this method and sketch lines of inquiry, and also give notice of a fuller study in the making.

A "HUMANISTIC" METHOD

A chief objective in embarking on this project is to drive a methodological wedge between a certain kind of scientific approach to understanding – an approach that is clinical, one-dimensional, and depersonalized – and the wholistic ("humanistic," if you will) procedure I am adopting. For too long have the methods of the humanities sought to conform to that of the natural and physical sciences, with an enormous loss of self-esteem and understanding of what they should be about in consequence. By trying to ape the "scientific method," and to engage in misguided debates about their own "scientific" credentials for discerning "truth," the humanities have undermined their credibility and appreciation of their proper capacities and goals. Study of the humanities involves systematic study of human subjects from a human point of view; as such, it must devolve an appropriate methodology to achieve its ends.

A crucial feature of this methodology must be to extend as comprehensively as practicable the range of human discourse, and to apply the implications of this extension, that is, its rational, affective, imaginative and empathetic dimensions; only then will the humanities begin to do justice to the labyrinthine complexities of their human subject matter. This method will be rigorous and precise in its own way (there will be no place for unsubstantiated speculation, just as there is no place for fantasy in the "hard" sciences). It will operate with a paradigm of truth that is based on experience; it will weigh up documentary evidence, strive to discern (and contextualize) the "facts," resort to observation, assess testimony, respect logic, remain open-minded, hold up its conclusions for verification. Yet this will be a paradigm that is neither literalist (viz. "truth can only be expressed in literal declarations") nor quantitative (viz. "truth can only be expressed in mathematical statements"). In short, this paradigm of truth will be as authentic in its own sphere as any that might obtain in the sphere of the sciences.

This chapter is indeed a case of work in progress, but a start must be made. My purpose is to use *love* as the symbol, vehicle, messenger, of creative understanding between the great traditions of Christianity and Hinduism, with special reference to the way love of God,[6] in both subjective and objective senses of the possessive, has been understood in these faiths, but without in the process doing violence to the integrity of either. In the course of my study, I will strive to be wholistic in a way that will unfold gradually. First, however, we must consider an objection.

An Objection to Comparative Study

There is a view that people live in self-contained worlds of their culture's making, that the language they use and the experiences it conveys enclose them in a self-referencing web of meaning, and that there is no way in which there can be really meaningful dialogue between two such webs or at least between webs that arise out of historically disconnected cultures. The categories of thought of a particular web act virtually as one-way semantic filters with regard to what is perceived beyond the web (or at least webs with historically disparate origins). Thus, speaking religiously, expressions like "creation," "God" and even "salvation," "providence," "incarnation," and "sinfulness" may well be stepping-stones to meaningful dialogue within the Abrahamic faiths (though "incarnation" here might become a meaningful stumbling-block), but they cannot be used as access points for constructive exchanges between these faiths and the historically disparate non-Abrahamic religions. The conceptual interactions possible between historically correlative linguistic-cultural webs are not possible between thought-worlds that developed quite separately. In the first case there may be a genuine basis for assimilative cognitive exchange, while in the second case there cannot be, for – to change the metaphor – the possibilities for cognitive osmosis between disparate linguistic-cultural skins are highly limited.

In the context of Christianity and Hinduism – traditions which grew to maturity without significant historical reference to each other – there is no basis for mutual transformation through constructive dialogue. In seeking to understand the divine love for us and its ramifications for human relationships, the contextual confrontation of words such as *agape* and *karuna/anugraha, avatara* and incarnation, "faith" and *bhakti/prapatti,* salvation and *moksha* – not to mention ideas for which there may well be no such apparent counterparts (e.g. "redemption" and "atonement," perhaps, on the Christian side, and *guru* and *prasada* on the Hindu) – cannot be bridged. One is really talking at cross-purposes in the attempt to do so; any similarity is superficial and deceptive. Contextualization in each tradition demands that there are more grounds to separate the juxtaposed meanings involved than to unite them. Here dialogue, at best, can lead by way of empathy to mutual understanding, but not to cognitive exchange and assimilation. The distortion that would be the price of decontextualization would be too high.

This objection overreaches itself, and suffers from a number of defects. Here I can do no more than indicate how it can be overcome. The assumption that linguistic-cultural webs are more or less self-contained structures is defective on both historical and philosophical grounds. Let us start with the philosophical. B-A Scharfstein, in an article entitled "The Contextual Fallacy," has pointed out that any discourse, from ordinary conversation in the home to more precise forms of communication, requires a continuous process of contextualization and decontextualization to be viable.

> Caution slips easily into hypercaution, which deserves the name because it is sterile. For those interested in comparative thought, it is therefore impor-tant to recognize that an extreme emphasis on context can be unreasonable and intellectually expensive enough to be considered a fallacy.
>
> A little reflection should persuade us that understanding is often injured if we try to confine it to appreciation of the nuances that make texts or any-thing else unique ... The very perception that discloses uniqueness discloses similarity. If it were not for the perceptual ability to disregard differences, our experiences would never become cumulative; we would never learn from them, because there are inevitable differences in any of the experiences we undergo. The question is not whether the differences exist ... but what we should make of them, and the answer often lies in the conscious or unconscious decision ... to make use only of the criteria that fit our need at the time, that is, to intuit or hypothesize or discover the context that is most pertinent to our need ...
>
> Contextualism is too easy a refuge from analysis ... The parochialism it encourages is itself a form of misunderstanding, intellectually little [more than] myopia raised to the status of virtue ... The fullest attempt to under-stand distant thought may be, in effect, both to insert it into and extract it from context.[7]

Thus comparative analysis, even of distant original contexts, if done with alertness and sensitivity, is liable to create new contexts, relationships and meanings for the material analyzed, and to enrich and expand understand-ing of the original contexts involved. It is the way that new discoveries are made, paradigm-shifts initiated, and perceptions and lifestyles transformed. This is because the (nodal) "words" rather than the "terms" compared are precisely embedded in context in the first place, and hence capable, when comparatively recontextualized, of systemically radiating semantic change in their original contexts in the understanding of the comparative analyst. It is a way – the only way – of going ahead in a communicationally interactive world. Thus, in this study, we celebrate context, rather than belittle it. What we do not celebrate is a stultifying contextualism.

There is a further consideration that enlarges the point already made. The words we use in discourse that matters to the living of our lives – especially religious discourse – are pervaded by patterns of speech – metaphor, analogy, narrative, paradox, parable, to name but a few – that are inherently resistant to a process of substitutionary literalism. That is, the meaning they are perceived to convey cannot be reduced to language that is simply literal. Tropes carry what has been described as a "surplus of meaning" that cannot be replaced without remainder by language that is literal.[8] In other words, in a significant way they are semantically open-ended. This open-endedness arises from our constitutional open-endedness as human beings to experience different forms of life and to be shaped variously by this experience on the one hand, and to experience vicariously, on the other, by means of what I have called constructive empathy – that is, the attested capacity we have to enter non-intrusively by a disciplined imagination into perspectives and situations that otherwise would be the terrain of "the other" – and it is this, I contend, that enables dialogic understanding and subsequent cognitive assimilation across such boundaries to take place by the creation of viable comparative contexts.[9] This is why it is necessary to include tropes in the dialogic process; but by doing so, we are only doing what is natural, and allowing language to function in its proper and fullest capacity.[10]

The Open-endedness of Religious Traditions

What I have given so far is a philosophical marker of a larger, more sustained argument justifying informed comparative, even distant comparative, contextualization, or rather recontextualization. Now to empirical considerations in support of our view. One has only to study the religious traditions to observe that in the developments of their conceptual and experiential histories the principle of open-endedness that I have spoken of above has been implemented with unfailing regularity. This implementation has taken place not only internally, that is, by means of

ongoing controversies about practice, precept and meaning within particular communities, but also externally, viz. through debate with groups who
hold different, sometimes apparently incompatible, fundamental assumptions and presuppositions. The boundaries of so-called self-referencing
and self-authenticating webs of sense and sensibility are regularly trans-
gressed in these encounters.

Christianity itself classically exemplifies this open-endedness. Indeed,
Christianity, supposedly a linguistic-cultural web in its own right, is itself
the product of the interaction of at least two quite disparate cultural mat-
rices – the Hebraic and the Hellenistic (not to mention others, e.g. the
Persian). Yet the Christian tradition has by definition (in terms of the
objection) become an integrated system of thought and meaning per se.
On a variety of subjects crucial to the development of Christian faith –
ideas of God, personhood, creation, providence and so on – protracted
debates, not only among Christian philosophers and theologians themselves, but also "outside the camp" – with those who have eschewed basic
Christian assumptions in articulating their views, viz. various kinds of
humanists, scientists and atheists – have continued to the present day,
leading to reappraisal and restructuring of Christian self-understanding.[11]
All the other major world faiths have developed in similar fashion, and one
could point to many instances of productive interaction among them.[12] I
do not think there are solid grounds then for defending the self-referencing
insularity of different faith traditions.

One final procedural consideration. We are to "compare" Christianity
and Hinduism. But who speaks for Christianity, and who for Hinduism?
Framed thus, the question is wrongly put. Hinduism and Christianity are
not homogeneous, monolithic entities. Under each designation exists a
wide plurality of religious options and forms of life, interconnected, no
doubt, by overlapping and frequently shared frameworks of meaning,
speech and behavior.[13] No single voice can speak adequately or representatively for each faith. But this is all to the good, for we shall listen attentively
to a spectrum of voices from each tradition, the better to appreciate their
rich variety and the experiential range of the tradition they invoke. Our
only criterion of recognition will be a broad consensus from within each
faith that the voice concerned emerges from the normative strands or
mainstream of that faith, though this does not mean that, where it seems
appropriate, we will not also listen to voices that appear to be more
marginal. Whether we will be able to detect particular harmonious patterns
within each tradition as also between the two religions of our study will be

a matter for personal discovery. The advantage of this method is that rather than resorting to facile generalizations, we will try to let each voice speak for itself, and attempt to discern for ourselves what it is that each may be saying both within and across boundaries.

CHRISTIAN *AGAPE*

Let us now consider a Christian self-perception rooted in scripture – that the God of the Gospel-message is, above all, a God of love – to use the word of the Greek text, a God of *agape*. Through story and teaching attributed to Jesus himself, and in New Testament commentary on this teaching – central to the subsequent articulation of the faith – it is the *agape* of God that emerges as a, if not *the,* defining divine attribute. I need hardly point out that the parable of the prodigal son (Luke 15:11f.), and statements such as John 3:16 ("For this is how God loved (*ēgapēsen*) the world … "[14]), Romans 5:8 ("So it is proof of God's own love for us, that Christ died for us while we were still sinners"), and I John 4:8, 16 ("Because God is love (*agape*)"), have acted as the basis for identifying the word *agape* with the nature of God's love for the world.[15] But what has *agape* been understood to mean here? The parable of the prodigal son can start us on our inquiry.

The story is well known. The younger of two sons, who is usually understood to represent the frailty of the human condition, the ordinary wrongdoer (or "sinner"), in distinction from the elder brother, who stands for the self-righteous orthodox, takes his inheritance from his father and goes off to a distant land where he squanders his wealth. In dire straits, he comes to his senses and resolves to return repentant to his father, ready to give up any filial rights he may have. All he seeks is his father's protection in return ("I no longer deserve to be called your son; treat me as one of your hired men"). But the father, who had been looking out for him, saw him "while he was still a long way off" and "ran to the boy, clasped him in his arms and kissed him." Not only did he reaffirm him as his son but held a feast in his honor to celebrate his safe return. For as the father said to the elder brother who questioned this welcome, "Your brother here was dead and has come to life; he was lost and is found." It is the purpose of the story to teach that the father acts as God would whenever a repentant sinner seeks forgiveness, no matter how great his (or her) sinfulness; God does not care only for the so-called righteous.[16]

I pass over the ancient Jewish nuances of this parable; its more general teaching is clear enough. The divine *agape* or loving-kindness is for all, not least the stricken and outcast; it is likened to a parental and therefore personal and individual love, and it is anticipative and unmerited.[17] How much is contained, both cognitively and affectively, by the image in the words: *"While he was still a long way off,* his father saw him ... He *ran* to the boy, clasped him in his arms and kissed him."* The personal, individual restorative warmth ("your brother here was dead and has come to life; he was lost and is found"), here expressed in parental terms, is an important originative, that is, scriptural, component of divine *agape,* and has often been lost in the traditional philosophical and theological analyses of its meaning.[18] We will have occasion to invoke it when we examine Hindu notions of divine love.

But this understanding of *agape* is still fundamentally incomplete. For in Christian ethics, the divine *agape* is the original criterion (the "primary analogue" to use philosophical jargon) of human love, the standard on which human relationships are to be judged and measured. As such, it is a prescriptive love – a moral imperative – and the encompassing context of other forms of love. No kind of loving is morally viable if it violates agapeistic love. According to this standard, the love of *agape* is inherently other-regarding, irrespective of the sex and other personal circumstances of the other, and irrespective of any expectation of return in kind. *Agape* is not predicated on reciprocity. This is the nature of God's basic love for us, and this is the love that is to ground all moral human relationships.

Gene Outka, in his careful study, describes neighborly *agape* as follows (one must overlook the sexism of writing in an earlier period):

> The principle of equal regard enjoins man not to let his basic attitudes towards others be determined by the disparities in talent and achievement and the inequalities in attractiveness and social rank which differentiates men. He is not, for example, to value his neighbor, in accordance with the value of that neighbor's social position. He is to attempt to get behind social, political and technical titles which are the all-too-evident tokens of inequality. He is not to confuse the differences in instrumental value which various titles doubtless often reflect with the irreducible value of the well-being of the holders of these titles. He is enjoined to identify with the neighbor's point of view, to try to imagine what it is for him to live the life he does, to occupy the position he holds.[19]

The last sentence indicates that the practice of *agape* need not be dispassionate in the sense that it lacks affective content, unfortunately a familiar characteristic of its philosophical description. In fact, neighborly *agape* should be suffused with compassion, based on a cultivated sense of human solidarity with the other. This seems to be indicated repeatedly in the biblical contexts of its expression. Its divine analogue is almost absurdly intimated in the story of the prodigal son: "absurdly," because according to the classical philosophers and theologians, God – the initiating subject of *agape* in the parable – has no "passions" or affective life like a human subject, and "almost," because it is precisely the function of narrative, as a linguistic vehicle, to make its point by the use of figures of speech – metaphor, allegory, paradox – that in general are intended to carry extended, usually convergent, meanings. The purpose of the parable is to illustrate by appealing to the hearer's mind, heart, and imagination, the range and extent of God's loving-kindness for us, and this it does incomparably (with regard to non-tropic language, that is) by intimating that the divine *agape* is proportionately or analogically (to use another technical expression) as complete and efficacious as the fullest recognizable personal human (parental) love can be.

Here we cannot overlook the real hint of vulnerability in the divine love for us that the biblical teaching seems to incorporate. This has been suppressed by classical Christian thinkers in particular in their development of a conception of a loving, yet apparently adamantine, impassible deity. There have been reasons for this, but it has failed to do justice to its Jewish roots. The Bible reveals throughout an interactive, involved God, deeply concerned for his creation and susceptible to rejection and betrayal by humankind. We cannot develop this point here, but it is a matter of regret that to do so would be to go beyond the traditional view in particular of Christian philosophical theology, and this is not the purpose of this chapter.[20]

Now it may be objected that the story of the prodigal son may demonstrate the quality of God's love for us, but is this sufficient grounds for providing the encompassing norm of our love (in terms of *agape*) for each other? Does the fact that God loves us in this way imply that we ought to love one another similarly?[21] This is a crucial question, and it is here that Christian theology gives the cue to Christian ethics.

Let us start again from scripture, this time from the parable of the good Samaritan (Luke10:29–37). This too is a favored story in the history of Christian self-understanding for demonstrating the neighborly *agape*, the selfless other-regarding love, that must lie at the basis of all human relationships. Once more, I can only sketch the story. This time some of the ancient Jewish nuances are more pertinent to our inquiry.

Once, during a journey, a Jew was attacked by bandits and left half-dead on the roadside. In turn, a priest and a Levite, both supposedly model representatives of traditional Jewish law or righteous living, passed the victim by without assisting him. But then a Samaritan, a traditional enemy of the Jews, came that way and "was moved with compassion" when he saw the injured man.[22] After carefully tending his wounds, he "lifted him onto his own mount and took him to an inn and looked after him." On the following day he paid the innkeeper to continue to care for the man, promising that on his way back he would make good any extra expense that the innkeeper might incur. As Jesus declares, the moral of the story is "Go, and do the same yourself."

So neighborly *agape*, in so far as it is *agape*, must not be governed by the personal circumstances of the other, but is a form of active benevolence that does not expect a return in kind. Once again, the Gospel passage does not speak of a dispassionate love; rather, it is a love born of solidarity or compassion and is attentive to individual needs. *Agape* is also a faithful love, in the sense of being constant over time, regardless of any sense of expressed or felt reciprocity on the part of the recipient. The father looked out for and took back the prodigal son despite the latter's errant ways, and the good Samaritan was prepared to express a practical benevolence not only to a stranger but to someone from a traditionally hostile people who seemed in no fit state to reciprocate, and for as long as it took to bring that particular act of benevolence to its conclusion. The advantage of the method I am trying to inculcate is that it allows tropic patterns of speech to convey the full resonances, semantic and otherwise, of the ideas being expressed, which cannot obviously be conveyed by a bland literalness.

It is noteworthy that the New Testament notion of *agape* does not come out of the blue. It has its bases in the earlier part of the Bible (the so-called "Old Testament"). One such linking strand is the notion of faithful constancy in the loving subject, exemplified first and foremost by God's constancy to the people of Israel in and through his covenant with them come what may, but also in recurrent images of faithful love between individuals throughout the Hebrew Bible. It is no accident, I believe, that in some of the noblest expressions of human love in Western literature – a literature that certainly up to its late medieval phases, at least, was more or less consciously inspired by Christian principles – it is this characteristic of potentially unrequited constancy that is lauded. Here is an expression of this trait by one of the greatest playwrights of Christendom:

Love is not love
Which alters when it alteration finds,
Or bends with the remover to remove.
O, no! it is an ever-fixéd mark,
That looks on tempests and is never shaken;
It is the star to every wand'ring bark,
Whose worth's unknown, although his height be taken.
Love's not Time's fool, though rosy lips and cheeks
Within his bending sickle's compass come;
Love alters not with his brief hours and weeks,
But bears it out even to the edge of doom.
If this be error and upon me prov'd,
I never writ, nor no man ever lov'd.[23]

This mark of unswerving constancy is also a keynote in the exchange of marriage vows during the Christian nuptial ceremony,[24] stressing the relationship of *agape* that undergirds the mutuality of requital in marriage.

But we have still not dealt with the theological reasons for neighborly *agape* in Christian ethics.[25] These reasons are diverse, and we cannot be exhaustive here; nevertheless, it would be important to include: (1) the role of scriptural injunction; (2) the example and role of Jesus; and, as a grounding concept, (3) the idea of the *imago Dei* or the "image of God" in the development of Christian thinking. Here it will be possible only to look briefly at each of these points.

Firstly, the scriptural injunctions concerned are not as straightforward as they might seem. Let us begin with what has been called "the greatest commandment." In Matthew's Gospel Jesus says: "You must love (*agapeseis*) the Lord your God with all your heart, with all your soul, and with all your mind. This is the greatest and the first commandment. The second resembles it: You must love (*agapeseis*) your neighbor as yourself. On these two commandments hang the whole Law, and the Prophets too" (22:34–40).[26] Note again how this teaching is legitimated with reference to ancient Jewish tradition and practice ("the whole Law, and the Prophets too"), as also the wholeness of the love enjoined ("with all your heart, with all your soul, and with all your mind"). Another important passage is Luke 6:27 in which Jesus teaches: "Love (*agapate*) your enemies, do good to those who hate you … Treat others as you would like people to treat you … love your enemies and do good to them … and you will be children of the Most High, for he himself is kind to the ungrateful and the wicked." We are to follow God's example and treat one another in the same loving non-self-interested way in which God treats us, regardless of whether such love is merited or requited. And we cannot forget, of course, that great paean to *agape* of I Corinthians:

> Love (*agape*) is always patient and kind; love is never jealous; love is not boastful or conceited, it is never rude and never seeks its own advantage ... Love does not rejoice at wrongdoing, but finds its joy in the truth. It is always ready to make allowances, to trust, to hope and to endure whatever comes. Love never comes to an end ... Make love (*agape*) your aim. (13:4–14:1)

In passing, we note here again the implied vulnerability of *agape* in human relationships – it is a love that makes allowances, that trusts, hopes, endures – which, it must be said, has had a history of clearer acknowledgment in its treatment by Christian thinkers than in the case of its divine analogue. There is a need for fundamental theologians to provide a better match for the two.

Analytically, however, a problem has arisen in respect of the self-referencing love implied by the injunction to love our neighbor as ourself, to treat others as we would like others to treat us. What is the nature of this self-love? What are its limits and implications? Some thinkers have found a connection here between *agape* and an idea of basic justice, a recognition of equal worth in regard of all human beings (including oneself) in so far as all are human, irrespective of particular talents and accomplishments. Others have interpreted the injunction as implying that *agape* cannot come to fruition unless there is some form of genuine interaction, if not mutuality, between the persons involved, while still others argue that the golden rule implies that it is an other-regarding self-sacrifice, if necessary to the point of giving up one's life, that is the essence of *agape*.

It is not to our purpose to enter these discussions. I do not think, however, that any notion of what Outka calls "nefarious self-love" has been countenanced in Christian ethics in general in the interpretation of this dictum, still less that condition which he refers to as "psychological egoism." "The single word which best connotes those attitudes and actions characteristic of nefarious self-love," he writes, "is, I think, *acquisitiveness*."[27] "The underlying thesis [of psychological egoism]," Outka continues, "is that acquisitive self-love constitutes de facto the sole spring of behavior, identical for every man ... If [human] behavior at times seems ostensibly altruistic, this is only disguised acquisitiveness ... At the deepest level, all aims are genetically derived from and may be reductively analysed into one and only one."[28] Christian thinkers have in general eschewed psychological egoism as either an explanation for or basis of altruism.[29] It has been seen to make nonsense of the biblical injunctions quoted which are taken to imply a core of genuine human ethical freedom, and perhaps more important, it would make a nonsense of the life and example of Jesus, who in mainstream Christian thinking, has always been regarded as a fully human, and as such, authentically free, incarnation of God.

Secondly, Jesus is, of course, the paradigm of *agape* in Christian tradition: the paradigm not only of wholehearted love of God and neighbor but the *paradigm* also (in the sense of "pattern" or "representative") of God's complete love for us. A doctrine of true incarnation has been seen to fulfill these expressions of love. As truly divine and truly human, Jesus, by his life and death, is (a) the fruition of God's *agape* for us, (b) the model of neighborly love, and (c) the exemplar of our love for God. Jesus is the fruition of God's love for us, for as John's Gospel declares, God sent his Son into the world not to judge the world but so that through him the world might be saved (3:17). Jesus also exemplifies how we are to love one another: individually, personally, tenderly, enduringly, hopefully, selflessly. Episodes from the Gospels, in particular Jesus' words and deeds at the Passover meal with his disciples before he died (or "Last Supper") at which in the apparent knowledge of his impending death he offered himself in a renewable and commemorative way as the food and drink of a universal binding love[30] ("Take … and eat … this is my body … Drink from this … for this is my blood … poured out for many for the forgiveness of sins … Do this in remembrance of me"), exemplify all these traits.

Indeed, it is in Jesus' life and death that we see how *agape* is to deal with evil in our lives and in the world. Violence, suffering, disappointment, and evil cannot be avoided, but it is in Jesus' death on the cross and his resurrection from death by the power of God that we have the key to facing and overcoming natural and moral evil without compromising the imperatives of *agape*. *Agape* must be constant and uncompromising, for individuals or groups, even in the face of unremitting suffering or moral evil. In this respect, Christians lay central emphasis on the virtue of wholehearted forgiveness; it is forgiveness that allows *agape* to achieve its fruit of healing and reconciliation. Forgiveness is the cutting edge of agapeistic love. Through the person and work of Jesus, God's love reconciles the world to himself, and we are enabled to forgive each other from the heart. Further, even after death, through the Spirit of the divine love Jesus will be present in the world, reaching out through his followers to draw the whole creation to

God. Finally, Jesus shows us how we are to love God: by embracing what is perceived to be his will for us, even to the point of a humiliating and forsaken death.

We have done no more than list some Christian commonplaces, and all these ideas have been nuanced and interpreted in endless variety in the history of Christian theology, of course; nevertheless, it cannot be gainsaid that the doctrines of Trinity and Incarnation in their wider ramifications lie at the heart of the Christian idea of *agape,* and that the articulation of Christian ethics in this respect cannot stand without reference to its theological implications. This *contextuality* of Christian ethics has not been appreciated sufficiently by Christian philosophers. They often write as if the rightness of the Christian idea of neighborly love is self-evident to careful, rational reflection. This, I think, is a delusion. There is no such thing as a free-standing, universal "rational" Christian ethics of love; the plausibility of such an ethics is rooted in its theological context.[31] And this plausibility has been traditionally developed by our third consideration.

This is the idea of humans as the "image of God,"[32] an idea that is already expressed in the "Old" Testament, but which is developed in the New and then in subsequent Christian reflection.[33] David Cairns distinguishes three senses of this expression in Christian tradition: (a) the sense that all human beings express, in so far as they are human, an important similarity with, or characteristic of, the divine being; (b) the sense that some human beings express a special likeness with God in so far as they enter into a special relationship with Christ who is God's "Son," that is, a unique expression of the divine reality; and (c) the sense that Christ is a unique (and some would say, unrepeatable) expression of the divine likeness in that he is the Incarnation of God.

Note that the first two senses are both universal in some respect: (a) applies to all human beings simply in virtue of the fact that they exist as human beings; (b) applies in reality to some (viz. those who are actually in the special relationship mentioned), but potentially to all in that all human beings are called by God to enter into this relationship. Only (c) is confined to Christ alone. We need not go into the theological controversies surrounding the precise meanings of these three senses (for example, whether sense (a) refers representatively to men [rather than to women] or, in a gender egalitarian way, to "a responsible presence in the world" or "the capacity to reason and will," as being key reflections of the divine reality,[34] or in what way each human being is called to enter into special relationship with Christ). Our point is that the Christian idea of the image of God grounds a Christian ethics of neighborly *agape* in an interesting way, viz. it ultimately bestows a crucial and equal worth and dignity upon each human being such that every human being becomes the object of neighborly *agape* for every other. For this the actual universality of sense (a) and the potential universality of sense (b) are sufficient. Further, note that the equal *agape*-grounding worth of which we speak is a bestowed worth, bestowed, that is, not by some arbitrary human source or choice, but in virtue of the fact that we are the image of God. It is thus a derived worth (to be discerned by the appropriate religious and moral guidance), and the divine nature is its originative ground, not human nature per se.

This seems to give a paradoxical quality to this understanding of *agape*. On the one hand, there is a largesse, a kind of superabundance to neighborly *agape* in so far as it takes its cue from God. God has created us in the divine likeness. We derive our agapeistic worth from God and, as such, are an expression of God's unnecessitated, overflowing creative loving act.[35] In the way that God loves us with a fulsome, universal parental love as individual images of himself, notwithstanding our human frailties and aberrations (cf. the parable of the prodigal son), so we must generously love one another – as the parable of the good Samaritan teaches us.[36] There is a generosity to this love which goes beyond the bounds of exactitude that attend most notions of justice.

On the other hand, *agape* is also a kind of just love in that it is based on a perception of equal human worth, regardless of individual status, personality or merit. In this sense it is a giving to every individual his or her due on the basis of their being the image of God in an egalitarian sense. Thus – and this is where *agape*'s paradoxical nature comes into view – there is, as it were, a sort of necessity, a moral imperative, that characterizes neighborly *agape*. In this sense, because of the kind of beings we are as God's image (in senses (a) and (b)), we ought to love one another as we love ourselves, and in doing this, whether we realize it or not, we are also loving God, the divine exemplar and source of our being (so I John 4:20 can say: "Anyone who says 'I love God' and hates his brother, is a liar, since no one who fails to love the brother whom he can see can love God whom he has not seen").

There is another way in which *agape* seems to be paradoxical. On the one hand, its benevolence is predicated on the equal worth of all humans *qua* human in the manner described above. In this sense it is not attentive to differences of wealth, sex, personality or talent; it is not a love based on the perception of some particular quality of the other or for the sake of personal gain. On the other hand, it is this very even-handedness, if you like, its egalitarian nature, that allows us to recognize the uniqueness of the other *qua* other. In acquisitive or self-regarding love a uniqueness is also perceived in the object loved. Thus one can love some other uniquely for the sake of a particular gratification that only that other seems able to render, but this uniqueness exists only in so far as the object loved is perceived to be a particular source of gratification. It is unique because of what it means to the selfish lover (from the viewpoint of the lover this is a self-referencing distinctiveness), whereas the object of *agape* is appreciated as unique in a non-self-referencing way, in its own right. *Agape* frees the selfless lover to love the other in the other's uniqueness. Thus *agape* is at the same time both egalitarian with respect to the other and attentive to the unique distinctiveness of the other. This is another way of saying that the practice of *agape* does not favor an attitude of emotionless dispassion; rather it calls for an individual benevolence.[37]

To clarify matters further, let us conclude this part by reference to a distinction made in an important work (written in the 1930s) by the Swedish theologian, Anders Nygren. The title of this work, *Agape and Eros*,[38] points to the distinction we have in mind. In Nygren's way of thinking, there seems to be only two kinds of love: *agape*, taught for the first time consistently in the New Testament and of which the exemplar and source is the love of God for us through the life and death of Jesus as revealed in that text, and *eros*, the type of every other kind of love.[39] *Agape* originates from God, is spontaneous (that is, it is not motivated by any quality of the beloved), seeks the welfare of and bestows an irreducible value on the beloved, initiates and grounds an attitude of neighborly love, and seeks to draw the beloved into a relationship of fellowship with God and the neighbor. It is a love of unalloyed self-giving.[40] So far so good. In general, these are the accredited attributes of *agape* in the Christian understanding. *Eros*, however, for Nygren, is acquisitive love, what Outka has described as "nefarious" self-love: it originates from human beings, is "ego-centric" (that is, invariably seeks its own advantage), is attentive to *differentiae* of status, talent, and worth in its object, and is infected with *hubris* or arrogated self-worth.[41] Though *agape* and *eros* are fundamentally incommensurable and irreconcilable, they are the only two kinds of love possible, and usually co-exist in intimate and sometimes inextricable union (in individuals and in movements of history, e.g. the Christian Church). Further, *agape* is the rightful preserve of ideal Christian teaching and living, while *eros* is the domain of every other form of religio-cultural or moral system (including "Old" Testament Judaism).

I believe that it is Nygren's puerile (and indeed, hubristic) desire to claim for Christianity the radical novelty of teaching and practicing *agape*,[42] supported by a (particular form of Evangelical) theology affirming the inherent depravity of human nature – a claim and a theology running throughout his work – that has vitiated his study of love in terms of the mutually exclusive yet exhaustive distinction described above. With respect to the ethics of human relationships (to which he extends the scope of *agape*), he seems not to have considered adequately, for instance, another kind of love – neither *agape* nor *eros* as understood by him, yet apparently quite viable, which we may formulate as follows: "I love you with a special love because you are my friend. I love you not only because you are a human being deserving of my benevolence *qua* human, but also because of the pleasure, support, companionship, and example that you give me (and no one else). In this love and because of this love, I am prepared to give up my life for you if necessary." In part, this is clearly a gainful kind of love. Yet it seems counter-intuitive to describe it as "ego-centric" or "acquisitive" or "possessive" *tout court* (Nygren's epithets), for let us assume that it is prepared to show all manner of self-restraint and sacrifice – in terms of the very attributes listed for *agape* in I Corinthians 13 (patience, kindness, not being jealous or boastful or conceited or rude or seeking a predatory advantage, or taking undue offense, etc.) – at its noblest to the point of death if necessary. It is a love of giving as much as of taking, indeed, perhaps more of giving than of taking. In fact its overall intention may be to give rather than to take, though it survives in so far as it entails a special relationship of reciprocity between two persons (a good example would be a certain kind of married or parental love) in which a particular value is bestowed mutually. Though not egalitarian in contrast to *agape*, it is clearly agapeistic. It would also be counter-intuitive (and pleading a special case), I think, to describe it as a combination of two separate kinds of love: *agape* and *eros* (in Nygren's sense). It is a single love with essentially "agapeistic" and "erotic" features. And it seems that Nygren's thinking can make little good sense of it.

Nor, it seems, can his position comfortably accommodate the following kind of love: "I love you not (only) because you are a human being deserving of my benevolence *qua* human (=*agape*), nor indeed because I seek to gain something by loving you (=*eros*), but because I simply recognise in you as lovable the virtues of kindness, goodness, and truthfulness." Now strictly speaking this is not what has been called "the love of friendship" (*amor amicitiae*), because one does not necessarily seek (perhaps to gain by) the other's friendship. One cay say: I love you because I recognize in you something particular that is lovable, which yet others may not possess, and which I do not seek for personal advantage. Let us call it the "love of virtue" (*amor virtutis*). Nygren's disjunction does not accommodate such love. This is because he has a theological axe to grind, and so has come up with a view that is tendentious, somewhat arbitrary, insufficiently nuanced, generally insensitive, and one may say, somewhat inhuman (since for him *agape* is fundamentally opposed to human nature which is inherently depraved). While Nygren's study is useful in important ways for its articulation of the meaning of *agape*, it is seriously deficient in its understanding of other kinds of love (which he lumps under *eros*), and we may dispense with it and the sense he gives to the latter term.[43]

Let us return instead to key features of (religious) *agape* that run throughout our analysis: its divine origin, its spontaneous character, its egalitarian nature, its quest for fellowship between the divine reality and humans, as also between humans themselves, on the basis of a value transcendentally bestowed, and a note of inherent vulnerability, at least in its biblical expression. I hope to show phenomenologically that in religious Hinduism too such a manner of loving is accorded a crucial role, though interestingly differently nuanced and contextualized. To this task we now turn.

HINDU *BHAKTI*

Recall again the point made earlier about the diversity that passes for that federated cluster of religions we describe as "Hinduism." Note too that there are numerous strands running through this diversity that are more or less distinctive, localized and popular (what anthropologists sometimes refer to as the "little traditions"), and strands that are more formalized, normative (attested to at least by way of lip-service), self-consciously articulate and hence "orthodox" (the so-called "great tradition"). Hinduism is less homogeneous than Christianity, one chief reason for this being its characteristic and deep-set feature of orality (notwithstanding a longstanding tradition of many written-down texts), which resists the standardization that an ecclesiastical faith such as Christianity (with its historical stress on the precise and inerrant formulation of doctrine and dogma, and the consequent issuing of anathemas) generates.

The great normative tradition in Hinduism is the Sanskritic tradition,[44] itself varied and in aspects adaptable and even subversive of accredited norms. Because the Sanskritic tradition contains the perhaps most developed features of systematic and reflexive articulation of Hinduism (viz. most of its full-fledged philosophies and theologies) – which is indeed the role of a normative orthodoxy – and as such has positively or negatively exercised a profound and lasting influence on the phenomenon of Hinduism as a whole, we shall draw most, but by no means all, our material from the Sanskritic tradition; when it seems called for, however, we shall also make use of vernacular or folkloric sources.[45] But inevitably, amid the bewildering plurality of the Hindu religions, there must be some selectivity to the material drawn upon. Perhaps all we can aspire to in this chapter is to give, within the comparative matrix of our concerns, a characteristic flavor of Hindu notions of religious love.

Let us begin with reference to the Bhagavadgita, widely recognized in Sanskritic Hinduism as a seminal text for understandings of the love of God (in both the subjective and objective senses of this expression). The Gita, as it is usually called – in its received form a text of 18 chapters and 700 verses – can be dated to about the beginning of the Common Era (interestingly, about the time of the New Testament).[46] It is in the form of a dialogue between the warrior-king Krishna, who progressively reveals himself as the supreme person (*purushottama*) of all, the origin, conserving power and End of all being, the Lord of the universe who has descended in human form into the world, and his friend and comrade, the warrior Arjuna. Krishna does most of the speaking, yet the dialogue format is significant as being the first medium in Sanskritic Hinduism for a sustained expression of divine love. It is a fitting vehicle for a teaching of responsive love between persons, but it is also a characteristically open-ended medium. Conversations are notable as much for what is left unsaid or cannot be said as for what is said. Their spaces leave room for development of ideas, for spontaneity of thought and expression, for fulfillment in action.[47] They are also suitable points of departure for (more systematic) commentaries. And so it has been with the Gita: it has been the basis for rich traditions of continuing reflection and theology, as well as practice, to the present day.[48] This takes us back to our original idea of using a range of linguistic resources to inform our discussion.

The immediate context of the Gita is Arjuna's war-chariot, in which Arjuna is the combatant and Krishna the charioteer,[49] positioned between two great armies about to do battle. Confused, Arjuna is reluctant to fulfill his duty as a righteous warrior, for the army confronting him includes relatives and others for whom he has high regard. After Arjuna has placed himself in the appropriate role of receptive (but not unquestioning) disciple of Krishna as teacher – thus enabling the "true teaching" to be imparted[50] – Krishna reveals, for the first time in Hinduism, the nature of the divine love and the response it invites.[51] It is a love that in the first instance is a form of spontaneous benevolence, seeking the welfare of all irrespective of circumstance, and not as a response to any human overture. As such, it exemplifies and grounds an ethic of egalitarian regard and self-less action; yet at the same time, it is a personal and compassionate love, seeking the salvation of the beloved and inviting a wholehearted response, but not without serious moral implications.

Krishna is a God who cares for the well-being of all existence, without fear or favor. Not only this, he is the exemplar of this universal benevolence:

> Whatever the best does, others will do the same.
> Whatever standard he sets, the world will follow.
> There is nothing that I must do, Arjuna,
> in the three worlds,
> nothing unattained that I need attain,
> yet I continue in action ...
> If I were not to do my work, these worlds would collapse,
> and I would bring about disorder;
> I would destroy my creatures.
> (3:21–22, 24)

Unless Krishna acts first, there would be neither the possibility to follow his example nor indeed the example itself. His descent (*avatara*) to earth then is an extension of this initiative.

Early in the fourth chapter, Krishna describes the nature and the manner of the teaching he has come to impart in his bid to rescue the world from evil, confusion and disorder:

This unshakeable disciplined way (*imaṃ yogam avyayam*), I had declared to Vivasvat [long ago] ... it has now been lost over a great period of time ... This ancient disciplined way is now told to you by me, for you are devoted (*bhaktaḥ*) to me, you are my friend. It is the highest mystery ... Though unborn, of changeless self, and the Lord of beings, yet by having taken up (*adhisthaya*) material nature which is mine (*prakṛtim svām*), I now come to be [in human form] by my wonderful power (*ātmamāyayā*). For whenever there is a decline of right living (*dharma*), Arjuna, and the rise of unrigh-teousness (*adharma*), I generate myself [anew]. To save the virtuous and destroy evil-doers, and to establish right living, I come to be age after age. (4:1–8)

Thus, rather than when it seems to be merited, it is when right living (*dharma*) is in decline that Krishna takes action. This is by way of an embodied descent into the world (*avatāra*) to renew an ancient teaching. Krishna declares that he descends again and again, though he does not specify the manner of his repeated descents. This has given scope for a doctrine of multiple *avataras* in different forms (human and non-human).

Many have commented on the difference between *avatara* and incarnation: that the former is many while the latter is one, that the purpose of the *avatara* is more diffuse than that of the incarnation, that incarnation is human while *avatara* may be human and non-human (though the human *avataras* of Rama and Krishna have commanded the greatest devotion), that the doctrine of the Incarnation has played a more integrative role in Christian self-understanding as a whole than its counterpart in Hinduism, and so on. I do not wish to gloss over these suggestive differences.[52] Here I am concerned to point to the basic features of *avatara* as it emerges consequentially on the Hindu scene. It is depicted as a saving initiative of the deity, revealed in a context of love ("You are devoted to me, you are my friend").

Though moral in tone, viz. though it distinguishes robustly, as in Christianity, between righteous and unrighteous, good and evil, it is also implicitly a universal initiative. By it Krishna comes to impart anew an ancient teaching, the "highest mystery," by which he reveals the path of loving union with him as the best way of all – and by implication, for all. Krishna is the terminus of all devotional religion, whether one knows it or not; but it is in knowing it – as in Christianity – that such religion attains its perfect end, irrespective of sex or status.

> But to you I will declare this most secret knowledge … knowing which you will be freed from evil … I am the father of this world, its mother, sustainer, its very founder (*pitāmahaḥ*) … Arjuna, even those devotees of other gods (*anyadevatābhaktā*) who worship possessed with faith, in fact worship me, though not in the appointed way. For I am the recipient and Lord of all sacrifices, but because they do not know me in truth, they are reborn … I exist, impartial, in all beings; there is in me neither aversion nor favour. But those who (knowingly) worship me with love (*bhaktyā*) abide in me and I in them … For those who have taken refuge in me, though they be of harmful birth – women, traders, even serfs – tread the supreme path. (9:1, 17, 23–24, 29, 32)

Notwithstanding cultural specificities, of course (e.g. reference to particular modes of worship, to rebirth, and to caste and gender prejudices) – indeed, it may well be said that it is in terms of these specificities that – there is clearly discernible in this excerpt an implied teaching of salvation available for all.[53]

Yet this impartial benevolence is withal warm and regenerative: it has been likened felicitously to a fire. Paraphrasing the words of Krishna in 9:29, the great classical theologian, Shankara (eighth century CE) says: "I am like a fire. Just as a fire does not banish the cold from those who stand afar, but dispels it from those who come progressively nearer, so do I welcome devotees." In other words, the warmth of a fire exists equally for all, but there are some who come closer to it than others, and still others who choose to live in the cold, outside its pale. And those who, supported by Krishna, knowingly abide in Krishna, are consumed by his love: "My devotee (*bhakta*), having realized this [teaching], attains to my being (*madbhāvāyopapadyate*) ... Having realized me in truth, he enters into me at once" (13:18; 18:55). The love of God is a consuming, absorbing love.[54]

Just as Krishna acts as the impartial exemplar of universal benevolence, even to the point of working toward bringing all to their final destiny of abiding in him, so we are instructed (through Arjuna, the type of the faithful devotee or *bhakta*) to act with impartial altruism towards all: "You must work with a view to the welfare of the world ... Just as the ignorant act with attachment to action, Arjuna, so the one who knows should desire to act without attachment, for the world's welfare" (3:20b, 25).[55] In chapter 12, entitled "The Yoga of Devotion" (*bhakti-yoga*), Krishna declares: "The person[56] is dear to me who is the same to enemy or friend, impartial to respect or disdain, to heat or cold, pleasure or suffering ... who is contented ... loving (*bhaktimān*)" (12:18–19).[57] Yet it is not a cold, unfeeling love: "That person is dear to me who does not hate any being, but who is friendly (*maitraḥ*) and kindly (*karuṇaḥ*), non-acquisitive (*nirmamaḥ*), non-egoistic (*nirahaṃkāraḥ*) ... forbearing, contented ... restrained (*yatātmā*) ... " (12:13–14). It is an altruism that is "friendly" and "kindly,"[58] a devoted love (*bhakti*) which can be (and has generally been) seen to be founded on the deity's immanent, sustaining presence in all being.[59] Indeed, in addition to the contextual differences indicated already, this fundamental benevolence appears to have a wider explicit scope than the *agape* of Christian tradition. It extends to every being – a familiar idea in the Gita. I do not think that it can be doubted, then, that the Bhagavadgita advocates a fundamental imperative of agapeistic love in the mode of Christian *agape*.[60] This primary teaching of *niṣkāma karma*, that is, selfless benevolent action, has had an immense influence in the discussion and practice of Hindu ethics right up to contemporary times. For example, it was the bedrock on which so significant an individual as Gandhi based his life's work.[61] Many similar examples could be given.

The word in its various forms that stands out in the Gita to express the loving relationship between Krishna and his faithful devotee is *bhakti*.[62] In the course of time the *bhakti* tradition developed in a variety of ways and with numerous refinements in Hinduism. A well-known text that can be regarded as having taken stock of this development in succinct fashion at a judicious point in history, and also as having acted as an important basis for consolidating and reinforcing the *bhakti* tradition in its different aspects, is the *Narada Bhakti Sutras*. As the name implies, this text is ascribed to the ancient sage Narada; however, it seems to be the work of more than one hand and can be dated to the tenth–twelfth centuries. It is only 84 verses or *sutras* in length. Though the *Narada Bhakti Sutras* is Vaishnava in tone (it echoes some of the key expressions and ideas of the Gita), it can conveniently be seen to summarize the love of God in general in Hinduism.

The first four *sutras* may be translated as follows: "Now, therefore, we shall explain devotion [to God] (*bhakti*).(1) It is of the nature of supreme love (*parapremarūpā*) in this world.(2)[63] It is also of the very nature of immortality.(3) Having obtained it, a person becomes perfect, immortal, fulfilled.(4)"[64] Note the introduction of the word *prema*. *Prema* is an emotional love, a love that implies wholehearted commitment. It is a love in which the whole person is caught up. As the highest form of such love (*paraprema-*), the *prema* of the *Narada Bhakti Sutras* is not carnal, but leads to immortality and fulfillment. It is as if to confirm this that *sutras* 5 and 7 say: "Having attained it, one doesn't hanker for anything, one doesn't grieve or hate or get excited or keen [as in carnal love] … It is not concupiscent, for it is of the nature of warding off [what's selfish]."[65]

It is an unselfish love. "Who crosses, who crosses this deceptive world (*māyā*)?" cries the text (*sutra* 46), and it answers: "The one who gives up attachment … who is non-acquisitive (*nirmamaḥ*) … who gives up the fruit of action (*karmaphalam tyajati*) … It is such a one, such a one indeed who crosses, and enables the worlds to cross as well" (*sutra* 50). So this love has a social dimension; it is not just individualistic. This idea is expanded in subsequent *sutras*. When one attains this love of God, one need not give up living in the world; one should only give up the fruits of action (*sutra* 62). Such single-minded lovers of God sanctify their families and the world, and validate sacred places, good works and the scriptures. Indeed, the ancestors rejoice, the gods dance, and this earth gets its protectors. Where they are concerned, there are no distinctions of birth, learning, appearance, family, possessions, livelihood and so on. Their love is even-handed, selfless, concerned, efficacious and beneficial to all.[66]

The Hindu traditions tend to stress a feature of such benevolence in a way that seems distinctive: viz. it entails a new perception of the world and of human relationships. As indicated already, ordinary non-agapeistic living becomes more or less deceptive if not delusional (*"māyā"*), with non-salvific consequences. Altruistic love of God and neighbor throws the world into a new light, and brings peace and deep joy. It is a life of total surrender, requiring no external proof; it is a self-validating experience. Lack of space prevents a more extensive discussion of this theme, though it must be noted here that a number of thinkers, both classical and more contemporary, have argued the point on both epistemological and psychological grounds.[67] So in addition to the two kinds mentioned earlier, from what has just been noted it seems that another form of paradoxicality emerges in agapeistic love of the deity, viz. seeing the world anew. Its sameness is reconfigured; what was alloyed or unalloyed sorrow before now becomes a source of overriding joy, even though a stratum of pain or sorrow may remain. The devotee can still suffer pain or grief (through sickness or bereavement, for example), but the dominant experience is one of peace and joy.

The purified and purifying nature of *bhakti* or *prema* is the cue for all sorts of metaphors and types of human loving (which ordinarily may well be expected to involve a degree of carnality) to act as symbols of the love of God. It is here that the experience of erotic, sexual love can help us to explore anew the richness of agapeistic love. In fact, a characteristic feature of devotional Hinduism seems to be to use, sometimes almost with startling or reckless freedom (or so it may seem to more prudish Western susceptibilities), usually erotic images of love as pointers for our understanding and expression of the intensity or abandon of the love of God.

This is how the medieval Bengali poet Chandidasa (ca. fourteenth century)[68] describes a kind of ardent mutual longing between the soul and God, erotically typified by the love Radha, Krishna's favorite lover, and Krishna have for each other.

> Suddenly I am afraid.
> At any moment, [Krishna's] love for me may cease.
> A building can collapse because of a single flaw –
> who knows in what ways I, who desire to be

a palace for his pleasure, may be faulty?
And few are those who can restore
what once is broken ...
Distracted, I wander
from place to place, everywhere finding
only anxiety. Oh, to see
his smile!
  My love,
whoever brings down the house of our love
will have murdered a woman!
Chandidāsa says, O Rādhā, you reflect too much;
without your love he could not live a moment."[69]

This is a sample of imagery that can be more erotic and protracted in describing the love-relationship between the individual and God.[70]

Yet this love is also a love of constancy. Its ardor is often said to have lasted through many births, as if contemplating the alternative of there not being a time when God was the object of wholehearted love, is unbearable. One of the most popular models of this unswerving fidelity to God is the sixteenth-century woman-saint of Rajasthan, Mirabai. As has been pointed out, Mira's popularity is pan-Indian, and the songs attributed to her have a direct, folk-like simplicity.[71] "Life without Hari [Krishna] is no life, friend," she says plaintively,

And though my mother-in-law fights,
my sister-in-law teases ...
A guard is stationed on a stool outside,
and a lock is mounted on the door,
How can I abandon the love I have loved in life after life?[72]

But such images are far from exhaustive of the recognized forms of *bhakti*. In an important verse, the *Narada Bhakti Sutras* lists eleven accredited forms of *bhakti:*

Bhakti though really one, is eleven-formed: of the form of attachment to the greatness of the (divine) attributes; of the form of attachment to the (divine) beauty or form; of the form of attachment to the worship (of God); of the form of attachment to (continuous) remembrance (of God); of the form of attachment to (the divine) service; of the form of attachment to the (divine) companionship; of the form of attachment (to God) through parental love; of the form of attachment of the Beloved; of the form of attachment of self-offering; of the form of the attachment of being suffused; of the form of attachment of the deepest separation.[73]

Thus *bhakti* is of the nature of a "sticking to," of attachment (*āsakti*). As such it must be a faithful, constant love, whatever its various modes. Here we cannot go into a more detailed analysis of these modes as listed above, interesting (and intriguing) though they may appear.[74] In this chapter, we have been concerned primarily with sketching out the scope and features of *bhakti* in general terms, and more detailed discussion of several specific modes of bhakti appears in subsequent chapters.[75]

CONCLUSION

One final point needs to be made. From our study it appears that the love of God is a "captive" love in more than one sense. By becoming available to human thought and experience in a number of ways – through the revealed texts of scripture, the manifestations of incarnation and *avatara*,[76] and the subsequent example and teaching of saintly men and women – the transcendent and ineffable One is present in recognizable ways in space and time to the supplicant in a supportive relationship of mutual accessibility. And as the devotee progresses in this relationship of mutual giving, she/he feels ever more incapable of living outside it.[77] But the traditions warn against a captivity of complacency. Such an attitude (on the part of the devotee, of course) leads to loss. Recall Radha's anxiety at the possibility of losing Krishna's love in the passage quoted earlier. This is why, especially in Hinduism, the love of God, primarily through its erotic images, has been depicted as an adventurous love, turning new corners, undergoing new trials as it runs its course. This is perhaps the greatest paradox of all: though ancient and recurrent, it restores, refreshes, renews.

It is now time to conclude this disquisition. In it I have tried to show, or at least to indicate, by a method that takes account of idiom that is tropic as well as non-tropic, what the chief features of that love called *agape* in Christian tradition seem to be, and its ethical grounds and implications, and also that such a manner of loving, though contextualized differently in a number of ways, plays a central role in devotional Hinduism.[78] It is regarded as the ideal form of loving, the foundation of uplifting human relationships, that is, of those relationships in this tumultuous and unsteadying world that make us authentically human.[79] This mode of love has been striven after, and attained in greater degree on a consistent basis, by persons commonly regarded as moral and religious exemplars, but to a lesser extent it has been attained by everyone who, directly or indirectly, has been inspired by the higher ethics of loving of the two civilizations we have considered. As such, surely it is deserving of careful study, and, so far as is practicable, of assiduous emulation in its various forms, the better to preserve all that we regard as ennobling in our civilized worlds.

NOTES

1. A version of this chapter was presented as the 1998 George Dana Boardman Lecture at the University of Pennsylvania, and another version as the Huntington Lecture at Chapman University, Orange, CA, shortly thereafter. This chapter combines and enlarges both lectures. I am grateful to the University of Pennsylvania and to Chapman University for the invitation to lecture.

2. The occasion would have had a legal context. Note that according to John 19:20f. the inscription written by Pilate and fixed to the cross of Jesus was in Hebrew, Latin, and Greek.

3. The problems of translation, as times and perceptions change, are fraught with consequence. A note of irony emerges in Pilate's response (*satya! satya ābār kī?*) in the acclaimed recent Bengali translation of the New Testament (*Maṅgalbārtā,* by Sajal Bandyopadhyay and Christian Mignon, S.J. [Calcutta: Xavier Publications, 1984]) which seems to be absent in the Greek, or indeed in the Sanskrit translation (*pīlātaḥ tam aha satyaṃ kim*) of The Bible Society of India and Ceylon (*The New Testament in Sanskrit,* 1962).

4. The authorial intention of the text, important though it is, is not germane to the point I am raising, which takes the incident described at face value.

5. See *The Intercultural Challenge of Raimon Panikkar,* ed. by J. Prabhu (Maryknoll, NY: Orbis Books,1996). The quotation is taken from Panikkar's *Response* (p. 287).

6. "God" is to be understood as a designation for the supreme being with such attributes as benevolence, originative power, omnipotence, omniscience and so on, rather than as a proper name for some particular deity, though in the course of this essay, the meaning of "God" will take on particular connotations as context demands.

7. B-A Scharfstein, "The Contextual Fallacy," in *Interpreting Across Boundaries: New Essays in Comparative Philosophy,* ed. G. J. Larson and E. Deutsch (Delhi: Motilal Banarsidass, 1989 Princeton: Princeton University Press, 1988), pp. 86, 94.

8. In this regard, see the study on metaphor by Janet M. Soskice, *Metaphor and Religious Language* (Oxford: Clarendon Press, 1985), and my "Śaṃkara on Metaphor with reference to Gītā 13:12–18," in *Indian Philosophy of Religion,* ed. R.W. Perrett, (Boston: Kluwer Academic Publishers, 1989).

9. I have developed this idea in "Philosophy and World Religions," in *Philosophy of Religion: A Guide to the Subject* ed. Brian Davies, (London: Geoffrey Chapman, 1998).

10. This indicates why I find G. Lindbeck's argument in *The Nature of Doctrine: Religion and Theology in a Postliberal Age* (Philadelphia: Westminster Press, 1984) deeply problematic. On the one hand, Lindbeck wants doctrine to function mainly, if not purely, as "communally authoritative rules of discourse, attitude and action" (p. 18); on the other, he sees religions as "comprehensive interpretive schemes, usually embodied in myths or narratives and heavily ritualized, which structure human experience and understanding of self and world" (p. 32). But by then giving doctrinal formulation with little or no cognitivist value such a central role in religion (its non-cognitivist function hardly justifiable in historical context, one might add), he goes counter to his description of religion as an *interpretive* scheme, for which conceptual content must, of course, be crucial. In any case, by according primacy to doctrine in the religious enterprise, Lindbeck undervalues so much else (e.g. narrative, myth, etc.) which he himself admits is central for a religious shaping of our lives.

11. In the article mentioned in note 9, I have exemplified this point by reference to the doctrine of the Trinity, which received seminal formulation at the Council of Nicaea in 325 on the basis of an already considerable history of development of the ideas of deity, substance, personhood, relation, etc. integrating, *inter alia*, Hebraic and Hellenistic components. This development continued apace, and in the course of time was, and still is, influenced by "dialogue" with sources not necessarily based on Christian assumptions.

12. For example, between Hinduism and Buddhism, Islam and Hinduism (consider the origins and growth of Sufi beliefs and practices), Islam and Sikhism, and so on.

13. I have argued in other writings that "Hindu" is essentially a cultural rather than religious term (see e.g. my *Hindus: Their Religious Beliefs and Practices* [London: Routledge, 1994], chapter 1). However, because of the overwhelming and persistent role of religion in the historical development of what "Hindu" means, we are here using "Hindu" as a convenient marker of religious identity.

14. Biblical quotations are taken from *The New Jerusalem Bible*.

15. Though the word *agape* does not occur in the Greek text of the parable of the prodigal son, there can be little doubt that the story has functioned as a classic locus for expressing what God's love means for us. See also the quotation in note 17.

16. This is to regard the elder brother in the story as self-righteous, a hackneyed interpretation of the character. But it is not necessary to resort to this interpretation for the parable to carry its point. I have always had a sympathy for the brother who stayed by his father's side and did not

abandon his home, and find telling the father's words: "My son, you are with me always and all I have is yours" (15:31). As we shall note later, there is a significant place for *constancy* in the expression of love.

17.   "Here the reference is quite indubitably universal ... The prodigal is the personification of lost sinful man in general, and he is thought of, not only as a prodigal, but also as a son. And if the prodigal is every sinner, then God is the loving Father of all, who seeks all": D. Cairns, *The Image of God in Man* (London: Collins Fontana Library, 1973), p. 59.

18.   Space does not permit more than a comment here on gender terms used for God. In Christianity these are overwhelmingly masculine, though it is a theological truism that the divine being is sexless. Theologically, therefore, God's love for us prescinds from sexual considerations; *psychologically,* however, the situation is very different. The situation is analogous with respect to Hinduism which is more heterogeneous than Christianity and which has a major strand (Shakta religion) where the supreme being is depicted as female (the Goddess). In this essay the gender of pronouns referring to the deity will follow the religious conventions of the faiths being considered. To explore these issues in the Hindu context see chapters 4 and 12.

19.   Gene Outka, *Agape: An Ethical Analysis* (New Haven: Yale University Press, 1972), pp. 262–263.

20.   For a fine, sustained attempt at this see Keith Ward, *Religion and Creation* (Oxford: Clarendon Press, 1996).

21.   Or to couch this in more philosophical terms: "From a factual statement such as 'God is love' one cannot logically conclude, 'therefore ... one *ought* to love one's neighbour'" (Outka, *Agape*, p. 186; emphasis added), for (quoting R. M. Hare, *The Language of Morals*, p. 28) "No imperative conclusion can be validly drawn from a set of premises which does not contain at least one imperative" (ibid.).

22.   "Was moved with compassion": this is how *The New Jerusalem Bible* translates the *kai ... esplagchnisthē* of the Greek text here (verse 33), the very same construction that appears at a similar point in the story of the prodigal son, but there rendered somewhat inconsistently by "(His father) was moved with pity".

23.   William Shakespeare, Sonnet 116.

24.   The well-known formula: "I ... take thee ... to my wedded husband/wife, to have and to hold, from this day forward, for better, for worse, for richer, for poorer, in sickness and in health, till death do us part, and thereto I plight thee my troth" typifies this commitment.

25.   A context which Outka must admit, though he does so only tangentially, in his mainly philosophical treatment: "Religious beliefs may provide ... a background of intelligibility for *agape*. They serve to define the total arena within which actions are viewed and assessed. A certain sort of

world is seen to lie behind the life of love, a world which will finally not prove indifferent, unsupportive, or hostile to such a life" (*Agape,* p. 185).

26. See also Mark 12:28–34, and Luke 10:25–28.

27. Outka, *Agape,* p. 56.

28. Ibid., p. 60.

29. If pressed they might well resort to distinguishing as follows (in the words of Outka): "It is one thing to say that some [nefarious?] self-love is unavoidable, another that it alone is always determinative. It is one thing to say that the agent is unable to love others without [implicitly?] loving himself, another that loving them is simply a way of [acquisitively?] loving himself". (ibid., p.287).

30. Instructing that this sacrificial act be repeated as the mark of an abiding friendship.

31. This does not preclude its nobility – in terms of a conveyed sense of uplifting rightness – from being appreciated across religio-cultural borders. But this appreciation is preconditioned, I would argue, by a responsive sense of rightness cultivated analogically in the religio-cultural context of the appreciator. We are speaking here of commonalities in differences, and perhaps of convergent resonances amid a distinctive plurality. Teasing out some of these mutualities is the purpose of this chapter.

32. The expression is being used here generically, without reference to further distinctions that have been made in this respect, such as those between "image," "likeness," "vestige," etc.

33. Cairns argues that the Old Testament references are important, and have a far-reaching significance. See *The Image of God in Man,* chapter 1.

34. In e.g. the influential Christian theologian, St. Thomas Aquinas' treatment of the subject (thirteenth century), the basic sense in which all human beings are the image of God is that they have an innate capacity to reflect God's Trinitarian mode of being in their mental acts, especially of knowing and willing. See his *Summa Theologiae,* Ia, 93.

35. An act that has been predetermined and preplanned from the very beginning, and which came to fruition in due course with the origination of human beings in the process of the world's "evolution" (here scientific explanations of the development of matter and life may well come into play). In other words, God's creative act, according to Christian teaching, both originates the world and continually sustains it in being.

36. This "fulsomeness" of *agape* has sometimes been taken as the basis for arguing that *agape* has a preferential option or corrective outreach towards the disadvantaged, marginalized or vulnerable members of society.

37. Acquisitive love can also be said to be paradoxical with regard to uniqueness, but in a different way. One could say that one loves every other equally only in so far as the other can gratify one, yet distinctively, in so far as each other can provide a unique gratification. Panikkar, in distinguishing between the "loving approach" and the "scientific approach,"

notes this attribute of uniqueness, but without making further distinctions: "Love ... entails the discovery of the uniqueness of a thing. A 'scientific' jar is a single specimen among many jars. If it breaks I can replace it by another one ... If I love a particular jar, that jar is for me unique ... It has something irreplacable . . . The loving approach to things is of another kind than the scientific one. Modern science has to exclude love from its approach to things ... It needs to abstract individuality. Love has no place in it. It approaches things in an impersonal and quantifiable manner" (*The Intercultural Challenge of Raimon Panikkar*, ed. J. Prabhu, p. 271).

38. Nygren, *Agape and Eros*. First published in Swedish in two parts in 1932 and 1938–9 respectively. My references are to the full English translation under the same title, trans. Philip S. Watson (London: SPCK, 1953). According to Outka, "one may justifiably regard [Nygren's] work as the beginning of the modern treatment of the subject" of the ethics of love (*Agape*, p. 1).

39. No doubt Nygren is writing primarily in a *religious* context, but in so far as he intends his comments to apply also to the ethics of human relationships, *eros* can be seen to be the type of every other form of love.

40. Nygren, *Agape and Eros*, passim, esp. pp. 75f.

41. Ibid., esp. p. 210.

42. This emphasis itself tends to violate a primary concern of Christian theologians, viz. to affirm that the coming of Christ and the Christian message (viz. which embody God's love for the world) was not a historical "bolt from the blue," but the culmination of – and prefigured in – the "salvation history" of the "Old" Testament.

43. Outka, *Agape*, devotes a discussion to "Karl Barth on Agape" (chapter 7). If Outka's analysis is correct, Barth also regards *agape* as (potentially) universal, but in actuality as "a universal love for Christians" (p. 210), and "erotic" love – in a "positive" sense – as "being-with" the other in humanness and gladness, and also "the particular love" between a man and a woman which encompasses "understanding, self-giving and desire"; *eros* in a negative sense is "a grasping, taking, possessive love" (see pp. 223–224). The Nygren disjunctive between *agape* and *eros*, based as it is on a particular kind of theology, has cast a long shadow. *Eros*, of course, is a contentious word and has a history of loaded connotations. In a stimulating article, Joseph Runzo also gives *eros* a positive sense, and indeed insists that divine love and "the highest human love" must include a "dimensionality of eros" (see his "Eros and Meaning in Life and Religion" in *The Meaning of Life in the World Religions*, ed. Joseph Runzo and Nancy M. Martin, [Oxford: Oneworld, 1999]). Runzo speaks of "seraphic [burning] love" as the ideal and of "*agape* and *eros* as the two poles of seraphic love, two poles in a dynamic tension." While I do not object to attempts to rescue *eros* from negative connotations, any such attempt must first show

due sensitivity to the word's troubled history. We shall have occasion to resort to the quality of vulnerability suggested by the sexual connotations of erotic love in the next section of this chapter. A more encompassing understanding of agapeistic love than Nygren's is evident from the following statement in a letter by Pope Paul VI to the kidnappers of his friend Aldo Moro in which he pleads for the latter's release: "I have no mandate to speak to you, and I am not bound by any private interest in his regard. But I love him as a member of the great human family, as a friend of student days and – by a very special title – as a brother in faith and as a son of the Church of Christ." Peter Hebblethwaite, *Paul VI: the First Modern Pope* (London: HarperCollins, 1993), p. 703.

44.   "Sanskrit" being generally regarded as the inherited language of high culture, learning, and the religious and social elite.

45.   For a study of key themes in Hindu religious tradition with reference to Sanskritic and other sources, see the author's "A Hindu View of Life," in *The Meaning of Life in the World Religions*, ed. Joseph Runzo and Nancy M. Martin (Oxford: Oneworld, 1999).

46.   The Gita has been especially influential in strands which focus on some form, aspect or intimate of Vishnu or Krishna as supreme (i.e. in "Vaishnava" religion). The important theistic Shvetashvatara Upanishad, which has been dated to about the same period and which seems to have Shaiva leanings, is more philosophical in tone and is hardly a devotional text.

47.   The Gita has sometimes been accused of being inconsistent and lacking in coherence (one might lay a similar charge against most major scriptures). But the Gita has been couched in the framework of a conversation, not of a philosophical treatise. In this essay, the Gita will be approached, phenomenologically, as it generally has been in Hindu devotional and theological tradition, viz. as a unitary text.

48.   For a good introduction to the Gita in context, and also the uses to which it may and has been put up to contemporary times, see the contributions in *The Fruits of our Desiring: An Enquiry into the Ethics of the Bhagavadgītā for Our Times*, ed. J. Lipner (Calgary: Bayeux Arts Inc., 1997).

49.   These two battle-positions symbolize respectively the type of the faithful devotee and the supreme being's guiding and saving role in life's spiritual and moral combat (in which we are all perforce engaged).

50.   Gita 2.7: "I ask you, with mind confused concerning righteous action, what is the better (path)? Tell me that surely. I am your disciple; teach me who come devotedly to you": *pṛcchāmi tvā dharmasaṃmūḍhacetāḥ; yac chreyaḥ syān, niścitaṃ brūhi tan me; śiṣyas te'haṃ, śādhi māṃ tvāṃ prapannam*. Translations in this essay are by the author, unless stated to the contrary.

51.   The Gita is the first Sanskrit text to give a sustained and explicit theistic treatment of divine concern for the world. The canonical Veda (dated to ca.1200 BCE in its earliest received form) may well be (and has been)

thought to have an inherent theism in interaction with human affairs, but it is a theism that is couched in poetic and obscure terms. H. H. Farmer's claim that "the notion of an avatar [is the notion] of a divine being who merely drops into the human scene in an embodied form from the realm of eternity, unheralded, unprepared for, without roots in anything that has gone before in history ... " (*Revelation and Religion: Studies in the Theological Interpretation of Religious Types* [London: Nisbet & Co. Ltd., 1954], p.196) may be somewhat premature. It fails to take account of the fact that traditional "Hinduism" is not only not a monolithic phenomenon but also that it is an essentially oral one. In the strand of devotional Hinduism represented by the emergence of the Bhagavadgita, there may well have been a preceding and developing oral tradition of considerable extent.

52.   See my article, "Avatāra *and* Incarnation?" in *Re-visioning India's Religious Traditions: Essays in honour of Eric Lott,* ed. David C. Scott and Israel Selvanayagam, (Bangalore: ISPCK, 1996).

53.   If even the disadvantaged can walk the highest path, it is implied, how much more those supposedly best placed to do so – devout Brahmins and noble seers (see 9:33).

54.   It was the image of the consuming fire that St Thérèse of Lisieux chose to express the intensity of a loving relationship with God: "It was in 1895 that I received the grace to understand ... how much Jesus longs for us to love him ... and from the bottom of my heart I cried: 'O my divine Master ... surely your merciful love has need of victims too ... the hearts on which you long to lavish it turn towards earthly creatures ... instead of running to your arms to be consumed in the enrapturing furnace of your infinite love ... It seems to me that if you found souls offering themselves to your love as holocausts, you would consume them speedily ... O Jesus ... consume me in the fire of divine love, your little holocaust." See *The Story of a Soul: The Autobiography of Saint Thérèse of Lisieux,* ed. Mother Agnes of Jesus, trans. Michael Day (London: Burns & Oates, 1957), pp. 106–107.

55.   This is the essential teaching of chapter 3: *lokasaṃgraham evāpi saṃpaśyan kartum arhasi ... saktāḥ karmaṇy avidvāṃso yathā kurvanti, Bhārata, kuryād vidvāṃs tathāsaktaś cikīrṣur lokasaṃgraham.* See also 2.47: "Your entitlement pertains to action, never to the fruits [of action]; let not your motive be for the fruit of action, nor should you be attached to inaction" (*karmaṇy evādhikāras te mā phaleṣu kadācana; mā karmaphalahetur bhūr, mā te saṅgo'stv akarmaṇi*).

56.   Or "man" (*naraḥ*) in the sense of representative or type of human beings.

57.   It is not clear who the precise object of *bhaktimān* is intended to be, Krishna or others in general.

58.   Cf. "Those who have come to know (*paṇḍitaḥ*) see the same thing with regard to a learned and virtuous Brahmin or a cow or elephant, or even

a dog or the outcaste who eats the dog" (5:18). One of the chief aims of the Gita is to show that the ideal of impartial regard of the traditional yogi finds its fulfillment in an ethic informed by loving devotion to God.

59. A theme running through the Gita. So Krishna can say in 7:4–5 that he has two natures (*prakṛti*), a lower, "material" nature, and a higher spiritual one (*parāṃ jīvabhūtām*), out of which all things develop. This divine source is the basis of all creaturely value which as such is a bestowed value.

60. This is why I use the term "agapeistic," but agapeistic is not the same as *agape.*

61. The following medley of quotations is taken from *The Moral and Political Writings of Mahatma Gandhi (vol.1),* ed. Raghavan Iyer (Oxford: Clarendon Press, 1986). "For me, [the *Gita*] is a spiritual dictionary. Whenever I am in doubt as to what I should or should not do, I fall back upon it, and so far it has never disappointed me (p. 97) ... When, thousands of years ago, the battle of Kurukshetra was fought, the doubts which occurred to Arjuna were answered by Shri Krishna in the *Gita;* but that battle of Kurukshetra is going on, will go on, for ever within us; the Prince of Yogis, Lord Krishna, the universal *atman* dwelling in the hearts of us all, will always be there to guide Arjuna, the human soul (p. 21) ... The *Gita* teaches that one should cultivate the state of *samatva* [sameness] and explains with every manner of argument the means of doing so, namely *bhakti* accompanied with *jnana* [wisdom], that is, service of every living creature without thought of reward (p. 84) ... I want to identify myself with everything that lives. In the language of the *Gita* I want to live at peace with both friend and foe. Though, therefore, a Mussalman or a Christian or a Hindu may despise me and hate me, I want to love him and serve him even as I would love my wife or son though they hate me (p. 19)." These quotations range from 1924 through 1936 (the latter year about a decade before Gandhi's death).

62. It is generally derived from the root *bhaj,* which means to share with, to give freely, to enjoy together, to have recourse to, to possess: all components of a composite sense that can connote a form of agapeistic love.

63. Or: "It is of the nature of supreme love with respect to this One (*asmin,* viz. God among us)."

64. The disciples of the sixteenth-century saint, Chaitanya, distinguished between *prema* and *kāma* or concupiscence thus: "*Kāma* is the desire for the satisfaction of the self, but *prema* is the desire for the satisfaction of the senses of Kṛṣṇa. The sole object of *kāma* is the pleasure of the self, but *prema* has as its only object the pleasure of Kṛṣṇa"; in *Sacred and Profane Dimensions of Love in Indian Traditions as Exemplified in the Gītagovinda of Jayadeva,* by Lee Siegel (Delhi: Oxford India Paperbacks edition, 1990), p. 69 (first published in 1978). Siegel is quoting from E. Dimock's *Place of the Hidden Moon,* which is citing the *Caitanya-Caritāmṛta, Ādi.*iv.139f.

65. Cf. *sutras* 67–72.

66. *Sutras* 59–61.

67. For example, the great champion of devotional theism, Ramanuja (eleventh–twelfth century), contends that a proper understanding of the scriptures teaches that all predication of "naming words" (e.g. "cow," "horse," "tree") reveals that Brahman or the supreme being is their ultimate referent in so far as their immediate referents, viz. the objects themselves, can be viewed as the "body" of Brahman (and therefore wholly dependent on Brahman), and that an experiential realization of this truth, which entails a life of total loving surrender (*prapatti*) to God, has radical cognitive (including emotional) consequences: "When one is freed from karma in its form of ignorance, this same world [formerly experienced as more or less sorrowful], but now experienced as an expression and attribute of Brahman-with-attributes, becomes nothing but joyful" (*karmarūpāvidyāvimuktasya tad eva jagad vibhūtiguṇaviśiṣṭabrahmānubhavāntargataṃ sukham eva bhavati*). See the *Śrībhāṣya*, 1.3.7. See also the author's *The Face of Truth: A Study of Meaning and Metaphysics in the Vedāntic Theology of Rāmānuja* (London: Macmillan, 1986).

68. The corpus of poetry ascribed to the figure of "Chandidasa" doubtless contains the work of more than one individual. It has played a significant part in the development of popular *bhakti* in Bengal.

69. *In Praise of Krishna: Songs from the Bengali*, trans. E. C. Dimock and D. Levertov (New York: Anchor Books, 1967), p. 49.

70. A good example of such an extended analogy in Vaishnava tradition is the well-known and highly influential Sanskrit love-poem by Jayadeva, the *Gitagovinda* (twelfth century). See B. S. Miller, *Love Song of the Dark Lord: Jayadeva's Gītāgovinda* (New York: Columbia University Press, 1977). See also Lee Siegel, op.cit. Notwithstanding Siegel's remarks in chapter 5, there can be little doubt, as the *Narada Bhakti Sutras'* view on *prema* indicates, that from the beginning the poem was susceptible to being interpreted both analogously *and* allegorically, though Siegel is right to point out that the poem's vogue has depended on its power to evoke the appropriate love-sentiment (*rasa*). A full treatment of love symbolism in Hinduism would require some analysis of its tradition of aesthetics (Siegel gives an account in chapter 2). Erotic imagery also symbolizes love for God in Shaivism. The twelfth-century woman-poet Mahadevi, who from an early age "betrothed herself to Śiva and none other (p. 111) … enlists the traditional imagery of pan-Indian secular love-poetry for personal expression" (*Speaking of Śiva*, translated with an introduction by A. K. Ramanujan [Delhi: Penguin, 1973], p. 113). She describes the intimacy of her love for Siva thus: "He bartered my heart, looted my flesh, claimed as tribute my pleasure, took over all of me. I'm the woman of love for my lord white as jasmine" (p. 125).

71. "Her songs are sung all the way to the southernmost tip of the sub-continent by people who otherwise have little command of Hindi": *Songs of*

the *Saints of India,* by J. S. Hawley and M. Juergensmeyer, (New York: Oxford University Press, 1988), p. 120.

72. Ibid., p. 134.

73. *Sutra* 82. The Bhagavata Purana (ca. ninth century), a lengthy (Sanskrit) text of great importance for the understanding and propagation of devotion in Vaishnava circles, lists nine forms of *bhakti* (see 7.5.23–24), with considerable overlap: viz. *śravaṇam kīrtaaṃ viṣṇoḥ smaraṇaṃ pādasevanam; arcanaṃ vandanaṃ dāsyaṃ sakhyam ātmanivedanam – 23. iti puṃsārpitā viṣṇau bhaktiś cen navalakṣaṇā; kriyeta bhagavaty addhā tan manye'adhītam uttamam – 24.*

74. Some explanation of each is given in my book, *Hindus,* pp. 307–321.

75. See chapter 4: "Loving the Goddess in Hinduism" by Nancy M. Martin and chapter 12: "Krishna and the Gender of Longing" by John Stratton Hawley.

76. Not least in the form of the images of temple worship in Hinduism.

77. "Cripple me, father, that I may not go here and there. Blind me, father, that I may not look at this and that, deafen me, father, that I may not hear anything else ... " yearns another twelfth-century devotee of Shiva, Basavaṇṇa (Ramanujan, *Speaking of Śiva,* p. 70).

78. Notwithstanding the Vaishnava slant of this essay.

79. It is important to note that we have focused on ideal forms of love with regard to God and human ethics, that is, those forms of love that provide the normative matrix for the validation of what have been recognized as "lower/inferior" if no less authentic forms of loving (referred to, in Hinduism, where God is concerned, as the "lower *bhakti*"). The latter is a needy love, God being supplicated on the basis of human desire and genuine need, and graciously responding on that basis. Such love of God is not improper, though as a self-centred love to some extent; it is inferior to the (predominantly) selfless or decentered, higher *bhakti.* Analogous to the lower *bhakti* (which may be more or less self-centered) are various kinds of human love (e.g. the *amor amicitiae* mentioned earlier in the chapter).

Plate 4 Sculpture of the Great Goddess Durga, in the act of slaying the buffalo demon Mahisha, the latter shown here transforming from animal to human form at the moment of decapitation. Osian, Rajasthan, India. Photo: *Nancy M. Martin.*

4

LOVING THE GODDESS
in HINDUISM

Nancy M. Martin

L ove is a primary way of understanding the religious life in Hinduism. The cultivation of love is valued as a transformative religious practice, moving human beings out of the predictability of dharma and the laws of karma and into dynamic relationship. The religious practitioner becomes *bhakta* or devotee, and ultimate reality is experienced as profoundly personal. Human modes of loving become both mirror and an emotional training ground for Divine–human love and provide a language to articulate the intensely personal relationship developing between devotee and Divine–parental love, friendship, the loyal and respectful love of servant for master, and the passionate union of lover and beloved.[1]

Human beings enter such relationships with other humans as embodied and *gendered* beings, and when these dimensions of love are explored and deepened in the devoted love of human and Divine, this experience, too, is shaped by social constructions of gender and articulated in gendered language. The Divine is son, daughter, father, mother to the devotee who takes the corresponding role, often set in the eternal drama of mythic narratives. Devotee and Divine may also meet as devoted friends, most often articulated in the form of same-sex relationships – Krishna's cowherding male companions or the (male) Vitthala's taking the form of a servant woman to assist the Maharashtrian saint Janabai in her back-breaking domestic labor.

The Divine–human encounter also may be experienced and expressed in the even more intimate mode of erotic love. There is an implied equality in such a meeting, and the gendering of this can be problematic, given the power differential in human relations. If God is conceived of as male, it seems acceptable for the human devotee to assume the role and attitude of a female lover. After all, devotion (in its many faceted meanings) is a definitive element in the complex construction of femininity in Hindu contexts, and in such a relationship the devotee steps up from an inferior position to meet God who steps down to make the meeting possible. The devotee does indeed take such a feminine stance in devotion to Shiva and to Vishnu, particularly in his form as Krishna, and Hindu devotional literature richly explores this "feminine" perspective.[2]

But what if ultimate reality is experienced as female, as Goddess? How is love for Goddess in Hindu traditions experienced and expressed? Who is she? In what sense is she feminine? And on what terms does a human man or woman approach her?

ULTIMATE REALITY AS FEMININE

Even as there are devotional strands of Hindu tradition directed toward Vishnu and his avatars and toward Shiva, so, too, a strand of devotion develops oriented toward the Devi or Goddess. There is evidence that goddesses may have been worshiped on the Indian subcontinent by the great civilizations of the Indus Valley as early as 2500 BCE, and there are a vast number of goddesses, ranging from very local village deities to the consorts of the great pan-Indian gods to the independent Great Goddess, Mahadevi.[3] The principle textual (puranic) declaration of her cosmic ultimacy, The *Devi Mahatmya*, dates to the sixth century CE, and the emerging theology proclaims that the Goddess is ultimate reality itself.[4]

A perception of the Oneness of reality underlies much Hindu thinking, and at the theoretical and abstract level that ultimate reality is beyond gender. However, the first movement from that one absolute reality into manifest multiplicity is articulated in gendered language. This level of differentiation is seemingly so fundamental in the experience of human beings that it enters immediately into the picture when *any* talk of distinction does, becoming emblematic of duality, relationality, and manifestation itself.

In early layers of myth (and I use "myth" in Wendy Doniger O'Flaherty's sense of shared stories that express a community's deepest truths about themselves and the world[5]), the emerging active creator is a male god – although the constituents of created reality, its creative yet also illusory or deluding nature, and the life force within it are perceived as feminine.[6] In later Goddess traditions, these first creative potentialities, powers, and substrates are affirmed as feminine and positively valued, but the movement into multiplicity, generated by a distinctly feminine force.

Here the Goddess is described as materiality, embodiment, in the form of *prakriti* (inextricably tied to the male consciousness of *purusha* and seen as lesser or even negatively valued in Samkhya philosophy but now given preeminence). She is also *shakti*, the empowering energy that enlivens all that is and makes all life possible (no longer merely a feminine aspect of the male gods, but the force which enables the gods to act at all in the various ways they do). And she is *maya*, the creative power that generates this wondrous world and which, though it may delude us (and is viewed negatively in Advaita Vedanta, for example, because of this), makes possible the experience of bliss. All reality is divinized as the manifestation of the Devi, and in the multiplicity of manifestation, love and relationality are made possible.

The Goddess reigns supreme, but is there any role left to maleness in such a view? Not necessarily but if there is, the masculine can only be the quiescence of the Godhead; the unmanifest, unrevealed Divine; the hiddenness of God (though not the wholeness of the Divine). And indeed such a fundamental masculinity in the form of Shiva is affirmed within strands of Goddess tradition. That which precedes the manifest world itself is said to be constituted by Shiva *and* the Goddess as Shakti. Thus, the inner relationality of the Divine, too, is articulated in gendered terms, suggesting that maleness and femaleness are in some sense together constitutive of embodied, manifest existence in a complementary way. Within such a vision, gender is recognized as perhaps the quintessential symbol of both difference or distinction and relationality. The use of images of gender difference in this context holds within it the possibility of generating and reinforcing a dualistic and oppositional view of the world, deluding us into a sense of absolute and often hierarchical understanding of difference, reflected in and reflective of social relations. But it also offers a possible wedge to break open the heart of human ignorance, offering a potential avenue into a non-dual and whole experience of reality as it is, in which such distinctions remain but are experienced in a radically non-hierarchical and "non-othering" way. According to Shakta or Goddess theology, the path to experiencing the whole of reality and becoming whole ourselves involves loving and becoming the Goddess, who is paradoxically at once femaleness and wholeness, transcendent and immanent.[7]

LOVING THE GODDESS IN PRACTICE

How does one relate to such a Goddess? If we turn to worship practices associated with her, we find people calling the Devi "Ma" and conceiving of her as a mother figure. When Kathleen Erndl interviewed people going to pilgrimage sites associated with various goddesses in the Punjab region about why they worshiped the Goddess, they spoke in explicitly "motherly terms" of her great power, her demanding nature coupled with deep compassion and abundant responsiveness to her devotees' wishes and needs (in a way that only a mother might), and the inner peace they found in her presence.[8] To enter many of the Devi temples, one must first complete the ordeal of climbing to the top of a high mountain and then crawl through a small opening into a cave-like (sometimes a literal cave) temple, returning as it were to the womb to encounter the divine mother. The symbolism is lost on no one. Similarly, Rachel McDermott found Shakta devotees in Bengal speaking of the Goddess, even in the outwardly horrific form of Kali, primarily as "the all-compassionate Mother" (see plate 8).[9]

In addition to pilgrimage practices, the Devi is glorified through the mantra-like recitation of the *Devi Mahatmya*[10] and worshiped in temples and homes with singing and offerings. During communal gatherings she may come into the presence of her worshipers through possession, playing and speaking among them, often through particular women who are her regular vehicles, some of whom become religious leaders and even great gurus.[11] The Goddess's involvement with her devotees is thus intimate and immediate. Watching devotees as they approached Ammachi (a south Indian woman who now has an international following) when she was embodying the Goddess, I saw clear adoration on their faces, and she responded with what appeared to be a motherly affection and sometimes motherly discipline. In such circumstances, love of a spiritual teacher or guru and love of the Goddess become one. (It is interesting to note that in her early days she was also possessed by Krishna, but her devotees overwhelmingly demanded to experience the Goddess through her, and she has ceased to manifest Krishna in recent years.)[12]

The Devi comes also in collective and spontaneous possessions during communal ritual performances. For example, this occurs among the tribal Bhils as they reenact her fierce salvific intervention on the part of their people during forty days of Gauvari performances in the hot season. The possessed must sometimes be physically restrained from hurting the actors playing the demons and other enemies during such performances.[13] She is embodied, too, as the fierce Bhadrakali to slay the demon Dharika in the *mudiyettu* dance of Kerala performed by male ritual specialists as a ritual offering, dispelling the Goddess's anger (and, Sarah Caldwell suggests, her sexual frustration and erotic danger) and unleashing her blessings.[14] Each of these complex phenomenon have multiple religious, cultural, political, social, and psychological dimensions and specific interpretive communities, but all show the Goddess as immediate and accessible to her devotees, intimately involved and embodied in the material world.

In more everyday practices, many women take up specific fasts associated with goddesses like Santoshi Ma, asking for help with family difficulties – oftentimes an unsettled husband or son – and continue these practices long after the initial problem has been resolved, saying that the practice gives them peace of mind.[15] In my own conversations with women in India, they have articulated a sense of security, of at-homeness, and of being in the care of an all-powerful and compassionate being when in the presence of the Goddess.

But she can also be demanding. Some fasts cannot simply be abandoned – special rituals must be carried out to end the vow or another person must be recruited to continue the practice. And there are stories also of the Goddess's demands on her devotees, particularly male ones: they must demonstrate their devotion by offering what is most important to them – their dearest family members, their horses, even their tongues or heads (all of which she always restores).[16] Animal sacrifices are still made to her in some temples (although elsewhere vegetable substitutes have been made). The image of "Mother" resonates with this kind of unbreakable bonding and mutual responsibility, if not its violent manifestation. The latter is perhaps indicative of a fierce maternal protectiveness on behalf of a child, but also suggests that the path to life and the Source of Life will almost certainly require a coming to terms with death and with ourselves as well.

THE LANGUAGE OF DEVOTION

What language might be used to describe the relationship between the Goddess and her devotees, particularly when that relationship is marked by an intimate and abiding love? The articulation and enhancement of the inner experience of love of the Divine is the specialty of the poet–saints of devotional Hinduism. The eighteenth-century Bengali saints Ramprasad Sen and Kamalakanta Bhattacharya are perhaps the two best-known early examples of such devotional voices addressing the Devi, although shakta and tantric forms of worship of the Goddess had been going on for centuries. These poets draw heavily on preceding mythology and iconography, ritual practices and theology, as they give expression to the very personal and intimate relationship between devotee and Goddess.[17]

Many themes in these poets' devotional songs are found in the songs of other saints, whether they are devoted to God or Goddess manifest in a particular form or beyond such limitations: admonitions to the mind so easily caught up in illusion; embittered cries against the difficult struggle of life in the embodied state fettered by sensual desires; rallying calls to pay heed to death's imminent approach; impassioned pleas for refuge and active intervention by the Divine on behalf of the devotee; self-congratulatory exposures of the Divine magician behind *maya*'s deluding creativity; and ridiculing critiques of outward forms of religiosity when the Divine is present everywhere. Other themes are shared only by those who approach Ultimate Reality in manifest form – bewildered awe-filled descriptions of the mystery of an embodied approachable Divine who is at the same time all and all, the cosmic totality, and expressions of the devotee's love, spoken in the languages of human intimacy and imbedded in mythological narratives.

When we reach this last stage of myth and relationship, the traditions around the Devi begin to diverge from those of Vishnu or Shiva. The Devi does not have a unified mythologically grounded identity in the way that Vishnu or Shiva do. She is fundamentally and seemingly infinitely multiple. In the defining narrative of the *Devi Mahatmya*, three distinct stories are told with the heroine of each described in decidedly different terms and with multiple goddesses emerging from the heroine and being absorbed back into her. This is something quite different from Vishnu's avatars, although both are said to enter the world in various forms to assist their devotees. All goddesses – from those of pan-Indian fame such as Lakshmi, Parvati, Durga, Kali, Sita, Ganga, Saraswati, and Radha (each with her own elaborate mythic biography) to those of very local worship at the village and caste level – merge in her. Not only is she "all in all" – the same could be said of Vishnu – but all female manifestations of the Divine are seen as inseparable from the Great Goddess, expressions of this gendered ultimacy. The mythic resources to speak about the Devi are then theoretically as endless as are her names, though devotion more often focuses on Kali and related manifestations of the Goddess that tend to be associated with Shiva – that is, Parvati or Uma, Durga, and Tara – while many of the other goddesses appear essentially as manifestations of Kali in the ten Mahavidyas.[18]

Devi as Mother

What forms of human love and relationship might provide a language and an entry point into loving the Goddess, especially given her various mythic identities? The love between parents and children is preeminent. As we have seen, the Goddess is addressed as "Mother" or more intimately as "Ma," a term used in human society for one's biological mother, for one's female guru, or for any other respected and/or well-loved older woman. The title resonates with qualities of nurture, care, comfort, and fierce protectiveness and with the provision of abundance and physical and psychic nourishment (though darker psychic resonances in child–parent relations may also be struck – the fear of the withholding of the above, anger at deprivation).[19] Admittedly the title might also merely designate respect. The title "Ma" seems to be universally applied to Hindu goddesses, some of whom are very unmotherly, in a manner that often has little or nothing to do with the human experience of this relationship, such as the Matrikas who appear to assist Devi in her battle with Sumbha and Nisumbha in the *Devi Mahatmya.* We must therefore be careful about assuming an automatic homology between the Goddess and cultural constructs of motherhood.

Nevertheless, in calling her mother, devotees' individual experiences of mothers may shape their experiences *and* description of the Devi (just as surely as speaking of God as Father may). Deep-rooted psychological fears of unmeetable maternal demands may find articulation here, as well as the assumed infantile experience of oceanic and blissful oneness with a seemingly omnipotent mother and the opposite fear of engulfment and loss of individuality (and, for the male devotee, of masculinity). In the myths and practices of Goddess worship, we can find what appear to be reflections of the psychological process of individuation and developing gender identities, particularly of sons in relation to mothers in a cultural context where this relationship is often highly emotionally charged, where the intimacy between husband and wife may be perceived as a possible danger to the stability of the extended family and the birth of sons is seen as absolutely essential to defining a woman's status.[20] Expressions of maternal anger as well as care and male fear of mature female sexuality appear to be threads woven into the tapestry of ritual practices and narratives associated with the Goddess, and admittedly may be a subterranean current in the male devotee's childlike approach to her, particularly in her more horrific forms.

In the rich array of both beautific and horrific forms of the Goddess and mythic stories associated with them, we find a rich source of reflection on Indian constructions of gender and gender relations, allowing the exploration of and commentary on these issues in addition to the cultivation of encounter with the Divine. Understanding the psychological power of these images is essential to understanding their *religious* function. Object relations theory and feminist psychoanalytic insights offer some explanatory potential with regard to the radically different forms in which the Goddess appears, and also to the paradox of both deep respect for and severe oppression of women in the Indian context and elsewhere.[21] Dorothy Dinnerstein and others suggest that children who first experience the limitations and frustrations of existence in the presence of female primary caregivers, come to associate these characteristics at some level with women, while the more distant male caregivers (and by inference all males) seem untouched by such things. Women end up bifurcated (as the Devi does), on the one hand all-giving goddesses and on the other demon-like – witnesses to our shame, frustrators of our desires, etc.[22]

Certainly the centrality of gender in the worship of goddesses makes these myths and practices ideal locations to work out psychological woundedness and gendered dimensions of the struggle for wholeness and healing. These myths and practices provide narrative structure and a ritual form for neuroses and psychoses as well as healthy emotional development, as the Indian Psychoanalyst Sudhir Kakar has reported from his clinical practice, and for wider social articulation and control of fear without any real resolution, as Sarah Caldwell has suggested with regard to the *mudiyettu* performances and John Stratton Hawley has suggested with regard to the gendered longing of Krishna devotion.[23] No doubt all these psychological levels are operative in loving the Goddess. Jeffrey Kripal's research suggests that Ramakrishna, perhaps the Goddess' most famous devotee, traversed dramatically gendered and mountainous psychic terrain in his spiritual journey (though Ramakrishna is much better-known for popularizing Vedanta in the West together with his disciple Vivekananda than for his devotion to Kali).[24] A human's relationship with the Divine can be as balanced and fulfilling or as dysfunctional and self-deceived as all other human relations. But it is also in relationship that healing occurs, that we can come into wholeness and the fullness of being. The call to love the Goddess often seems to be initiated by a need for healing, and it may ultimately be a call to lose control (or admit our lack of it) and to face our reality and our own fears.

The explanatory power of psychological analysis is helpful but limited. We must examine ways in which religious imagery and practices interface with psychological development and sociological constructions of gender in order to understand their true meaning and power in maintaining or challenging inequality and injustice. But they should not be reduced only to this. Cracks begin to appear immediately when we try to apply the notion of the bifurcated feminine to Indian goddesses – there are not two types of goddesses but many and complexly defined forms, and there is a fundamental multiplicity rather than a simple dualism that defines the feminine Divine and reality generally within this worldview.[25] Further, though the feminine Divine and more generally gender distinction itself are emblematic of manifestation – the movement away from Oneness – human–divine relations cannot be reduced to the human psychology of individuation.

In what sense do the poet–saints Ramprasad Sen and Kamalakanta Bhattacharya speak of the Goddess as mother to the child devotee? Both do address her as Mother, but their poems tend to contrast her actions with those of a human mother, in order to point out the painful depths of her seeming indifference to her devotees and to call her *into* motherly affection. It is absence of which they speak, the utter devastation of a child deserted by its mother. And who is more pitiable and thus more irresistible than the motherless child? The poets play the image both ways – chiding the Goddess and calling her into the role of mother. There is a mythic precedent for this approach as well: Shiva is able to stop Kali's mad dancing in one telling by becoming an infant and suckling at her breast, instantly getting her attention and calming her as well as dispelling her destructive power. Ramprasad cries out to the Devi in frustration:

> Mother, You lured me into this world,
> You said, "Let's play," only to cheat
> My hope of its hope with Your playing …
>
> Ramprasad says: In this game
> The end is a foregone conclusion.
> Now, at dusk, take up Your child
> In Your arms and go home.[26]

Elsewhere he insists:

> When a child cries out, calling the precious name
> Of mother, then a mother takes it in her arms.
> Everywhere I look I see that's the rule,
> Except for me …

> There are many
> Bad children, but who ever heard
> Of a bad mother?
>
> There's only one hope
> For Ramprasad, Mother – that in the end
> He will be safe at Your feet.[27]

Paradoxically it is the Goddess who brings the devotee into this world of pain and delusion and she who is our only hope of liberation from it. She is the source of all that is, indeed she is all that is, so where else can a human find ultimate refuge and on what grounds can she reject her child devotee? Ramprasad will not let her off the hook easily, saying:

> You are the mother of all
> And our nurse. You carry the Three Worlds
> In Your belly.
>
> So am I some orphan fallen out
> Of the sky? And if You think I'm bad,
> Remember, You're the cord connecting
> Every good and evil
> And I'm a tool tied to illusion.[28]

There is a recognition here that ultimate reality is experienced often as impersonal, as uninvolved or self-involved, non-relational, unengaged with human beings. And the Devi is this – all in all – good, bad, ignorance, knowledge, life, death, luck, misfortune. At times she seems cold as stone, unmoving as her Himalayan father, to Ramprasad. She is the cause of disease which seems to afflict its victims randomly. Yet she is also the healer of disease, answering her devotees' prayers, and she is experienced as personal, lovingly engaged with the world, and fundamentally and essentially relational. Calling her "Mother" then is a way of affirming her loving engagement but also of taming other aspects of her character (and of reality itself) and of reigning in indifference and turning it into interested inter-relationship.

Beneath these complaints is an assurance of relationship and love and a genuine intimacy. How else would a devotee dare to speak to the all-powerful Goddess in such tones? He knows she could destroy him in an instant, but he speaks out none the less, not unlike the prophets of the Hebrew Bible who sometimes challenge God's actions on grounds of justice. Here, the child devotee's anger and sense of betrayal parallels that of Radha when

Krishna forgets their rendezvous and comes to her after spending the night out, the marks of another's love on his body. Both presume an existing singular intimacy and love and express the devastation of the human bereft of a sense of divine presence.

Ramprasad sings:

> I'm not calling you Mother anymore,
> All You give me is trouble.
>
> ... I'll beg before I come to You,
> Crying "Mother." I've tried that
> And got the silent treatment.
> If the mother lives should the son suffer,
> And if she's dead, hasn't he got to live somehow?[29]

He demands more than indifference; he demands relationship, care, nurturing, comfort, love (and specifically motherly love for a child):

> You think motherhood is child's play?
> One child doesn't make a mother if she's cruel ...
>
> When a child is bad, his parents correct him,
> But You can watch Death come at me
> With murder in His heart
> And turn away yawning.
>
> ... [D]on't call Yourself
> The Mother.[30]

To be "mother" is to be compassionate, to heal, to provide abundantly as the Goddess Annapurna does, even to discipline and teach, and thus to be in ongoing relationship with one's children. All these are characteristics of the Goddess, though she seems at times as indifferent as the forces of nature, blind to the human plight.

Ramprasad pulls out all the stops, drawing from the deep well of parental guilt and the fear of what others will say about such a parent, to articulate his feelings:

> What's so good in You
> That You deserve to be called Mother?
>
> ... Twice-born Rampradas says: people mock me.
> They say: "If your mother is Annapurna,
> Why isn't there food in your father's house?"[31]

Beneath these complaints, in addition to the desire for relationship and love, is genuine need. The child cannot survive without parental care, nor can the human live without the enlivening *shakti* of the Devi nor find release without divine intervention or without encountering the full reality contained by the Goddess, including death itself:

> I clutch You, Mother,
> But with all my bungled karma, can't hold on.
> Prasad cries out: Mother, cut this black narl
> Of acts, cut through it. Let life, when death
> Closes down, shoot rejoicing up
> Out of my head like a rocket.
>
> Ramprasad says: Call the Mother,
> She can handle Death.[32]

The poet–saint portrays this relationship as passionately interested, on both sides – and his arguments would not work if it were not. (In this sense it is paradigmatic of Joseph Runzo's characterization of Divine–human and ideal human love as "seraphic love" which includes passionate involvement, and also supports Julius Lipner's movement toward a redefined notion of *agape*.[33])

Mythic narratives do not provide much direct support for this explicitly motherly dimension of the salvific human–Divine relationship. Goddesses do not bear children by ordinary means if they are mothers at all, and iconographically, Kali (whom these two poet devotees primarily address) would definitely be an embarrassment to the devotee as a mother, dancing naked and standing on the naked and inert body of her consort Shiva.

The awkwardness of calling Kali "Mother" is not lost on the poet saints. Kamalakanta sings:

> Who is this,
> Dressed like a crazy woman,
> Robed in the sky?
> Whom does she belong to?
> She has let down her hair,
> Thrown off her clothes,
> Strung human hands around her waist,
> And taken a sword in her hand …
>
> Mother, are you going to rescue Kamalakanta
> In *this* outfit?[34]

Ramprasad expresses a similar feeling:

> Kali, why are You naked again?
> Good grief, haven't You any shame?
> Mother, don't you have any clothes?
> Where is the pride of a king's daughter?
> And, Mother, is this some family duty –
> This standing on the chest of Your man?
> You're naked, He's naked,
> You hang around the burning grounds.
> O Mother, we are dying of shame.
> Now put on Your woman's clothes.[35]

Clearly she is no ordinary mother or woman, though the power of this vision plays off the radical reversal of notions of proper behavior for a woman and wife, and off a child's embarrassment and frustration at his/her inability to control a parent's behavior. The discomfort of the poets seems mirrored by twentieth-century devotees, who Rachel McDermott notes, in Bengal have largely abandoned this portrayal of Kali for a beautiful version of her.[36] But discomfort is not necessarily a bad thing, containing within it the seeds of change and transformation, and this disjuncture between the use of the language of mother–child relations and some of the characteristics of the Devi reminds us that this language is being used symbolically.

Goddess as Daughter

Other gendered human relationships also provide images and templates for loving the Divine. Seldom in the devotional songs associated with male gods is fatherly love invoked in any detail, although in Maharashtra a regional form of Krishna, Vitthala, is compared to a mother cow pining for her calf in his love for devotees. The reverse role, where devotee is parent to the child god, is explored extensively, however, especially with regard to Krishna in light of the elaborate stories of his childhood among the cowherding people of Braj.[37] (A Christian parallel might be imagining oneself to be Mary or Joseph caring for the child Jesus.) In goddess devotion, it is the mythology of Parvati or Uma, as the daughter who insists on marrying the disreputable ascetic Shiva (every parent's nightmare son-in-law), that provides the narrative base for the devotee's parental love of the Divine. Both Ramprasad and Kamalakanta sing of the child goddess's desire for the moon, finally fulfilled when her father sits her on his lap and gives her a mirror to view her own luminous face (paralleling a similar story of the child Krishna).[38]

The majority of songs in this genre, however, develop the bittersweet love and longing of mother and daughter after the daughter's marriage when she moves away to live with her new husband and in-laws. Her visits home are precious moments, anticipated and cherished by both, and love and longing in separation is epitomized here by the mother–daughter relationship and the deep bonds between women. In the songs we hear of Uma's mother's insistence that her unfeeling and literally unmovable mountain father go to Shiva and ask that Uma be permitted to return, Uma's insistent pleading with her husband to let her go, the joy of the reunion of mother and daughter as well as the other women of the village who run out to kiss and embrace her, and mother and daughter's desperate sorrow at parting. These poems of love's longing emphasize mutual care, particularly between women. Such songs and emotions come to the fore during Durga Puja, as the Devi is welcomed like a daughter come home, only to depart at the end of the festival, abandoning the clay images which are then submerged in ponds or rivers where they dissolve back into the material world, itself the Goddess's manifestation or body.

Images of Women's Friendship

The friendships of women and the relationship of servant maid and mistress offer further models for loving the goddess. Although these themes apparently were not developed extensively by Ramprasad and Kamalakanta, the *Devi Bhagavata Purana* (a second major text associated with the Goddess that was composed sometime between the eleventh and the sixteenth centuries) relates how the gods Brahma, Shiva, and Vishnu approach the Goddess on her island paradise and are immediately transformed into beautiful women. They can come to her in female form and serve her, oiling her hair, helping her to dress and put on her ornaments, applying her make-up, even as devotees are called to do in other shakta texts (and as are the *manjaris* and *sakhis* of Radha in Vaishnava tradition).[39]

Here there may be a measure of the same identification of femininity with devotion operative that characterizes Krishna devotion, and the author of the *Devi Bhagavata Purana* is clearly aware of and responding to Vaishnava traditions. But the situation is quite different because there remains *no* male on the scene and no goal of erotic union, vicarious or otherwise, though the interactions are extremely sensual. The phallic god Shiva acknowledges his desire to remain in this "feminized" state, for he knows that maleness would exile him from intimacy. Clearly this might be psychologized as male emasculation in the presence of the sexual mother, but it seems more importantly a banishment of any hint of lust or dominance, traits that perhaps almost inevitably shadow maleness under such circumstances.

Gender Transformation and Erotic Love

The *Devi Bhagavata Purana* includes other tales of gender transformation, radically relativizing gender identity and revealing what Wendy Doniger O'Flaherty refers to as the "serial androgyny"[40] of humans across multiple rebirths – an androgyny that still preserves gender distinction in specific embodiments. Such androgyny also suggests in the final analysis that the Devi herself is inclusive of male and female, beyond gender in her ultimate form (as indeed ultimate reality must be if it is truly all in all and One). However, this is one pair of opposites that are not mentioned in the hymns to the Great Goddess in the earlier *Devi Mahatmya*. Although she is praised as both ignorance and knowledge, auspicious Lakshmi and inauspicious Alakshmi, hunger and satiation, life and death, deluder and savior, she is not addessed as male *and* female.[41]

Yet she is able to take on specifically male forms. The poet Kamalakanta addresses her genderedness, singing:

> You don't realize this, mind,
> But Kali, the Prime Cause,
> Is not only female.
> Sometimes,
> Taking the color of a cloud,
> She transforms herself,
> and emerges
> Male.[42]

She who is at one moment Kali appears as Krishna playing his irresistible flute in the forests of Braj. She is at once female, male, beyond gender, creator, destroyer, preserver, mother, sufferer of the world's pain, taking any form you believe her to have, indwelling divine presence in the lotus of the heart. Such roles maintain both her transcendent and immanent nature and her radical and passionate involvement with the world. Kamalakanta suggests that she is caught up in her own *lila* or divine creative play and both suffers the pains of the world and becomes male to make love to her "female" devotees as Krishna.

Her primary identity remains decidedly feminine, however, and she takes desirable female forms as well. Describing her once again in her frightful Kali form, Kamalakanta goes on to say,

At other times
You take a flirtatious pose,
And then even the God of Love is outdone.

... You are terrifying,
You are death,
You are a beautiful woman.

Thus assuming various forms,
You fulfill the wishes of your worshippers.[43]

Can this beautiful Goddess who is also terrifying death be approached by a devotee as a lover? Kamalakanta asserts that she takes various forms to fulfill the wishes of her devotees – dare they have such a desire?

In myth, we do find models for gods loving goddesses and vice versa. Shiva's tragic love for his first wife Sati leads him to wander through the world inconsolably carrying her dead body, until Vishnu is able to cut it away bit by bit, each dismembered part dropping to deify the earth and form a future goddess pilgrimage site. Sati had immolated herself when her husband was dishonored by her father, and she is reborn as Parvati who sets out to win Shiva's heart through extremes of asceticism and meditation rather than the seduction of beauty. Then when this quintessential ascetic (who despises Kama, the God of Love, but is himself represented by the *linga* or phallus), finally gives in to Parvati, their passionate love-making threatens the stability of the world, and the gods must conspire to stop it. In some tellings Rama's love for Sita leaves him utterly incapacitated after her kidnapping by Ravana, and Krishna pines for Radha as deeply as she longs for him. Such myths reveal multiple dimensions of the Indian constructions of romantic love and gender relations.

But dare a human devotee aspire to the role of these gods in his/her love of the Devi? Other mythic models are discouraging. Kali is most often portrayed naked and standing over the inert body of Shiva, his phallus erect. When approaching her sexually, even this god appears as a corpse to calm her destructive dancing. Ramprasad speaks in what might be construed as Oedipal terms about wanting what Shiva his father has, but it turns out to be only the touch of the Devi's feet, as the poet and the tradition play fast and loose with human psychology and expectation, reflecting not naiveté but a sophisticated level of awareness.

The demons who approach the Goddess with lust on their minds in the *Devi Mahatmya* fair much worse than Shiva. She laughs at their desires, claims she will marry only the man who can defeat her in battle, and kills them with ease, usually by decapitation (see plate 4). To approach her sexually is a fatal proposition for demons, and in all likelihood for humans with similar motivations.

Yet Kamalakanta speaks explicitly of her love-making with Shiva, calling the Devi "Shyama," the Dark One, and saying:

> Sweating with the fun of reverse sexual intercourse
> Young Syama's flesh thrills
> On top of you Siva,
> Her boat amidst the deep ocean of nectar.
> Her long hair reaches down to the ground.
> She is naked,
> Ornamented with human heads and hands.
> Kamalakanta watches their beautiful bodies
> And sheds tears of bliss.[44]

Such a description resembles Bengali songs of Radha and Krishna's joyous union where she too takes the upper position, but different power relations, other energies, and alternate interpretive communities are involved when one speaks of Kali in this manner.[45] Radha's riding of Krishna's body demonstrates their equality and the fulfillment of love within the reality of Krishna. Kali, on the other hand, is arrayed in horrific attire rather than the ornaments of desire, and her love play is suggestive of dominance and self-amusement. Like the coupling of Radha and Krishna, that of Kali and Shiva images a relationality within the ultimate – here the cosmic union of Shiva and Shakti. But this latter coupling also images another union said to take place within the individual in tantric practice in which the feminine kundalini energy of the indwelling Goddess is understood to rise through the *chakras* of the body to union in the thousand-petalled lotus at the top of the head where Shiva rests, generating a non-dual experience of reality and a liberating freedom that sends bliss cascading down through the practitioner's body in an inner integration and wholeness. The "erotic aesthetic" employed here (to use Joseph Runzo's term) describes the inner relationality of the Divine and the indwelling presence of the Divine within the human.

To approach the Goddess as lover, as Shiva does, requires heroism and a willingness to give her the upper hand; this is the prerogative of the male tantric practitioner who understands himself to be meeting her thus in ritual encounters with female practitioners. Tantric practices include the recitation of sacred mantras and the performance of elaborate rituals and visualizations, designed to win *darshan* of the Goddess and to cultivate a realization and an actualization of the Goddess's multifaceted presence within each individual (male and female).[46] When properly prepared and sufficiently spiritually advanced, the male tantric may also dare to approach the Devi as a lover, though he will in all likelihood have to meet her on a cremation ground and will worship and love her in the body of an equally advanced female practitioner in ritualized sexual intercourse. Such a path purports to lead to the dissolution of dualistic ways of thinking, in part by transgressing the boundaries of pure and impure, life and death, high and low, human and Divine, and so entering the realm of the forbidden and the repulsive as well as of pleasure and desire. In its highest stages, male and female practitioners ideally meet, acknowledging the Divine within each other and combining their energies toward their mutual liberation. (Although the erotic language here is decidedly heterosexual, we need only look back to the gender transformations of the Goddess affirmed by Ramprasad and Kamalakanta and of her devotees in the tales of the *Devi Bhagavata Purana* to see that gender is a fluid concept and that there is room here for considerable flexibility.[47])

From this perspective, the Goddess is uncensored reality, where life and death are inextricably intertwined, and the Divine pervades the material realm, energizing and manifesting the play of existence. According to tantric teachings, to love this Goddess is to realize our own divinity, and to short-circuit what David Kinsley playfully calls "a hardening of the categories," freeing the devotee/lover into a liberating existence that is at once passionate and blissful.[48] To love the Goddess in this most intimate of ways would be in the final analysis to immerse oneself in the whole of Reality.

Beneath this kind of erotic encounter with the Divine is a fundamentally gendered way of understanding reality that affirms difference and an egalitarian complementarity that preserves relationality. Ramprasad says, "I want to taste sugar; I don't want to be sugar."[49] Merger is not the goal, and manifestation (fundamentally identified with the feminine but also characterized by male and female) is seemingly the only game in town. Sexual union marks one of the deepest ways that human beings know of meeting another, of tasting another, of experiencing another as not other than ourselves and yet fully and wonderfully distinct. The practice of ritual sexual union in tantric Hinduism is understood to be in part a daring act of return to the female for the male, who thereby shows a willingness to take down the ramparts of separation and "othering" that have also come to be identified with maleness. And for both male and female it should be a profound affirmation of both human beings' full humanness *and* our divine nature.

It is in sexual union that human beings might perhaps be vulnerable and most exposed and where there is therefore the potential for our deepest psychic wounds to be healed.[50] And it is the love of the Goddess which is manifest here, in tantric ritual practice.

Gender is recognized in tantric practice as one of our most hardened categories and its psychological formation as perhaps a foundation for other forms of "othering" and delusions of self. There is a kind of spiritual affirmative action operative in this tantric understanding, one which works through the psychology of individuation and gender identity formation, that has in varying cultural forms shaped us all, and offers the possibility of a reconciliation with human vulnerability and sacredness and a vision of wholeness for men and women. In requiring the worship of the Goddess in women, tantra seeks both to raise the feminine and to lower the masculine, and through this to overturn the hierarchy of difference and shatter our illusions of control, absolute autonomy, and purity, potentially replacing them with an experience of radical freedom.

Kamalakanta acknowledges that the Devi is "matter, spirit, then complete void,"[51] but she is also fundamentally feminine and embodied. In fact Ramprasad says,

> You'll find the Mother
> In any house.
>
> Do I dare say it in public?
> She is Bhairavi with Shiva
> Durga with Her children,
> Sita with Lakshmana.
>
> She is mother, daughter, wife, sister –
> Every woman close to you.[52]

Loving the Goddess in Hinduism offers a vision of and a possible path, which is by no means guaranteed, into loving and mutual relationships between men and women through the transformation of gender hierarchies and the affirmation of the divinity of all and the sacredness of embodied difference. And further, this tradition offers a broader challenge and a hope, suggesting that wrestling deeply with issues of love, sex, and gender may be itself a spiritual discipline, one that contains seeds not only for social liberation but also for spiritual liberation, whether or not one chooses to follow this particular Hindu religious path.

NOTES

1. See Nancy M. Martin, "Love and Longing in Devotional Hinduism," in *The Meaning of Life in the World Religions*, ed. Joseph Runzo and Nancy M. Martin (Oxford: Oneworld, 1999), pp. 203–219.
2. See for example, A. K. Ramanujan's translations in *Hymns for the Drowning: Poems for Viṣṇu by Nammalvar* (New Delhi: Penguin Books, 1993) and *Speaking of Śiva* (London: Penguin Books, 1973) and Edward Dimock and Denise Levertov's translations in *In Praise of Krishna: Songs from the Bengali* (Chicago: University of Chicago Press, 1965).
3. See David Kinsley, *Hindu Goddesses* (Berkeley: University of California Press, 1986).
4. Thomas Coburn, *Devi Mahatmya: The Crystallization of the Goddess Tradition* (Delhi: Motilal Banarsidass, 1984) and *Encountering the Goddess* (Albany: State University of New York Press, 1991); C. Mackenzie Brown, *The Triumph of the Goddess* (Albany: State University of New York Press, 1990).
5. Wendy Doniger O'Flaherty, *Other People's Myths* (Chicago: University of Chicago Press, 1985).
6. See Tracy Pinchman, *The Rise of the Goddess in the Hindu Tradition* (Albany: State University of New York Press, 1994); see also Rita Das-Gupta Sherma, "Sacred Immanence: Reflections of Ecofeminism in Hindu Tantra," in *Purifying the Earthly Body of God*, ed. Lance Nelson (Albany: State University of New York Press, 1998), pp. 89–131.
7. David Kinsley has been the most influential interpreter of Kali in Western scholarship and details the way in which her integration of oppositional forces (including death and life) leads the devotee to a new-found wholeness. See Kinsley, *The Sword and the Flute* (Berkeley: University of California Press, 1975); *Hindu Goddesses*; and *The Goddesses' Mirror* (Albany: State University of New York Press, 1989). Rachel McDermott points out that he has been heavily influenced by tantric readings of the Kali in her "Popular Attitudes toward Kali and Her Poetry Tradition," in *Wild Goddesses in India and Nepal*, ed. Axel Michaels, Cornelia Vogel-sanger, and Annette Wilke (Bern: Peter Lang, 1997), p. 385.
8. Kathleen Erndl, *Victory to the Mother* (Oxford; New York: Oxford University Press, 1993), pp. 9–10.
9. McDermott, "Kali and Her Poetry Tradition," pp. 385, 393–396. McDermott makes the point, however, that devotees' ritual actions and attitudes suggest also fears and somewhat more ambivalence toward her.
10. Cynthia Humes, "Glorifying the Great Goddess or Great Woman?: Hindu Women's Experience of the Ritual Recitation of the *Devi-Mahatmya*," in *Women and Goddess Traditions in Antiquity and Today*, ed. Karen L. King (Minneapolis: Fortress Press, 1997), pp. 39–63.
11. Erndl, *Victory to the Mother*, pp. 84–134.

12. Swami Amritaswarupananda, *Ammachi: A Biography of Mata Amritanandamayi* (San Ramon, CA: Mata Amritanandamayi Center, 1994); see also Linda Johnsen, *Daughters of the Goddess: The Women Saints of India* (St. Paul: Yes International Publishers, 1994). I observed her disciples at a gathering in Oakland, California in 1994.

13. Komal Kothari, personal communication, 1998.

14. Sarah Caldwell, "Bhagavati: Ball of Fire," in *Devi: Goddesses of India*, ed. John Stratton Hawley and Donna Marie Wulff (Berkeley: University of California Press, 1996), pp. 195–226.

15. I have been told this numerous times by women I have interviewed in Rajasthan; see also Anne Mackenzie Pearson, *"Because It Gives Me Peace of Mind": Ritual Fasts in the Religious Lives of Hindu Women* (Albany: SUNY Press, 1996).

16. For example, see the story of Queen Tara recounted by Erndl, *Victory to the Mother*, pp. 93–96.

17. The following analysis is drawn from selections of Ramprasad Sen's poems found in *Grace and Mercy in Her Wild Hair: Selected Poems to the Mother Goddess* (Boulder: Great Eastern, 1982), trans. Leonard Nathan and Clinton Seely, and from translations of selected poems of Kamalakanta by Rachel Fell McDermott, "Bengali Songs of Kali," in *Religions of India in Practice* ed. Donald Lopez (Princeton: Princeton University Press, 1995), pp. 55–76.

18. David Kinsley, *Tantric Visions of the Divine Feminine: The Ten Mahavidyas* (Berkeley: University of California Press, 1997).

19. David Wulff, "Prolegomenon to a Psychology of the Goddess," in *The Divine Consort*, ed. John Stratton Hawley and Donna Marie Wulff (Boston: Beacon, 1982), pp. 283–97; Dorothy Dinnerstein, *The Mermaid and the Minotaur: Sexual Arrangements and Human Malaise* (New York: Harper & Row, 1976).

20. Here I am drawing on the work of Sudhir Kakar, Jeffrey Kripal, and Stanley Kurtz as John Stratton Hawley also does in analyzing the language of longing within Krishna devotion in chapter 12. See Sudhir Kakar, *Intimate Relations: Exploring Indian Sexuality* (Chicago: University of Chicago Press, 1989) and *The Inner World: A Psycho-analytic Study of Childhood and Society in India*, second ed. (Oxford: Oxford University Press, 1981); Jeffrey Kripal, *Kali's Child: The Mystical and Erotic in the Life and Teachings of Ramakrisha* (Chicago: University of Chicago Press, 1995); and Stanley Kurtz, *All the Mothers are One: Hindu India and the Cultural Reshaping of Psychoanalysis* (New York: Columbia University Press, 1992).

21. Dorothy Dinnerstein, *The Mermaid and the Minotaur*; Nancy Chodorow, *Feminism and Psychoanalysis* (New Haven: Yale University Press, 1989); Karen McCarthy Brown, "Fundamentalism and the Control of Women," in *Fundamentalism and Gender* ed. John Stratton Hawley (New York: Oxford University Press, 1994) and "Comment: Good Mothers and Bad

Mothers in the Rituals of Sati," in *Sati: The Blessing and the Curse*, ed. John Stratton Hawley (New York: Oxford University Press, 1994).

22. See also Veena Das, "The Goddess and the Demon: An Analysis of the *Devi Mahatmya*," *Manushi*, 30 (1985), pp. 28–32.

23. Kakar, *The Inner World*; Caldwell, "Bhagavati: Ball of Fire"; Hawley, "Krishna and the Gender of Longing" (chapter 12 of this volume).

24. Kripal, *Kali's Child*.

25. There are other problems as well. These theories have also been developed in the context of a nuclear family. Family structures in India are quite different, changing the dynamic. Further they assume infants experience the world in a particular way, but we do not actually know what an infant experiences.

26. Ramprasad Sen, *Grace and Mercy in Her Wild Hair*, p. 23.

27. Ibid., p. 24.

28. Ibid., p. 28.

29. Ibid., p. 35.

30. Ibid., p. 32.

31. Ibid., p. 45.

32. Ibid., p. 21.

33. Joseph Runzo, "Eros and Meaning in Life and Religion" in *The Meaning of Life in the World Religions*, ed. Runzo and Martin, pp. 187–201; Julius Lipner, "The God of Love and the Love of God," chapter 3 of this volume.

34. Kamalakanta, "Bengali Songs of Kali," p. 66.

35. Ramprasad Sen, *Grace and Mercy in Her Wild Hair*, p. 46.

36. Rachel McDermott, "The Western Kali," in *Devi: Goddesses of India*, ed. John Stratton Hawley and Donna Marie Wulff (Berkeley: University of California Press, 1996), p. 299. See also McDermott, "Kali and Her Poetry Tradition."

37. See John Stratton Hawley, *Krishna, the Butter Thief* (Princeton: Princeton University Press, 1983) and "Images of Gender in the Poetry of Krishna," in *Gender and Religion*, ed. Caroline Walker Bynum, Steven Harrell, and Paula Richman (Boston: Beacon Press, 1986). As Hawley shows, this relationship also has erotic dimensions when it is extended to the mothering cow-herding gopi women whose butter the child Krishna is always stealing and who become his lovers when he reaches adolescence.

38. For an extended discussion of this relationship in Ramprasad's poetry, see Malcolm McLean, *Devoted to the Goddess: The Life and Work of Ramprasad* (Albany: State University of New York Press, 1998), pp. 95–107.

39. June McDaniel, *The Madness of the Saints: Ecstatic Religion in Bengal* (Chicago: University of Chicago Press, 1989), pp. 114–115; C. Mackenzie Brown, *The Triumph of the Goddess: The Canonical Models and Theological Visions of the Devi-Bhagavata Purana* (Albany: State University of New York Press, 1990), pp. 206–212.

40. Wendy Doniger O'Flaherty, *Women, Androgynes, and Other Mythical Beasts* (Chicago: University of Chicago Press, 1980), p.129, cited by C. Mackenzie Brown, *The Triumph of the Goddess,* p. 211.
41. Brown, *The Triumph of the Goddess,* p. 216.
42. Kamalakanta, "Bengali Songs to Kali," p. 67.
43. Ibid., p. 68.
44. Ibid., pp. 72–73.
45. Edward Dimock and Denise Levertov, trans., *In Praise of Krishna: Songs from the Bengali* (Chicago: University of Chicago Press, 1965), p. 56.
46. *Darshan* implies both a vision of the Goddess and a real coming into her presence such that she also sees the devotee.
47. Jeffrey Hopkins takes up this issue in his discussion of Tibetan Buddhist tantric practices in chapter 14.
48. David Kinsley, *Tantric Visions of the Divine Feminine,* p. 251.
49. Ramprasad, *Grace and Mercy in Her Wild Hair,* p. 62.
50. Miranda Shaw writes of Buddhist tantric union in a way that seemingly also applies to Hindu forms, suggesting:

> Ultimately, since the heart is the site of the deepest fears, hatreds, and self-centered distortions of reality, the openness, mutual transparency, and total trust required by the yoga of union make it an ideal discipline to bring the negative emotions to awareness and transform their poison into the ambrosia of enlightened awareness.

Shaw, *Passionate Enlightenment: Women in Tantric Buddhism* (Princeton: Princeton University Press, 1994), p. 147.
51. Kamalakanta, "Bengali Songs to Kali," p. 70.
52. Ramprasad, *Grace and Mercy in Her Wild Hair,* p. 60.

Plate 5 The Wailing Wall in Jerusalem, the only remnant of the Second Temple of Judaism, rebuilt after being destroyed in 587 BCE by the Babylonians and destroyed again in 70 CE by the Romans. In 1988 women delegates to the First International Jewish Feminist Conference challenged entrenched custom at this traditionally male-only site of religious practice by praying here with the Torah. Photo: *Anne D. Martin.*

5

TAMING THE POWERS *of* DESIRE: LOVE *and* SEX IN JEWISH CULTURE

Charlotte Elisheva Fonrobert

INTRODUCTION

In a famous kabbalistic or mystical text from the end of the thirteenth century, we find the following exegetical passage expounding the esoteric meaning of the biblical creation of humanity:

> This is the secret of [the verse] "Let *us* make man in our image and our form" (Gen. 1:26). That is to say, "I [God speaking], too, am a partner in the creation of a human being."
>
> This partnership is due to the fact that all the organs of the body are drawn from the father and the mother, and the Holy One effuses the soul in it, "And breathed into his nostrils the breath of life" (Gen. 2:7). And it is said, "And the dust returneth to the earth as it was, and the spirit returneth unto God who gave it" (Eccl. 12:7).
>
> And you who have power to see and understand, is it possible there is something unseemly in that of which God is a partner? If so, the union of a man with his wife, when it is proper, proves to be the mystery of the foundation of the world and its civilization [*sod binyan 'olam ve-yishubo*], and through the act they become partners with the Holy One Blessed be He in the act of creation. This is the mystery of what the sage said, "When a man unites with his wife in holiness, the Shekhinah [God's presence] is between them in the mystery of man and woman."[1]

The medieval text from which this passage is taken is a meditation on the nature of the sexual union between husband and wife. Primarily, *The Holy Letter* or *Epistle* [*Iggeret ha-Qodesh*], as this text has come to be known, presents its addressees with practical advice as to the "proper" performance of the sexual act. The anonymous author's concern about "propriety" here is directed both toward requiring moderation for the sake of the individual's religious integrity, as well as toward the product of the sexual act, children. As one important interest of the epistle, therefore, we can define the concern about eugenics, introducing the epistle:

> You have asked me, my brother, to show you the way in which a man may consummate sexual union with his wife so that it will be for the sake of heaven, *and thereby merit sons learned of the law, worthy of accepting the yoke of the Kingdom of Heaven.*[2]

Proper sexual relations are the precondition, if not the guarantee, for the perfect child. However, beyond this "pragmatic" or utilitarian aspect of the letter which it shares with earlier Aristotelian medical literature, its theological intent lies on the surface. The epistle is permeated by the repeated insistence that the union between a man and a woman, as husband and wife, is emblematic of the order of the universe itself: "On all these matters of which we have spoken, they are the mystery of the arrangement of the order of the universe, and its structure in the likeness of males and females in the secret of the giver and the receiver."[3] The existence of two genders and their unification in the sexual act is considered to be not merely an anthropological fact but a reflection of the dual structure of the cosmos. The intent of the epistle on this level is to initiate the addressees into this mystical aspect of the sexual act.

To address the task at hand, that is, to reflect on the configurations of love and sex in Jewish culture, it is instructive, by way of introduction, to focus for a moment on the polemical thrust of the epistle. This polemical intent can be gleaned from the passage cited above, in the rhetorical question it asks: "And you who have power to see and understand, is it possible there is something unseemly in that of which God is a partner?" The basis of the whole epistle is the insistence not only on the goodness of sexual desire and its consummation (albeit in the context of marriage only, as will be discussed), but also on God's participation in it and on its theological and religious importance.

In this, the epistle's specific polemical target is the Aristotelianism of Moses Maimonides (1135–1204), the slightly earlier philosopher and *halakhist* (Jewish lawyer) whose controversial philosophical tractate *The Guide to the Perplexed* had begun to be disseminated in this period. Thus the author of our *Holy Letter* opens his reflections:

The matter is not as Rabbi Moses (Maimonides) of blessed memory said in his *Guide to the Perplexed*. He was incorrect in praising Aristotle for stating that the sense of touch is shameful for us. Heaven forbid! The matter is not like the Greek [i.e. Aristotle] said. It smacks of imperceptible heresy, because if the accursed Greek believed the world was created purposely, he would not have said it. But we who have the Torah and believe that God created all in his wisdom [do not believe that he] created anything inherently ugly or unseemly.[4]

It is the Aristotelian disdain for the bodily or physical and sexual aspect of life, now beginning to be introduced into the Jewish intellectual world via Maimonides,[5] which raised the ire of the epistle's author and provoked him to write a tractate in praise of sexual union between husband and wife as the very structure of the world itself.

The Holy Letter may serve as an entry-way into our reflections on the role of love and sexual desire in the religious culture of Judaism. In the first part of this chapter, I will focus on the "simultaneous" religious affirmation and restriction of sexual desire. I will discuss this stoic moment of classic Judaism as what I want to call "taming strategies" with respect to sexual desire. The first of these primary taming strategies is the construction of the marital relationship as willed by God, as a commandment incumbent upon every Jew. Within this strictly defined framework, sexuality finds its legitimized place in Judaism. The other primary taming strategy concerns the focus of the rhetoric of love and passion into the context of the relationship between God and Israel or the individual. The hermeneutic and cultural basis of this strategy is, of course, the allegorization of the biblical Song of Songs as a poem on the love between God and Israel. In the second part of the chapter, I will turn to the problem of engendering this ideology and will present a critique, or qualification, of the structure analyzed in the first part as primarily an androcentric model, a model in which men or the male perspective is constructed as the subject that desires and women or the female as the object of desire.

TAMING STRATEGIES

Marriage

JUDAISM AS A CIVIC CULTURE

Judaism, as framed by the rabbis of the talmudic period based on biblical culture, is in a very fundamental sense a civic religious culture. That is to say, the rabbis and almost any other Jewish cultural formation post-dating them understand it to be a divinely ordained mandate for humanity to settle the world and cultivate it as it is humanly known. One of the most significant aspects of this mandate, if not the most important one, is reproduction. Thus the rabbis of the talmudic period (the second through seventh century CE) consider the first divine commandment in biblical literature to be the commandment "to be fruitful and multiply" (Gen. 1:28).[6] This commandment included every man[7] without exception and, encoded as divine will and thus religious law, came to form the basis for Jewish society.

The most scholarly and the most saintly man is as obligated to reproduce as the regular householder. *The Holy Letter* builds with its kabbalistic language on this rabbinic framing when it says: "If so, the union of a man with his wife, when it is proper, proves to be the mystery of the foundation of the world and its civilization, and through the act they become partners with the Holy One Blessed be He in the act of creation."[8] Accordingly, the sexual union of husband and wife as world-building has cosmological significance. Its theological significance lies in the understanding of sexual union as an act of continuing God's creation of the world.

In *The Holy Letter*, the discussion of sexual desire is encoded almost exclusively in the rhetoric of reproduction. Sexual desire is validated as a God-given aspect of human life but exclusively with respect to its reproductive function in the context of marriage. *The Holy Letter* rests on the foundation laid in rabbinic Judaism. The rabbis produced a number of narratives that addressed the tension between the inherent goodness and world-building function of sexual desire and the need to channel this desire into the proper framework of marital relations and reproduction. It is this tension that a number of scholars have recently discussed as the "dialectics of desire" in Jewish culture.[9]

The following talmudic text on the struggle with personified "Desire" is beautifully emblematic of this tension:

> [The returnees from the Babylonian exile] said: "Since this is a time of [God's] favor, let us pray regarding Desire for sexual sin [to gain control over it]."
>
> They prayed and he [Desire] was committed into their hands. He [God or the personified Desire] said to them: "Be careful, for if you kill that one [Desire], *the world will end.*"
>
> They imprisoned him for three days, and then they looked for a fresh egg in all of the Land of Israel, and they did not find one.
>
> They said: "What shall we do? If we kill him, *the world will end.* If we pray

for half, in heaven they do not answer halfway prayers." "Blind him and let
him go." At least, a man does not become aroused by his female relatives.
(Babylonian Talmud, Tractate Yoma, 69b, my emphasis)

In rabbinic theology it is human or, more specifically, Israel's transgression
that causes God's punishment, as expressed in the destruction of Jerusalem
by the Babylonians. Therefore, the returnees from the Babylonian exile
want to gain control over those desires that provoked Israel to transgress in
the first place and to become idolatrous, that is, to fall in love with other
gods. In a certain way, this presents, of course, the desire to reverse the story
of the Garden of Eden. The rabbinic story presents the people who suffer
from the consequences of their own transgressions as praying for the liberation from the capacity to perpetrate evil.

But the lack of desire will cause the world to come to an end. Again,
sexual desire is conceived of as world-building, as having cosmological significance, albeit in less mystical terms than in *The Holy Letter*. Desire is the
engine of fertility, of reproduction and, hence, of the continuity of life.
Without desire no egg, the ultimate symbol of fertility, can be found. After
realizing the existential importance of libidinal energy, the people in our
story consider praying for retaining only half of desire, which Rabbi
Shlomo ben Yitzhaq (1040–1105), the most important medieval commen-
tator on the Talmud, interprets as wanting to retain desire only for licit,
marital sex.

The rabbinic authors of the tale do not construct sexual desire as inherently negative and destructive. On the contrary, as a force of creation and
reproduction, it is a necessary part of the fabric of human life. Yet desire,
understood to be a simultaneously potentially destructive force, will lead to
sexual transgression – that is, adultery and incest – if left uncontrolled and
untamed. As to the latter, the rabbinic narrative in its "mythical mode of
thinking"[10] claims that the desire for incestual sex has been overcome,
emblematized in the blinding of the "Evil Inclination": "At least, a man no
longer becomes aroused by his female relatives." Sadly enough, we know
that this is far from reflecting the reality of human life. But as far as the
desire for adultery is concerned, the talmudic tale acknowledges its continuing potent force. Since sexual desire has to remain a part of the fabric of
human life to preserve the continuity of life, its transgressive potential has
to be accepted as part of the package deal. Hence, to the rabbis, a desire for
adulterous sex, or the potential temptation by it, is ingrained in the (male)
psyche. Regarding the negative pole of the dialectic – the desire for illicit

sexual relations – the rabbis of the talmudic period thus devote much of their energies to combating the transgression of adultery. Marriage is constructed as the proper channel for consummating sexual desire.

The Holy Letter is close to the earlier rabbinic sensibility in terms of the language of sexual moderation and control. However, its emphasis with respect to the negative pole of the dialectic lies much more on the analysis of sexual desire itself, even within the marital framework. The distinction that it makes is not so much between marital and illicit (i.e. extramarital) sex, as between proper and improper consummation of sexual desire within the context of marriage. To the author of The Holy Letter, improper desire means desire for self-gratification, gratification of mere physical desires, whereas proper desire means desire for both the creation of the perfected fetus – the guarantor of an Edenic future – and for the proper relationship to God.

> It is said concerning the act of creation in the Garden of Eden: "And they were both naked, the man and his wife, and were not ashamed" (Gen 2:25). All this was prior to their sinning. They were engaged in intellectual matters, and all their intention was for the sake of heaven. For them, the sex organs were only like eyes or hands or the other organs of the body. However, when they lusted after bodily pleasures, and their intentions were not for the sake of heaven, it is said about them: "And they knew that they were naked" (Gen 3:7).[11]

Again, the Edenic past is turned into an ideal, and the ideal is to consummate sexual desire in a manner that equates the sexual act with intellectual discourse.[12] That is, one should not let oneself be overwhelmed by the powers and pleasures of desire, and one should demystify the sexual organs. This portrayal is devoid of lust, passion, and pleasure, and in the end even devoid of the sense of the electricity of touch. Sex "for the sake of heaven" is understood (in mystical terms) as an act of partnership with God.[13]

This is, then, what I would describe as the stoic moment of Judaism. Human life in its *physical* reality infused by sexual desire, human life as a collective to be reproduced via sexual desire, is affirmed as the basis of all Jewish *religious* culture. Sexual desire is acknowledged as part of divinely created human life and, therefore, is not to be fought against or to be transcended and left behind in a realm devoid of the Divine. At the same time the various religious leaders – rabbis, mystics, philosophers, writers – extol in various ways the demand that this human life, with its pleasures and needs, has always to be related to the reality of the Divine.

STRUCTURING OF MARITAL LIFE

Since marriage has, therefore, not only a legitimate role in Jewish culture but one that is religiously endorsed and even considered to be divinely ordained as an obligation, discussions of marital relationship take up considerable space in Jewish classic literature. Sexual life within the marital context is actually highly regulated. For example, talmudic Judaism and subsequently Jewish law famously regulate the number of times that a husband is obligated to have sex with his wife, depending on his profession.[14]

Again, *The Holy Letter* echoes the classic rabbinic concern: "Speak to her so that your words will provoke desire, love, will, and passion, as well as words leading to reverence for God, piety, and modesty."[15] As mentioned previously, the intent is a eugenic one, but let us consider the following passage also:

> A man should never force himself upon his wife and never overpower her, for the Divine Spirit never rests upon one whose conjugal relations occur in the absence of desire, love, and free will. The Shekhinah [the manifestation of God's presence] does not rest there.[16]

To summarize what we have learned so far, classical Judaism lays the foundation for later Jewish culture by making marriage and reproduction a divine commandment. With the framework of marriage sexual desire has a positive and constructive function, and only without this framework is it considered to turn into evil desire. The medieval discourse on sexual desire then attributes mystical and theological meaning to the act itself, as reflecting the structure of the universe and God's participation in it.

The Song of Songs and Its Allegorization

Having discussed the first strategy to tame the potentially chaotic and dangerous force of sexual desire in Jewish culture – i.e. its affirmation and simultaneous regulation – let us turn to what I discern as the second major one. Let me begin with the observation that the rhetoric of love and passion is primarily invested in the context of descriptions of God's relationship with Israel or the individual or vice versa.[17] This is an aspect that characterizes almost all areas of classic Jewish literature, such as rabbinic-narrative literature, philosophical and mystical literature. The language of passion that is lacking in the context of describing, narrating and legally circumscribing human erotic relationships is plentiful in the context of the metaphoric divine–human relationship. Thus, sexual desire is tamed by investing passion in descriptions of the love of God. The root of this phenomenon, I would suggest, is located in the traditions of reading and interpreting the Song of Songs.

THE RHETORIC OF LOVE IN JUDAISM

The Song of Songs is one of the few books in the biblical canon which does not mention God once. Various contemporary scholars have characterized this book as a secular love poem. In the traditional Jewish[18] context, however, the Song of Songs has always been read as a love poem praising the love between God and Israel. In the Mishnah, the earliest rabbinic text of the end of the second century, we find the following famous passage:

> No man in Israel ever disputed about the Song of Songs [that he should say] that it does not render the hands unclean,[19] for the entire world is not worth the day on which the Song of Songs was given to Israel; for all the Writings are holy, but the Song of Songs is the Holy of Holies. [Mishnah, Tractate Yadayim 3:5]

It was Rabbi Akiva, one of the greatest sage–heroes in rabbinic culture, who championed the uniqueness of the song in the context of a discussion about its canonical status. Some of Rabbi Akiva's disciples and friends suggested that the question of whether the Song of Songs does "render the hands unclean," a feature characterizing the rest of scripture, had been a point of contention. Rabbi Akiva vehemently protested against the very possibility of any such protest ever having arisen.[20] From the very beginning of its inclusion in the canon, the book is understood to describe the relationship between God and Israel. However, the early rabbis in their commentary literature do not understand the song to describe this relationship generically. Rather, to them the poem is concerned with a particular "historical" moment in this relationship – that is, the moment of the Exodus when Israel is standing at the Red Sea and beholding the miracle of the splitting of the sea[21] or the moment of the revelation of the Torah on Mount Sinai. The rabbinic commentaries describe these moments as the engagement and the wedding of God and Israel.

Among scholars, the debate about Rabbi Akiva's designation of the Song of Songs as the Holy of Holies of scripture revolves around the question of whether this declaration is linked to the mystical, esoteric interpretation of the poem or whether the passionate love of God is upheld as a normative religious value.[22] It may be that some aspects of the poem's interpretation are linked to esoteric interpretations. However, given the fact that the poem is recited once a year in public during the celebration of Passover – that is, the celebration of the Exodus – the reading of the poem as the love story of God and Israel is firmly inscribed in the Jewish community's consciousness.

In the later kabbalistic and hasidic (mystical) literature, the motif of the passionate love between God and Israel or God and the individual mystic becomes, of course, much more prevalent, again often in connection with readings of the Song of Songs. In the Jewish mystical literature, the emphasis is shifted to the analysis of the love relationship between the individual and God, especially the (feminine) soul and God, as in this text by the founder of the Chabad sect of Hasidism at the end of the eighteenth and the beginning of the nineteenth century:

> "How beautiful and how pleasant are you, O love with delights" (Song of Songs 7:7).
> There are two kinds of love for God. One is "love with delights." This is a state of wondrous delight in God, with a great, a mighty joy, the joy of the soul to the very limits of its strength, in experiencing that God is good … One cannot attain this by effort, like the fear of God … which depends on arduous effort, as one who searches for a great treasure … But this great love with delights descends on a person as a grace from above …
> The second level of love for God is the soul's yearning to cleave to God, to be included in the source of life. The nearness of God is her good, and she desires it and it is painful for her to be separated from Him by a barrier formed by worldly involvements.[23]

This text, as Jewish mystical literature in general, often uses explicitly sexual love, or the love of husband and wife, as a metaphor for describing the relationship of the soul and the Divine.

Again, it is important to remember that this language and its love poetry are not necessarily restricted to the inner mystical circles of the elect few initiates, but that it is disseminated into the ritual life of the community. As an example, we may think of hymns sung for the celebration of the Sabbath by the community in the synagogue on Friday evening, such as *Yedid Nefesh* (Beloved of my Soul), a poem that has its origin in Jewish mystical literature:

> Beloved of my soul, merciful father, draw Your servant towards You. Let your servant run as a hind to bow before Your glory. Let Your affection for him be sweeter than a honeycomb or any other delicacy.

Glorious one, most beautiful splendor of the world, my soul is sick with love for You …

Reveal Yourself and spread over me, beloved one, the shelter of Your peace. Let the earth sparkle with Your glory; we will rejoice and be happy with You. Be quick, beloved, for the time has come …

Hence, Jewish literature and liturgy is permeated with language and imagery that describes and elaborates the deep passion of the religious individual and the community for God. Erotic desire thus gets channeled into the other primary relationship in Jewish religious culture – the relationship between humans and the Divine. Within this framework there are no bounds to passion and love, while at the same time the individual is not allowed to withdraw from sexual relations with his wife.

THE CONTEST BETWEEN LOVE OF GOD AND LOVE OF WIFE/FAMILY

Having discussed briefly the rhetoric of love and passion as centered on the relationship between God and Israel or the individual, we need to consider a dynamic that evolves from this. This dynamic could be thought of as a contest between love and devotion for God (and what this can stand for) and attachment to one's wife or family which are – at least in theory – endowed with equal value.[24] This contest takes place on a metaphorical level, as well as on a sociological level. The metaphorical contest has immediate consequences for the structuring of society.

Rabbinic (classic) Judaism attempts to strike a balance between the two. The Talmud is quite conscious of the potential conflict between these "religious" commitments. Love of God in talmudic literature takes the form of love of Torah, the manifestation of God in a text, and hence devotion to the study of Torah with a sage or at the *Beit Midrash* (the House of Study). In metaphorical terms, the love of Torah is, again, often described in terms of a relationship of lovers, between the student and the Torah, the latter representing the female pole of the relationship.

Rav Shmuel the son of Nahmani expounded: Why is it written [in the biblical text], "Loving hind and a graceful doe; let her[25] breasts satisfy you at all times …" (Prov 5:19)? Why is the Torah compared to the hind of love? To tell you: Just as the hind has a 'narrow womb' and stays as desirable to her mate each time as she was the first time, so the Torah always stays as desirable to those who study her as she was the first time." (Babylonian Talmud, Tractate Eruvin 54b)

The study of Torah is not just a duty; it is conceptualized in terms of a passionate love relationship. Subsequently, talmudic literature invests a considerable amount of energy in the attempt to strike a balance between this passionate love and marriage to a woman. On the legal (*halakhic*) level, discussions evolve around the question of whether a man should first go and study or marry, in order to fulfill both commitments. On the narrative (*aggadic*) level, story after story is told about the sometimes fatal consequences for the scholar who forgets himself in his studies and fails to return home to his wife in order to give her the sexual and emotional satisfaction that is her right. Thus, talmudic literature can conceive of the two commitments only as exclusive of each other, and they have to be balanced in terms of dividing time, one's life-time, into periods of "total" commitment to study or periods of "total" devotion to the family.[26] The precarious nature of the balance is reflected in all those narratives in which the overzealous student of Torah is killed because of neglect of his wife.[27]

In later Jewish cultural formations both this contest and solutions to it can take different forms. For example, in hasidic circles in Eastern Europe at the end of the eighteenth and the beginning of the nineteenth century, the love of God and his Torah takes the form of devotion to one's *Rebbe* or charismatic leader. The conflict between this devotion and the obligation to build a family remains the same, resulting in a world in early modern Eastern Europe in which wives became responsible for raising the family while their husbands studied Torah or lived at their *Rebbe's* residence.[28] A different solution, again in Jewish mystical circles and hasidic circles, is to suggest that the balance between devotion to the Divine and devotion to one's family is not found in division of one's time but in psychological sublimation. That is, the mystic, who emphasizes cleaving to God constantly, has to strive for a level of consciousness in which he can engage in any "worldly" activity whatsoever and regard himself as not having lost his communion with the Divine.

> Therefore, the sages said: "Is it possible that when they [the patriarchs] were involved with food, drink, sex, and other bodily functions, the words of Torah were uncared for?" The answer is, through all these bodily matters, their intentions were directed *always* for the sake of heaven, and their thought was not separated from the upper light, *even for a single moment*.[29]

This solution is perhaps equally precarious. Jewish mystical literature tends, therefore, to be much more cautious as to bodily desires than classic rabbinic literature.

To summarize, the fundamental tension built into Jewish religious culture is the tension between passionate love for God (or the manifestations of God in the Torah and in study) and the obligation to build a family. Jewish tradition has provided two solutions. On the one hand, rabbinic Judaism discusses the solution in terms of splitting one's actual time between study and engagement of the Divine and family life. Mystical literature raises a second possibility that internalizes the process of combining the two poles of desire. A pious person thus is supposed to perfect and control his spiritual life to such a degree that he is internally perpetually devoted to the Divine, while at the same time being engaged in the physical world. The balance, that both solutions try to strike, is obviously rather difficult to maintain and cast as a life-long process of adaptation.

ENGENDERING DESIRE

In the final portion of my reflections, I would like to move to a brief critique of this model of desire. The critique emerges from the raising of the question of gender – or the gendered nature of the religious discourse(s) of Judaism – which was the engine driving many of the transformations of Judaism in the past century.

It is a somewhat obvious truth that most of the literary, philosophical, kabbalistic, theological, and liturgical creations in Judaism have been produced by men, certainly up to and including the nineteenth century. The constructions of sexual desire and love that we have discussed above, therefore, are the products of an androcentric culture, androcentric at least on the level of literary production. In most contexts women remain the object of desire, and the Torah as an object of desire is feminized.

I do believe that the crucial question for Judaism in this new century (which is not the twenty-first century in the Jewish calendar) is how to create new spaces – and by this I mean both imaginary spaces and actual social spaces – that allow for the transformation of the traditional gendering of Jewish discourse. In other words, the crucial task for Judaism is to transform women from objects into subjects of religious and theological discourse and desire.

We need to experiment with thinking about the question of what happens when women desire God, Torah or each other as teachers and students. What happens to the culture of study that has defined Judaism? This entails also the task of creating "religious" space for "new" relationships, and by "new" I mean relationships that are left almost entirely unarticulated in the past, relationships that have not been ritualized, articulated,

praised, critiqued, etc. Such relationships would be mother–daughter relationships and friendships between women. Similarly – and here men and
women have to do the creative thinking together – cross-gender relationships need to be (re)created theologically, such as the father–daughter
relationship, the son–mother relationship, and ultimately the relationship
between lovers and partners as well. This task I like to call "the decentering
of androcentrism." How this will change the face of Judaism I do not think
we can predict. But the genuine transformation can only come from those
who are intoxicated by the love of Torah.

I would, therefore, like to conclude with a suggestion by a poet who is
also a teacher of Talmud: "We have not yet discovered the Torah written by
women. The Torah that we know was written by men. Thousands of men
participated in the making of the Written Torah and the Oral Torah."[30] We
have had two thousand years of study and love of Torah by men. What
needs perhaps to happen now is another two thousand years of study and
love of Torah by women, before we learn what Torah is really all about.

NOTES

1. *The Holy Letter: A Study in Medieval Jewish Sexual Morality*, bilingual
   edition, ed. and trans. Seymor J. Cohen (New York: KTAV Publishers,
   1976), p. 60.
2. Ibid., p. 28.
3. Ibid., p. 58.
4. Ibid., pp. 41–42.
5. For example, in his *Eros and the Jews: From Biblical Israel to Contemporary
   America* (Berkeley: University of California Press, 1997), David Biale discusses the work of Isaac ben Yedaiah, a disciple of Maimonides. Biale
   writes: "Quoting Maimonides, Isaac labels the sense of touch as 'disgrace'
   and proclaims that 'a man should not be drawn after this shameful thing
   even with his wife, for it confuses his intellect' " (p. 94).
6. See the discussion of the history of this commandment in Jeremy Cohen,
   "Be Fertile and Increase, Fill the Earth and Master It": *The Ancient and
   Medieval Career of a Biblical Text* (Ithaca, NY: Cornell University Press,
   1989).
7. Women were not commanded to reproduce. On the *halakhic* (legal)
   reasoning for this, see Cohen, *Be Fertile and Increase*.
8. *The Holy Letter*, p. 60.
9. See Daniel Boyarin, *Carnal Israel: Reading Sex in Talmudic Judaism*
   (Berkeley: University of California Press, 1993) and David Biale, *Eros and
   the Jews*.
10. Boyarin, *Carnal Israel*, p. 62.

11.   *The Holy Letter*, p. 46. David Biale analyzes the closeness of this text to Augustine's portrayal of sex in paradise: "In its view of sex in the Garden, the *Iggeret* [*The Holy Letter*] was very much at home in the medieval Christian milieu. The Christian arguments were based on Augustine, who held that sex between the first couple was under the complete control of the will and without lust" (*Carnal Israel*, p. 104).

12.   As Biale points out: "The philosophical term our author uses and the activity he describes are remarkably similar to Maimonides' description of Adam and Eve in the Garden" (*Eros and the Jews*, p. 104). In spite of its anti-Aristotelianism, the epistle ends up being much closer to the Greek philosopher than the author would like to admit.

13.   This structure is repeated throughout the letter. As another example consider this text: "Is it possible that when they [the patriarchs, Abraham, Isaac and Jacob] were involved with food, drink, sex, and other bodily functions, the words of Torah were uncared for? The answer is, through all these bodily matters, their intentions were directed always for the sake of heaven, and their thought was not separated from the upper light, even for a single moment" (*The Holy Letter*, p. 126).

14.   This is found already in the Mishnah, the earliest rabbinic document from the late second and early third century CE, in Tractate Ketubbot 5: 6. For a discussion of the marital duties of a husband to his wife, see Rachel Biale's *Women and Jewish Law: An Exploration of Women's Issues in Halakhic Sources* (New York: Schocken Books, 1984), pp. 125–128.

15.   *The Holy Letter*, p. 140.

16.   Ibid., p. 142.

17.   This is not to say that this is the only place. The language of love we find again exalted in the ritual of a traditional Jewish wedding ceremony, as reflected for instance in the seven blessings pronounced on the couple. One of the blessings is the following: "Grant perfect joy to these loving companions, as You did to the first man and woman in the Garden of Eden. Praised are You, O Lord, who grants the joy of bride and groom."

18.   And Christian context as well, ever since Origen's allegorical commentary on the Song of Songs!

19.   Only books that are considered to be holy render hands impure. On the paradoxical relationship between "holiness" and "impurity," see Jacob Milgrom, *Leviticus 1–16: A New Translation with Introduction and Commentary, The Anchor Bible* (New York: Doubleday, 1991).

20.   See Marc Hirschman, *Rivalry of Genius: Jewish and Christian Biblical Interpretation in Late Antiquity* (Albany, NY: SUNY Press, 1996), p. 83.

21.   Thus, the Song of Songs is recited in the synagogue once a year during Passover, the celebration of the Exodus.

22.   See Ephraim E. Urbach, *The Sages: Their Concepts and Beliefs* (Cambridge: Harvard University Press, 1987); Hirschman, *Rivalry of Genius*; Saul Lieberman, "The Teaching of Song of Songs" (Hebrew) in *Jewish*

Gnosticism, Merkabah Mysticism, and Talmudic Tradition, ed. Gershom Scholem (New York: Jewish Theological Seminary of America, 1965); and Daniel Boyarin, *Intertextuality and the Reading of Midrash* (Bloomington: Indiana University Press, 1990).

23. Ben Zion Bokser, *The Jewish Mystical Tradition* (New York: The Pilgrim Press, 1981), pp. 218–219.

24. See D. Boyarin's analysis of this contest in his *Carnal Israel.*

25. The biblical verse refers to the words of personified wisdom in general which the rabbis transfer to the Torah as a specific form of wisdom.

26. In this, rabbinic culture is not so different from early Christian culture. In his magisterial *The Body and Society* (New York: Columbia University Press,1988), Peter Brown discusses the discourse of devotion to the Divine in Christianity in terms of single-heartedness. Early Christian circles often regarded the devotion to the Divine as completely non-compatible with family life and reproduction and, therefore, abnegated family life and consummation of sexual desire altogether. Rabbinic Judaism, on the other hand, even though it seems to agree that devotion to the Divine, i.e. Torah, is compatible with family only with difficulty, avoids this route and tries to reconcile the two.

27. For a discussion of this material, see Boyarin, *Carnal Israel.*

28. For an extended discussion see Biale, *Eros and the Jews,* pp.121–149.

29. *The Holy Letter,* p.126. Of course, there are endless examples for this in hasidic literature. Further, see the mystically inspired *Mesillat ha-Yesharim,* an eighteenth-century text in the genre of moralistic literature, whose author Moses Hayim Luzzato writes that "communion is a state in which one's heart clings so closely to the Blessed One that he does not strive for and is not concerned with anything outside of Him ... The end of this trait is that a man be *constantly* united with his Creator in this manner. At the very least he will, if he loves his Creator, certainly engage in such communion during the time of his Divine service" (B. Z. Bokser, *The Jewish Mystical Tradition,* p. 249).

30. Ari Elon, *From Jerusalem to the Edge of Heaven: Meditations on the Soul of Israel,* T. Frymer-Kensky (Philadelphia: The Jewish Publication Society, 1996), p. 53.

Plate 6 Papa Gede, the spirit associated with sexuality and death, possessing a Vodou priest and taking a comic mock karate stance. Port-au-Prince, Haiti. Photo: *Chantal Regnault*

6

LOVE, SEX, *and* GENDER EMBODIED: THE SPIRITS *of* HAITIAN VODOU

Elizabeth McAlister

If you ever visit Haiti and are lucky enough to be invited to a *dans*, or religious service, you must prepare yourself to view something like a long, danced opera. If you are not yet initiated, you will be seated in a hard-backed chair in a place of honor, facing the ritual space where you can view the drummers on one side, and the chorus of worshipers singing and dancing on the other. There you will sit all night, doing your best to follow the complex and beautiful ritual, which passes from a "cool" regal dance into a "hot" fiery one. You will arrive mid-evening, so that by five o'clock in the morning it will be hard to keep your eyes open despite the music, heat, and closeness of others sitting next to you.[1]

It is in these wee hours of the morning that the Gede spirits (pronounced GEDD-eh) will come to "*monte*" (ride) the dancers (see plate 6). And what a change there will be from the decorum of last evening. Both women and men will powder their faces white, don sunglasses missing one lens, and let out strings of unspeakable words in a nasal whine: "*zozo-koko-eya-eya-eya*" ("cock-pussy-yeah-yeah-yeah"). And they will direct the greatest vulgarities at the most respectable people present as they sing.

Women, "ridden" by the *lwa* (spirit), will become men. Grasping walking sticks – some with penises carved at the top – they will begin the *gouyad*, a grinding, *wining* dance of the Banda, a stylized parody of sexual intercourse. Judging by the songs some of these women-turned-men are singing, you will guess they have become homosexual men. As the songs for the Gede continue, men will also seem like *masisi*, "faggots." One man even seems to have become a woman, who is busy gossiping primly to a group of her fans.

All of the Gede whirling around the room hips first are bawdy, irreverent jokers. If they are not embarrassing you, they are making you laugh. If you are a visiting professor and make the mistake of introducing yourself as "Dr. so-and-so," the Gede spirits will tell you that their *zozo* (penis) hurts, and ask you for a treatment. The congregation around you will howl with laughter. If you are pregnant, the Gede will perform a special blessing over your womb, since these spirits live in the cemetery and are specialists in ushering souls from one world to the next. Gede are living corpses, great healers, great workers, and the ultimate drama queens in a divine theater of power and gender.

The Gede spirits display, mimic and caricature gender and sexuality in order to get at cultural knowledge and memory, the pain and truth of which only they can withstand. The Gede are almost always dark-complexioned spirits of former colonial slaves, and if you get to know them, they will tell you how they were tortured, how they suffered, and how they died. At the ceremony, after you have been ridiculed and forgotten and as you rise to leave the next morning, you will still be able to hear the Gede inside, singing with nasal voices, "*Miyò miyò miyò*, faggots and dykes, Oh …"

A central project across academia has been to examine the ways in which class, race, gender, and sexuality are constructed, and indeed are mutually constitutive. Scholars have been interested in the ways these aspects of culture and identity change in historical process, as well as across diverse localities. Only too rarely does such work take religion into account. This is ironic, since religious systems are in the business of constructing the world and then naturalizing its meaning as "true." It stands to reason that we cannot fully understand the ways in which love, gender, or sexuality operate in a given society without attending to the role of religion and its multiple powers.

This chapter, like the others in this volume, seeks to examine the complex relationship of religion to the construction of love, gender, and sexuality. What religious processes produce particular emotional, sexual, and gendered practices? And what are the meanings of particular practices in any certain location? Here I explore how the adherents of the Afro-Haitian religion called Vodou shape their identities using historical, national, and transnational tropes of love, gender, and sexuality. To speak of gender and sexuality within Vodou is a charged subject, since Vodou has too often been hypersexualized by foreign writers. Since the colonial period, the sexual lives of Africans have been the object of fascination for outsiders. It is true for Haitians that "the exoticization of colonized peoples was achieved by the eroticization of their lives."[2] I argue here that in Haitian Vodou, the terms of a specific construction of gender and sexuality exist apart from, yet in conversation with, dominant (Catholic) discourse. Inscribed through religious ritual and performative understandings of supernatural forces, these creole constructions of gender and sexuality reveal how power takes hold of and constructs bodies in particular ways.[3]

The physical body is at the center of Vodou, akin to shamanistic systems and other so-called spirit possession religions. When the spirits come to *monte* ("ride") their *chwal* ("horses"), they transform ordinary people into divinities capable of teaching, healing, and transcending the here and now. While most academic studies of religion center on textual analysis – on texts usually written by elite males and recorded as revelation or prescription – Vodou has no such texts. Or if it does, its texts are the altars, the operatic danced rituals, and the songs created by ordinary women and men *and* by the spirits dancing in their heads. To interact with Vodou elders, or with spirits who have possessed them, is to open oneself up to learning, potentially even to epiphany. The body is always the site of instruction and learning, as Vodou is an initiatory system whose *konesans* or "knowledge" is arrived at through direct experience.

Vodou is a religious system, but it is more than that. As in other agricultural societies, philosophy, cosmology, medicine, religion and justice systems are often rolled into one worldview. The majority of Haitians are agriculturalists and have been for the whole of their nation's difficult history. Begun as the French colony of Saint-Domingue, Haiti was the site of brutal torture as the plantation system generated immense wealth for planters and utter misery for enslaved people. These African peoples, versed in various African religions, met with the conversion practices of the French Catholic Church. What gets called Vodou is actually a variety of practices from diverse nations in Africa (including the Dahomean, the Yoruba, and the Kongo) in forced conversation with the Catholicism of the colonial masters. Their God is the same – a high God who created the world. But *Gran Mèt-la* (God) is remote and uninvolved, while the spirits are immediate and responsive to their *sèvitè* (human "servants").

In a country with a literacy rate of fifteen percent or less, Vodou has grown into a creolized blend of African and (to a lesser extent) European knowledge, focused not on texts but on embodied forms of spirit work. Rather than speak about "a religion called Vodou," practitioners will more likely explain that they *sèvi lwa* ("serve the spirit"). Afro-Haitians work with a complex pantheon of divinities who both shape and reflect the world for their spiritual "children." What outsiders and academics know of this complex system is arrived at through engagement with the religion and its practitioners – through ethnographic fieldwork.

"IF YOUR HUSBAND DIES, YOU'LL FIND ANOTHER"

In its early phases, the academic study of gender focused on women's experiences, while constructions of masculinities and other gendered structures were not yet under investigation. Accordingly, most fieldwork and writing on gender and sexuality in Vodou focuses on the spirit or goddess Èzili. Split into many versions of female divinity, Èzili has two main faces: Èzili Freda and Èzili Dantò. Together, their stories reveal how the racialized and sexualized histories of certain types of bodies can shape religious meaning.

Èzili Freda is depicted as light-skinned, wealthy and dripping with gold. She is pathetically childless, for she had a baby, but she sold the baby for jewels. She is called "the goddess of love" and is known as *Metrès* or "Mistress," a term that goes quite directly back to slavery days. Then, the mulatta creoles of Saint-Domingue formed a class apart of mistresses, concubines, and sex slaves of the wealthy white planter men. On the eve of independence from France, out of seven thousand mulatta women counted in the colony, five thousand were "kept" by white men.[4] Freda recalls these mulatta prostitutes, who were famous for their beauty and high style, and dressed in silks and laces in the competitive decadence of Saint-Domingue.[5]

Women (and more uncommonly, men) who are "ridden" by Èzili Freda dress in pink satin and ask for mirrors and perfume. They mimic the decorum and postures of today's wealthy, light-skinned, elite women who are the historical descendants of the creole mulattas. Freda is above all an icon of romantic love, a coquette and a fiercely heterosexual femme. She parades around the ritual space batting her eyes at the men, blessing them and asking their hands in marriage.[6] Queen of overblown drama, she typically spurns any women present, appraising them as possible rivals in the enterprise of heterosexual romance. She has a special relationship with effeminate gay men and is often considered their *mèt tèt* (patron spirit, literally "master of the head").[7]

How can we understand this heterosexual femme goddess, this bejeweled yet miserable paramour? What does she mean for poor Haitians who "serve" her? Surely she is the product of a specific female experience of brutal subjugation, of torture, even, by virtue of her female body and her in-between racial status. Historian Joan Dayan invites us to recall the domination mulatta women often experienced "under another name, something called 'love.' In that unnatural situation where a human became property, love became coordinate with a task of feeling that depended to a large extent on the experience of servitude."[8] Dayan reads Èzili Freda as a remembering of a certain kind of sexual violence and bondage dressed up as *eros* and romance. The bodies of the Vodouists enact this, remembering through the ritual of spirit possession where romantic love and its props of courtship are exalted and made divine.

The way that Èzili Freda embodies both romance and frustration can be read as a kind of critique of the real lives of poor Haitian women and men. In fact, poor Haitian women are quite unlikely to find themselves objects of romantic subsidy. Women typically support children and male relatives in an economy that devalues male labor. For the growing numbers of country people displaced to the cities, even traditional systems of *plasaj* ("living with") have been disrupted. In a culture where women have long been market vendors and family treasurers, it is poor urban males who now find themselves unemployed and unable to contribute to family finances. This scenario is all the more frustrating for poor men, who see the nation's wealthy men carrying out traditional Western patriarchal roles of provider and head of the house. Love, courtship, and couplehood are difficult to sustain in these conditions.[9]

In her classic wisdom, the Vodou priestess Mama Lola comments to her biographer Karen McCarthy Brown, "Poor people don't have no true love. They just have affiliation." Brown comments that "romance – its language, its style, its wardrobe, and its dance – belongs to the top ten percent of the Haitian population that controls the lion's share of Haiti's wealth."[10] Èzili Freda also embodies a kind of critique of class inequalities while at the same time she becomes a route to the experience of *eros* and romantic love for the disenfranchised poor.

Love relationships, along with the economic advantage couplehood can bring, are a deep desire for many Vodouists. The scores of priests and priestesses I have interviewed all maintain that clients most typically seek their help for one of three main reasons: money, health, and love. Numerous *wanga*, or spiritual "works," are effected to "make somebody see you, make them love you. Once they love you, the spirits can make them stay with you and only you."[11] In these cases clients seek the help of a priest or priestess privately for a session in the inner altar room of the temple. There, *wanga* can also reconcile two lovers, make a wayward spouse faithful, or break apart a budding adulterous liaison. In most relationships, however, romantic love and sexual pleasure are only one part of a complex exchange that inevitably involves finances or resources. "Americans can afford to marry for love," a Haitian friend once commented. "We Haitians have to marry for money."[12]

One spirit or goddess who is not searching for romantic partnership is the other important Èzili, Èzili Dantò. She is in many ways an opposite of Freda: dark-complexioned, strong-willed, independent, poor, and a single mother. Depicted in Catholic iconography as the "Black Virgin," Our Lady of Czestochowa, Dantò bears a scar on her cheek and carries a child in her arms. I can remember how thrilled I was when somebody explained to me who the child was. The child she carries is not the baby Jesus and is not even a boy. Her baby, significantly, is a little girl. This Èzili, her daughter, and her mother, Gran Èzili, recall the triple aspect of the child, crone, and mother goddesses of other traditions, and present womanhood in multiple roles.

When Dantò "rides" her devotees, she manifests as a fierce and powerful force. She sometimes asks to hold the doll that represents her daughter, embodying the image of mother-and-child that is in many ways the most primary and most lasting relationship in Haiti. When she manifests as her more fiery self, Èzili *ge wouj* or "red-eyed Èzili," she stammers "*ge-ge-ge-ge.*" They say her tongue was cut out as she fought for freedom in the Haitian revolution. Closely associated with the military tropes of Haitian nationalism, Dantò wears the blue and red of the Haitian flag.

Unlike Freda, Dantò's persona is that of Haitian poor women. She ultimately presents a picture of female strength and independence – a fighter who provides for her children. Dantò can also be read as a psychic remembering of slavery, where dark-complexioned women suffered specific kinds of brutality centered on overwork, physical torture, and sexual abuse but nevertheless fought in the struggle for freedom.

Èzili Dantò and her daughter manifest the fruits of the highest value in Haitian personhood: fertility. Motherhood is one of the few roles available to poor women and crucial in a culture where children provide one's support in old age. Everyone – whether single, disabled, or homosexual – all women and men are expected to have children. Èzili Dantò is a divine representation of the Haitian wisdom that the mother-child bond is far more important than the bonds of romance and marriage. One of the prayer songs for Èzili reminds us that while lovers may come and go, the mother is irreplaceable:

Èzili, if your mother dies, you will cry. (×3)
If your husband dies, you'll find another one.

Èzili, si maman'w mouri, w'ap kriye. (×3)
Si mari'w mouri, w'a jwenn yon lot, O.

Dantò "works" for people in ways different from Freda. Concerned with maternal bonds and women's independence, she protects women from domestic abuse and sex abuse.[13] She can be heterosexual, but she can also be a *madivin*, or *madivinèz* ("lesbian"), and men and women who are homosexual are considered to have been "blessed" or "worked" by her. As Freda is a heterosexual femme figure, Dantò performs independent, woman-centered sexuality and financial control.[14] Although Èzili Dantò is a spirit who is pro-homosexual, I have never heard any elaboration on who her female spirit lovers might be.

As in many societies, being labeled a lesbian in Haiti is one of the worst stigmas and is usually an insult reserved for women whom particular men find too powerful or too independent. While it can ruin reputations at the national political level, among the poor who practice Vodou, many women consider themselves to be *madivin* and will acknowledge it in discreet ways. In some congregations I have visited, virtually all of the worshipers – both men and women – are homosexual. I have also met two lesbian priestesses who each had several sexual partners, in the polygamous style of the rural Haitian man. One of these women also had a husband who lived in Miami. As poor women struggle to cobble together lives that include both resources and pleasure, fixed identities are less important than the ability to be fluid and adaptable in both economic and sexual partnerships.

While the term *madivin* translates as a pejorative term for women who engage in erotic relationships with women, it is unclear what the full range of meanings for this terms really is in the context of Vodou. Of all the anthropologists who have been fascinated with Vodou, none has taken its (homo)sexualized aspects as a serious topic of study and theorizing. It will not do simply to accept Dantò as a "lesbian," since sexual acts may have different meanings and social significance depending on how they are understood in different cultures. There is no certain relationship between sexual acts, meanings, and sexual identities, since sexual acts do not carry with them a universal social meaning.[15]

One thing we *can* see is that Freda and Dantò represent a range of gendered possibilities that are not offered by Roman Catholicism. Whether she comes as heterosexual paramour, as her daughter's mother, as lesbian, warrior, or grandmother, the Èzili are more complex and present far more diversity than the female figures of the New Testament. Unlike the Virgin Mary, the Èzili are sexual beings who lead complicated mythological love lives.

Although their official state religion has always been Catholicism, Haitian women have drawn knowledge from both Catholic theology and from Vodou. The spirits offer Haitian women creolized understandings of love, gender, and sexuality apart from the dominant French-based Catholic culture. In a society that is oppressive to women in multiple ways, the two worst insults that can be hurled at a woman in Haiti are *bouzen* (whore) and *madivin* (lesbian). It is significant that two major spirits or goddesses are divine recuperations of these stigmatized identities.

"I AM A SOLDIER, I WILL NOT SLEEP"

While the female divinities of Haiti are known for their emotional and familial relationships, the male spirits have two main associations: work and militarism. Generally speaking, each male spirit controls a different expertise, whether it be blacksmithing, agricultural work, or sea captaining.[16] Most are also soldiers in an invisible spiritual army within an elaborate web of military designations.

Ogou is one of the oldest male spirits and is now one of the most "served." In great numbers Vodou temples are devoted to him, initiates are adopted by him as spiritual children, and women marry him in elaborate spiritual marriages both in Haiti and its diaspora. He can be traced all the way back to the Yoruban and Dahomean kingdoms that were undone by events leading up to the slave trade. The Yoruba knew him (and know him) as Ogun; he was (and is) Gu in Dahomey (now Benin). He is a divine blacksmith, a master iron-worker and keeper of the secrets of metalwork and forging. He is also known as a god of war.[17]

In Haiti, Ogou is a military officer who represents engaged battle, discipline, and self-control. In the Catholic imagery associated with him, he appears as Sen Jak (Saint James) atop a rearing white horse. In these Catholic icons Saint James brandishes a sword, triumphing over the bodies of infidels lying trampled beneath his horse's feet. Haitians reading this image recognized military triumph, and for them Sen Jak recalled Ogou, the powerful god of war. Just as there are many Èzili, there are also many Ogou.

Ogou's masculinity lies in his physical strength, high military rank, and self-discipline. Generally speaking, when Ogou "rides" an initiate, he asks for two red scarves to be tied around his arms in an instant uniform, broadcasting strength and authority. He also often asks for a sword or machete, which he ritually brandishes during the ceremony. Above all, Ogou is in control and in command of both the people around him and of many of the other spirits. He is a divine version of a "big man," a leader with many loyal followers. To pledge allegiance to Ogou is to receive blessings, protection, and a psychic masculine "shoring up." "*Met gason sou ou*," (literally, "put on your maleness") I once heard him say.

While Papa Ogou has many "children" – initiates – he has no mythological children, nor is he particularly known for being a lover or husband.[18] A childless, wifeless *patron*, his masculinity is nevertheless heterosexual and hinges on his independent "big man" status as a martial force. Papa Ogou will tell you that he loves you, but it is the distant love of a strict and exacting father.

Karen McCarthy Brown characterizes Ogou helpfully as an exploration of the constructive and destructive uses of power.[19] We can also read his domain as particularly that of normative Haitian masculinity, concerned with public politics, war and policing. Given the history of Haiti, it is not surprising that this warrior divinity has become a dominant masculine force in Vodou. Haiti won its independence from the French colonists in the only successful slave revolution in history. Since that long war, the country has been ruled by one military president after another, culminating in the infamous thirty-year Duvalier dictatorship.

This prayer song for Ogou portrays him as a "man of war" who is a sentryman on a night watch:

> Ogou Badagri what are you doing?
>   On watch, they put me on watch
>   I won't sleep, Feray I won't sleep
>   I'm a warrior, I couldn't sleep
>   I was at war, they put me on watch
>
> *Ogou Badagri sa w' ap fè la-a?*
>   Se veye, yo mete'm veye
>   M' pap dòmi Feray m' pa dòmi
>   M' deja gason lagè m' pa sa dòmi
>   Nan lagè'm te ye yo mete'm veye

Here Ogou is a sentryman put on watch against the enemy, and like a responsible "big man" he will not sleep and abdicate his duty. A *nèg serye* ("serious man"), he has been given a job to do which he takes seriously and lives up to. As a watchman in wartime, Ogou is in charge of the national security of an entire people in a hypermasculine protector role.

One thing about the cryptic nature of many Vodou songs is their flexibility for use in different contexts. It is sure that songs for Ogou carry a different valence during each political era in Haiti. During the coup against President Jean-Bertrand Aristide in 1991, for example, this song was used in Carnival as a *pwen* ("point" or "message"). It used the divine authority of this masculine warrior to indicate the need for witness and for struggle on the part of the Haitian majority who opposed the coup. Carnival musicians segued from this song into a second Ogou song that said, "I'm a warrior, an iron rod. What can they do to me? Guns don't scare me!" (*"Se nèg lagè m'ye, se baton fè anye. Ki sa yo ka fè mwen? Kanno pa fè mwen pè!"*) In the context of the political crisis in Haiti, Ogou served as an encouragement for people to acknowledge their opposition to the coup and to recall their history of freedom struggle.[20]

GEDE'S SEXUAL PARODY: CRITIQUE AND LIBERATING LAUGHTER

Urban Vodou ceremonies usually finish with appearances by the Gede, so let us now return to these most explicitly sexualized divinities in Vodou. The ultimate destabilizers, Gede mediate yet disrupt dichotomies. They manifest as *malere* (poor) but are the spirits of money who nevertheless prefer gifts of cigarettes or *kleren* (cane liquor). Spirits of the dead who live in the cemetery, they usher the living in and out of this world. They feel no physical sensation, yet they are spirits of sex. Androgynous yet vulgar, they perform an ambiguous gender scheme where both femininity and masculinity are parodied and ridiculed. Linking sex irrevocably with satire, the Gede are the ultimate social critics in Vodou, uniquely able to make political commentary both in domestic and national arenas.

Just as Ogou has historical roots in West Africa and has creolized into an American entity, so does Gede begin as the Yoruban Eshu-Elegbara and the Fon Legba. This trickster divinity is crippled but nevertheless displays a large erect phallus. Owner of crossroads and doorways, first to be invoked in prayer, the African Elegba is also divine mouthpiece between the living and the dead. Papa Legba, in Vodou, inherited this station at the crossroads, but his phallus and social satire seem to have been passed on to the descendents of the Dahomean Guede-vi.[21]

In Haitian cosmology, the Gede are the closest spiritual beings to humans, since they were once ancestors who lived real lives. Many were slaves in the French colony. "They cut off my legs for running away, and I bled to death," one Gede told me. "I was eighteen years old." The persona of the Gede is usually that of a poor person, and occasionally they "walk with" other spirits as their servants or slaves. Known for their untiring capacity to "work," the Gede are usually the primary healing spirits for working priests and priestesses. They may be invoked on a daily basis for clients behind the scenes, to do works for health, money or love.

In possession appearances Gede will don old clothes, sit on the floor, and drink liquor (which they call their "medicine") straight from the bottle. "That's my wife," said one heterosexual male Gede possessing a lesbian priestess. He/She pointed to the wild boar with protruding incisor teeth on the Gordon's Gin label. Peals of laughter was the response from most present, while a few sucked their teeth in friendly disdain.

While Èzili Freda is a melodramatic romantic, Gede parodies both the sentiment and the sentimentality of love. Assigning it to the false and hypocritical realm of all things French, one Gede spun love into a mock French lesson: "... singing in childish syllables, 'I love, you love, he loves, she loves, What does that make? (Chorus, drawn out) 'L'Amour.'"[22] Very like drag queens in the United States, the Gede are brilliant social critics of gender, are inveterate gossips, and are capable of a quick "read" of the politics of either domestic or national power. The Gede are also quick to satirize the ruling order in general, and with it, anybody in authority or in positions of respect. Donald Cosentino writes of an amusing and elaborate display in Port-au-Prince by the chief of the Gede family, Bawon Samdi:

> Bawon mounted his godson Edner, in Gesner's *ounfò* [temple]. He held his phallic cane like a baton, leading a troupe of Gedes through a martial display, every few steps pausing to execute a bump and grind. The brass band hired for the occasion was playing "Jingle Bells." Gesner's *ounfò* had been a favorite of Baby Doc, and the crowds were roaring in derision at this parody of the military that had replaced him.[23]

How do the Gede spirits work across the seemingly contradictory fields of religion, sexuality and political satire? What is it about sexuality that lends itself to performances of social critique? Part of the answer has to do with the politics of "high" and "low" culture and the way that in Christian cultures sexuality is assigned to the latter and religion to the former. The Gede spirits in particular use sexuality as a sort of language of knowledge, embodying a type of Haitian, the *vakabon* or undisciplined sexual male. Whenever the Gede make appearances, they inevitably use the form of Kreyòl speech called *betiz* (humorous vulgarity). To *di betiz* (say vulgarities) is to enter the deep Kreyòl of *vakabondaj* (male sexual prowess). This kind of language is the special province of the Gede and is also reserved for Carnival and Rara songs, and for some Konpa (popular music).[24] At its sophisticated best, *betiz* is full of double and triple entendres, making for multiple layers of humor.[25]

I see Gede as a counterpart to the heterosexual masculinity and the "big-man-ism" of Papa Ogou. Gede can be understood as sort of queer "small man" who occupies the lowest end of the divine/social order. He displays one side of the personality of the poor male in Haiti who is usually unemployed and socially devalued. While most Haitian men maintain heterosexual identities in a homophobic society, Gede parodies even that hetero-normativity. While Gede spirits are usually male, it is not uncommon for them to be ambiguously gendered and ambiguously sexual.[26]

When the Gede (or the boisterous Carnival bands) sing *betiz* songs, they are enacting a form of popular laughter that comprises the only public form of speech possible for the disenfranchised poor. Under military rule, oppositional political speech is repressed and becomes impossible. Under these conditions, Gede's sexualized *betiz* songs affirm not only the existence but also the creative life of a people in the face of the brutality and everyday violence of their countrymen. Sexualized popular laughter constitutes a kind of national politics in which divine "small men" use sexual imagery to "read" gender relations and also the social order. Gede's *betiz* songs are political "readings" at the deepest level of Haitian Kreyòl.

From this perspective, Gede's sexualized satire can be seen as the last bastion of uncensored speech in Haiti. Herein lies one of the ironies of Gede's great power: the spirits of former slaves who are still harnessed by the living for spiritual work are the harbingers of a particular kind of freedom. Not only does Gede call the gendered body into question, but he also questions the entire social order from the bottom to the top. Through Gede's jokes and *betiz*, the freedom to question, to parody, and to laugh is enacted on a daily basis. While Gede's politics is not an engaged political movement, it is a politics of liberation nonetheless. Gede opens a philosophical space for opposition and rejection of the suffering of the world through laughter. Gede are very much the spirits of slaves, but they can also be seen as transcendent *mawon* (maroons, runaways from slavery) who use gender to reject even the most basic terms of the social order.

The official religion of the social order in Haiti has been Roman Catholicism, ever since colonial times. But the Afro-Haitian religion of the majority operates with drastically different premises from those of Christianity. For Haitians, scripture does not represent the word of God, or if it does, it is not as immanent as the many spirits who populate the universe, claim initiates, and work on their behalf. The spirits are not beings in whom it is necessary to have faith. Rather, they materialize from time to time in the bodies of their initiates and in the works they perform. Vodou is ultimately a moral system, and it involves taking responsibility for desires and actions and working within social bounds.[27]

While many priests and priestesses of Vodou attend mass regularly and observe the Catholic sacraments, the Gede spirits are decidedly not Catholic. For the Gede, the divinities, priests, trappings, and teachings of the Church are "high culture" authorities it is best to parody. They sing obscene parodies of Catholic hymns, often beginning in French but delivering their ridiculous sexualized punch-lines in Kreyòl. Here *betiz* is used in a classic form of the "code-switch," where the alternating use of "high" and "low" language is employed strategically for humor (or anger, or seduction). Gede always uses "low culture" to perform rebelliousness toward bourgeois Catholic culture. In this way, the sexualized silliness of Gede depends on Catholic decorum for its humor.

I like to understand this sexual explicitness in the context of conservative morality as a politics undermining order. It is a metaphysical revolt against the ruling powers and reminds people that there is an alternative way to imagine authority. Gede presents a psychic and philosophical attitude that works in the face of generations of military rule where outright resistance was met with violence and death. For Gede even death – especially death – is an enormous cosmic joke that he has come to help humans play.

LOVE, GENDER, SEXUALITY, AND RELIGION

To try to analyze all of the ways that love, gender, and sexuality work in any one religious system would require far more space than a single chapter in a volume. Here I have suggested some possible ways to understand these processes in the context of Afro-Haitian religion. Not a purely African or purely European tradition, Haitian Vodou creates and presents a creolized set of gendered structures. It is a religious culture that arose out of the institutionalized violence of slavery and still remains embedded in a system of unequal relations of power. The diverse personalities of the spirits reveal an autonomous set of values that are in dialogue with the hegemony of Catholicism but which are separate from it. These values and structures can be understood as religious and philosophical encounters with power in its many forms.

The spirits of Vodou present clues to historical realities in Haiti, and the ways in which power was enacted, acted upon, and reacted to. Many of the historical and present struggles are over people and their bodies. In Vodou, knowledge about love, gender, and sexuality is focused and enacted not in texts, but on and through the bodies of practitioners.

I have argued several main points. Following the work of Karen McCarthy Brown and Joan Dayan, I have described how heterosexual romantic love is imagined as an upper-class prerogative in Vodou. Romantic love carries specific historical class associations, and its trappings of courtship and economic exchange in a universe of childlessness leave it outside the reality of the Haitian majority. Still, the power of the history of sexual slavery and the enduring images of romance in Western culture make the spirit Èzili Freda a potent presentation of its possibilities.

Èzili Dantò, in contrast, presents a more realistic portrait of the poor Haitian woman's life. She is a strong, fierce, independent spirit, representing the love relationships between women, particularly mothers and daughters, that are the glue of Haitian families and lives. Dantò also embodies a fluidity in sexual identity and pleasure not present in the dominant heterosexual discourse.

Ogou and Gede, I suggested, are counterparts in a conversation about masculinity. Ogou presents a militarized "big man" who recalls the war for national independence while Gede is a "small man" who subverts the dominant order with sexualized laughter. Ogou is a dominating, heterosexual male hero, while Gede performs an ambiguous sexuality open to homosexual possibilities. Both spirits use their sexualized personas to present ways of knowing and ways of acting in the world that are different from Catholic narratives.

Vodou is a case where structures of gender and sexuality cannot be understood without attending to the role of religion, as well as history. In Haiti, spiritual beings represent diverse sexualities to create a key language that articulates an alternative, creole philosophical stance in the face of the structures of domination. The entry of the life-affirming value of sexuality is a direct challenge to the dominant Catholic discourse which would banish it from the religious sphere except in terms of condemnation and control. Sexuality can be a language of independence, of shock and reversal, of laughter in the face of suffering, and of affirmation of life when survival is in question.

NOTES

1. The way that religious rituals proceed is actually quite different across the various regions of Haiti. The characterizations in this piece refer to the urban ceremonies of Port-au-Prince and its outpost, New York City.
2. Evelyn Blackwood and Saskia E. Wieringa, ed., *Same Sex Relationships and Female Desires: Transgender Practices Across Cultures* (New York: Columbia University Press, 1999), p. 43.
3. See Blackwood and Wieringa, ed., *Same Sex Relationships and Female Desires*, p. 2 and Moira Gatens, "Power, Bodies and Difference," in *Destabilizing Theory: Contemporary Feminist Debates*, ed. Michele Barrett and Anne Phillips (Stanford University Press, 1992), p. 132.
4. C. L. R. James, *The Black Jacobins* (New York: Vintage, 1963), p. 32; cited in Joan Dayan, *Haiti, History and the Gods* (Berkeley: University of California Press, 1995), p. 57.
5. Dayan, *Haiti, History and the Gods*, p. 57.
6. Quite a few of the spirits can marry people in elaborate marriage ceremonies modeled on the Christian hetero-normative model. They then serve as special protective forces for their human spouses. In this article, I do not describe the elaborate kinship networks in the religion among humans – "fathers" and "mothers" who initiate "children" who become "twins," and the ways that spirits "marry" people. Nor do I have space in this chapter to describe how the schemes of love, gender, and sexuality presented here in Vodou work in the daily lives of Haitian people. For a more complete picture, see Karen McCarthy Brown, *Mama Lola: A Vodou Priestess in Brooklyn* (Berkeley: University of California Press, 1991). Also see Ira P. Lowenthal, "Marriage is 20, Children are 21: The Cultural Construction of Conjugality and Family in Rural Haiti" (Ph.D. dissertation, Johns Hopkins University, 1987).
7. For fuller discussions of the spirits and their attributes, see Brown, *Mama Lola*; Dayan, *Haiti, History and the Gods*; and Leslie Desmangles, *The Faces of the Gods: Vodou and Roman Catholicism in Haiti* (Chapel Hill: University of North Carolina Press, 1992).
8. Dayan, *Haiti, History and the Gods*, p. 56.
9. Brown, *Mama Lola*, p. 234.
10. Brown, *Mama Lola*, p. 246; cited also in Dayan, *Haiti, History and the Gods*, p. 132.
11. Interview with Manbo Camille, Brooklyn, 1986.
12. Interview with Sanba Legba, Manhattan, 1997.
13. Mambo Racine, personal communication, Port-au-Prince, 1993.

14. I do not mean to argue that Dantò is necessarily a feminist goddess. Though she is a defender of single mothers, she does not particularly advocate alliances among women, nor does she shy away from "working" for the interests of men.

15. Carol Vance, "Social Construction Theory: Problems in the History of Sexuality," in *Homosexuality, Which Homosexuality?*, ed. Dennis Altman et al. (Amsterdam: An Dekker/Schorer, 1989), pp. 13–34; cited in Gloria Wekker, "What's Identity Got to Do with It? Rethinking Identity in Light of the Mati Work in Suriname" in *Same Sex Relationships and Female Desires*, ed. Blackwood and Wieringa, p. 119.

16. These *lwa* are Ogou, Kouzen Azaka, and Mèt Agwe, respectively.

17. See Suzanne Preston Blier, *African Vodun: Art, Psychology and Power* (Chicago: University of Chicago Press, 1995) and Sandra T. Barnes, ed., *Africa's Ogun, Old World and New* (Bloomington: Indiana University Press, 1989).

18. Certain Ogou are said to be consorts of certain Èzili, but these relationships are not performed in ritual nor depicted in art in the way of other Vodou couples, like Danbala and Aiyda Wedo and Kouzen and Kouzinn Azaka.

19. Karen McCarthy Brown, "Systematic Remembering, Systematic Forgetting: Ogou in Haiti," in ed. Barnes, *Africa's Ogun*, p. 70.

20. This version is abridged; the whole version can be heard in the 1993 Boukman Eksperyans carnival song "Jou Malè", on their album *Libete Pran Pou Pran'l/Freedom Let's Grab It*. Compact Disc published by Island Mango, 162–539946–2 (1995).

21. For Dahomey, see Blier, *African Vodun*; for the Yoruba, see Henry Louis Gates, Jr., *The Signifying Monkey* (Oxford: Oxford University Press, 1988).

22. Maya Deren, *Divine Horsemen: The Living Gods of Haiti* (New York: Chelsea House, 1953), p. 103; cited in Donald J. Cosentino, ed., *The Sacred Arts of Haitian Vodou* (Los Angeles: Fowler Museum of Cultural History, 1995), p. 412.

23. Cosentino, *The Sacred Arts*, p. 411.

24. For work on Carnival and Rara see Elizabeth McAlister, *Rara! Vodou, Power and Performance in Haiti and its Diaspora*, (Berkeley: University of California Press, forthcoming).

25. The popular Konpa singer Coupe Cloue was a particularly sophisticated master of sexual double entendre, and in one song ("Madame Marcel") he is introduced as "Papa Gede." Many of his songs were ballads that contained multiple, drawn-out jokes. The jokes had double and triple entendres but were "clean" to the innocent ear.

26. Within the Haitian majority population there is a range of gender practices and sexualities. However it is unclear (to us outsiders) how these creole sexualities are practiced by Haitians and what their meanings are. More research is needed on the full practices and meanings of Haitian gender and sexuality, and their relationship to religion.

27. The full relationship between Vodou and Catholicism is far too complex to address here. See Brown, *Mama Lola*; Desmangles, *Faces of the Gods*; and Elizabeth McAlister, "Vodou and Catholicism in the Age of Transnationalism: The Madonna of 115th Street Revisited," in *Gatherings in Diaspora: Religious Communities and the New Immigration* ed. R. Stephen Warner (Philadelphia: Temple University Press, 1998), pp. 123–160. For a more detailed discussion of Vodou as a moral system, see Karen McCarthy Brown, "Haitian Vodou: The Distinct Self and the Relational World," in *The Meaning of Life in the World Religions,* ed. Runzo and Martin, pp. 235–250.

Plate 7 Stained-glass window of the Christian saint Julian of Norwich (1342–c.1413) in a side chapel that was later added to the magnificent Norman cathedral at Norwich, England, originally built between 1096 and 1136 CE. Photo: *Nancy M. Martin.*

7

LOVE'S SACRED GROVE: H.D.'S POETICS *of* SPIRITUALITY

Clare B. Fischer

> We have to uncover much that has been hidden, left out or forgotten; it
> means that we have to remake, rewrite and reinterpret much that has gone
> for the history of our religious traditions.
>
> Ursula King[1]

Feminist spirituality emerges in the context of Western Christianity out
of the perception that women have been systematically objectified,
oppressed, and erased within this tradition and out of the desire of women
to both recover and create a spiritual tradition that affirms women, embodiment, and human wholeness and in which women's voices may be heard
and women's spiritual transformation facilitated. Many women have
chosen to work within their religious traditions to transform them, but
other women have determined that it is necessary to step outside these
established traditions – seen as irretrievably patriarchal – to find a space for
women's personal and spiritual development.

Although differences of opinion among writers concerned with feminist spirituality are commonplace, there is general agreement that the
recovery of memory is an essential step in resisting the historical hegemony
of patriarchy. This is particularly true for those probing the character and
interpretation of feminine *eros* that traditionally has been associated with
passivity, receptivity, and objectification. Recent writers attest to both the
misrepresentation of women's expression of love and the harm brought
about by the values embedded in these dominant perspectives. Yet the feminist writer must enquire whether it is sufficient to identify women as

victims – of both historical interpretation and social practices – and to what extent women are free from essentializing understandings of "the person who loves."

For centuries, women's erotic experience has been expressed in terms of another's desiring – women as objects of pleasure rather than as experiencing subjects. Recognizing the distortion of this perspective, it becomes abundantly clear that there is need for an alternative view as well as greater clarity about the connection between engendered expressions of love and spirituality. Some writers attempting to develop a feminist spirituality offer maternal devotion as a positive alternative to an objectifying heterosexual erotic love, but the desiring subject remains out of focus so long as love is solely defined in terms of motherhood, reproduction, and early childhood socialization. In this chapter, I will approach feminist spirituality with a consideration of an embodied subject – women loving in ambiguity and in spite of patriarchal constructions. In order to make my case I depend upon the substantial contribution of the American poet known as "H.D." (Hilda Doolittle). Little known among readers outside literary critical circles interested in modernist women writers, H.D. offers a spirituality of *eros* that both conforms to and refines some of the insights inscribed in current feminist spirituality literature. Moreover, she presents a novel way of understanding women's resistance to the victim ideology so pervasive in our culture.

The irreverent expressions of a poet might seem an unlikely site for the construction of a feminist spirituality worthy of comparison with non-Western religious traditions. H.D. was indeed defiant in her use of images, her objectives, and her interpretations. Yet her contribution fosters a sense of commonality between men and women in our time and those figured in a distant past. She was absorbed in the project of revisioning the meta-narrative of heroic conquest and woman's subjugation to the victor; she took up the serious encounter of Eris as discord and Eros as abiding and triumphant love. In her life-long poetic of spirituality, H.D. revisited the actors so vibrantly portrayed by the Greek tragedians and Homer, and probed how love might counter violence, how the typecast roles of conqueror and objectified booty (women) might be shattered. Hers was a religious perspective and sometimes a mystical one. She wove a complex spiritual cloth. Threads from her Moravian Christian childhood experiences were combined with her classical readings. The "love feasts" at Christmas time in her family's Moravian church offered memories of a ritual life that reached back to the radical Protestant Reformation. On the other hand, she translated and interpreted Greek literature and found the vigorous accounts of ancient Egyptian deities compelling. Her revisions richly adapted mythic characters, goddesses, and shadow forms of lovers into a poetry of yearning.

Her works are daunting to her readers, requiring attention to symbol, image, and historic event. Her scope of interest and erudition demand much but prove to be a superb source for students of spirituality. She wrote of armed conflict, well-qualified to do so after having lived through both World Wars and experienced first-hand the cost of battle and blitz. H.D. attested to human suffering, expressed in disillusionment and fragmented relationship, associating these manifestations of modernity with a spiritual crisis. She asked through much of her poetic expression: "Where is home? Is there a map that will guide humanity toward a peaceable, egalitarian world?" This was the stuff of her poetic imagination, never very distant from the realities of the social order and its flaws. Yet she offered a testimony to spiritual survival without sentimentality and anticipated much of the life-oriented optimism of contemporary feminist spirituality, frequently said to be "life-committed."

FEMINIST SPIRITUALITY

Ursula King's fine introduction to contemporary feminist spirituality allows me to locate my subject in this discourse.[2] Identifying three pivotal features of feminist spirituality (integration of body and soul, reclamation of a time past, and embrace of the Goddess), King suggests that recent writings align with more general feminist aspirations for wholism and the construction of women's selfhood. She notes that feminist spirituality departs from the conventional understanding of women and the spiritual life in representing devotional life as experimental and embodied – a clear departure from a tradition that emphasized disembodied practices of devotion and defined women's religious role in excessive terms, either as saint or sinner. The integrative approach of which King writes rejects dichotomous distinction, seeking to overcome assumptions of woman as an emotionally effusive actor, subdued by her beloved attachment to spouse and child. Hagiographic accounts of saints and mystics frequently contribute to the distortion of women's spirituality as well, depicting religious figures without physical appetite, especially sexual longing. Unfortunately, King does not take a critical stand regarding the privileging of maternal love, a view dominant in the spirituality literature but one that reduces women's *eros* to a biological expressivity. King, making an aside that women are more "other-centered," concludes that they exhibit a stronger proclivity than men for the spiritual life.[3] One of the benefits in reading H.D. against this text is a wariness about maternalism and the slippery side of essentialism. She carefully avoids any suggestion of women's moral superiority.

In King's triadic typology of feminist spirituality, in addition to the matter of integrity, reclamation of women's history is encouraged in order to assure repossession of women's agency in their own historical narrative. The task of re-membering, a formidable effort given the hegemony of the Western canon, raises innumerable problems not the least of which is the question of sources. What texts invite women to appropriate alternatives to the dominant tradition? The epigraph introducing this chapter reveals King's determination to discover what has been "hidden," "forgotten," and manipulated. In short, there is a need for "re-covery," which some feminist writers argue entails imaginative reconstruction of event and consequence. H.D.'s effort is, perhaps, best understood in this context. She is an archaeologist of sorts, probing the dry soil of Egypt, searching for shards that can be reconstructed into a whole piece. Her poetry assumes an ancient coherence that has been broken and buried in the course of Western history, recovering a sense of wholeness which is never completed. She proposes a history true to struggle and ambiguity.

In H.D.'s long poem entitled *Helen in Egypt* (the focus of my analysis of love and spirituality) a tradition of misrepresentation is challenged. She scrutinizes the agonal values of the past based upon a warrior code that makes men into metallic heroes and women helpless in the face of destiny. Depicted as vulnerable trophies of war or as excessive in their sexuality, women appear to be entrapped in texts and ideologies of negative determination. H.D. inscribes an alternative history derived not from theological text or traditional historical sources. She depends on literary sources that the scholarly community has dismissed over time as inappropriate evidence of truth. Today contemporary feminist writers identified with spirituality in the Western tradition (who share H.D.'s orientation toward rescuing women's history) often choose literary text. Joann Conn Wolski asserts that fiction is a particularly useful resource because:

> This literature demonstrates how women's spiritual quest concerns women's awakening to forces of energy larger than the self, to powers of connection with nature and with other women, and to the acceptance of the body.[4]

The third motif in King's summary of feminist spirituality is openness to non-Christian religious imagery with particular attachment to the figure of the Goddess – as the Great Mother and as a power evidenced by recon-structions from archaeological sites. King writes of this new interest in goddesses as a "second coming" rather than a return to historical record. Citing prominent proponents of this approach, including Carol Christ, she notes three aspects of attraction to goddess traditions.[5] The first is repre-sented as a psychological event involving the personification of a living goddess. The second and third refer to symbolic features such as life, rebirth, and power. The latter representation of Goddess power is certainly important to H.D.'s poetic; we read of Thetis as a divine being who can change shapes, modify realities, and abet in transformation of mortals.

Several feminist scholars who have probed the traces of ancient Goddess worship in Egypt are suspicious of the way in which this material can be interpreted and misdirected.[6] Springbord writes: "If ancient Egyp-tian texts suggest an unequivocally patriarchal kinship, nevertheless the feminine principle of empowerment is just as explicit." She asserts here a clear distinction between the physiological reproductive aspect of the Goddess (as an emblem of fertility) and a political arrangement entailing monarchial lineage. In other words, the reproductive capabilities of ancient goddesses cannot be embraced as the exclusive basis for constructing an alternate view of engendered power.

Associated with this third dimension of King's typology of feminist spirituality is the motif of transformation. The Goddess perceived as pow-erful is an enabling personification or symbol of change. Calling upon a female deity from antiquity generally suggests a calling forth of images of strength and courage, of resilience and survival. Clearly, H.D. deploys female mythic divines precisely in this way, inviting her readers to experi-ence the quality of persistence as abiding love.

H.D.'S POETIC VOCATION

> Her lifelong revolt against a traditional feminine destiny ... set her apart from the literary mainstream and led her ultimately to a woman-centered mythmaking and radical revision of the patriarchal foundation of western culture.[7]

A number of biographies are available providing compelling description and analysis of H.D.'s complex and fascinating life story.[8] Born in Bethle-hem, Pennsylvania in 1886, she grew up deeply immersed in the symbols and practices of her grandparents' Moravian church. In later life, as part of her personal recovery, she returned to memories of Moravian religious belief and ritual, especially its celebrations of love, the visible role of women, and impressions of Jesus Christ as a loving, feminine image. She moved to London in 1911 and never took up permanent residence in America after that time. Clearly, one aspect of her long life (she died in 1961) that has attracted much interest among students of modernist literature was her intimate association with such luminaries as Ezra Pound, D. H. Lawrence and Sigmund Freud, generally acknowledged to be protagonists in *Helen in Egypt*. It should be noted, however, that H.D., while infusing her poetic with personal history, avoided the confessional impulse found in the writings of some current feminist poets. She was committed to expression that was true to the "real," that conveyed what she termed "spiritual realism." I will explore this rubric below.

In a remarkable essay on poetic inspiration written as early as 1919, H.D. indicates a resistance to the spiritual crisis of modernism.[9] With attention to her own creativity, H.D. reflects on the integration of body and mind, intellect and emotion, that grounds her work. Examining her own "mental process" and the emotional significance of suffering, the poet writes of an "over-mind" as comparable to the womb containing new life. On her forehead rests a space "fluid yet with definite body" which is supplemented after the birth of her daughter, with a second site: a consciousness in "the love-region of the body or placed like a foetus in the body."[10] Creative energy is embodied and located in front of the brain and in her womb: "over-mind" and "love-mind" equally contribute to her poetics of spirituality. This unity reappears in *Helen in Egypt* in H.D.'s embrace of the intellectuality of ancient Greece and the *eros* of ancient Egypt. With this self-understanding of the rational and of love, the sensual embodied memory of birth is set side by side with an intellectual interpretation of how the poet grasps her creativity. Her reflections on womb-creativity, however, are not on the same order as the more essentialized perspectives of maternal spirituality resonating throughout a good deal of feminist spirituality. For H.D., birth is a trope for new life, for interior movement and external expression.

This integrative approach is also evidenced in H.D.'s notion of poetry as equally private and public. Experience is critical to the truth of a poet's vocation and, for H.D., must be tightly interwoven with threads of personal memory and identification of the self as witness. Her voice is of a time long past, and of a time not as distant but reflective of her earlier life, as well as the present, which serves to fuel her voice of anguish and hope. In reading the body of H.D.'s works, it is possible to decipher erotic encounters that were part of her life story as well as emotions of fear and sadness about the actual violence of nations throughout the twentieth century. Certain of H.D.'s critics emphasize her highly conflicted private life: the failed romance with Pound, the betrayal of her husband, Richard Addlington, the mysterious relationship with Lawrence.[11] In short, they examine these troubled loves as subtexts of H.D.'s poetry and perceive her poems as an excellent resource for discerning the poet's more intimate biography. There is little doubt that the painful consequences of each affair left traces on her work, but it would be a mismeasure of the poet's nuanced vocabulary and the complexity of her conceptual structures if one were to depend entirely upon the stuff of her lived experience. Her remarkable imagination, filled with visions, dreams, and memories suggests much more than a reactive and recuperative creativity.

Although her "romantic thralldom" (a term attributed to DuPlessis) was genuinely a part of her earlier efforts at poetry and acknowledged by H.D. as a dependence upon the poets who tutored her, there is much to be said for the poet as an exceptional, autonomous searcher. Her poetic and prose works can also be read as veritable records of a spiritual journey, a pilgrimage from site to site wherein she begins to discover her own voice. Her therapeutic exchanges with Freud, undertaken after a dry period in her creativity, indicate the emergence of a self, confident in her knowing and her ability to transpose the mix of actual experience and imaginative play into fine poetry. In a fascinating account of her meetings with Freud, she records a recognition of liberation from the benevolent but judgmental male tutors who seemingly dominated her early writings: "You might say, that I had, yes, I had something that I specifically owned. I owned myself."[12]

Reclaiming her experiences of love – affirming and rejecting – H.D. constructs the meaning of intimate connection. Her poetry folds in the emotional cost and pleasure of these loves. It also reclaims mythic female figures from antiquity, disabusing them of the flaws in character and fatalism that condemned them to objectification and made them, as exemplars of women's nature, weak and without subjectivity. This recovery effort relies upon other sources not used in the conventional appropriation of classical themes. H.D. incorporates her meditations based on her dreams, having learned much from her therapy about the interpretation of symbolic material embedded in the unconscious. She also incorporates visual images seen on trips to Greece and Egypt, particularly those of hieroglyphs, mysterious inscriptions requiring scrupulous decoding. Yet, H.D. read this language as a poet of imagist orientation and understood that these picture words were more than evidence of monarchial lineage and rule. She took them to be part of a magical tradition far different from that of the Greeks. Just as these inscriptions held her attention, so, too, did fragments from Greek poets: The incomplete pieces of poetry attributed to Sappho and Steisichorus are particularly privileged in H.D.'s poetic, in part, I suspect, because the fact of loss to us of their respective works must have resonated with H.D.'s concern for retrieval of evidence that might point to an alternative interpretation of engendered relations in antiquity. I add, with some haste, that both ancient poets provide a glimpse of a different Helen, the infamous beauty who is alleged through Western convention to have been the singular cause of the devasting Trojan War.

Memory plays a crucial role in H.D.'s compositions. Psychoanalysis, however abbreviated, underscored the importance for H.D. of childhood experience, especially those repressed moments that required interpretative work to recover. Narratives strung from shadows and images not quite accessible were part of the poet's creative recasting. One significant event, told to Freud, is H.D.'s endeavor to understand what she believed to be prophetic dreams and visions. These materials are eventually threaded into her post-World War II poetry. Visiting Corfu in 1920 accompanied by her female companion Bryher, she experienced "writing on the wall," a two-phased vision composed of pictures, like stencil drawings on a wall in her rooms.[13] The head of a helmeted warrior and a chalice are seen along with a tripod. H.D. interpreted these as suggestive of a tension between agonal and love ethics. The second phase of her Corfun vision included a ladder and the figure of Nike (Victory) ascending the ladder, which H.D. was to interpret as spiritual triumph over violence. While Freud questioned this vision and did not acknowledge it as evidence of H.D.'s prophetic capabilities, H.D. held fast to the truth of this extrasensory reality. In her configuration, then, of diverse sources, the poet exemplifies an experimental openness in her effort to convey "spiritual realism," a spiritual expression equally permeable to unusual experience and flexible in reading the signs of the times. In *Helen in Egypt*, the poet invites the reader to participate in a multi-textual reading: glyphs, memories, awakened voices from classical accounts, time, and place spiral without reference to the conventional chronology of narrative.

By way of summary, several observations about H.D.'s poetic vocation and vision have been offered. In general H.D. writes a poetic of spirituality that is reflexive but crisp, eluding the entanglements of self-pity or complacency found in certain expressions of spirituality. She is troubled by events in the world and discomforted by her memories of incomplete relationship. Her spirituality avoids coating fragile relationship with an optimistic veneer; distrust, hostility, rage reside alongside a deep yearning for transformation. Her reappropriation of antiquity and distant place suggests her dual motivation – to write in order to release herself and to free images from the fixity of traditional readings of engendered relationship in times of terrible combat. King's notion that "the central pivot" of feminist spirituality is, after all, freedom and transformation where wounds are healed and opposition harmonized hints at the impulse that nourished H.D.'s poetry. But there was another motive as well – writing and life were intertwined. She wrote in *Hermetic Definition*: " ...why must I write?/ ... She draws the veil aside,/unbinds my eyes,/commands, 'write, write or die.'"[14]

HELEN IN EGYPT: THE ENCOUNTER OF ERIS AND EROS

The search for identity; the role of the woman poet; the significance of dream visions; the adventures and misadventures of the questing self: these are the concerns in *Helen in Egypt*.[15]

The poetics of spirituality I am constructing in these pages focuses on H.D.'s poem that retrieves, integrates and provides a powerful vision of the ancient Goddess. *Helen in Egypt* is not the simple retelling of Homer's account of the Trojan War, *The Iliad*. Unlike the epic that has been retold innumerable times, locating beautiful Helen in Troy, H.D. takes her to Egypt and rejects the conventional perspective of the female as a catastrophic object of desire. More pervasive a figure than the biblical Eve, blameworthy for human sin, Helen is characterized throughout Western letters as scandalously desirable and thoroughly lacking in agency. Homer provides little information in his epic about Helen, but we meet her there as Paris's obsession and the rationale for Greek against Trojan. With no voice of her own, Homer's beautiful protagonist gives no hint of her desires, her fears, her understanding of the tragic waste of war.

H.D. approaches Helen sympathetically; her Helen is the woman maligned, woman known only through the male gaze. Preserved for centuries as an archetype of the dangerous female, few have challenged this stereotype or approached it with any concern for the larger question of women and love in the context of violence. H.D. interrogates: what was

Helen's memory of the war? How is it that she is unheard? And if she could speak, what would Helen tell of her loves? Thus, *Helen in Egypt* begins with inquiry; it is Helen who poses the questions that weave through the long poem. H.D.'s poetic myth-making can be read as a search for identity – real or phantom, culpable or without responsibility. This poem is about quest; H.D.'s principal literary friend acknowledges this in an interview a few years after her death. Pearson states that it is "the quest that counts, and it is the quest that gives the power and vigor to poetry."[16] The reader encounters maternal deities who are searching for their lost loved ones – Isis for Osiris and Thetis for Achilles. Helen similarly looks beyond her alleged destiny – death in Troy – eager to discover the beloved. Is it Achilles? Paris?

Earlier poetic attempts were made by H.D. to rescue Helen; a short version with this same title anticipated the ambiguity of identity embedded in *Helen in Egypt*. Here she maintains a distance, joining others who regard the figure as an object, neither an embodied woman nor an actor in the history of Greece. H.D. writes that "all Greece" hated her for her seduction of Paris but they also worshiped her as a frozen idol, immobilized in death, a marble figure. This version of Helen proved to be as unsatisfactory to H.D. years after its composition as the classical accounts that fostered a meta-narrative of heroic battle and tragic slaughter. Two ancient writers, translated by H.D. and to some degree inspiration for her later Helen, took a different position which removed the great beauty from Troy. Euripides and Steisichorus construct Helen as guiltless (and Sappho was to echo this insight) and far from the shambles that became Troy. However, these revisions still did not free Helen from the patriarchal values attached to marital fidelity. Helen, in both accounts, resumes her role as wife, retrieved from her exile in Egypt.

Steisichorus' *Pallinode* locates Helen in Egypt, telling his readers that only a phantom was taken to Troy. In writing this, he invites his readers to grasp that the war was fought for an illusion. H.D. locates Helen in Egypt, but she is unclear whether she is a phantom, transported to the Temple of Amen after the war or an embodied, alive woman. Book One entitled "Pallinode," which the poet explains in a short prose introduction represents a "defense, explanation or apology," examines Helen's boundaries and her assessment of what is real, of who is responsible for violent death. Helen-Helena of the first section encounters Achilles as a ghost and Thetis, his goddess mother, who assumes the role of a powerful mediator. Recalling her vision on the wall in Corfu, H.D. most certainly was responding to Freud's criticism of her interpretation of Nike as symbol of female victory, figuring the Goddess as a vital presence in the movement from confusion and anger to a new phase of understanding. At the time of H.D.'s discussion of her vision with Freud, he had shown her a small artifact – a sculpture of the wingless Nike – and asserted that this was woman: victory lacking a spear. At least one feminist critic interprets this encounter as Freud's response to the transgressive woman who attempts to exceed her sexual limits. In H.D.'s construction of Helen she is not a redeemed Nike, but one could argue that the poet recovers victory's wings and allows her protagonist to take flight from combat and visions of heroic triumph.

Clearly I cannot rehearse all of the layers of meaning in H.D.'s *Helen in Egypt* in this short space, but I will trace the passage of Helen through the pages of the poem and indicate how this intricate narrative of love, of war, of memory and transcendence undergirds a contemporary feminist spirituality. Recasting the three motifs enumerated by King, each of the Books of *Helen in Egypt* illuminates the notion of retrieval of women's history and the imaginative construction of what might have been, given the absence of source materials. The poem is an exercise in liberation from the deadly representations that lock women into roles that arrest self-knowledge. H.D. writes that the Phoenix, symbol of transformation, has vanquished the Sphinx. Riddles need not be solved; conclusive answers may be irrelevant. Thus, the "what" of loving relationship gives way to the "how" and allows the reader to enter into the spiral movement that starts with a dream-like state, shifting to an energetic re-membering, and concluding with a mystical recognition of the Divine. The narrative is thickened by the introduction of readings from the temple walls, glyphs signaling meaning that defies mundane understanding, and the appearances of deities whose investment in Eros and Eris further compounds Helen's quest for identity and the clarity of her love/s. We discover the significance of H.D.'s palimpsest reading, soon to recognize after reading the first chapters of "Pallinode" that a surface encounter with text will not yield up the richness of H.D.'s questing. What lies below the surface are half-forgotten, buried voices. Even if the reader of mythic material ignored the buried voices of the past, some trace emerges from under and transforms the present. Freud enabled H.D. to understand the persistence of memories half-remembered and the rupturing consequences of denial. In her Helen narrative H.D. recasts the erotic implications of the Trojan conflict at the same time that she scratches through her own surface notions of sexual love. Whether the poem serves to heal Helen or H.D. is cause for speculation, but it points toward reconciliation of all sorts of conflicting conditions.

Book One finds Helena (H.D.'s designation in this section) alone, wondering who she might be. Is she a dream? What is real? She encounters Achilles, believed to have been killed when an arrow pierced his vulnerable heel. Both are quizzical and find themselves radically separated by their different memories of the war. Helen insists upon her innocence at first; she asserts that she took no part in the sexual conspiracy that prompted the men of Troy and Greece to fight over her as property. Achilles, by contrast, is enraged and holds Helena responsible for the slaughter of his comrades in arms and for his own death. His anger mounts, eventuating in a violent loss of control where he attempts to strangle the woman who refuses to accept her guilt. His violence countered by her denials of blame is a prelude to how the poet will have her two protagonists continue their mutual search for clarity in their Egyptian encounter. The opposing forces – love and discord – are mediated, partly through the appearance of Achilles' divine mother, Thetis. He gains the capacity to speak of his memory of the deadly combat and his recognition of abandonment by his fellow combatants. "We were an iron-ring/whom death made stronger," he tells Helena, "but when the arrow pierced my heel, they were not there … what had happened? Was the command a lure to destruction?" This questioning of his warrior life and the betrayals that happen on the battlefield reveals how vulnerable a mortal can be. The vocation of soldier, in spite of the dominant ancient Greek notion of masculine destiny, will not assure a virtuous, protected life.

H.D.'s language of "the Command" used here, it is important to recognize, is intentionally anachronistic, referring to Hitler's forces. She would remind her readers, as a poet who is both witness and prophet, that here is lesson to be taken. Warriors persist throughout the ages bequeathing a violent lineage, father to son. Yet it is not the Command that failed Achilles; he recognizes that he placed himself in death's path by an exchange of glances with Helen on the ramparts. It was then that the arrow was shot into his mortal flesh. H.D. comments that it was "love's arrow" that made the lethal wound. Just as Achilles' death cannot be attributed to a single cause, Helena acknowledges the mystery of her "transport" to Egypt, the history that antedated her phantom present and the turning cycle of violence. Clytemnestra, her twin and mother of Iphigenia (promised to Achilles and sacrificed to guarantee Greek success) would avenge the murder of her daughter. Here was another violent response – a blood-taking that seemingly is without end. But Helena distinguishes her destiny from that of her sister, insisting that a peaceable existence is not without possibility – Eris need not lead to death, and Eros might prove victorious.

Book Two, "Leuke," locates Helena between the love of her youth and that of old age. No longer in Egypt, Helena departs from the site of picture-images and finds herself on the "white island," meeting Paris – her springtime lover. The impulsive taking of Helen from her home by the love-struck Paris was not an unwanted action; Helen acknowledges her passion for the Trojan. But Paris is not a stable, supportive lover desiring Helen's self-discovery. On the contrary, he is represented in "Leuke" as jealous, competitive and anxious to prove that Achilles is not the appropriate object of Helena's love. He denies that Achilles loves her and hopes to persuade Helena that she is a victim but he is a true partner. Vows have been taken, and she is bound by them to him. Confused and wanting to retrieve memory, Helena returns to Greece where she consults with her earliest lover, Theseus (often interpreted by H.D. critics as the elderly Freud). In his company Helena identifies her yearning for new life.

> Helen must be reborn, that is, her soul return wholly to her body ... 'The memory of breath-taking encounters those half-seen' must balance and compensate for the too intense primary encounter.[17]

It is Theseus who awakens Helena from a dream-like state and enables her to remember history. Here, H.D. represents Theseus as the Greek intellectual – rational and wise. He advises her to abandon her love for Achilles. H.D.'s poem allows for the expression of self-discovery at this moment: Helena is respectful of Theseus but clear that she will find an unmapped passage and reunite with an Achilles who will be transformed. "There is a voice within me," Helena asserts, "listen, let it speak for me."[18]

In this figurative move, from remembrance and courageous self-identity, we read of Helen (as she now emerges) in Egypt again – the site of her initial encounter with Achilles. The final book, "Eidolon" (referring to a wooden idol given to Achilles by Thetis), moves to a third state: not dream, not intellectual recounting, but a mysterious encounter in Formalhaut's Temple. In the site of Egyptian mystery Helen's sense of space and time now present an integration of heaven and earth, of human and divine realities. But separation is also experienced in Helen's recognition that Paris and Achilles are distinctive loves; she has found liberation from unclear testimonies about each and from an Eros that creates her as a dependent upon one or the other. Unheard, H.D. writes, is Helen's new voice which allows her to know the fullness of her humanity – memory, embodied desiring, and intellectual knowing begin to cohere, and she is full of life. She will give birth to two, the fruit of her love of Achilles, who is also transformed. He responds to a "new Command," not duty-bound to the battlefield but to the exploration of the sea.

There are several interpretations of how H.D. brings her long poem to a close. Some will urge the reader to recognize a reconciliation of forces otherwise experienced in opposition to one another. Hollenberg takes exception to this reading of transcendence, asserting that pain and death cannot be reconciled.[19] I am reluctant to choose one position over the other but agree with Hollenberg's notion of a lasting pathos – Achilles as "la Mort" and Paris as "L'Amour" do not merge into a unity; rather they represent a cycle, a mysterious movement where two parts share in an unfinished narrative of life following death.

Each of the poem's books attests to H.D.'s persistent quest for spiritual renewal. With the interrogation of the protagonists of "Pallinode," the reader enters into a superrational space of glyphs, symbols, and conflicting memory. The setting is war; the yearning is for a way through such violence to a site where loving will not be for ever subject to false gesture, possessive domination, illusory purposes. "Leuke," the site of a double movement finding Helen between youth's passion and the sage's explanation, is not the space for love's consummation. In seeking, the poet finds that reclaiming a past is not assured by a chronological recounting. It is only in the last book that the idol, symbol of the warrior's attachment to his mother Thetis, palpably leads the reader to an unimagined geography where mystery prevails, and life is renewed.

CONCLUSION

> Love operates as a mystical life force that infuses all organic and spiritual things with the power of growth, synthesis and resurrection.[20]

"Spiritual realism," the term applied by H.D. to her own writing, provides a step forward in the discussion of contemporary feminist spirituality. In her effort to hold as much of the complexity of the human condition together as possible, H.D. inscribed a poetics of spirituality that embraced consciousness, unconscious drives, cosmic images derived from ancient myth, worldly memories of experience, and experiences lacking in accessible memory. The ambitiousness of her mission cannot be easily matched but does represent guideposts for those of us perplexed by the restlessness of soul, the yearning for a something more.

It is not sufficient to approach love and gender through the lens of a feminist spirituality that merely offers a disgruntled repudiation of Western tradition and its intricate repression of women. The critique of a past which represents woman as Eve or Mary – seductress or virgin – provides a point of departure, offering a deconstruction of a simple opposition having little to do with the lived experience of embodied female persons. Helen, not unlike the reductionist images of Christianity, could continue to be the perfect object of male desire and an excuse for agonal values. H.D. anticipated the feminism we have been discussing in the cultures of the West for the past three decades, discomforted by the double distortion of female beauty as the rationale for and justification of war. She was not interested, however, in reacting to the fixity of literary distortion alone. In her efforts to release Helen – "all Greece," which is all of us – from the bonds of hatred and distrust, she saw her mission as prophet and teacher. Her message, embedded in her revisioning of myth and the reality of wars, is of love that is never sentiment or nostalgic attraction.

In a small measure H.D. rescues Helen from misreading and the rest of us from a notion of *eros* that assumes enduring harmony. I have read her in relation to the implications of a feminist spirituality which all too hastily glosses over pain, suffering, confusion, and, most important of all, vulnerability. In her elaborate re-creation of ancient actors, H.D. writes of a layered recognition; assumptions of innocence and compassion must be read along with culpability and self-longing. None of the figures in *Helen in Egypt* are complete; none are exemplars of unobstructed agents. Paris loves and is unfree in his desire for a Helen who remains untransformed; Achilles is transformed into a man abandoning the warrior's path, but his is not a conjugal love for Helen – he is drawn to his love of the sea. A "new mortal" with a renewed attachment to his mother Thetis, he has forgiven Helen for any part she was alleged to have played in his death. Achilles' change is magical, associated with the "eidolon" (wooden idol) symbolic of his sea goddess mother. Helen, finally, has gained a clarity of meaning and mystery; the poet knows that some realities are ineffable.

The realism of H.D.'s spirituality is attached to both the social verities of a violent human history and the sites of peaceable resolution to difference. The refusal to communicate violence as the last word, annihilating love and the holy, emerges in "Eidolon." Yet it is not the healing balm of a love without shadows. In a poem entitled "Priest," H.D. invites us to experience its elusiveness: "Love is no easy thing to define,/ you take plummet and line and say,/ you touch depth ... you measure that love,/ it was so many hopes so many fears, nights and days."[21]

In her poetic of spirituality, language serves as an alchemical process.

This is not to say all is word, but it is a recognition that the poetic disrupts language that fixes and rules with tragic consequences. To speak of erotic attachment is the solution; while Troy and Greece may be placed in a new setting, Egypt does not reconcile Eris and Eros. Our reality is infused with magic and mystery and is never outside of the embodied, lived experience of human actors who struggle mightily to elude violence and find expression of an ecstatic energy which, in conclusion, I call love.

NOTES

1.   Ursula King, *Women and Spirituality: Voices of Protest and Promise* (London: Macmillan Education, 1989), p. 94.

2.   Ibid.; other titles for consultation include Joann Conn Wolski, *Women's Spirituality: Resources for Christian Development* (New York: Paulist Press, 1986) and Charlene Spretnak, ed., *The Politics of Spirituality: Essays in the Rise of Spiritual Power Within the Feminist Movement* (New York: Anchor/Doubleday, 1982).

3.   King, *Women and Spirituality*, p. 144.

4.   Joann Conn Wolski, "Women's Spirituality," *Cross Currents*, 30 (1980) p. 303.

5.   See Carol Christ, "Why Women Need the Goddess," in *Womenspirit Rising: A Feminist Reader in Religion*, ed. Carol Christ and Judith Plaskow (New York: Harper & Row, 1979), pp. 273–287.

6.   Judith Ochshorn, "Goddesses and the Lives of Women," in *Women and Goddess Traditions in Antiquity and Today*, ed. Karen King (Minneapolis: Fortress Press, 1997), pp. 392–401; see also Patricia Springbord, *Royal Persons, Patriarchal Monarchy and the Feminine Principle* (London: Unwin Hyman, 1990).

7.   Susan S. Freidman, *Psyche Reborn: The Emergence of H.D.* (Bloomington: Indiana University Press, 1981), p. ix.

8.   In addition to Friedman's superb biography, see Janice Robinson, *H.D., The Life and Work of That Struggle* (Bloomington: Indiana University Press, 1986).

9.   H.D., *Notes on Thought and Vision* (San Francisco: City Lights, 1982).

10.   Ibid., pp. 19–20.

11.   See note 7 for references.

12.   H.D., *Tribute to Freud* (Boston: David Godine, 1974), p. 17.

13.   Reported in *Tribute to Freud*, pp. 15–16.

14.   H.D., *Hermetic Definition* (New York: New Directions, 1972), p. 7.

15.   Angela DiPace Fritz, *Thought and Vision: A Critical Reading of H.D.'s Poetry* (Washington, D.C.: Catholic University Press, 1988), p. 15.

16.   Norman Holmes Pearson, "H.D.: An Interview," *Contemporary Literature* 10, 4, p. 439.

17. H.D., *Helen in Egypt* (New York: New Directions Book, 1961); prose introduction, p. 162.
18. Ibid., p. 175.
19. Donna Krolik Hollenberg, *H.D., The Poetics of Childbirth and Creativity* (Boston: Northeastern University Press, 1991), p. 203.
20. Friedman, *Psyche Reborn*, p. 266.
21. H.D., *Collected Poems, 1912–1944*, Louis Martz, ed. (New York: New Directions Press, 1983).

Part III

GENDER AND RELIGION

Plate 8 Life-sized image of Kali, the indomitable Hindu goddess who can even outlast her consort, the great male god Shiva, in the frenzied dance of creation and destruction, shown here just after being garlanded by a priest, perpetually devouring the entrails of a demon whom she has slain. Sri Krishnan Temple, Singapore. Photo: *Joseph Runzo*

8

TOWARD A GENERAL THEORY
of WOMEN *and* RELIGION

Arvind Sharma

INTRODUCTION

A general theory of women and religion is something that we badly need, but it is far beyond the reach of this short chapter. In setting out to address the question of women and religion, I am reminded of what Gwendoline Konie, the Zambian Ambassador to Germany, has to say about speaking on such a broad topic: "The beauty of having to talk on such a complex and evolving subject partly lies in this that one can turn it inside out or around till it becomes identical with what you want to say!" It is somewhat in this flexible spirit that I, too, move "toward a general theory of women and religion." Let me begin by selecting some key words out of this title and holding them up for inspection, as a way of entering into the subject.

"Toward"

My original intention had indeed been to provide a general theory, but then it shared the fate of the Indian poet who told his beloved:

> Your poet once thought of writing an epic,
> But it struck your anklets
> And broke into a thousand songs.

I, too, once thought of producing a general theory of women and religion, but it struck the rock of hard data and broke up into several distinct observations. So I will begin by rendering my task more manageable, by making it more modest. I will try to provide the *materials* for a general theory, thus moving *toward* a general theory of women and religion but making no claim to have yet produced such a full-blown theory.

"Religion"

With regard to religion, I would like to clarify three points. The first is that I use the word "religion" in the context of the *study* of religion. We must begin by recognizing a durable fact about the nature of the intellectual enterprise we call the study of religion. As scholars, we are, after all, students of religion, and the fact is that the study of religion, as we go about it, is basically a secular enterprise. If secularization means, in one sense, the withdrawal of religion from various spheres of life – state, society, and so on – then, in modern times, the process has been carried to a point where even "soteriology" itself has been virtually emptied of its religious content. New wine has been poured into this old bottle, and it has been given the label of progress. Why I advert to soteriology will soon become apparent. What I would like to emphasize at the moment is that unless we realize how thoroughly secular our approach to religion has become, we will not be able to do justice to the role of religion in its relationship to women. Note, for instance, that the charge that religions discriminate against women is to be located in the sociological approach to the study of religion.

Since the relationship of religion and women these days is primarily discussed in the context of the oppression, or at least subordination, of women in the various religions, let me put this question to you point-blank: were religions brought into being to oppress women? This question must be distinguished from another question: do religions oppress women? The question being raised is whether they were founded to oppress women. This leads one to the most fundamental question of all. What are religions for? More precisely, what do religions claim they are here for?

Why were religions founded? Was Christianity founded to subordinate women or to carry the saving gospel of Jesus to the four corners of the world? Was Islam founded to proclaim the word of God to human beings or to put women behind *purdah*? If you read the current discussions of the subject, you might well be left with the impression that Christianity was founded to lower women in the sight of men and Islam founded to put women out of sight of men. Yet, when one mixes with Christians and Muslims, one finds such a conclusion (that the be-all and end-all of these religions is to oppress women) often inconsistent with, in fact obnoxious to, the evidence of daily life. However, it is a fact that the rights of women have often been suppressed in Christianity and Islam, at least in some ways. How do we handle this situation? Or better still, how do we get a handle on this situation? We must distinguish here between intent and impact.

The castigation of religion for its complicity in the oppression of women seems to have reached a point where one may be forgiven for wondering if religions were indeed not set up with this goal in mind. They may have had this effect, this impact, but the clarifying question to ask here is: what do religions set out to accomplish by themselves? Or to be even more forthright, what is religion? What does it intend?

I would like to adopt the approach here that a widespread, if not universal, feature that makes religion unique is "its concern with what is variously called salvation or liberation."[1] Religions look upon themselves not as instruments of oppression of women but as avenues of salvation, of emancipation, for human beings. I propose then that for the purposes of our discussion we view a religion in terms of its soteriological intention and never lose sight of this fact. This is the second point I wish to make.

My third point has to do with the category of religion itself. By religion I mean world religions – not the world's religions nor religion in the abstract. This is important because it is in relation to the world religions, as distinguished from world's religions, that the soteriological claim I just alluded to has been made most explicitly. The seven religions conventionally listed as world religions comprise two religions from India: Hinduism and Buddhism; two from China: Confucianism and Taoism; and the three Abrahamic religions: Judaism, Christianity and Islam.

In sum then, we have identified the soteriological dimension of religion as its key dimension, in the sense that this is how religion perceives itself, with the recognition that religion is not a uni-dimensional phenomenon and also possesses a pronounced sociological dimension.

"Women"

The next term I wish to take up and clarify is "women." I shall not try to define "women." But I would like to suggest that the differences between men and women are a key issue here, and in this context I would like to make the following two points.

First, we must guard against the danger of overstating the difference between men and women. My standard way of making this point is to state that men have nipples too. The fact that they cannot flaunt them does not mean that they do not have them. There is more. Men have been known to

suffer from breast cancer. There is still more. They have even produced milk
in extremis. The Freudian slip of paper on which I jotted down the source
of this information is lost, but apparently it is so. In this respect I side with
the anonymous comment which appeared in Ann Lander's advice column
– that exquisite barometer of the pressures of American life and culture.
He, or she, wrote:

> Dear Ann, I'm tired of hearing references to the "female mind." The mind is
> not a sex organ. It has no gender. One might as well talk about the female
> liver. Get it?[2]

The point is not trivial because religions typically concern themselves with
the salvation of human beings in general – not so much with that of men
as such or of women as such.

Secondly, when I say that one should not overstate the difference
between men and women, I am not saying that we should understate it.
There are differences between men and women. When a woman says the
biological clock is ticking away, she usually means that she is slipping past
the age of child-bearing. When a man says that his biological clock is
ticking away, I have absolutely no idea what it means. I will say "my biological clock is ticking away" when I am about to die. So much for famous last
words. In view of this complexity, the question arises: what exact degree of
significance, if any, should we attach to the fact that arguably the first disciple of the famous modern Hindu woman saint, Anandamayi Ma, was her
husband Bholanath, and the first follower of Prophet Muhammad, his wife
Khadijah?

The point to be borne in mind is that just as with religion we discovered two tracks although from a distance it might appear as a single line –
the soteriological and the sociological, or at another remove, the secular
and the sacred – the category of women also conceals a duality, nay, even
paradox, just like that of religion. At one level, women are human beings
just like men. At another level they are human beings, different from men.

A GENERAL THEORY

The squaring of these two dualities within the categories of "religion" and
of "women" is the central task of a general theory of religion and women,
or women and religion. However, although we laid out a two-track
approach to the category of religion and a two-track approach to the category of women, the two tracks do not coincide. It is true that they run side
by side, that they fall within each other's magnetic range, and yet – and this

is the important point to make at this moment – they do not coincide. The image which comes to mind is of two separate tracks running alongside but sharing one rail in common – that of humanity. Religion, taking its stand on ultimate truth, addresses humanity soteriologically while sociologically men and women equally compose this humanity. But the tracks of religion and women share only one line in common – their other lines fall on opposite sides, on the distinction between the ultimate reality and human beings for religion and between the sexes for women.

This fact has a profound intellectual consequence. A general theory of "religion and women" is not interchangeable, is not synonymous, with a general theory of "women and religion." A general theory of "religion and women" will be primarily oriented towards religion as a soteriological structure and women as human beings, whereas a general theory of "women and religion" will be primarily oriented toward the social power structure and women in relation to men and toward the role of religion (and specially of its soteriological dimension) in this set-up.

The challenge to negotiate here is first to distinguish between the indivisibility of men and women at the level of the general theory of religion and women, so far as salvation or liberation is concerned, and the invisibility of women at the level of the general theory of women and religion, so far as the power structures are concerned, and then to take both into account. This raises the stupendous question: can the two approaches be considered simultaneously, or only successively?

At this point allow me to lighten the burden of our theme with a personal reminiscence. I was wrestling with this dilemma when I was invited to dinner by my friend and colleague, Katherine K. Young. Her husband is a scientist. As I sat down next to him, he asked, "What are you working on these days? You look run down." "I am feeling debilitated as a result of the prolonged conceptual struggles I am engaged in," I said. "I am trying to develop a general theory of women in world religions." He seemed shocked, almost speechless. Then he began to laugh as he said, "Even Einstein started out with a special theory before he dared to develop a general one." As often happens in these matters, light had come from an unexpected quarter. I apparently had two special theories on my hands rather than a general theory: a theory of "*religion* and women" and a theory of "*women* and religion."

I have now to offer to you a package of two special theories: of religion in relation to women and of women in relation to religion. Each of these I shall offer under five headings: (1) statement; (2) illustration; (3) complexification; (4) limitation; and (5) insight conveyed by the theory.

A Theory of Religion and Women

STATEMENT

The position of women is a soteriological variable. It is a function of the relationship of women with the structure or structures of salvation or liberation found in the religion.

ILLUSTRATION

Eve is associated with the Fall in Christianity and is therefore viewed negatively, but Mary, as the mother of Jesus, is viewed positively, giving rise to her description as the "new Eve" and even to her worship, because she is the medium through which the agent of salvation appears in the world. Neat – too neat, I hear you murmur. You are right. And that brings us to the need to indicate the complexity of this theory, or rather, thesis.

COMPLEXIFICATION

With a social power structure already in place, salvation or liberation may have to find its way around the power structure of society. Soteriology can be subdued by society. The example here is provided by two female figures from the Lingayata movement from medieval India. This movement was "innovative in the sphere of gender relations," and the two "best known women poet–saints" of this movement are Akka Mahadevi and Muktayakka. It is noteworthy in this movement,

> ...that women participated in religious life, theological debates, et cetera, on a par with their male coreligionists; but this does not mean that women's overall position in society changed instantaneously. The life story of Akka Mahadevi can be read as a tale of individual revolt against the kind of male chauvinism that regards women as objects of lust; but we must note that Mahadevi's way out of the problem was to abandon worldly life altogether and to follow a mystic path of self-realization – society and the religious life are here placed in opposition to each other. Muktayakka, on the other hand, did not follow Mahadevi's radical path, and the statements in her *vacanas* are correspondingly less confrontational and extreme. Even her *ankita* (the short phrase, or word, which the authors of *vacanas* insert in their compositions as a mark of their authorship), which refers to her brother, indicates a compliant subordination, just as other female authors refer to their husbands. Obviously, there were limits to feasible change, given the circumstances of that time. [3]

LIMITATION

The impression the foregoing discussion might create is that, although a religion sets out to redeem all human beings, it is not able to fulfill this promise as it gets trapped in the structures of society, where the differences between men and women block or at least complicate its unfettered operation, and the operation of the soteriological impulse is compounded, and even confounded, by the distinction of the sexes.

We must not forget, however, that this distinction between men and women is not the only distinction bifurcating, and dissipating, as it were, the soteriological flow, tempting as it might be to think so. Distinctions of class – that is, distinctions between men and men and women and women – can muddy the waters as well. Sometimes sexual distinction itself becomes assimilated to a class. In classical Hinduism, for instance, both the female sex and the *shudra* class were denied access to Vedic literature. One must be careful here. They were not denied access to salvation; they were denied access to salvation through Vedic study. My point here is that the denial was not confined to women.

INSIGHT

We have stated the thesis, illustrated it, complicated it, delimited it. Now the time has come to ask what insight it offers that otherwise might elude us. To gain this insight we will have to first work our way around a commonly held view that the spiritual, at its highest, is a solvent of gender distinctions.

It can be plausibly argued that most religions of the world openly assert the annulment of male-female distinction at the highest spiritual level. Thus in Christianity it is asserted, in a famous biblical passage, that in Christ there is neither male nor female; according to Islam, Allah neither begets nor is begotten; in Buddhism, enlightenment possesses no gender and the Buddha-nature inheres in all irrespective of physical difference, while in Hinduism the ultimate reality is often indicated by the word Brahman in the neuter gender. I do not wish to deny this point. But I would like to move toward another, impelled by the theory as it were. This point has to do with structures of ultimate reality. Most religious traditions, however, generally regard ultimate reality as beyond the reach of words if not concepts. So, to be more accurate, let me clarify that what I really mean by the structure of ultimate reality is the structure of the imaging of ultimate reality.

If we thus speak imagistically rather than analytically, then ultimate reality has been imaged in what might be called "He" terms and "She" terms, as male or female. It is widely acknowledged that ultimate reality is predominantly represented in "He" terms in the Abrahamic religions, and prominently represented in "She" terms in Taoism and in some forms of Hinduism and Buddhism such as Tantra.

Now, to the extent that the imaging of the ultimate reality in "He" terms or "She" terms may be implicated in patriarchy and needs to be transcended, one route out of this situation could well lie in emphasizing that God's gender is grammatical and not metaphysical. But I would like to introduce another possibility here: that ultimate reality could – and perhaps should – be imaged in terms of the feminine principle for both men and women. I would now like to claim that God is Mother, as a metaphorical truth-claim, may have more truth to it as a claim than the other, that God is Father.

My argument in favor of this position runs as follows. Ultimate reality has been imaged both in masculine and feminine terms. In masculine terms it has often been imaged as Father and in feminine terms often as Mother. But while maternity is a fact, paternity is only a presumption. When I first made this statement in a presentation, the woman scholar who spoke after me went on to say that it is not even a presumption – it is only an opinion. Tempting as it might be to view the history of humanity as a story of its failure to regulate human sexuality, especially in our overheated times, I hesitate to go that far. Suffice it to say that there may be more solid grounds for imaging God as mother than as father, for both men and women.

A Theory of Women and Religion

STATEMENT

The position of women in religion is a political variable, in the sense of having to do with the distribution of power between men and women in society. It is a power variable that appears dressed in the rhetorical vestments of a religious or even soteriological vocabulary. In point of fact it determines, or at least colors, this soteriology.

ILLUSTRATION

In my view, two of the most remarkable social innovations of human ingenuity are the institutions of marriage and monasticism. Perhaps every human being should savor both during a lifetime, though there might be some contention about the order in which they should be experienced. Be that as it may, my purpose in mentioning them here is not to encourage speculation on them as lifestyles but to point out that both have been closely associated with religions, although they involve opposite, even diametrically opposite, perceptions of gender roles. The institution of marriage recognizes their interdependence, while monasticism recognizes their independence. Marriage seems to make the statement that men and women cannot live without each other, or at least should not, while monasticism seems to make the statement that they can, or at least should.

Now, what is interesting from the point of view of the religious cultures of the world is that, be it marriage or monasticism, both have historically involved the subordination of women as a principle of organization. This brings us to the threshold of a paradox. As human beings, religion offers women salvation, but as women it offers them subordination!

COMPLEXIFICATION

A society may adopt several possible attitudes towards existing socio-religious realities, especially if they discriminate against women. It may ignore them. In this it may have the support of religious orthodoxy, if it is true as is widely believed that "Orthodoxy tends to support the status quo whatever it may be."[4] It may try to reform them, as often happens in the case of new religious movements, typically in their early phases before stagnation supersedes the first fine fervor for social change or even revolution. It may try to put the religious abuse to use. This is the most complex maneuver of them all, but encouraging a prevailing practice of religious infanticide, especially female infanticide to control population growth, for instance, is one such possibility. The look of excited horror I always see when I mention this dissuades me from developing this unwholesome point further, except to say that society perhaps can be as pathological, or at least as cynical, in its exploitation of religion, as religion of society.

LIMITATION

The limitation of this theory was brought home to me in a somewhat surprising manner. I once submitted an anthologized account of women saints to a university press for publication. The anonymous reviewer remarked:

> As a text that shows women achieving spiritual heights comparable to those of men within the traditions, this manuscript is situated in a middle ground in a number of current academic controversies, as well as personal conflicts for women. The manuscript offers a middle position between proponents of

feminist or womanist spirituality who argue that traditional religions are irredeemably spiritually bankrupt because of the patriarchal choke-hold that they maintain on women's lives, and proponents of traditional religions, who claim that women can still find a wealth of spiritual treasures within those traditions despite their clearly belittling attitude towards half of their adherents. By showing ways in which women have triumphed within the traditional spiritual pathways, the manuscript provides both evidence in favor of the spiritual value of the traditions for women, and evidence of the abusiveness of traditions, both toward women, and in general.

This passage further clarifies two important points. First, when one addresses the question of the position of women in world religions, that train of investigation must run on two tracks: of women as women and of women as human beings. Second, religions have been more successful in offering spiritual salvation or liberation to women, or liberty, shall we say, rather than equality.

INSIGHT

What insight have we gained by this exercise? We have advanced our discussion further by engaging in it, but in a subtle way. Permit me to explain. It is a common frustration of feminism that women all over the world, in all religions, do not make a common cause – rise as one "man," as it were, against men, when all presumably suffer from the same patriarchal domination. This frustration is similar to the communist frustration that workers all over the world did not rise against all capitalists the world over simultaneously. That German workers should have gone to war with Russian workers, when both of them should have been jointly overthrowing their respective capitalist exploiters, is the ultimate scandal of and in Marxism.

Why then do Hindu women not join hands with Christian women to overthrow male domination both in India and in the U.S.A.? Why do some Hindu feminists criticize Western feminists as cultural imperialists instead? The conventional explanation has been that religion is a marker of cultural identity. In the Indian response to Western colonialism, Hinduism – no matter how internally repressive – became a symbol of identity of the people in their struggle against the external oppression represented by British Rule. The eighteen thousand Indian women who were imprisoned during the Salt March were not about to join British suffragettes just because they were all women – national and cultural difference overwhelmed gender identity.

The new perspective I am advocating suggests that this explanation, although important, may also be incomplete and that at least part of the reason why Indian and British women could not join hands is because Hindu women did not merely derive their national identity through Hinduism but because Hinduism may have met their soteriological needs in a way other religions do not. And that is why they remain Hindu and not merely for reasons of identity. I am not denying the question of cultural identity, but I am claiming that there might be more to the Hindu identity than just "identity," something qualitatively "Hindu" as well. If such were not the case, we should have had more Pandita Ramabais than we have.

Pandita Ramabai was a high-caste Hindu widow, proficient in Sanskrit learning, who converted to Christianity almost a hundred years ago, and our theory enables us to appraise her case in a new light. To many of her contemporary Hindus, her conversion amounted to an act of betrayal. Our theory enables us to say that this response is perhaps understandable, given the unfortunate political relationship existing between India and Britain at the time, but offers a very limited perspective on her case, for it overlooks the fact that she may have converted to Christianity not merely to escape the structures of oppression which traditional Hindu society imposes on a widow but also because she may have found salvation more easily within her reach in a church than in a temple.

CONCLUSION

Now you are bound to want to ask me where the truth lies, or the same question in a more personalized form – where do I think the truth lies? Which of the two theories is true or at least possesses more explanatory power – the theory of "religion and women" or the theory of "women and religion"? My answer to the question at this stage of the game must be that I do not know! The answer is, I admit, a "cop-out," an evasion of truth perhaps. Or is it? I am reminded here of physicist Böhr's famous comment: "The opposite of a profound truth is also profound."

The universe, as we know it, hangs out there (wherever "there" is) as an ambiguous entity. One can offer a plausibly naturalistic explanation of it. One can also offer an equally plausible theistic, or let us say religious, explanation of it. If the universe itself is so ambiguous in this way, should we be too surprised that elements within this universe are equally ambiguous? I am not saying that things within the universe have to be ambiguous, just because the universe is ambiguous. I am saying that this ambiguity regarding institutions in relation to soteriology – as to whether socio-economic and political structures control a soteriology or whether a soteriology is versatile and potent enough to capture them for its own purpose – can be viewed, in a sense, as a scaled-down version of a larger problem.

If we regard the current and regnant view that religions are exploitative of women, as a version of the sociological approach to the study of religion, then the following remarks made by John Hick, some of which I anticipated a moment ago, become relevant:

> I believe that the universe is religiously ambiguous, in the sense that complete and coherent religious interpretations, such as are offered by the different religious systems, and also complete and coherent naturalistic interpretations of it, whether sociological, psychological or biological, or all three together, are alike possible.
>
> Neither a religious nor a naturalistic understanding of the universe can be objectively established. Both have the status of faiths. Neither the fact that at one time most people lived within a religious worldview, nor the fact that in our own society today most people live within a naturalistic worldview, takes those worldviews out of the category of faiths. The justification for a religious response to the mystery of the universe lies (in my opinion) in the basic empiricist principle that it is rational to trust our experience, except when there is specific reason not to, and the extension of this principle, impartially, to religious experience.[5]

Earlier on I raised the question of where the truth lies. I said that I did not know the answer, but I would now like to suggest that although we are not any closer to finding an answer to the question, we may have moved, by now, a little closer, not to answering the question to be sure, but to facing the dilemma posed by the question more squarely. The question now becomes: what should be one's approach to questions of women's rights as "believers," so to say, in either a religious tradition or an academic tradition of studying religion.

If we accept the empiricist principle proposed by John Hick, then its application yields two results. If we consult our experience in the matter, then both these statements seem to have the status of facts: (1) that the religious structures associated with religions have often compromised the rights of women; and (2) that these same religions have brought salvation; or if not salvation, then solace; and if not solace, then certitude; or if not certitude, then at least larger structures of meaning, to millions of their followers, men and women. As we move toward a general theory, then, we must necessarily take both of these facts into account, and must include within our general theory the insights of both the special theories of "women and religion" and of "religion and women."

NOTES

1. John H. Hick, *Philosophy of Religion*, fourth edition (Englewood Cliffs, New Jersey: Prentice Hall, 1990), p. 3.
2. *Gazette* (Montreal), 3 February, 1998, p. D4.
3. Robert J. Zydenbos, "Virasaivism, Caste, Revolution, Etc." *Journal of the American Oriental Society,* 117, 3, 1997, pp. 533–534.
4. Ibid., p. 531, note 36.
5. See "The Subjective and Objective Dimensions of the Study of Religion: A Panel Discussion," in *Religious Traditions,* vols. 18–20, 1995–1997, p. 106.

Plate 9 Main altar of the Kuan-Yin Hall at the Chuang Yen Chinese Buddhist Monastery. On the left is a wooden image of Kuan-Yin, the bodhisattva of compassion, from the Tang dynasty (618–907 CE) and in the center-back a Ming dynasty (1368–1644 CE) image, the largest porcelain Kuan-Yin in the world. Avalokiteshvara, the male bodhisattva of compassion from India, underwent a gender transformation in China, becoming the feminine Kuan-Yin. Carmel, New York State, U.S.A. Photo: *Joseph Runzo.*

9

THE REAL TROUBLE *with* CONFUCIANISM

Vivian-Lee Nyitray

Scholars of Chinese religions will immediately recognize the title of this paper as a reference to *The Trouble with Confucianism*, in which Wm. Theodore de Bary suggests that the greatest difficulty Confucianism faces as it moves into the twenty-first century – indeed, has always faced – is the tension produced when an elite group of scholars, steeped in moral philosophy and imbued with a vision of a perfect(ed) society, find themselves laboring uncomfortably under the auspices of an authoritarian political system not of their own making.[1] Characterizing Confucian scholars as "prophets," de Bary sees such individuals as the traditional holders of moral conscience and the modern defenders of human rights and dignity – struggling against authoritarian and hierarchical governmental structures.

While not denying de Bary's thesis, I have long held a different view of "the trouble with Confucianism." I suggest that the Confucian vision, clear and well-focused in its inception, came over time to betray a peculiar myopia – a shortsightedness that, although understandable, has left its modern heirs facing a series of challenges that may prove its undoing. The "real" trouble with Confucianism today is that it has not yet addressed complex questions of sex, gender, and human relationality that occupy modern civil societies.

CAUTIONS AND CAVEATS

In surveying the Confucian sex-gender system, this chapter can do little more than "look at the flowers while galloping on horseback." It cannot begin to address alternative religious paths for women found in Taoist,

Buddhist, or shamanic traditions, even though it is rarely helpful and almost never tenable to discuss any single Chinese religion by itself. A myriad of competing religious, philosophical, and socio-cultural elements impinged on Confucianism throughout its history, forcing varying degrees of accommodation and refutation. Accordingly, we must be careful not to conflate Confucianism with Chinese culture, or with the cultures of Korea, Japan, and Vietnam, despite the tremendous weight of Confucian thought and practice in all these areas.[2]

This brings us to a second caution: despite a strong tendency toward intellectual conservatism, we must be careful not to project a monolithic continuity upon the tradition. The term "Confucianism" suggests a single or unified entity, but it would be far more accurate to speak of a plurality of "Confucian traditions" evolving over time. History demonstrates that the ambivalent Confucian regard for women's capabilities and the circumscribing of their spiritual potentialities varied greatly, expanding and contracting in response to shifts in state ideology, local culture, economic circumstances, general literacy rates, and levels of male scholarly anxiety.

The aims of this chapter are, first, to display something of the historical vicissitudes of the Confucian sex–gender system, and secondly, to speculate as to whether contemporary Confucian traditions have the resources to adjudicate conflicting desires to honor intellectual precedents and yet craft practical responses to questions about the real trouble it now faces.

ORIGINS AND EVOLUTION

Confucius himself had virtually nothing to say about women – merely describing them as "difficult to deal with" (*Analects* 17: 25), presumably because their relative lack of education in ritual matters and in the cultivation of virtue left them unable to negotiate social relations with grace. Such difficulties notwithstanding, there is little in the early texts of the school to deny women access to the education which would make them virtuous and ritually refined. In the *Book of Changes* (*Yijing*), women are considered to be the human manifestation of the *yin* cosmic principle, identified with the hexagram *kun*, "the receptive, the earth." The notable characteristics of the hexagram are its yielding devotion and quiet perseverance, in contrast to the activity of *yang*-identified heaven. The key image is one of an overarching complementarity of *yang*-heaven-male and *yin*-earth-female, with the latter in the yielding or deferential position.

Elsewhere, this early ideal of female submission is displayed in the differential treatment of infants described in the *Book of Odes* (*Shijing*):

> A son will be born
> And put to sleep upon the bed.
> He will be wrapped in fine robes
> And given a jade scepter to play with.
> A daughter will be born
> And put upon the ground.
> She will be wrapped in cloths
> And given tiles to play with.[3]

Confucian ritual texts such as the *Book of Rites* (*Liji*), compiled during the early Han dynasty (202 BCE–8 CE), also stressed the importance of maintaining distinctions between men and women. Except at sacrifices and funerals, they should not hand items to each other, nor should they share the same mat when lying down. They should not wear similar clothing, or even hang their garments upon the same stand, peg, or rack. A house where propriety was observed was one in which women did not come out into the exterior apartments but remained secluded in the inner quarters.[4]

Few non-elite households followed these restrictions closely, but the general principle of maintaining distinctions between males and females was widely adhered to. The devaluation of daughters was more commonplace, as it derived from a desire to regulate bloodlines through surname exogamous marriage, i.e. marrying a spouse with a different surname. Given the relatively low number of surnames in China, this practice often entailed village exogamy as well, for it could happen that everyone in a small village held only one or two surnames. Girls were thus only temporary residents in their natal homes, raised for their labor value and future bride price.[5]

Once married, a woman's principal duty was the production of a son and heir. Other overt religious duties for women concerned preparing sacrificial altars by setting up the requisite ritual implements; preparing the liquors, sauces, and preserved foods used in the rites; and observing the ceremonies. In these ways, women's performance was understood to reflect and thereby complete the actions of male participants. Women, together with men, were to find spiritual fulfillment in the performance of ritual activities and in the cultivation of harmonious social relations; in this way, they would assist in the transforming powers of Heaven and Earth.

While Confucian tenets were contested and codified during the Han dynasty, the ambiguity of women's roles and status persisted. Women were socially subordinated to men, but they were capable of demonstrating a broad spectrum of virtues, both moral and intellectual. The archivist Liu Xiang (77–6 BCE) compiled his *Biographies of Exemplary Women* (*Lienü zhuan*), a collection in which virtuous women exemplified filiality, loyalty, and other core Confucian virtues; they were shown to adeptly criticize husbands, sons, and on occasion, even their rulers for failure to heed good advice or fulfill their responsibilities.[6]

Of all the virtues displayed, the text underscores the role women play as primary educators of the young by presenting lives of virtuous mothers as the first chapter. So encompassing is this responsibility that it begins at conception; an expectant mother should see her body as a conduit and expose the fetus only to uplifting sights and sounds (1.6). The domestic example of a wife and mother is thus crucial for the development of a family's moral standards and its public stature.

The most famous maternal exemplar is Mother Meng, widowed mother of Mencius (371–289 BCE?), the great interpreter of Confucian thought. Foreshadowing her son's later emphasis on the crucial role of environment in the cultivation of innate moral potential, Mother Meng shifted her residence three times in search of the most edifying influences: their first home abutted a cemetery (where young Mencius and his friends played at the unseemly game of conducting funerals); their second house was close by the marketplace (where Mencius played shopkeeper and devised cunning methods of enhancing his profits); and their third adjoined an academy (where Mencius now played at performing sacrificial rites and emulating scholarly etiquette). In another incident, Mother Meng provide an object lesson in the need for industriousness by ripping up her own weaving – the source of their livelihood – when Mencius fell lax in his studies. Later in life, Mencius entered his wife's chambers and, finding her less than fully dressed, threatened to divorce her for lack of decorum; his mother dissuaded him by asserting that the fault was his for having gone in unbidden and unexpectedly (1.11).[7]

Unfortunately, such edifying examples of female potential were overshadowed during the course of the later Han (25–220 CE) through the syncretic appropriation of *yin-yang* cosmology. The grafting of *yin-yang* theories onto the core of Confucian ideas on morality, ritual, and human relationship during this period led to a proliferation of gender hierarchies within the tradition. Han cosmology favored the hierarchy of *yin-yang*, perhaps to underscore the qualities of the ruler (*yang*) over the ruled (*yin*). As many scholars have noted elsewhere, the unfortunate consequence was

that *yang* (strength, growth, light, life) was given primacy over its comple-
ment, *yin* (weakness, decay, darkness, death). Although the human
heart–mind was seen to possess both rational and emotional qualities, the
latter was ascribed to *yin* and thought to cause disorder and error; *yang* was
accordingly more highly regarded and ultimately seen as morally superior.[8]

Pre-Confucian customs of patrilineality and patrilocality fused with the
Confucian imperative to educate, cultivate, and control the self – to the
detriment of traits and persons associated with *yin*. Thus by the end of the
Han, although women were not perceived as without potential for either
virtue or knowledge, the essentializing tendency to associate them with *yin*
worked to undermine their accomplishments or to valorize them primarily
in the service of larger family or state needs.

Examples of this trend toward the conflation of sex and gender are
readily found in didactic texts for women, the earliest of which was Ban
Zhao's (c.48–c.120 CE) *Instructions for Women* (*Nüjie*). Such texts reinforced images of female subordination drawn from classic texts such as the
Book of Odes and the *Book of Rites* and symbolically consigned women to
the domestic sphere. Ban Zhao was an imperial tutor who decried the trend
in her own day to neglect women's education beyond an elementary level,
yet she herself promulgated an unambiguous view of women's primary
duty as "humbling herself before others" (*Instructions for Women* 1).
Tellingly, her call for girls' education stemmed not from a belief in the
ability of women to progress toward sageliness or moral nobility but rather
from her belief that unless women were educated the efficacious performance of family rites would be jeopardized.

During the Six Dynasties period (420–589), the dominance of Confucian ideology collapsed under foreign rule and the displacement of court
intellectuals. The subsequent Sui-Tang dynasties (589–907) witnessed the
rise of Taoist and Buddhist influence, both of which provided alternative
understandings of sex, gender, and abstract notions of "the feminine." The
exemplary biographies of this era emphasized filiality for both men and
women, thereby acknowledging the emotional ties that bound women to
their natal families. Widow remarriage was not prohibited, and a generally
extended concept of family was reflected in the Tang legal code, in which
even married-out daughters could inherit property in certain circumstances.

Once again, the ambiguity of women's roles was clear. Subject to the
constraints of "thrice following" (*san cong*), i.e. following the dictates of
father, husband, and eldest son over the course of life, women were

nevertheless granted some legal recognition and were placed on a pedestal as "moral custodians" of their households.⁹ This dual sensibility is illustrated in the early eighth-century *Classic of Filial Piety for Women* (*Nü xiaojing*), wherein the narrator, in the voice of Ban Zhao, enjoins women to lead their fathers, husbands, and sons to improve their character through their own modeling of virtue and through their artful use of ritual and music (2.17).

The Song dynasty (960–1279) witnessed the revitalization of Confucianism. Self-cultivation now incorporated meditation and other forms of quiet sitting borrowed from Buddhist and Taoist interior spiritual practices – a shift that increasingly emphasized the need to eliminate distraction and quell one's passions. Not surprisingly, ambivalence toward women increased. As essentialized representations of *yin*, they required regulation and restriction lest they instigate male passion; this was to be accomplished through strictly prescribed education for women in matters of family ritual and domestic routine.¹⁰

Close reading of Song documents, especially the manuals of "family instruction" privately produced by scholars, yields a sense of a tradition straining to reconcile appreciation for womanly talent with the need to constrain female sexuality by advocating such concepts as "chastity" (*jie*) for both the unmarried and the widowed. Typical of the sentiments of the time are the words of the late twelfth-century pragmatist Yuan Cai. He admitted that some women with stupid, unworthy, or inept husbands somehow managed their families on their own, e.g. keeping the accounts and not allowing others to take advantage of them. These were "wise and worthy women."¹¹ It was regrettable when women had to assume public duties, but Yuan admitted that the alternative – prohibiting women from assuming control of a household – would yield grave and unacceptable consequences for the family.

The early Neo-Confucian philosopher Cheng Yi (1033–1107) sought to preserve family integrity by condemning widow remarriage, even when the woman had no means of support: "To starve to death is a very small matter; to lose one's integrity, however, is a grave matter."¹² Soon after, Zhu Xi (1130–1200) brought his formidable intellect and scholarship to bear on the problem of reinvigorating Confucianism. In his compilation of the teachings of earlier Neo-Confucian masters, Zhu reproduced Cheng Yi's dictum regarding widow remarriage in the hopes of discouraging a practice that was still widespread during the Song, even among those of the upper class.¹³ Zhu expressed his admiration for widows who committed suicide rather than submit to remarriage or who mutilated their faces to make themselves unmarriageable.[14]

Zhu's role in delineating Confucian attitudes toward sex and gender cannot be overstated. His was not the only voice, but it was his edited versions of two chapters of the *Book of Rites* ("Centrality and Commonality" and "The Great Learning"), along with the *Analects* and the writings of Mencius, that came to be elevated as the "Four Books." When Neo-Confucianism was again established by the state in the later Yuan and Ming dynasties (1280–1368–1644), the Four Books formed the basis for the imperial examination system. For centuries thereafter, Zhu's word was orthodoxy, and his visions normative.[15]

Several recent studies analyze Zhu's understanding of sex and gender. Ping-cheung Lo argues that the Cheng-Zhu school had a strong ascetic tendency, leading most later "Chinese intellectuals" to adopt "a rather negative and mortifying attitude toward sexual desire."[16] Zhu Xi does not explicitly discuss sexual matters, but Lo sees Zhu's extensive commentaries on "preserving the heavenly principle and mortifying human desires" as constituting an implicit sexual ethic. Lo concludes that Zhu Xi's condemnation of the erotic ballads of the *Book of Odes*, his understanding of marriage as undertaken for the survival of the family rather than for companionship, and his general advocacy of eliminating "selfish desire" combine to render romantic love obscene and licentious (even between a married couple), and sex acceptable only for procreation.

Bret Hinsch details Zhu's expectation that men could find heavenly principles within themselves through self-mastery and introspection, whereas women's inferior *yin* nature dictated their dependence on the actions of fathers, husbands, and sons "to force them into conformity with cosmic order."[17] For Zhu, the path to human tranquility and cosmic harmony was through adherence to the natural hierarchical distinctions of *yang* over *yin*, male over female, and men over women. Hinsch further suggests that Neo-Confucian philosophers melded classical references with both traditional and new cosmologies to provide explicit justification for the social subordination of women and *yin*-identified individuals, based sometimes – although not necessarily in the case of Zhu Xi – on their own antipathies toward the powerful women, eunuchs, and homosexual favorites who were their rivals in palace politics.[18]

Over the course of the Ming dynasty (1368–1644), the strictures proposed by Neo-Confucian literati permeated the broader social structure. Household instructions and regulations proliferated; the number of stipulations on women exceeded Song times by far, with restrictions on women becoming ever more tedious and severe. For example, by the age of eight, a daughter was expected to learn the *Instructions for Women* and *Biographies of Exemplary Women* by rote. Ban Zhao's call for women's education centuries earlier was thus ironically realized; instead of clarifying and promoting regard for women's status, however, her work (or one similar) was often their sole curriculum. Illustrated and easy to read, such primers became extremely popular, even among commoners.[19]

The definition of womanly virtue in terms of wifely fidelity or chastity advanced through the Ming and into the early-mid Qing dynasty (through the mid-nineteenth century). During this period of Confucian intellectual dominance, the Qing interest in "Han learning" differed from earlier revivals in that its reach extended directly down to the commoner class and was focused less on the personal cultivation of sageliness than on discerning the contours of ideal family life. State-supported "Han learning" promoted the reexamination of classical texts to discern and define these ideals, with chastity becoming the most vaunted moral quality for women. So valued was chastity that under the 1646 rape law, rape victims could be forced to defend their chastity with their lives.[20] Stories and portraits of women cutting their flesh to feed their in-laws were omnipresent, as were images of chaste young widows languishing in the deep recesses of the inner quarters (or committing suicide rather than be forced into remarriage). These ideals of the "virtuous wife and good mother" became deeply rooted in the popular imagination, the product of continuous oral transmission and of literary reproduction in almanacs, popular morality books, and primers.[21]

Yet even in these more repressive eras, discordant notes were sounded. The otherwise conservative text of the *Training for the Inner Quarters* (*Neixun*) upheld the Neo-Confucian claim that all people can become sages, here extending the notion to include women, urging them to keep watch on their thoughts and to cultivate sageliness, a jewel more precious than pearls or jade (3.22).[22] Scholars such as Lü Kun (1536–1618) advocated complementarity rather than hierarchy as the defining characteristic of the marital relationship; Yu Zhengxie (1775–1840), a prominent critic of footbinding and widow chastity, invoked a classic Han dynasty text, *Discourses in the White Tiger Hall* (*Bohu tong*), to support his refutation of women's subordination in marriage; and, most radically, the late Qing visionary Kang Yuwei (1858–1927) outlined an overhaul of social practice that included advocacy of free choice of marriage partners, no-fault divorce, and the positing of the mutuality of friendship rather than the hierarchical division of labor as defining the marital bond. His reform efforts caught the imagination of the young Guangxu emperor in 1898, but it was a mere hundred days before they were quashed ruthlessly by the empress dowager.[23]

Scholarly efforts notwithstanding, it was the Confucian-sanctioned images of the good wife, obedient daughter-in-law, virtuous mother, and chaste widow which prevailed at the turn of the past century, and against which feminists and socialists railed. Beginning in the 1910s and 1920s, social reformers rallied against the degradation of women, typified for them by footbinding, female infanticide, and the wholesale trade in women as brides, concubines, and slaves. None of these practices was inherently Confucian, but together they were emblematic of the subordination of women endemic to the Neo-Confucian sex-gender system.

REFORMS AND RETRENCHMENTS

Both the Nationalist and Communist political parties held that changes in women's status was a fundamental condition for China's modernization; however, on both sides of the Taiwan Straits, drives to dismantle Confucian patriarchy proved to be a movement of both forward and backward momentum. Not uncommonly, efforts to improve the condition of women fell into disarray or were coopted into some larger ideal. The experience of the early Communist Party provides an instructive illustration. Despite their commitment to gender equality, the liberation of women had more symbolic than actual import, and the party often reinscribed traditional gender models. Women who did reach positions of power were either childless or else sent their children off to be raised by relatives; barring this, they found themselves cast in support roles – organizing and nurturing their comrades in ways compatible with maternal experiences.[24]

It is true, however, that once ensconced in power, the Party revamped the Chinese educational system to afford women greater access. What Party leaders underestimated was the degree of resistance such changes would encounter, as demonstrated by the differential impact of these policies in rural versus urban areas: after a decade of implementation, the proportion of girls in primary schools increased only modestly, from 25 percent in 1949 to 30 percent in 1958. Beyond the primary level, few rural girls went on to middle and high schools, as these were located in the cities. Moreover, "peasants in particular were still reluctant to 'waste' education on girls."[25]

The 1950 Marriage Law similarly aimed to improve the status of women by abolishing "the arbitrary and compulsory feudal marriage system which was based on the idea of the superiority of man over woman and which ignores the interests of children." Free choice of marriage partner, monogamy, and the rights of both parties to divorce were mandated, and concubinage, child betrothal, interference with the remarriage of widows, and betrothal gifts were outlawed. However, as sociologist Margaret Ann Franklin has observed, it was here that the full force of conservative resistance appeared. Husbands did not want to lose wives for whom they had paid good money, and mothers-in-law did not want to lose daughters-in-law; peasant families saw their economic security threatened by divorce proceedings. All these parties brought pressure on women to drop their divorce cases, and women who persisted were often harassed, driven to suicide, or murdered. By 1955 it was estimated that 70,000 to 80,000 women were

> dying annually as a result of disputes with their families. Faced with the fact that most peasants, male and female, were not prepared to sacrifice the security of the family for the happiness of any individual member, the Communist Party abandoned its policy of making divorces easy to obtain.[26]

In 1956, the Party introduced "The Five Goods Program," which emphasized the importance of good housekeeping, advising women that "to diligently and thriftily manage a home" was as much a woman's job as building the nation.[27] Promulgation of this campaign coincided with the Party's efforts to respond to conservative social forces and with an economic downturn that made it difficult for women to find employment outside the home; the "Five Goods" campaign met these competing needs by valorizing traditional notions of the virtuous wife and good mother while now declaring her a model citizen as well.

The tide appeared to turn in 1958 when the "Great Leap Forward" brought a reversal of these ideals. The shift toward industrialization and the establishment of communes created a need for "Iron Girls" to "hold up half the sky," and the rampant iconoclasm of the Cultural Revolution (1966–76) seemed to sound the death knell for Confucian "feudalism." Why then did the 1980s see the resurrection of the traditional image of wife and mother, only slightly transformed into a consumer-oriented model?

Harriet Evans' recent studies of efforts during the 1950s to provide the public with a "scientific" understanding of sex suggest that the "evidence" of these campaigns continued to define popular attitudes toward sex and gender through the 1980s (and on up to the present).[28] Claiming to advance "scientific" knowledge that would foster women's emancipation, the official 1950s discourse on sexuality perpetuated the essentialist conflation of sexuality and gender. Free-choice monogamous marriage was implemented to protect women from male abuse; however, as the only legitimate expression of sexuality, the monogamous relationship sharply defined gender behavior.

Monogamy was also represented as the wife's obligation to

> support her husband's interests and service his needs, whether as the self-sacrificing manager of his domestic affairs or as his moral guide. Women who went too far in questioning the implied gender constructs by postponing marriage, by "refusing to see their husbands" for fear of becoming pregnant, or by spending too much time trying to acquire an education were constructed as the equivalent of gender deviationists – women who through betrayal of their proper gender attributes brought disruption and conflict.[29]

Notably, heterosexuality is portrayed as natural and thus the only sanctioned sexuality; sexuality is conflated with reproduction; and gender characteristics of women are inseparable from their reproductive functioning. Evans' analysis further exposes the gender distinctions presented in discussions of reproduction and contraception as replicating the traditional asymmetry between *yin* and *yang*: male desire is sudden and powerful, but female desire is gentle and responsive. "Indications that female desire could exist independently of male stimulation were associated with danger, abnormality, and harm."[30] Female sexuality is thus defined in relation to the dominance of masculinity and male desire.

The final aspect of Evans' work that commands attention concerns the 1950s promotion of sexual hygiene during menstruation and pregnancy, in which advice on hygenic practices

> reinforced the view that women were particularly vulnerable to disease because of their reproductive function. Despite the assertion that menstruation was a "normal physiological function," medical opinion continued to place women in what Charlotte Furth [has] called the "not-quite-well" category [in her studies of Qing dynasty views of menstruation and pregnancy].[31]

For all the "scientific evidence" marshalled in these campaigns, the essentialist identification of women with reproduction continued, as did the designation of women as "naturally" weak, yielding, and in need of male stimulation and/or assistance. In short, women were defined as inferior against a masculine norm, both biologically and sociologically.

Thirty years later, biology is still destiny. Women, not men, are restricted from some occupations for fear that their reproductive capacities will be damaged – even as the state attempts to implement its "one child" policy.[32] Moreover, women, not men, are punished for out-of-quota births, and women are subjected to the "three surgeries" (abortion, IUD insertion, and sterilization). Male contraceptive use lags far behind.[33]

Across the Straits in Taiwan, the story is much the same. The grip of traditional notions of sex and gender has tightened and loosened over the decades. Particularly during periods of political entrenchment or economic hardship, Confucian dictates for women were either relaxed or promulgated of necessity. Following the traditional ideal of the "virtuous wife and good mother" sometimes required women to work outside the home to assist in the tasks of nation-building, as when the Nationalists were establishing their base-in-exile on Taiwan during the 1950s. At other times, as in the economic boom years of the 1970s, women were urged to stay home and enjoy the benefits of middle-class prosperity – as well as free jobs for young men who might otherwise emigrate. Emphasizing Taiwan's role as custodian of tradition, the government stressed preservation of the "Three Bonds" of respect for ruler-state, father, and husband, thereby effectively joining Nationalist patriotism to Confucian patriarchy.

In 1974, Lu Hsiu-lien published *New Feminism* (*Xin nüxing zhuyi*), arguing that patriarchal values continued to control women's lives and calling the Confucian tradition to accountability. Its texts, she said, were written by men for men, and its goals were impossible for women to pursue.[34] Lu was castigated for "encouraging promiscuity," and her criticism of "one-sided chastity" was read not as a condemnation of male behavior but as an incitement to female wantonness. She was accused of wanting to destabilize society, a task which she planned to carry out by "encouraging disputes between husbands and wives of high-ranking officials so as to break up their marriages."[35] Eventually, Lu's dual involvement with feminist causes and the Taiwan independence movement led to her imprisonment. After her release, she continued her feminist activism and was eventually elected to the Executive Yuan, the legislative branch of office. Victories are always contextual, however, as proved by Lu's experience as section chief of the Commission on Law and Regulation: for one half day every month, she had to recess from her legislative duties to fulfill her obligation as a patriotic woman by sewing pants for soldiers.[36]

PROBLEMS AND POSSIBILITIES

The introduction to this chapter suggested that modern Confucians face a series of challenges that may prove to be the undoing of the tradition. As we have seen "while galloping on horseback," problems concerning sex, gender, and human relationality are multiple and persistent. Rather than reiterate them at length, it is worth considering in the space that remains just why Confucian ideals are so stubbornly present and vociferously defended – and whether or not the tradition possesses the resources necessary to craft a new vision for itself.

We know that every individual life is ineluctably touched by the dictates of historical circumstance, locale, and the differential appropriation of religious and social ideals occasioned by class. We know too that notions such as "valuing boys and slighting girls" held by the common people always differed from the concept of "male superior and female inferior" held by the educated upper classes and promoted by elite Confucian culture. Rural families historically relied on female as well as male labor for productivity, and their expectations of women's behavior were tempered by practical concerns. Therefore, although we may generalize that from Song times onward, the concepts of "thrice following" and "four virtues"[37] were widely accepted, we also know that such ideals were mutable.

It is not unreasonable, then, to find that modifications of traditional formulations of sex and gender continue to arise. In the People's Republic, population control billboards exhort expectant parents to believe that "Girl or Boy, either is fine!" Similar slogans adorn buses in Taiwan. Son preference is weakening as factors such as retirement pensions and the need for greater mobility in search of jobs and housing render patrilineal ties less compelling. The trend away from son preference has been accompanied by the increasing prevalence of a neolocal pattern of residence after marriage, i.e. the married couple live separately from either set of parents. Neolocal residence is now more common than the traditional patrilocal arrangement, although popular sentiment for the patrilocal form persists.[38]

Due to the increasing prevalence of nuclear families and to economic developments that facilitate the maintenance of natal ties, filial daughters are again prominent and distinctly appreciated. Over the past two decades, daughters have assumed broader and longer-term responsibilities for their parents as well as parents-in-law. Filiality now extends far beyond a woman's "maiden years," and offers the potential for increased valuation of women that encompasses more than their fertility.[39]

The five cardinal relationships of the Confucian system offer no images of women in relation to each other beyond the mother-daughter bond (traditionally valued most highly in its altered form of mother- and daughter-in-law).[40] "Sisterhood" is not natural to this system, and the bond of "friendship" for women was historically fragile and often fleeting, dependent for maintenance on factors beyond women's control. Hierarchy rather than lateral ties characterize women's relations with each other, and there is little discussion of women as peers, equals, or "sisters." Throughout Confucian East Asia, "women" as a category of analysis separate from class or kinship is a recent construct. Under whatever rubric, however, women are increasingly politically active, especially in educational, consumer, and environmental affairs understood to be extensions of their concerns at home. Once inaugurated, the growth of "women's consciousness" is perhaps less likely to recede as women increasingly gain emotional sustenance from each other as well as through the traditional Confucian roles of daughter, wife, and mother.

As the classical boundaries of domesticity are expanded, the tradition moves ever closer to reconfiguring the basic social unit of the family. And it is here, I suggest, that the tradition will either stand or fall. The greatest challenge to Confucianism today lies in renegotiating a sense of family in a conceptual environment besieged by the forces of industrialization, urbanization, education, population growth policies, and appeals to Enlightenment-based notions of autonomous individuals in a civil society. Traditionally, and as diagrammed in "The Great Learning," the fruits of Confucian self-cultivation radiate outward in ever-widening circles of influence. The family is where one first learns ritual interaction and is the first recipient of one's cultivated virtue. Thus, far from being merely a political or economic unit, in Confucianism the family is understood to be a profoundly religious unit, a venue for self-transformation and the springboard to public application of one's personal virtue.

At this point, we reach a critical observation, namely, that any rethinking of Confucianism in order to address gender issues will necessarily require acceptance of the deeply and specifically religious aspects of that tradition. There have been several "New Confucians" who have made explicit their sense of Confucianism as a religious tradition, among them the late Mou Zongsan and, currently, Tu Weiming.[41] Tu is also attentive to feminist questions, although there has yet to appear a lengthy feminist analysis of Confucianism in specifically religious – rather than economic, political, or "familial" – terms.

Confucianism is not termed a "religion" (*zongjiao*) in Chinese, that designation being reserved for Buddhism, Christianity, Islam, Judaism, and some forms of Taoism. Whether or not Confucianism is called by a word or phrase which translates into a Western language term for "religion," however, has no bearing on the fact that it has always functioned as one in Chinese culture. Recognizing Confucianism as a religious system accounts for the inherent power and seeming "naturalness" of its values, and for the longevity of its deeply rooted symbolic structures. In constant conversation over the centuries with prevailing socio-cultural currents in China, what we call "Confucianism" has exhibited a remarkable and paradoxical tension between resistance and accommodation in its adaptations to pressures from competing intellectual and pragmatic systems; it has weathered waves of encounter with Buddhism, urbanization, technological change, and both socialism and capitalism, while maintaining its ideal images and core values. Failure to discuss the tradition as religious thus truncates analysis and forestalls potentially illuminating comparisons with other world religious traditions.[42]

Central to the Confucian tradition is the notion that human beings differ from animals in that our "heart–mind" – seat of rational and emotional faculties – has the capacity to create orderly, harmonious, and aesthetically pleasing relationships among ourselves. Indeed, the highest virtue, *ren* (often translated as humaneness), is that of living in concert with others. The underlying theoretical imperatives are shared respect and deference, as well as mutual responsibility to and for the other. This is the religious ground of Confucianism that can be foregrounded and stripped of centuries of accreted correlative cosmologies, politically inspired concepts of hierarchy and privilege, and plain old human insecurity in the form of male anxiety.

In revisiting Confucian history, and in emphasizing the religious nature of mutual responsibility within the tradition, new possibilities for appreciating human community emerge. To take the issue of sexuality as but one example, it becomes clear that male homosexuality was historically tolerated if it did not displace the marital bond. Today, a curious amnesia exists regarding the long history of homosexuality in China; only the need to face the dangers of HIV and AIDS has forced official recognition of its existence. Of lesbians, even less is said. Ping-cheung Lo has argued that austere attitudes toward sex are as untenable today as they were to the common people of the Ming dynasty, as attested by the proliferation of pornographic materials at that time. And in fact, there were Ming Confucians who expressed their dissatisfaction with the segregation of human desire from "heavenly principle," among them Wang Fuzhi (1619–1692), who articulated the notion of heavenly principle as immanent in human desire. Writing today, Lu sees Wang's vision as a resource for a more plausible Confucian sexual ethics.[43]

It is reasonable to assume that revisiting Lü Kun, Kang Yuwei, and a host of others not named here would provide fertile grounds for reconceiving many aspects of the tradition. Were the conflations of sex, gender, and reproduction undone, a "family" might acceptably comprise working wives and mothers with stay-at-home husbands, childless couples, single parents, and even same-sex partners. Although not adhering to orthodox familial forms, such unions would be valued for their positive contributions to the harmonious functioning of a larger society, and, more important, the individuals involved would be validated in their explorations of new expressions of the traditional virtues of reciprocity, conscientiousness, filiality, and humaneness. New Confucians of recent years have begun to do just this, but the work is far from complete. Resources abound, but trouble lies in the will to discover and in the determination to enact.

There is a Chinese maxim that says, "A woman too well educated is apt to cause trouble." I should like to close this chaper as I began it, with reference to Professor de Bary's praise for modern Confucians as defenders of human rights and dignity. Taking seriously this image and working towards the reenvisioning of traditional ideals, New Confucians might one day find it possible to update this folk saying as follows: "A person well educated is apt to both cause and resolve trouble" – to which we might then add "as all prophets are wont to do."

NOTES

I should like to thank Savita Bal, Matt Center, and Jonathan H. X. Lee, for their research assistance, and I especially want to thank Douglas Oliver for his enthusiasm, patience, and many valuable suggestions.

1.   Wm. Theodore de Bary, *The Trouble with Confucianism* (Cambridge, MA: Harvard University Press, 1991).
2.   The present study will focus primarily on the Chinese cultural areas of the People's Republic of China and Taiwan, although brief mention will be made of Korea and Japan.
3.   *Shijing* Xiaoya II.iv.V.8–9; James Legge, trans. *The She King or The Book of Poetry*, vol. IV, *The Chinese Classics* (Oxford: Oxford University Press, 1871; reprint Hong Kong University Press, 1970), pp. 306–307.

4.   For a complete translation, see James Legge, *The Texts of Confucianism,* vol. 27, *Sacred Books of the East,* ed. F. Max Müller (Oxford: Clarendon, 1885), pp. 454ff.

5.   For detailed analysis, see Du Fangqin, "The Rise and Fall of the Zhou Rites: A Rational Foundation for the Gender Relationship Model," in *"The Chalice and the Blade" in Chinese Culture: Gender Relations and Social Models,* ed. Min Jiayin [for the Chinese Partnership Research Group] (Beijing: China Social Sciences Publishing House, 1995), p. 175.

6.   For further details, see Marina H. Sung, "The Chinese Lieh-nü Tradition," in *Women in China: New Directions in Historical Scholarship,* ed. Richard W. Guisso and Stanley Johannesen (Youngstown, OH: Philo Press, 1981), pp. 63–74; and Lisa Raphals, *Sharing the Light: Representations of Women and Virtue in Early China* (Albany: State University Press of New York, 1998).

7.   Some feminist scholars, especially in the West, are weary of the revisiting of "Mencius' mother" as valorized exemplar. See, for example, Charlotte Furth, "The Patriarch's Legacy: Household Instructions and the Transmission of Orthodox Values," in *Orthodoxy in Late Imperial China,* ed. Kwang-ching Liu (Berkeley: University of California Press, 1990).

8.   For an excellent illustration of the complexity of the Han synthesis, see Terry Woo, "Confucianism and Feminism," in *Feminism and World Religions,* ed. Arvind Sharma (Albany: State University of New York Press, 1999), pp. 120–132. See also Nyitray, "Yin/Yang Polarity," in *Encyclopedia of Women and World Religion,* ed. Serinity Young (New York: Macmillan, 1998).

9.   The concept of *san cong* originated in the *Book of Rites* 1.441, dictating that females "follow" (*cong*) father, husband, or son, in the sense that women were socially ranked at the level of the male head of the household. Later interpretations expanded the notion into a demand for women's submission to authority, leading to its translation as "three obediences." Arguing that this model of total dependence oversimplifies the relationship between the Chinese gender system and Confucian ethics, Dorothy Y. Ko has advocated the use of "thrice following," which I have adopted. See *Teachers of the Inner Chambers: Women and Culture in Seventeenth Century China* (Stanford, CA: Stanford University Press, 1994), pp. 6ff.

10.   Bettine Birge, "Chu Hsi and Women's Education," in *Neo-Confucian Education: The Formative Stage,* ed. Wm. Theodore de Bary and John W. Chaffee (New York: Columbia University Press, 1989).

11.   Cited in Patricia Ebrey, "Women in the Kinship System of the Southern Song Upper Class," in *Women in China,* ed. Guisso and Johannesen, pp. 115ff.

12.   Bret Hinsch notes that Cheng contradicted his own injunction in approving the marriage of a cousin's widowed daughter, a match

arranged by Cheng's father, in "Metaphysics and Reality of the Feminine in Early Neo-Confucian Thought," *Women's Studies International Forum,* 11, 6 (1988), p. 594. I would add that the incident provides an illustration of the sometimes conflicting demands of filiality and propriety.

13. See Wing-tsit Chan, trans., *Reflections on Things at Hand: The Neo-Confucian Anthology* (New York: Columbia University Press, 1967), p. 177 (6.3a).

14. Discussed in Hinsch, "Metaphysics and Reality of the Feminine in Early Neo-Confucian Thought," p. 594.

15. Hinsch has noted that the anti-feminine overtones of Song thought are clearly demonstrated in what he calls the "chilling effects" of the importation of Neo-Confucian doctrines into Korea which included the reversal or destruction of rights women had traditionally enjoyed. Ibid., pp. 591ff.

16. Ping-cheung Lo, "Zhu Xi and Confucian Sexual Ethics," *Journal of Chinese Philosophy,* 20, 4 (December 1993), p. 465.

17. Hinsch, "Metaphysics and Reality," p. 595.

18. Ibid., p. 598.

19. Katherine Carlitz, "Desire, Danger and the Body: Stories of Women's Virtue in Late Ming China," in *Engendering China: Women, Culture, and the State,* ed. Christina Gilmartin (Cambridge, MA: Harvard University Press, 1994). In opposition to these works, Lü Kun (1536–1618) updated the Han text of *Biographies of Exemplary Women* in an effort to augment increasingly prominent images of decorous maidens and chaste widows by resuscitating earlier images of wise wives and mothers.

20. Vivien W. Ng, "Ideology and Sexuality: Rape Laws in Qing China," *Journal of Asian Studies,* 46, 1 (1987), p. 65.

21. On the proliferation of illustrated biographies, see Carlitz, "Desire, Danger and the Body"; on handbooks and primers, see Tienchi Martin-Liao, "Traditional Handbooks of Women's Education," in *Women and Literature in China,* ed. Anna Gerstlacher et al (Bochum: Studienverlag Brockmeyer, 1985).

22. Cited by Theresa Kelleher, "Confucianism," in *Women in World Religions,* ed. Arvind Sharma (Albany: State University of New York Press, 1987), p. 157.

23. On Lü Kun, see Joanna F. Handlin, "Lü K'un's New Audience: The Influence of Women's Literacy on Sixteenth-Century Thought," in *Women in Chinese Society,* ed. Margery Wolf and Roxane Witke (Stanford, CA: Stanford University Press, 1975). On Yu, see Mann, "Grooming a Daughter for Marriage: Brides and Wives in the Mid-Qing Period," in *Marriage and Inequality in Chinese Society,* ed. Rubie Watson and Patricia Ebrey (Berkeley: University of California Press, 1991), p. 211; and Paul Ropp, *Dissent in Early Modern China: Ju-lin Wai-shih and Ch'ing Social Criticism* (Ann Arbor: University of Michigan Press, 1981), pp. 144ff. For a

provocative introduction to Kang, see Jonathan Spence, *The Gate of Heavenly Peace: The Chinese and Their Revolution, 1895–1980* (New York: Viking, 1981).

24. Christina Kelley Gilmartin, *Engendering the Chinese Revolution: Radical Women, Communist Politics, and Mass Movements in the 1920s* (Berkeley: University of California Press, 1995).

25. Margaret Ann Franklin, "The Chinese Sex-Gender System, Party Policy, and the Education of Women," *Women in International Development Working Paper #176* (East Lansing: Michigan State University, 1989), p. 5.

26. Ibid., p. 5.

27. Ibid., p. 6. The Five Goods were: to cooperate with one's neighbors, to handle one's own household sanitation, to bring up one's children well, to encourage one's husband and children to study well, and to study hard oneself.

28. Harriet Evans, "Constructing Difference: The 'Scientific' Construction of Sexuality and Gender in the People's Republic of China," *Signs* 20, 2 (1995) pp. 357–394. See also her 1991 Ph.D. dissertation, "The Official Construction of Female Sexuality and Gender in the People's Republic of China" (University of London).

29. Evans, "Constructing Difference," p. 362.

30. Ibid., p. 372.

31. Ibid., p. 381.

32. A significant corollary exists in both Korea and Japan, where the conditions of a woman's employment are often explicitly linked to her marital and reproductive status. See Eiko Shinotsuka, "Women Workers in Japan: Past, Present, and Future" and Sandra Buckley, "A Short History of the Feminist Movement in Japan," in *Women of Japan and Korea*, ed. Joyce Gelb and Marian Lief Palley (Philadelphia, PA: Temple University Press, 1994).

33. Nancy E. Riley, "Chinese Women's Lives: Rhetoric and Reality," *AsiaPacific Issues*, 25 (September 1995), pp. 5ff.

34. Lu Hsiu-Lien, *Xin nüxingzhuyi* (Taipei: Yu-shih, 1974), pp. 154ff. For an English-language introduction to her thought, see Barbara Reed, "Women and Chinese Religion in Contemporary Taiwan," in *Today's Woman in World Religions*, ed. Arvind Sharma (Albany: State University of New York Press, 1994), pp. 227–232.

35. As recounted by Lu in "Women's Liberation: The Taiwanese Experience," in *The Other Taiwan: 1945 to the Present*, ed. Murray A. Rubinstein (Armonk, NY: ME Sharpe, 1994), p. 303, note 16.

36. Lu, "Women's Liberation," p. 303, footnote 17.

37. The "four virtues" for women are proper virtue, speech, carriage, and work (*Book of Rites*, chapter 44).

38. Martin King Whyte, "Sexual Inequality Under Socialism: The Chinese Case in Perspective," in *Class and Social Stratification in Post-Revolution*

China, ed. James L. Watson (Cambridge: Cambridge University Press, 1984), p. 234.

39. There is potential for additional oppression of women in this new configuration, with adult daughters sometimes required to care for two sets of parents as well as for their own child(ren).

40. The remaining four relationships are between ruler–subject, parent–child, older and younger brothers, and friends. All of these bonds are defined as reciprocal or complementary, but an implicit hierarchy is evident in each case.

41. For a succinct introduction to New Confucian thought, see John H. Berthrong, *Transformations of the Confucian Way* (Boulder, CO: Westview, 1998), pp. 185–200.

42. An interesting illustration of Confucianism as covert religion is provided by studies of religion in public school textbooks in Taiwan. Not included on the list of "world religions," Confucianism nonetheless becomes the standard by which other traditions are judged. See Jeffrey Meyer, "Teaching Morality in Taiwan Schools," *China Quarterly*, 114 (June 1988), pp. 267–284, and "The Image of Religion in Taiwan Textbooks," *Journal of Chinese Religions*, 15 (1987), pp. 44–50.

43. Lu, "Women's Liberation," p. 473. The most complete studies on the homosexual tradition are in Chinese, but readers are directed to Bret Hinsch, *Passions of the Cut Sleeve: The Male Homosexual Tradition in China* (Berkeley: University of California Press, 1990) and to Evans, "Constructing Difference."

Plate 10 Roman Catholic representation of the crucifixion with Jesus in the role of savior and reconciler as well as ideal person to be emulated. The Virgin Mary stands below him to the left. Our Lady and the English Martyrs Catholic Church (built in 1885–90), Cambridge, England. Photo: *Joseph Runzo.*

10

GENDERED IMAGERY *in* EARLY CHRISTIAN THEOLOGIES *of* SALVATION

Karen Jo Torjesen

Roman religion was mostly a public affair. Festivals were civic events, and religious processions were public parades. Temples adorned city squares, and priests and priestesses were city officials. Celebrations and rituals that honored the patron gods and goddesses of a city benefited the whole populace. When Christianity made its entrance into the Roman world, it was viewed at best as a sect and at worst as a cult. It was not a religion practiced openly in the familiar style of Roman civic religion. The earliest Christians gathered in homes and celebrated their new religion over a common meal with prayers and readings and exhortations. They modeled themselves on family life, calling each other brother and sister and designating themselves the household of God. They undertook familial responsibilities for each other such as payment of burial costs, support for the poor among them, and care for the sick.

These young house churches encouraged diverse forms of leadership. The householder in whose home a house church met acted as a patron, providing not only space but also food and, depending on his or her social status, connections and protection. Prophets and teachers imbued their communities with a sense of being in direct communication with God through their words of revelation and exhortation. The role of the overseer (*episcopos* in the masculine and *episcope* in the feminine) was consistently modeled on household. "If someone does not know how to manage a household, how shall they care for God's church?" is a rhetorical question posed by the writer of I Timothy.[1] There were also leaders who were on the road – evangelists or apostles who often traveled as couples and itinerant prophets.

Because Christianity as a new religion was born and nurtured in the household and in fact remained there until the middle of the third century, Roman notions of male and female roles within the household influenced the new religion. The household-based model of leadership adopted by the early churches created a space for women's leadership. From the perspective of Roman politicians, philosophers, and rhetoricians, society was divided into two spheres: the city, a public male space, and the household, a private female sphere. Public life centered on the politics of the city. Its spaces were those outside the boundaries of the households. The household was considered private, circumscribed, and the domain of women's activities but also of female authority. Philo, an Alexandrian intellectual, expresses this oft-repeated theme thus:

> For the nature of communities is twofold, the greater and the smaller; the greater we call cities and the smaller households. As to the management of both forms, men have obtained that of the greater, which bears the name of statesmanship, while women have obtained that of the smaller which goes under the name of household management.[2]

From a juridical perspective, the male householder represented the household in the eyes of his fellow citizens and linked the household and the city. The centrality of the male householder in this sense leads to a corresponding marginalization of his wife as subordinate. However, when the household was considered from the economic perspective, the roles of men and women within the household were complementary. The duties of each of the partners who ran the household were complex because households were both social units for the preservation of a family's lineage and status and economic units for the creation of a family's material wealth. The household was something like an agricultural factory. The agricultural side – the planting of crops, the cultivation of vines, the tending of olive groves, fruit trees, and livestock – was the work of the male household manager, while the factory side – converting grain to bread, grapes to wine, olives to oil, and wool to textiles – was the work of the female household manager. In both cases men and women supervised the work of slaves.[3] Since women's authority within the household had cultural legitimization, it is not surprising that Christianity's earliest records, the letters of Paul, reveal that about a third of the leaders of the house churches in Rome were women, that women traveled as evangelist-apostles, and that a woman named Phoebe, herself the head of a house church, was Paul's patron.[4] Further, Paul's letter to the Corinthian church reveals that women were prophets and teachers.

Over the next three centuries Christian house churches proliferated. Along with the growth came an improvement in social status as wealthier members of the cities joined. Even civic benefactors who were not Christians offered gifts and financial support to the Christian churches that had come to be recognized as valuable contributors to city life. By the third century wealthier house churches were able to purchase houses to be used exclusively for worship. Taking out a wall to create a larger room, enlarging the entrance to make it more ceremonial and adding a portico transformed these homes into places of assembly. The effect of these changes was that Christian worship moved out of the dining room and into the assembly hall. The centerpiece of Christian worship was no longer the meal but the public address. Placed at the head of the hall on a podium sat the bishop's chair, signaling a new concentration of authority in the hands of the bishop overseer and symbolizing the transition from communal debate and discussion to the exegetical sermon delivered in the style of the rhetor.[5]

Through this process the space of Christian worship became a public space, and the leadership functions of the church became public offices. During the third century women's leadership was contested on the basis that public space was male space and public office was a masculine prerogative. Tertullian, an African theologian of the mid-third century, captured the sense of the church as public space by explaining that the clergy, like the civic leaders, possessed certain rights: the right to baptize, the right to teach, and the right to offer the Eucharist. Although these had once been ministries, in Tertullian's view they had become legal rights and privileges. Since, according to the gender ideology of the public man and the private woman, women could not hold public office or exercise public function, then neither could they exercise any of these rights in the body politic of the church. Tertullian insists that a woman may not hold an office, for it is a "manly" function.[6] The particular privileges of the public, available to men but not to women, were public speech, the power of the podium, and public office. The Roman notions of the public man and the private woman, thus, had their greatest impact on the Christian churches in the third and fourth centuries as Christian worship moved out of domestic space and into public space.

The ideas of public man and private woman did create space for women's leadership and legitimated female authority during the first two centuries of the church's growth. However, another set of Roman notions about gender – male honor and female shame – created a dangerous undertow even during this period for women in leadership roles. The legal subordination of wife to husband was a tenet of Roman law, but the social inferiority of women to men was a tenet of Roman society. The subordination of wives to husbands and the exclusion of women from public speech and public office were legitimated through deeply held beliefs about masculine superiority (honor) and female inferiority (shame), that reinforced the loss of women's leadership within the church in the centuries that followed.

It was this set of beliefs about male superiority and female inferiority that triggered the passionate debates over gender in the early centuries which were formative for Christian theology. Did the message of Christianity have implications for gender roles? For gender identity? Did "becoming a new creature in Christ" also transform what it meant to be male or female? Were there differences between the way men and women thought about salvation? The impact of ancient Roman beliefs about gender went deeper even than what roles men and women should carry out on behalf of other Christians. It touched profoundly on the concept of Christian salvation itself, on what it meant to live the resurrection life now, and beyond that it touched on what masculinity and femininity meant for the heavenly existence for which Christians waited. Before moving on to this debate, it is critical to understand the deep background behind the ideas of male honor and female shame.

THE SINGLE-SEX THEORY OF GENDER

Notions of gender difference in Roman society seem familiar on first reading, but the statements made were based on a quite different model of sexual differences. The ancient Greeks and Romans held to a "single-sex" theory that posited women simply as incomplete or imperfect men. We moderns assume that gender differences are based on anatomical differences between male and female which in turn are construed as irreducibly different and complementary. What secures the seeming irreducibility of that difference are the reproductive organs and reproductive systems themselves. However, Thomas Laqueur alerts us to the uniqueness of an older perspective in which the self-evident, natural truths on which gender differences rest were not anatomical but self-evident natural philosophical truths such as "male is active, female passive" or "male potency creates form, while female passivity contributes only matter." [7]

The biological differences so important to post-enlightenment thought between penis and vagina, testicles and ovaries, semen and menstruation, were understood as relative and contingent differences up until the seventeenth century. Gender differences were simply relative positions on a single scale ranging from more perfect to less perfect. A man might be more or less masculine, a woman might become more or less feminine, depending on how close or far either was from the single ideal of a perfected masculinity. Sexual differences were represented as degrees of differentiation along a single spectrum.[8]

But how did they understand what we assume to be radical difference as a continuum? Semen was thought to be blood that had been concocted into sperm by the greater heat of the male body. Semen possessed an intrinsic power to produce life, form and order. Menstrual blood, which was thicker and heavier, was not capable of producing life because the cooler female body could not heat it sufficiently. Through a theory of the interconversions of bodily fluids, food, blood, phlegm and semen, Greek medical theorists interpreted substances ejaculated by male and female as hierarchically ordered versions of one another.[9] But only one sex was able to convert food into its highest life-engendering state, that of true sperms.[10]

The sex organs themselves were treated as further evidence for the "one-sex" theory. According to the second-century physician Galen, the cervix and the vagina could be thought of as an inverted penis with the ovaries lying alongside of it in the same positions as the testes. "Think of the uterus turned outward and projecting, would not the ovaries then necessarily be inside of it? Would it not contain them like a scrotum? Would not the neck, the cervix and the vagina have the two concealed inside the perineum, but now pendent, be made into the male member?"[11] Another second-century physician Soranus gives an even more detailed description of the points of identity between the male and female reproductive systems.[12] He equates the cervix with prepuce and imagines the "vagina and external structures as one giant foreskin." The sciences of biology and medicine in this time were simply scientific elaborations of the single-sex theory of gender differences. They began with this assumption and interpreted the data of physical bodies within this frame of reference.

The commonality of male and female does not imply equivalence in this scientific analysis. The male organs are the more perfect. Galen compares the female reproductive organs with the unseeing eyes of the mole because the female genitalia do not open. Biological femaleness represents a lower evolutionary stage than biological maleness, or as Laqueur puts it, the vagina is "seen as eternally precariously unborn penis, the womb a stunted scrotum."[13] "Women are inverted, hence less perfect, men."[14]

ristotle gives a certain philosophical sophistication to such popular
efs.[15] While granting that male and female belonged to the same species,
he positioned them as opposites, not complementary opposites whose
nature and function together create a wholeness and balance, but rather
contrary opposites like hot and cold. One is a privation of the other: cold is
a privation of heat and femaleness a privation of maleness. In fact, according to Aristotle, there is one human essence and that is maleness. Hence
femaleness is an imperfect manifestation of maleness.

SYMBOLIC FEMALENESS AND SOCIAL FEMALENESS

What are the theological and social implications of such an understanding
of gender? In his history of the sexed body, Laqueur does not discuss the
slippage between anthropology and theology, the eliding of the human and
the Divine. But there are definite theological implications to Aristotle's
claims. If femaleness is the absence of masculinity – if it is absence and not
presence, then femaleness has more in common with matter than form.
Form is the power to shape, order, and give life. If femaleness is absence and
male is presence, and if female is matter and male is form, then male is also
active agent and female is passive and acted upon. As active and form-
giving, it is the masculine that has the greater affinity with the divine. With
this move, the male is then something better and more Divine than the
female. The male is the principle for movement and for the generation of
the things for which the female serves only as their matter.[16] What Aristotle has done here is to coopt the female power of giving birth and invest it
with an essentialized masculinity. The result is an emasculation of the
female.

The notion of essential maleness as having the power to form and shape
life and femaleness as privation is worked out in Aristotle's reproductive
biology. "The male and female are distinguished by a certain ability and
inability. Male is that which is able to concoct, to cause to take shape, and
to discharge semen possessing the principle of the form ... female is that
which receives the semen, but is not able to cause the semen to take shape
or to discharge it."[17] The power of the female of all species to produce life
is appropriated by Aristotle to become the defining characteristic of essential maleness, in both biological and philosophical terms. A corollary of this
act of appropriation is the obliteration of the distinctiveness of the group
which suffered the expropriation. Females of all species, in spite of pregnancy, delivery and nurture of the young, can no longer claim the power of

generation, of giving life. The expropriation of this power is an attempt to destroy this seemingly fundamental evidence.

Correspondingly, female reproductive (menstrual) fluid is understood to reflect the lack of autonomy and agency in the prescribed gender roles for human females in ancient Greece – it is nothing without the shaping power of the masculine. Aristotle's single-sex theory is further supported by the observation that "a boy actually resembles a woman in physique and a woman is, as it were, an infertile male."[18] Aristotle even interpreted baldness as a sign of an excess of semen: "Women do not grow bald because their nature is that of children, both are incapable of producing seminal secretions. Eunuchs do not grow bald because of their transition to the female state."[19]

From the vantage point of a century two thousand years later, Greek philosophy and medical science is not just a description of "the way things are" but also simultaneously a system of symbols that describes and reinforces social identities, social relationships and social status. Ultimately reproductive biology and philosophical theories of gender are about politics, the arrangements of power in a social system. Greek theories of procreation explained not only how life comes into being and the physiology that makes it possible, but the same science also defined what it meant to be a person, what it meant to be male or female, and how gendered persons were related to each other and to the cosmos.[20] Aristotle's and Galen's theories of sexuality and reproduction created a "symbolic universe through which gender relations could be visualized and a symbolic system through which they could be rationalized."[21] The inability to produce the "heat" needed to create seed capable of both order-giving form and life-producing force revealed through the symbols of the reproductive body was used to justify and rationalize women's lack of potency in the social and political order.

Just as women had no agency in reproduction, they were also denied agency in the political domain. The heat of the male body symbolized male potency, energy, drive, and initiative. Expressed philosophically, the active animating principle is male. The cooler, moister, more phlegmatic female body signified woman's passivity and inertia and her fixity, her enclosure and immobility within the domestic domain. Women's social inferiority was institutionalized in law, both in the form of women's legal dependence on fathers, husbands, and tutors and their legal subordination to husbands within marriage. The rationalization given by the jurists for both was women's supposed inferior moral and intellectual judgment.[22]

Female Shame as Inherent

What we might call Aristotle's "physical biology" articulates an ontological schema of maleness and femaleness. Within it, femaleness is defined as a deficiency – a lack of heat, inadequately developed sex organs, and the incapacity to produce life. When these philosophical/biological "facts" formed the basis for a social identity, a distinctive Mediterranean concept of femaleness emerged. This ontological deficiency of woman (her lack of maleness) is expressed culturally in the notion of female shame. At its core the concept of female shame signifies the recognition of this status of deficiency, the awareness of a lack, a consciousness of the kind of power and potency which a woman does not possess and an acquiescence in that lack.[23] Anthropologist Carol Delaney elaborates the connection between femaleness and shame:

> Women ... are, by their created nature, already ashamed. The recognition of their constitutional inferiority constitutes the feeling of shame. Shame is an inevitable part of being a female; a woman is honorable if she remains cognizant of this fact and its implications for behavior, and she is shameless if she forgets it.[24]

For a woman to feel shame implies an acknowledgment. A woman who has a sense of shame, of modesty, of humility is one who understands and acquiesces in what she does not possess – masculine honor, masculine agency, masculine authority. The psychological state produced by the internalization of female shame and by the socialization of women and of girls into a female identity is revealed in feelings of bashfulness, embarrassment, and awe, and in shyness, timidity, and passivity.[25]

Female shame is institutionalized in both Greek and Roman society through the enclosure of women within domestic space, and through their exclusion from public political power. Their "deficiencies" were thought to render them incapable of full participation in the public sphere. Their exclusion was defined in terms of women's incapacities, a deficiency of either rationality, authority, strength, or power.

Female Shame as Sexual Reputation

There is an intrinsic connection between a woman's inferiority and her sexuality.[26] If she preserves her sexual reputation, she enjoys the particular form of honor a woman can enjoy. A woman's honor was her reputation for chastity. Her chastity showed that she had a sense of shame, of her proper place in the social order. It was not an honor that could be enhanced or advanced. It was a passive form of honor that must be defended. A woman was constantly at risk of losing her reputation for chastity, so her quest for honor focused on the preservation of her sexual reputation. A shameless woman had no concern for her reputation and therefore had lost her honor. If a woman restricted her activities to the household, she could protect her sexual reputation. If she participated in public life, she could be accused of being unchaste, of "running around." Contemporary anthropologists describe the female personality in the Mediterranean, that is the goal of the socialization of little girls, in the following way. A woman should be discreet, shy, restrained, and timid by temperament. Those qualities were necessary to safeguard female chastity, and they were the same qualities that demonstrated a woman knew her place in the gender hierarchy.

WOMEN'S LEADERSHIP AND FEMALE SHAME

Paul's letter to the Corinthians reveals the contours of an early debate over the meaning of gender in the light of conversion to Christianity. His letter represents one position in this debate; his opponents' position, however, can be read between the lines. By analyzing Paul's rhetoric and correcting for his bias, the other side of the debate can be reconstructed. Paul takes the Corinthian prophet–teachers to task for their failure to observe the conventions of gender. His ire is directed particularly at the women prophets who do not wear veils while prophesying. The fact that women are in positions of leadership, exercising authority and enjoying the honor that comes through leadership undermined the notions of male superiority and female inferiority. Paul does not contest their leadership roles, but rather insists that they observe the conventions of gender while they are exercising leadership. "A woman prophesying unveiled dishonors her head," even as a man who prophesied with a veiled head would be dishonored.[27]

In Paul's view, the veil is a cultural symbol of women's subordination. If a woman exercises authority unveiled, she offends the honor of the men present and thereby dishonors and disgraces herself. Paul represents the Christian God as authorizing this understanding of gender by explaining that "the head of every woman is her husband" and "the head of every man is Christ." A man should not cover his head because he is the "glory and image of God;" however, a woman should cover her head because she is only the "glory of man."[28] Paul insists that the societal gender distinctions continue even when one assumes the new Christian identity. There are men prophesying and women prophesying, there are male heads and female heads, and there is male honor and female shame even in Christ.

Furthermore, the social distinctions between male and female have even more important theological consequences. Gender identity is critical in the mediation of the Divine. The "head" or authority over woman is man; therefore, the power to mediate the Divine passes from God through men. Maleness, not common humanity, represents the image and glory of God. When women wear veils while prophesying, the veil symbolizes their subordination and makes clear symbolically that their mediation of the Divine does not bypass the divinely ordained hierarchy of God, man, and woman.

Paul's views represent one side of this debate. The other side must be reconstructed from his letter. The first clear conclusion to be drawn is that the Corinthian women prophets did not wear their veils. Through a rhetorical analysis of Paul's letter, Antoinette Wire has recaptured the voice of the women prophets and explicated their theology.[29] For the Corinthian women prophets their new religious identity transformed their social identity. Having been baptized into Christ meant that they assumed a new identity. This new spiritual identity transcended the social identities based on differential social value between Jew and Greek, slave and free, male and female. The new identity in Christ was also a communal identity understood as solidarity and equivalence among the baptized in which there was neither Jew nor Greek, slave nor free, male nor female.[30]

In their understanding of the Christian message, all were empowered to mediate the Divine. The spirituality of the women prophets celebrated their identity with Christ, their possessing the mind of Christ, their oneness with Christ, and culminating in their confidence that they could mediate the Divine in prophecy, prayer, and teaching. In their view, God's glory and God's honor were realized through the presence of the Divine on which Paul insisted. In the self-understanding of the women prophets, baptism into Christ deconstructed their old gendered identities. Becoming a "new creation" in Christ resulted in a regendering of femaleness. In their new understanding of gender, femaleness was invested with honor, wisdom, and authority. They signaled their new understanding by taking off their veils.

GENDER SYMBOLISM IN EARLY CHRISTIAN THEOLOGIES

The use of gender symbolism in early Christian writings on gender and salvation must be interpreted against this conceptual system of a single-sex theory of a perfected masculinity articulated through reproductive theory, biological beliefs, and philosophical doctrines. Just as they did for physicians like Galen and Soranus and for philosophers like Aristotle and political theorists like Plato, sex and gender functioned as a powerful symbol system through which to explain a myriad of other relationships for early Christian writers. These writers often used gender as a way of describing realized personhood in various understandings of salvation and of describing (from that vantage point) what was wrong with the cosmos and humanity. In this process, however, their use of gendered imagery strained, ruptured and sometimes transformed the conceptualization of gender itself.

The earliest writings of Christians, those of the first and second centuries, were letters to the churches, collections of sayings, gospel memoirs and acts of the early apostles, and revelations. All of these types of writings made their way into the Christian canon. Once Christianity became a religion protected by the emperor and supported by the empire, the process of making a definitive and authorized collection of Christian books began in earnest. Out of this process came the present New Testament canon which included the books now familiar to us, but excluded many others. However, the Christians of the first through fourth centuries read and used the broader collection of writings. Among the various strains of early Christianity were a cluster of theologies that used gender extensively to explain the various stages in the formation of the cosmos, the crisis of the fall, and the plan of redemption. Several of these non-canonical gospels, acts, and revelations were found recently in a collection in Nag Hammadi in upper Egypt and were classified as Gnostic Christianity because of their use of myth to develop theology and a distinctive representation of the fall as a cosmic event.[31] Other acts and revelations had been preserved as devotional literature of the church after an authorized canon was formed. In these "extra-canonical" writings we find more evidence of the early debates over gender and salvation.

Cosmic Gender Crossing

Gendered imagery is used to articulate notions of sin and salvation within early Christian writings such as the Gospel of Thomas and the Gospel of Philip, and there we find what we might call "cosmic gender crossing."[32] In some of the earliest versions of Christianity, salvation was expressed as "the overcoming of sexual difference." In a single-sex conception of gender difference, this would mean becoming a perfected human being and thus in some sense "male," although the use of this imagery within the texts is highly nuanced, and this is not the only option. When Peter challenges Mary Magdalene's right to be counted among the apostles in the Gospel of Thomas, saying: "Let Mary leave us because women are not worthy of the life," Jesus responds: "Behold, I myself will lead her so as to make her male that she may become a living spirit like you males, for every woman who makes herself male will enter the kingdom of heaven."[33] Peter was asserting the social hierarchy of men over women. Since women were social inferiors, intellectually and morally deficient, they would not be appropriate candidates for the spiritual teachings which Jesus would disclose. The quest for perfection, in virtue or in politics is a male prerogative, because maleness is ontologically superior to femaleness. But the reply of Jesus at one and the same time acknowledges, contests and reframes this notion of gender. Jesus' rejoinder is that woman, qua woman, is indeed worthy of "the life," because her social identity as woman is not a hindrance to a spiritual identity, to the quest for perfection. Social femaleness is radically different from essential femaleness. In fact, both men and women are symbolically female until they have entered a state of salvation.

Femaleness in these texts signifies a spiritual state in which difference has not yet been overcome, a state of multiplicity. In the Gospel of the Egyptians, femaleness refers to lust, birth, death and decay.[34] Here unity symbolizes perfection; multiplicity and difference are understood as inferior or deficient modes of being. Becoming male signifies attaining a spiritual state in which difference is overcome and unity is restored: "When you make the two into one, when you make the inner like the outer and the outer like the inner ... and when you make the male and female into a single one so that the male and the female will not be female, then you will enter the kingdom."[35]

The single-sex theory of gender differences lies behind this innovative Christian theology. Namely, all human beings, men and women are gendered female because of their attachment to the material world. Salvation, understood as escape from the entanglements with the world, and a new identity – one that transcends traditional notions of gender – await the adept. The social meanings of gender, the limits they impose on human men and women are challenged and transformed. The symbolic meanings of gender, however, derive from the single-sex theory, and so symbolically both men and women are female before they enter into a state of salvation, and both are male afterwards.

Androgyny and the Cosmic Union of Male and Female

Another text, the Gospel of Philip, uses androgyny rather than "becoming male" as a metaphor for overcoming sexual difference. Here androgyny does not mean transcending masculine and feminine characteristics, but a restoration of the primal unity through union with the missing and separated part of the primal self. "When Eve was still in Adam, death did not exist. When she was separated from him, death came into being. If he again becomes complete and attains his former self, death will be no more."[36] Both Adam and Eve, that is, both male and female, must be reunited with their alter ego, their lost companion, in order to be restored to their original nature. Christians following the Thomas tradition celebrated an individual's entry into this state of primal perfection through a ritual of the bridal chamber.[37] In this gendered imagery, the bridal chamber symbolizes the union attained in the final state of perfection, the restoration of that original unity that preceded the fall into sexual difference. "Christ came to repair the separation which was from the beginning and again unite the two and to give life to those who died as a result of the separation and unite them. Indeed those who have been united in the bridal chamber will no longer be separated."[38]

In the Acts of Thomas a couple, newly converted to asceticism and abandoning sexual relations, is promised "an incorruptible and true marriage" in which each will be united to a heavenly mate and thereby be restored to their original androgynous nature.[39] Death itself is the consequence of the alienation of the self, symbolized in an original differentiation of the two genders in the fall.

A different version of the single-sex theory lies behind this theory of salvation. Plato recounts a myth of primal fall in which an original androgynous creature, the prototype of the human being, was split into two parts. Each part then spends its earthly sojourn trying to reunite with its lost other half. Plato's theory also explained the passionate desire of one sex for the other.[40]

Relativizing Social Difference, Reinscribing Cosmic Maleness

In using gendered imagery in their myths, Gnostic Christians ultimately sought to challenge the conventional social meanings of masculinity and femininity and to push their boundaries to suggest a different and radical understanding of maleness and femaleness. The Gospel of Philip attempts to explain it like this:

> Whereas in this world, the union is one of husband with wife – a case of strength complemented by weakness. In the aeon the form of the union is different, although we refer to them by the same names. There are other names, however, they are superior to every name that is named and are stronger than the strong. There are not separate things, but both of them are this one single thing.[41]

In this world, the union of husband and wife is not understood to be a union of equals. Masculinity was characterized by strength and femininity by weakness. It was precisely the hierarchical ordering of male and female that made the gendered imagery ultimately inadequate in its conventional form to articulate the idea of simultaneous complementarity and unity. This other way of naming masculinity and femininity was superior to the way they are named "in this world." Once masculinity and femininity have been understood in this superior sense, it is possible to grasp the nature of the primal self that "both of them are this one single thing."

Notwithstanding, even Gnostic writers continued to speak of the "perfect man" as the metaphor for the final state, just as the Gospel of Thomas speaks of "becoming male." The assumption here is that male is generic on the cosmic level and that socially gendered men and women can become cosmic males. The fact that it is male, rather than female, which symbolizes generic humanity, reflects, of course, the cultural assumptions of the single-sex theory in which masculinity is the realized form of humanness. Although the social construction of gender roles is challenged and done away with in the concept of androgyny as perfection, the old gendered meanings are reinscribed in the new symbolic order!

An Alternate Voice: an Early Two-Sex Theory

In the tradition of early Christian soteriologies, there was an even more radical thinker. Not surprisingly, it was a woman, Philoumene, who shared a similar view of salvation to those expressed in the Gospels of Thomas and Philip but gave their analysis of gender a new twist.[42] She is one of the very few early theologians who broke with the single-sex theory of gender. Philoumene's writings are lost, but she seems to have published either one or two books. Tertullian mentions *Phanerosis*, written by Philoumene. She is also said to have written her own *Apothegmata*, although these two works may be the same book under different titles. Apelles, initially a disciple of Tatian, abandoned his teacher to become her disciple and embraced her teachings. Philoumene taught that souls were originally created gendered, that their essential identity was a gendered one. In fact, it was the gendered soul that gave the body its gender.

Since her writings have not been preserved, there are few clues to her theories of salvation. If she used the model of androgyny as a metaphor for salvation, the union of a soul with its mate would not restore an original divine unity. Maleness and femaleness were part of the original and perfect creation, according to her. Neither represents a fallen state, rather salvation is a restoration to a primal, unfallen state of maleness and femaleness. According to her system of thought, male and female cannot be hierarchically ordered, either socially or symbolically. She, thus, holds to a two-sex theory of gender. Perhaps it is because she was a woman that she felt the need to rethink the fundamental framework of sex and gender for her time. Certainly her view is radically different from that of many of her contemporaries.

The single-sex theory of gender differences seems antiquated, quaint, occasionally amusing, and sometimes outrageous, especially when we confront it in the form of a medical science or reproductive biology. However, the philosophical and political assumptions that were based on the single-sex theory are still quite pervasive. In the disparity of pay scales of men and women, under the glass ceiling of corporate life, in the absence of women in the American congress, we find the stubborn persistence of the notion of male superiority and female inferiority, of public man and private woman long, long after the eclipse of the single-sex theory of gender difference.

NOTES

1.   I Timothy 3:5.
2.   Philo, *The Special Laws*, 3.170, trans. David Wilson, *Philo of Alexandria* (New York: Paulist Press, 1981), p. 280.
3.   Karen Jo Torjesen, *When Women Were Priests* (San Francisco: Harper-SanFrancisco, 1993), pp. 53–89.
4.   Romans 16; see Elisabeth Schussler Fiorenza, *In Memory of Her: A Feminist Theological Reconstruction of Christian Origins* (New York: Crossroad, 1989), p. 169. For Junia as an apostle, see Bernadette Brooten's "Junia, Outstanding Among the Apostles," in *Women Priests*, ed. L. and A. Swidlers (New York: Paulist Press, 1977), pp. 135–140.
5.   Under imperial patronage when the first Christian emperor Constantine financed the building of great Christian churches, the assembly hall became the basilica or throne room, a formal reception hall lined with columns and climaxing in an apse which held the throne for the emperor or a high official.

6. Torjesen, *When Women Were Priests*, pp. 155–178.

7. Thomas Laqueur, *Making Sex, Body and Gender from the Greeks to Freud* (Cambridge: Harvard University Press, 1990).

8. Laqueur's study builds on the work of feminist scholars who have long insisted that gender is a social construct, concocted out of the raw material of biological sexual difference. Recently feminist theorists like Judith Butler (*Gender Trouble* [New York: Routledge, 1990]) have pressed the claim that even biological sexual difference, that is the sexed body, is also a cultural construction.

9. Laqueur, p. 38.

10. Ibid., p. 29.

11. Ibid., p. 26. Galen, who had done surgeries and dissections, knew that the female also produced "seed." He had found eggs in the ovaries. This, however, did not dissuade him from his one-sex theory.

12. Soranus, *Gynecology,* 9.1.16.

13. Laqueur, p. 28.

14. Ibid., p. 25.

15. Intellectuals of antiquity reflected on gender in a variety of contexts, medical and biological being only two of these. For a rigorous and nuanced interpretation of the historical imagination on gender differences, see Sister Prudence Allen, RSN, *The Concept of Woman: The Aristotelian Revolution 750BC through 1250AD* (Grand Rapids, MI: Eerdmans, 1985). In examining early philosophical traditions on the nature of maleness and femaleness, Prudence Allen observes that questions about gender differences came into play in the context of four different philosophical preoccupations. In what would later be called metaphysics the question of what defined the essence of maleness and femaleness was discussed. Are they the opposite or the same? Are male and female natures equal, or are they ordered hierarchically? In what would later become the philosophy of science, philosophers attempted to understand maleness and femaleness in their reflections on generation, both in cosmic myths about the generation of the world and in scientific theories of reproduction. In the division of philosophy that would later be called epistemology, gender questions were raised with respect to wisdom, the capacity to know the highest orders of reality. Do men and women have the same capacity for learning? Should they study the same subjects or different ones? The fourth area in which the earliest philosophers asked questions of gender was ethics. Do men and women have the same virtues? Are their virtues related to their functions in society? See Allen, pp. 75–77.

16. Aristotle, *On the Generation of Animals*, 732A, 5.10 *The Basic Works of Aristotle*, ed. Richard McKeon (New York: Random House, 1941).

17. Aristotle, *On the Generation of Animals*, 765B.

18. Ibid., 728B.

19. Ibid., 783B.

20. See Carol Delaney, *The Seed and the Soil: Gender and Cosmology in Turkish Village Society* (Berkeley: University of California Press, 1991), pp. 1–20.

21. See Maryanne Cline Horozwitz, "Aristotle and Women," in *Journal of the History of Biology,* 9, 2 (Fall 1976), p. 207.

22. Jane Gardener, *Women in Roman Law and Society* (Indiana University Press: Bloomington, 1986), p. 21.

23. The social act of shaming operates along two registers. The obvious use of shaming is to shape social behavior and reinforce social norms. But if we examine the social context in which shaming is used, it becomes very clear that shaming is also used to actively put someone else in an inferior position. As contemporary anthropologists point out, shaming in Mediterranean culture is used most frequently within a hierarchical relationship: parents to children, elders to youngsters, guardians to wards. To be shamed is to be placed in the position of a social inferior to the one who is doing the shaming. Further, the meaning of shame, disgrace and humiliation itself is the diminishment of social worth. This is also the meaning of a woman's shame even in the positive sense. It is an acknowledgment of the lesser social worth of women within the hierarchy of gender.

24. Carol Delaney, "Seeds of Honor, Fields of Shame," *Honor and Shame and the Unity of the Mediterranean,* ed. David Gilmore (Washington, D.C.: American Anthropological Association, 1987).

25. Gideon M. Kressel, "Shame and Gender," *Anthropological Quarterly,* 6 (1992), pp. 34–46.

26. Torjesen, *When Women Were Priests,* pp. 135–154.

27. I Corinthians 3:14.

28. I Corinthians 11:7.

29. Antoinette Wire, *The Corinthian Women Prophets: A Reconstruction Through Paul's Rhetoric* (Minneapolis: Fortress Press, 1990).

30. Ibid., p. 124.

31. The classification of these writings as gnostic is a topic of heated debate. There was great diversity in the theologies of the first four centuries as intellectuals from different philosophical and cultural traditions explained the nature of Christianity to their communities. The writings labeled gnostic have much in common with other theological traditions of the second and third centuries; hence, segregating them into a class of their own and labeling them heretical is not an adequate description of them.

32. This section will deal with texts that, following the conventions of the patristic heresiologists, have been categorized as gnostic. This category was created as part of the polemical struggle of early theologians to claim authority for their respective visions of the Divine. The category gnostic

is hence quite problematic as much of their teaching is found in other "orthodox" Christian writings as well. This cluster of theological writings has attracted scholarly attention because they make rich use of gendered imagery. For earlier studies, see Dennis MacDonald, *There is No Male and Female: The Fate of Dominical Saying in Paul and Gnosticism* (Philadelphia: Fortress Press, 1981) and *Images of the Feminine in Gnosticism*, ed. Karen King (Philadelphia: Fortress Press, 1981).

33. Gospel of Thomas, Logion 114 in *The Nag Hammadi Library*, ed. James Robinson (San Francisco: Harper, 1978), p. 130.

34. Kristen Aspegren, *The Male Woman* (Stockholm, Sweden: Almquist and Wichsell International, 1990), pp. 123ff.

35. Gospel of Thomas, Logion 22 in *The Nag Hammadi Library*, p. 121.

36. Gospel of Philip II.3 in *The Nag Hammadi Library*, p. 141.

37. I am grateful to Donna Wallace for calling attention to a tradition of salvation as androgyny in the Gospel of Philip, Gospel of Thomas and Acts of Thomas in an unpublished paper, "From Thomas to 'Thecla: Androgyny as Salvation in Early Christianity."

38. Gospel of Philip II.3 in *The Nag Hammadi Library*, p. 142. See also p. 139.

39. Acts of Thomas, Logion 12–15 in *New Testament Apocrypha*, vol. 2, ed. Wilhelm Schneemelcher (Louisville, KY: Westminster/John Knox, 1992), pp. 339–341.

40. Plato, *Symposium*, in *The Collected Dialogues of Plato*, ed. Edith Hamilton and Huntington Cairns (Princeton: Princeton University Press, 1961), pp. 189ff.

41. Gospel of Philip II.3 in *The Nag Hammadi Library*, p. 145.

42. Ann Jensen, *God's Self-Confident Daughters*, trans. O. C. Dean, Jr. (Louisville, KY: Westminster/John Knox, 1996).

Plate 11 An all-male Islamic worship service, with the devout facing the prayer niche *(mihrab)* that marks the direction of Makkah, and the imam, who is leading the service, standing to the right. Mosque of Sayyidna Al-Hussein, one of the most sacred places of Shi'ite Muslim worship, revered as the final resting place of the head of Al-Hussein, grandson of the Prophet Muhammad, and built in 1878 CE Cairo, Egypt. Photo: *Joseph Runzo*.

11

POLITICIZING GENDER *and* RELIGION: LOVE *for* WOMEN, LOVE *for* ISLAM

Zayn Kassam

The purpose of this chapter is to introduce readers unfamiliar with gender issues in the Islamic world to some of the broader contours and discussions of the subject. The rapid increase of scholarly literature on women in the Middle East has made it almost impossible to keep up with this body of material.[1] My intention here is to provide an entry into the complexity of the subject and its relevance to problematizing the intense politicization of gender issues in the Islamic world, and to stimulate further exploration on the part of the reader.

It is critical to note that within the Islamic context – both in the medieval discourses on gender and in current representations – biblical understandings and colonial discourses were far from absent. The issue of gender in the Islamic world cannot be understood apart from these, in the first instance with respect to the appropriation by medieval Muslim minds of biblically derived – and patriarchal – models pertaining to gender construction, and in the second instance with respect to the colonizers' identification of Muslim women as epitomizing the backwardness of Islam, thereby both "othering" Islam and Muslims and – in a manner not always acknowledged by Muslims who subsequently signified women's comportment and dress as expressing quintessentially what it means to be Muslim – laying out the framework dictating the terms of the debate over gender issues within the Islamic world. While there are scriptural and intellectual resources within the Islamic tradition (understood here in all its diversity of expressions and articulations) to argue against an androcentric reading and application of the Qur'an, the encounter with colonization and the

Western world's media-assisted "othering" of Islam and Muslims presents a challenge, in that those seeking change in Muslim society run the risk of being identified with Western hegemonic agendas. Thus, Muslims – along with their global counterparts in other religious traditions and societies – seeking to ameliorate women's lives and equalize female access to legal, social, health, and educational institutions through intellectual discourses or activism are faced with the double bind of asserting their full membership in and loyalty to an Islamic polity while exploring various avenues through which gender attitudes, relationships and issues may be discussed and addressed.

SOURCES OF AUTHORITY FOR GENDER DISCOURSES IN ISLAM

Many Muslim apologists[2] would claim that Islam is an egalitarian faith that considers women to be equal with men, albeit different. Nevertheless, a reading of these works affirms the widely held notion that Islam, as with all the world's major religious traditions, has become associated with patriarchal practices. How did this situation arise? The research conducted by Gerda Lerner, Leila Ahmed, and Eleanor Doumato,[3] to mention a few scholars who have worked on this issue, shows that patriarchal structures and practices were well in place in both the Byzantine and the Persian empires that the Muslims conquered in the seventh and eighth centuries of the Common Era. The advent of Islam on the world scene simply perpetuated many of the institutions that treated women as second-class citizens in those areas of the world, and Muslims interpreted their tradition in a manner that was consonant with the reigning social and institutional codes of the day. For example, the practices of veiling and seclusion, both of which were restricted to the Prophet's wives during his lifetime, began to gain general currency among Muslim women in the generations after his death during the period of Islamic expansion into Byzantine and Persian territories directly as a result of upper-class Byzantine and Persian practices of the same. Given this upper-class cultural context in the subject territories, Islamic jurists moved swiftly to promote the model of the Prophet's wives' seclusion and veiling as pertinent to all Muslim women, in casual disregard of the qur'anic verse which affirms that the Prophet's wives are not like ordinary women (33:32).

Two sources of authority need to be distinguished in discussing the role of women in Islam: the teachings of the Qur'an itself and the later literature that provides interpretations of the Qur'an. The Qur'an, which is viewed as sacred scripture by Muslims worldwide, clearly stipulates the spiritual and moral equality and accountability of both men and women. Further, the sanctity of female human life is upheld in the face of the practice of burying female infants alive. Both males and females are constructed from a single soul, both will be rewarded for righteousness and good works, the labor of both is valued equally (3:195), and both will go to paradise if they so merit.

Statements such as these lead many Muslims to believe that God does not discriminate against women. However, despite the ethical and spiritual egalitarianism found in the Qur'an, there are nonetheless inequities in the legislative and social sphere that are also to be found there. Let me quickly add that such inequities must be viewed contextually, as many of the legal pronouncements – about a hundred verses or so – concerning women can be considered remarkable advances for that time. For example, in contrast to Western women who attained these rights only in the last century or so, Muslim women were allowed to own property, were provided for in the event of divorce, and were allowed to inherit as well as give legal testimony.

Nonetheless, from the point of view of a modern lens, there are many verses which can all be considered to be restrictive in various degrees with regard to women's economic and public mobility. For example, the fact that women may inherit only half the amount of property their brothers can (4:11); their legal status as witnesses is half that of men, so that two female witnesses count for one male witness; men are granted authority over women because they provide for them (4:34); if wives are rebellious they may be punished in various stages culminating in, according to traditional qur'anic interpretations, beating (4:34); women are expected to throw a cloak around themselves when leaving the house, and the Prophet's wives – who were viewed by later commentators as a paradigm for all Muslim women – were expected to stay in their houses, avoid strutting about, to pray and give alms and so forth (33:33). The commodification of women is further perpetuated in verses that declare that men are permitted polygamy up to four wives, provided they can treat them equally, but women are denied polyandry.

Now, what does one make of a religiously and socially authoritative document that upholds the moral and spiritual equality of both sexes, while at the same time proposing a less than equal social valuation of women? Here we run into the second issue, the problem of interpretation.

As with all other scripture, the Qur'an is a "thick" text, and its meaning not always clear. Qur'anic commentators therefore turned to a number of sources, which themselves were in the process of being constructed, in order to explicate and clarify the meaning and implication of verses that were self-evident as well as verses that appeared obscure in meaning. One such source was the *asbāb al-nuzūl* literature, which attempted to record in the generations after the Prophet's death, the historical occasion that prompted the revelation of each verse. A second source was the collections of *hadith*, where all known reports of the Prophet's actions and sayings are recorded. These collections constitute the second most authoritative source of guidance for many Muslims today. Sectarian and political issues played into the collection and transmission of the *hadith* literature. The authenticity of the *hadith* literature has been debated, with scholars reaching the consensus that if nothing else, this literature is representative of the values held by the early Muslim communities as well as being a possibly authentic reconstruction of what is significant in Muslim memory in the period from the seventh to the ninth centuries of the Common Era. By this time also, the Islamic empire stretched from Spain to India. The jurists, in their attempt to standardize the rule of law over a vast domain, developed theoretical frameworks that lay emphasis on the Qur'an and the Traditions as the primary sources for Islamic law, while also drawing upon other sources such as local customary practices and juridical reason.

In addition to the Qur'an and the Traditions, however, there is a third source that has had an impact on the development of legal frameworks in the Islamic world with respect to gender issues. Since the Qur'an acknowledged the common monotheism of Judaism, Christianity and Islam by referring to the followers of all of these as Peoples of the Book, and since there is a *hadith* in which the Prophet is reported as saying that Muslims may ask neighboring Jews and Christians for further information, elaboration and comment in order to understand many of the references in the Qur'an to biblical events and prophets, it was natural for qur'anic commentators and those learned men engaged in gathering Traditions to turn to their compatriots for information. The narratives or biblical lore they acquired, entitled the *isrā'īliyat*, were popularly used as the basis for a genre of works known as the Stories of the Prophets *(qiṣaṣ al-anbiyā')* and found their way into the classical qur'anic commentaries, and thence into some early legal frameworks. Later jurists attempted to discount the *isrā'īliyat* as foreign influences; however, they did so selectively.

The qur'anic commentators integrated Jewish and Christian Bible-related traditions wholesale into their commentaries on female figures mentioned in the Qur'an. They did not focus their energies at that time on differentiating the status and role of Muslim women from women in their subject cultures. Rather, as Barbara Stowasser's persuasive book on this subject suggests, the jurists interpreted the Qur'an in a manner consistent with the social structures prevalent in their society: "the theme of 'woman's weakness' with its paradoxical twin, 'woman as threat to the male and society,' dominated the Islamic scripture-based paradigm on gender throughout the medieval period, and in that isrā'īlīyat played a major part in its formulation."[4]

Woman's Fall from Equality

To illustrate, she examines the account of the events in the paradisical garden that lead to the fall of Adam and Eve. Eve is not mentioned in the Qur'an by name, nor are the circumstances of her creation detailed. All we are told is that God created "you from a single soul, and from it created its mate" (Qur'an 4:1; 39:6; 7:189: *khalaqakum min nafsin wāḥidatin wa ja'ala (in 4:1, khalaqa) minhā zawjahā li yaskuna ilayhā*).

There are several accounts of the Fall (2: 30–39; 7:11–27; 15:26–43; 20: 115–124; 38:71–85). In the earliest account (20), God's warning, Satan's temptation, and God's forgiveness are all directed at Adam alone, even though both man and woman eat of the Forbidden Tree and are expelled from the garden.[5] In a later account (7), both male and female are tempted and tricked by Iblis, or Satan, both succumb, both repent, and both are sent down, with the statement: There will be for you on earth a habitation and provision for a while. In the account held chronologically to have been revealed last (2:30–39), Satan is squarely blamed for the couple's expulsion from the garden, and the account ends with God's pledge that "whoever follows My guidance shall have no fear, nor shall they grieve."

Classical (that is, the period up to about 950 CE) qur'anic exegesis or commentary takes the bare outlines given in the Qur'an with respect to these events and not only fleshes it out with Bible-related lore but also drastically changes it with respect to the woman's role. Tabari (d. 923) fleshes out the story of woman's creation by incorporating all the biblical lore concerning woman's creation from one of Adam's ribs while he lay sleeping, and when he awakens, he names her Hawwa, from *hayy*, meaning a living thing. Then, although he quotes the qur'anic account of the temptation of the couple, he also cites an overwhelming number of Traditions that illustrate that Hawwa or Eve was the one to succumb to Satan's guile, and further, that Satan made her appear attractive to Adam, and when he desired her, she refused to obey until he first ate of the forbidden fruit; or, in another account, she gave him wine, and when he was drunk, she led him to the tree. The rationale here is that some explanation must be provided for the absence of Adam's rational powers at this crucial juncture: so Eve's sexuality or seduction or temptation must be responsible.

Tabari's account goes on to place God's curse on the woman and the serpent. On the woman it involves her constitution and mental abilities; she is condemned to bleed once a month, carry and deliver children against her will and be close to death at delivery. Further, although God had created her wise and intelligent, she was now made foolish and stupid. As for the male, he is not cursed, only the earth from which he was created, which would now be made to bear thorns where there once was fruit; and Adam is condemned to a life of want and work.

Again, although Tabari does record traditions in which both man and woman repent and are forgiven, he records a far greater number that indicate that Adam alone repented and was forgiven and promised eternal life, thus pointing to the lower moral consciousness of the female. A final element Tabari introduces into his narrative, departing from the qur'anic accounts, concerns the shame experienced by both partners. In the qur'anic accounts, after having eaten of the Tree, Adam and his partner perceive their shame and begin to sew leaves together to cover themselves. According to Tabari, however, after having eaten of the Tree, it is only Adam who feels shame, but not Hawwa.

The lower moral, mental, and physical nature of women, once it enters the Traditions by way of the isrā'īliyat, continues to be reproduced in all subsequent qur'anic commentaries, and is used to justify further male authority over the woman and her exclusion from activities outside the house. Illustrative is this piece of advice by one of the towering intellects in Islamic literature, the medieval jurist, theologian, mystic, and anti-philosopher (despite his use of philosophic methods) al-Ghazali (d. 1111 CE), whose works continue to be read and to inspire to the present day. He states: [6]

> ...[a man] should not be over-indulgent, lest his wife lose her respect for him. If he sees anything plainly wrong on her part, he should not ignore but rebuke it, or he will become a laughing-stock. In the Koran it is written, "Men should have the upper hand over women," and the Prophet said, "Woe to the man who is the servant of his wife" for she should be his servant. Wise men have said, "Consult women, and act the contrary to what they advise." In truth there is something perverse in women, and if they are allowed even a little license, they get out of control altogether, and it is

difficult to reduce them to order again. In dealing with them one should endeavour to use a mixture of severity and tenderness, with a greater proportion of the latter. The Prophet said, "Woman was formed of a crooked rib; if you try to bend her, you will break her; if you leave her alone, she will grow more and more crooked; therefore treat her tenderly."

The point here is not to blame the *isrā'īliyat* traditions for the essentialist view of woman that entered the Islamic commentarial consciousness, but rather to point out that this view directed and enforced the interpretation of verses in the Qur'an that need not necessarily have been construed in that light. Further, when the *isrā'īliyat* lore was incorporated both into the learned commentarial tradition and the popular *qiṣaṣ al-anbiyā'* or "stories about the prophets" literature, then it entered mainstream consciousness as well. In this respect, Muslims along with their Jewish and Christian counterparts are up against a centuries-long paradigm that views women in essentialist terms primarily, but not solely, through the reinterpretation of that most powerful of biblical stories, the expulsion of Adam and Eve from the blissful existence once intended for them.

THE POLITICS OF REFORM AND THE USES OF RELIGION

Now, the forum in which this essentialist view of women exercises far-reaching impact is in the area of legislation that governs issues pertinent to women. Throughout the course of Islamic political history, the state and the Muslim jurists effectively carved up areas of jurisdiction so that there was a dual system for the administration of legal justice. While I am simplifying the very complex machinery of the legal systems under the three Muslim empires, the Persian, the Ottoman, and the Mughal, the broad contours, nonetheless, hold, in that by and large, the caliph was granted a mantle of justification for his policies by being accorded the mandate to uphold the divinely revealed *shari'ah* or law and protect it. Under this mandate, state-controlled institutions oversaw business and commercial law, criminal law, real-estate law, and constitutional law, while the Muslim jurists controlled family law, inheritance law, and the laws governing religious endowments, along with all the laws pertaining to ritual performance and behavior. Thus, for centuries, family and inheritance law have been essential partners in the laws governing the rituals pertaining to one's religious duties as a believing Muslim, such as performing the *hajj* or pilgrimage to Makkah, prayer, alms-giving, fasting during the month of Ramadan, and so forth. The connection I am seeking to bring to the forefront is that while legal institutions under the control of the caliph remained dynamic, that is, absorbed and responded to the exigencies and demands of the particular legal situation, it appears that whatever remained thoroughly within the sphere of family law and ritual law did not undergo the same processes of change and revision.

In the current context, with the resurgence of purist movements, attempts have been made to extend the sphere of Muslim legal influence into areas that have by tacit consent been handled by the state, and examples of these can be seen in Pakistan, Egypt, Iran, and Afghanistan, to name but a few. Given the fact that family and inheritance laws have been so closely aligned with laws governing ritual expression, it is not difficult to see that any attempts to change family and inheritance laws to reflect a more equitable treatment of women might be considered tantamount to interfering with the heart and soul of Islam.

Thus, most nation states in the modern period in parts of the world with majority Muslim populations are faced with a double bind: how do they modernize their societies and make their countries economically viable in a shrinking global market, without being accused of Westernization? Westernization, as you may have guessed, is not a highly sought-after commodity, if for no other reason than the fact and memory of colonization. Indeed, under the Shah, Westernization was seen as a mere aping of the corrupting ways of the West and as an attempt to undermine Islamic culture, in continuity with what the colonizers themselves had attempted to effect. And feminism is seen as an element of Westernization.[7]

Insofar as this is relevant to the status of women and the formulations regarding their comportment and place in society, it is necessary to understand both colonial constructions of the "other" and the Islamists' need to define an identity that stands apart from that of current hegemonies, the cultural construct known as "the West."[8] As Ahmed, among others, has pointed out, "colonialism's use of feminism to promote the culture of the colonizers and undermine native culture has ever since imparted to feminism in non-western societies the taint of having served as an instrument of colonial domination, rendering it suspect in Arab eyes and vulnerable to the charge of being an ally of colonial interests. That taint has undoubtedly hindered the feminist struggle within Muslim societies."[9] Deniz Kandiyoti makes the link between colonial discourses and the current preoccupation with women's status in Muslim societies:

The identification of Muslim women as the bearers of the 'backwardness' of their societies, initially by colonial administrators and later by Western-oriented reformers, is mirrored by a reactive local discourse which elevates the same practices into symbols of cultural authenticity and integrity ... The privileged sites for such assertions of authenticity are, once again, the dress and deportment of women.[10]

The state's role in this is ambiguous:[11] it can promote change in women's legal, social and economic status, or it can be the sometimes complicit, sometimes unwilling ally of the growing numbers of Islamists, thereby preventing changes in the laws and social practices affecting women. In Egypt, Nasser gave women the right to vote in 1956, and the right to work outside the home in 1959 even though in practice women were channeled into "feminine professions, such as medicine and nursing," and primary school teaching jobs rather than secondary school jobs, leaving the men to teach history, science, logic and philosophy. However, Nasser also proposed a law which – in contrast to Islamic law under which women are allowed to inherit – would have bypassed women in favor of males or male children. In all of this research, it is becoming clear that for the state, religion was marginal in the perpetuation of women's subordinate economic and political roles.

Where religion did play a role was with respect to divorce law and polygamy. Women were still denied the right to divorce by the state's family law, and polygamy was retained on the books. When women activists approached Nasser regarding this, especially in light of his otherwise liberal agenda, he referred them to the religious scholars. *Shari'ah* is pulled out of the hat once again, despite the decision to ignore *shari'ah* when attempting to introduce a law of inheritance that would be prejudiced against women. Thus, it appears that while the state in some Muslim countries does attempt to create the social and institutional conditions under which its population can prosper, in some respects it joins its Western counterpart in its unwillingness to eradicate the discriminations against women globally, and it is at this point that the idea of the "immutability" of divine law is brought to the forefront. This despite the fact that *shari'ah* law is only as static as the generation that enforces it, that historically, *shari'ah* law has not only been a dynamic entity, but that to this day there are differences between the legal schools on many points. Besides, even older laws that have not been tampered with for centuries are still open to interpretation should the consensus of the community of Muslim jurists require it.

Indeed, we come full circle: unless societies change, legal institutions and codes will not change. If the role of the state remains ambiguous, at times supporting women's access to and participation in the public forum and at times not, then it is clear that state and society both play a role. And then how important is the role of religion in the formation of a public discourse? It is clear that with the Islamist revival in the twentieth century there are several discourses emerging. The traditionalist or purist Islamic position uses rhetoric similar to that of the medieval thinker al-Ghazali mentioned earlier and appeals to the "equal but different" argument to maintain that the woman's task is to bear and raise children.[12]

However, there is also the Islamist discourse, which is connected to traditionalist discourse, but not quite the same. Islamist discourse can be identified as a late-nineteenth- and early-twentieth-century form of Islamic expression that has taken its identity from its struggle against colonial powers and against state governments it considers to be secular and Western-inspired. For such groups, revolutionary and freedom-fighting activities have necessitated the full participation of women in politically emancipatory activities, such as those in Algeria, Egypt, Iran, and Palestine, to name a few. However, once the struggle has been won, women discovered to their dismay that they were expected to return to their homes while the legal and social structures around them tightened the noose with respect to women's rights – as was noted in Iran, when Khomeini ordered women out of some of the professions, for example, or in Afghanistan, where women are no longer allowed to go to school.

Despite these setbacks, there is an emergent Islamist discourse on women's participation in society that can be found in the works of Rashid al-Ghannushi, for example, that women "cannot be ignored or relegated to a secondary role. 'A movement whose aspirations do not go beyond teaching women to cover themselves and perform their religious duties will be elitist and not populist.' Women must be encouraged to possess the spirit of daring, not of fear and retreat. Nothing in Islam says that a woman must take care of the house or raise the children. If she chooses to do that, she is to be compensated. If she decides that she does not wish to be paid, then gratitude for her work must be expressed. Furthermore, the husband must help with the housework. This is the way of the Prophet, who used to help his wives."[13]

EVOLVING TRADITIONS OF INTERPRETATION AND ACTIVISM

In this vein, attention may be drawn, albeit too briefly, to some of the efforts being made to change the interpretive bias of verses that have been utilized to promote social and legal inequities in the *shari'ah*. For example, the verses that have traditionally been called upon to justify veiling for all women, as well as allowing males, in the final recourse, to beat their wives, have been identified by feminist interpreters as pertaining only to the Prophet and his household. (Let me add that by feminist interpreters I mean those who seek to correct the hitherto androcentric bias in interpretation.) The same goes for seclusion. Verses that support polygamy have also been similarly scrutinized to clarify that the Qur'an clearly stipulates that a male may marry more than one wife only if he is able to treat them all equally, and proponents of monogamy have argued that since it is humanly impossible to treat any two people exactly the same, the Qur'an was in fact supporting monogamy but was sensitive to the contemporaneous cultural context in which both polygamy and polyandry were in practice.

The problematic, for those looking for an egalitarian vision, qur'anic verse[14] is of course that which places men in charge over women owing to the excellence granted to them by Allah and also because they are responsible for their upkeep, and which has been interpreted as indicating, therefore, that the sphere of public and economic activity belongs to men, while the sphere of the hearth and childrearing belongs to women. In this regard, reinterpretive work emerging from Iranian women puts forward the argument that an analysis of the Arabic root of the term "superior" shows that it should not be traced back to *q-y-m*, which means guardianship of one over the other, but to *q-w-m*, which means standing for, that is, being supportive of another.[15] The above examples fall into the category of reinterpretation that is grounded in the view that the Qur'an, if understood properly, cannot be anything other than egalitarian in its treatment of women, and that is tacitly unwilling to accept that there is anything in the authoritative literature, primarily the Qur'an and the *hadith*, that Muslim women need to fear, and if these sources are understood properly, then the *shari'ah* will be what it properly should be, a legal instrument to protect women.

A more compelling theoretical framework was articulated by the modernist Egyptian jurist Muḥammad 'Abduh, who tacitly acknowledged the social and legal inequities for women found in the traditional sources by reasoning that the Qur'an contains eternally applicable verses that deal with matters of faith and ritual practice, as well as historically conditioned verses that deal with specific cultural practices known in seventh-century Arabia. Amina Wadud-Muhsin, an activist Muslim writer and academic, has further clarified this view in her work by stating that earlier qur'anic commentators engaged in androcentric modes of interpretation that were reinforced by their social and cultural contexts. In other words, they read into the text what were socially and culturally acceptable modes of behavior towards women. The implication of these lines of reasoning is that the Qur'an should no longer be used to oppress women in the name of religion. That aspect of *shari'ah* law which pertains to family law and inheritance is not immutable but a historical construct which now needs reinterpretation via the spirit of the Qur'an rather than its letter. This argument is predicated on the view that surely a just and merciful God would not have intended oppression using the authority of scripture for half a billion Muslim women.

Finally, in addition to the traditionalist and Islamist discourse, a third factor has the potential to exercise a tremendous impact on women's lives. Economic, political, and cultural realities have a role to play in effecting social change. Valentine Moghadam argues that Middle Eastern women "are not simply acting out roles prescribed for them by religion, by culture, or by neopatriarchal states; they are questioning their roles and status, demanding social and political change, participating in movements, and taking sides in ideological battles."[16]

Non-governmental organizations, or NGOs, which are relief and development agencies, continue to work alongside local, state, and international organizations to ameliorate the living conditions of women. These, together with local women's activist groups, are exploring the possibility of changing "the framework of debate." Rather than focusing on prescriptive discourses with regard to gender issues,[17] they respond to the reality of women's lives and the impact on women of modernization where the mode of production has shifted from the home to the factory or the marketplace or the business mall. The shift in focus away from religion was reflected in the 1994 document produced by the United Nations Economic and Social Commission for Western Asia, which includes most of the Arab world, in preparation for the United Nations Fourth World Conference on Women held in Beijing in 1995, which articulated the need for programs "which respect woman's rights as a human being and her participation in development and its benefits as a condition for comprehensive and sustainable development."[18] In other words, at the ground level there is an awareness by women and by organizations working with women that the realities women face in the economic, social, legal, educational, and health spheres far outweigh what some cleric sitting in comfort might prescribe as their role in life.

NOTES

1. Beth Baron, "A Field Matures: Recent Literature on Women in the Middle East," in *Middle Eastern Studies*, 32, 3, pp. 172–186.

2. See, for example, 'Abdur Raḥmān I. Doi, *Woman in Sharī'ah* (London: Ta-Ha Publishers, 1989), as well as the writings of Mawdudi and Khomeini.

3. Gerda Lerner, *The Creation of Patriarchy* (New York: Oxford University Press, 1986); Leila Ahmed, *Women and Gender in Islam* (New Haven and London: Yale University Press, 1992); Eleanor Doumato, "Hearing Other Voices: Christian Women and the Coming of Islam," *International Journal of Middle East Studies*, 23 (1991), pp. 177–199.

4. Barbara Freyer Stowasser, *Women in the Qur'an, Traditions, and Interpretation* (New York: Oxford University Press, 1994), p. 23.

5. Stowasser, *Women in the Qur'an*, pp. 26ff.

6. Following quotes taken from "Chapter Five: Marriage as a Help or Hindrance to the Religious Life," in Abu Hamid Muhammad al-Ghazzali, *The Alchemy of Happiness*, trans. Claud Field, revised by Elton L. Daniel (New York: M.E. Sharpe, Inc., 1991), pp. 45–56.

7. Afsaneh Najmabadi draws attention to the perception that women are simply the tools of a Western agenda aimed at destroying the integrity of the culture of the colonized. She states: "In this new Islamic political paradigm, imperialist domination of Muslim societies was seen to have been achieved not through military or economic supremacy, as earlier generations of nationalists and socialists had argued, but through the undermining of religion and culture. Woman was made to bear the burden of cultural destruction. As an editorial in a weekly women's journal published in Tehran described it: 'Colonialism was fully aware of the sensitive and vital role of woman in the formation of the individual and of human society. They considered her the best tool for subjugation of the nations … women serve as the unconscious accomplices of the powers-to-be in the destruction of indigeneous culture … woman is the best means of destroying the indigenous culture to the benefit of imperialists.'"See Afsaneh Najmabadi, "Feminism in an Islamic Republic," in *Islam, Gender, and Social Change*, ed. Yvonne Yazbeck Haddad and John L. Esposito (New York: Oxford University Press, 1998), p. 60.

8. While Edward Said's *Orientalism* (New York: Vintage Books, 1979) and *Culture and Imperialism* (New York: Vintage Books, 1994) are critical in framing the issues, there are works such as Sara Suleri's *The Rhetoric of English India* (Chicago: University of Chicago Press, 1992); Billie Melman's *Women's Orients: English Women and the Middle East, 1718–1918* (Ann Arbor: University of Michigan Press, 1992, 1995); Kumari Jayawardena's *The White Woman's Other Burden: Western Women and South Asia During British Rule* (New York and London: Routledge, 1995) (this work deals largely with Hindu women); and *Third World*

Women and the Politics of Feminism, ed. Chandra Talpande Mohanty *et al.* (Bloomington and Indiana: Indian University Press, 1991) that explore colonial legacies with respect to women.

9.   Ahmed, *Women and Gender*, p. 167.

10.   Deniz Kandiyoti, "Reflections on the Politics of Gender in Muslim Societies: From Nairobi to Beijing," in *Faith and Freedom: Women's Human Rights in the Muslim World*, ed. Mahnaz Afkhami (Syracuse: Syracuse University Press, 1995), p. 21.

11.   Attention to which has been drawn by Deniz Kandiyoti, ed., in *Women, Islam and the State* (Philadelphia: Temple University Press, 1991) and in Deniz Kandiyoti, ed., *Gendering the Middle East* (Syracuse: Syracuse University Press, 1996) as well as by Afkhami, ed., *Faith and Freedom*, among others.

12.   See, for example, the popular Egyptian preacher Muhammad Mutawalli al-Sharawi writing in the 1980s: "The Prophet said about the women that 'they were created from a crooked rib; the most crooked part is its top portion, and if you were to straighten it, you would break it (the break signifying divorce); so enjoy her as crooked as she is.' He was not blaming the woman when he said this, but was defining women's natural disposition and the preponderance of emotions over rationality, with which God has distinguished her, unlike the male in whom rationality surpasses the emotions. Neither man nor woman are inferior one to the other. The 'crookedness' in the hadith does not imply any corruption or imperfection in woman's nature, because it is this crookedness of hers that enables her to perform her task, which is to deal with children who need strong compassion and sympathy, not rationality. The words 'the most crooked portion of the rib is its uppermost part' signify the compassion which the woman feels for her child and the supremacy of her emotion over her rational mind. On this basis, her 'crookedness' has become a laudatory attribute for the woman, because this 'crookedness' is in reality woman's 'straightest' qualification for her task." Reported in Stowasser, *Women in the Qur'an*, p. 37.

13.   Yvonne Yazbeck Haddad, "Islam and Gender: Dilemmas in the Changing Arab World" in *Islam, Gender, and Social Change*, ed. Haddad and Esposito, pp. 20–21.

14.   Qur'an 4: 34: Men are in charge [*qawwāmūna 'ala*] of women, because Allah hath made the one of them to excel [*faḍḍala*] the other, and because they spend of their property. Translated by Mohammad Marmaduke Picthall.

15.   Afsaneh Najmabadi, "Feminism in an Islamic Republic," in *Islam, Gender, and Social Change*, ed. Haddad and Esposito, p. 66.

16.   Valentine M. Moghadam, *Modernizing Women: Gender and Social Change in the Middle East* (Boulder and London: Lynne Rienner Publishers, 1993), p. 27.

17. For example, Maha Azzam argues for going beyond the Islamic frame-
     work: "This would not necessarily undermine the importance of Islam,
     but it would allow us to analyse the role of Arab Muslim women with the
     use of analytical frameworks that, for example, draw on the sociology of
     religion and on the political and economic dynamics of nationalism and
     dependency ... By showing some of the contradictions that arise from
     remaining solely within the Islamic discourse, perhaps we can begin to
     answer some of the questions relating to Arab women." Quoted in Hijab,
     full citation below.

18. Nadia Hijab, "Islam, Social Change, and the Reality of Arab Women's
     Lives," in *Islam, Gender, and Social Change,* ed. Haddad and Esposito, pp.
     49–51.

Plate 12 Wall painting of the popular sixteenth-century Hindu *bhakti* saint Mirabai, singing her devotion and longing before an altar to Krishna, with the amorous god himself looking on from above. Charbhuja Temple (said to be the one where Mirabai worshiped during her childhood), Merta, India. Photo: *Nancy M. Martin.*

12

KRISHNA *and the* GENDER OF LONGING

John Stratton Hawley

That love is an illness comes as news to no one. What language lacks a poet who has made this point? What person has never felt queasy and unable to eat in the presence of that particular someone else? And it is scattered like curry powder through the literature of religion. Take, for example, the early American composer William Billings, who turned to the Song of Songs to find his text:

> Stay me with flagons,
> comfort me with apples,
> for I am sick of love.
> *Song of Songs* 2:5 (K.J.V.)

Billings' musical treatment of this verse and the passage in which it occurs is remarkable for several reasons. He arranges it as a dialogue between the "sons" and the "daughters." In the written text, the weight of language falls easily to the bride who has been, as the Song says, "brought ... to the banqueting house," but by often giving the vocal line to the men when the heroine describes her bridegroom, Billings shares the burden – well, the joy. He does the same with this verse too, which should by rights fall entirely to the bride. "Stay me with flagons," the women swoon. "Comfort me with apples," urge the men, as if they were ready to take a bite out of a big ripe Macintosh. And then both voices make a try at "For I am sick," before completing it in mixed-voice harmony: "For I am sick of love." Again there is the hint of swooning, but the overall line rises to a crest and settles into a great affirmative tonic. No hint of any minor key here. The Bible does recognize moments of deep estrangement between the allegorical Israel and her covenanted Lord (consider Hosea), but none of that intrudes as she waits for her Betrothed here – especially with all those delicious apples ripening on the branches just outside the church windows![1]

The story of divine lovesickness is not always told in this way. Where Krishna is the bridegroom – or rather, as almost always, the irresistible paramour – the mood is often quite different. Here too the poet–musicians tend to be male; at least these are the voices that predominate in the lyrics that survive from the great creative sixteenth and seventeenth centuries in the religious literature of Hindu North India. But when they speak of lovesickness, they project themselves almost exclusively into the voice of one of the women who wait for Krishna – before love-making or, even more likely, afterward. And although there is plenty of humor, there is a deep sense of longing and lament. This lament is echoed in the narrative line, for according to most versions, this love story has no happy ending: Krishna never really returns to the women he leaves behind. Whether one conceives it in the secular or religious sense (and these are not entirely separable), longing has a definite gender: it is feminine. And the metaphor of illness reigns supreme.

One can ask many questions here. Why should the paradigmatic lover, the image of God, be a man? Why should his mate, who shares much more in human limitation, be a woman? These things are hardly to be taken for granted, after all, even after one has intoned the word "patriarchy." For example, in the Islamic Mughal court that reigned throughout the region where Krishna was most intensely celebrated during this early-modern efflorescence of devotional literature, one met very different models, mostly Persian in origin. There the Divine was seen in the form either of a beautiful woman or of an elusive adolescent boy, and in both instances the human being was represented as male.

But certain members of the court also savored the Hindu, heterosexual construction of Divine–human love, and there further questions remain. Why should the illness in love be shouldered so preponderantly by the woman? And why should it so often be male authors who luxuriate in her distress? Some of these questions could be asked of Billings and the Song of Songs too, but they assume particularly sharp outlines in the worship of Krishna.

THE GENDER OF LONGING

We will come to the men in a moment, but for balance let us turn first to Mirabai, or Mira for short: Mira, the upper-caste Rajput woman poet who is said to have been smitten with love for Krishna from earliest childhood, and who is arguably the best known of the great "family" of Krishna poets who flourished in sixteenth-century North India. Famous as she is, only one poem bearing Mira's signature (encoded orally in the poem itself) seems to have survived from her own century. It was preserved by being recorded in the Kartarpur manuscript of what was to become the Sikh *Guru Granth Sahib*, a manuscript dated 1604. The Mira poem appears in a hand different from that of the scribe who wrote the main manuscript and its colophon, so it is possible that it was appended some years later, but in any case it has to be dated before 1642, when it was copied as part of the regular text of the *Guru Granth Sahib* – only to be cast out somewhat later, probably on theological grounds.[2] It is a poem of love and longing addressed to Krishna, and it is all about affliction.

> He's bound my heart with the powers he owns, mother –
>> he with the lotus eyes.
> Arrows like spears: this body is pierced,
>> and mother, he's gone far away.
> When it happened, mother, I didn't know,
>> but now it's too much to bear.
> Talismans, spells, medicines –
>> I've tried, but the pain won't go.
> Is there someone who can bring relief?
>> Mother, the hurt is cruel.
> Here I am, near, and you're not far:
>> Hurry to me, to meet.
> Mīrā's mountain-lifter Lord, have mercy,
>> cool this body's fire!
> Lotus-Eyes, with the powers you own, mother,
>> with those powers you've bound.

Like so many compositions attributed to Mira, the poem is relatively straightforward, a cry for help. The body is female, and love is a wound. The speaker appeals to a female friend, it seems, for she addresses her with the general and familiar expression "mother" (*māī*). Yet as she continues, it becomes increasingly clear that at a deeper level she is appealing to Krishna. Her friend may stand near her, but Krishna is the person she really hopes is "not far." This is who she really wants to meet. At the end, when she repeats portions of the title line as a delirious refrain, she seems to be addressing more him than her.

This makes sense, since it is actually Krishna who is equipped to do the healing. His tools are his intrinsic powers, the qualities or virtues (*āpne gun*) that have caused this woman to fall in love with him. Or to change the metaphor slightly, as Mira does herself, love is a disease – the affliction of being absent from one's beloved. The wound itself is in the nature of a bond, a bondage: the verb *bāndhiu* is cognate to both these English words. But paradoxically, this wound also *needs* to be bound. It needs bandaging – and in saying that, we are still within the semantic realm of the word *bāndhiu*. This is just right, for the only true treatment is the lover's return. Cause of the disease, he is also its cure and sole physician.

At a basic level, the gender realities here are stark and plain. It is the male who inflicts injury, whether that male be understood as love (the god Kama) or the lover (Krishna); and the injured party is female. Any gender confusions are ancillary, as when her friend's name lingers in her emergent appeal to Krishna. But matters become more complex when such confusions extend from the person being addressed to the person who is doing the speaking.

To demonstrate this, let us consider a parallel lyric attributed (through the signature, again) to the male poet Surdas – or Sur, for short. Like Mirabai, Sur is also a sixteenth-century poet, and he is the person regarded as the exemplar of poets composing in Brajbhasha, the language of the Braj region south of Delhi where Krishna is said to have spent his youth. In part for that reason, Brajbhasha was for many centuries the leading literary forum in the family of languages we nowadays call Hindi. Like the Mira poem, the composition we will hear can also be traced to the sixteenth century: it appears in a manuscript dated 1582. But far from being alone, like hers, it takes its place among some four hundred roughly contemporaneous poems attributed to Sur. A remarkable number of these – about half – depict the struggles and longings of women in love.[3] So marked is the theme that it is given a distinct name: *viraha*, which can mean both the physical fact of separation between lovers and the various emotions that accompany it. And most often it is the *virahiṇī* herself, the woman afflicted by love, who speaks. Listen:

> My eyes have become so greedy – they lust for his juice;
> They refuse to be satisfied, drinking in the beauty
>   of his lotus face, the sweetness of his words.

> Day and night they fashion their picture of him
> and never blink a moment for rest.
> What an ocean of radiance! But where's it going to fit
> in this cramped little closet of a heart?
> And now with raw estrangement its waters surge so high
> that the eyes vomit in pain:
> Sur says, the Lord of Braj – the doctor – has gone.
> Who can I send to Mathura to fetch him here again?[4]

In a certain sense, not much has changed from Mira's poem. The voice is still female, its object male; though here it is clearer that the woman speaks not to Krishna but to a friend, or perhaps to herself. Once again we recognize the lotus in Krishna, but this time it is his entire face, not just his eyes. Once again the vision is refracted through longing – "raw estrangement" (*birah ajīr*) – and this time the separation is given narrative specificity: Krishna has departed for the city of Mathura, leaving his love-lost cowherder women (*gopīs*) to pine away in the countryside of Braj. Once again their experience of his absence is represented as illness – a nausea of tears – and once again the doctor is also the cause of the disease. The identity of these two makes particularly good sense when one considers the kind of doctor Krishna is said to be: an Ayurvedic *baid* (Sanskrit *vaidya*, v. 6). His homeopathic practices deploy elements in the disease itself to effect their cure.

But what about the signature? What about the fact that the person singing this song announces himself as male – a male taking the voice of a female? Does this change the poem in any way? What does it mean that a sort of verbal cross-dressing has occurred, and that this cross-dressing is actually the norm in poems of this kind? And then there is our old question. Looking beyond the obvious fact that the sickness of love is here praised, romanticized, and emulated, what are we to make of a literature in which the normative condition of the female body is disease – a disease caused by and indeed consisting of the absence of the male?

THE FEMALE BODY AND THE BODY OF DISEASE

Drawing on the resources of earlier centuries, North Indian aestheticians in the period we are considering elaborated a complete taxonomy of the stages and types of love. While the hero (*nāyaka*) received his due, it was the heroine (*nāyikā*) whose states and moods particularly fascinated these theorists, resulting at one point in a calculus of 384 types of love-heroine.[5]

More to the point, one saw the emergence of influential independent texts such as Bhanudatta's *Rasamañjarī* (ca. fifteenth century) and Kriparam's *Hitataraṅganī* (1541) which focused entirely on the heroine. In a work like Rupa Gosvami's early sixteenth-century *Ujjvalanīlamaṇi*, these classifications were integrated with a theory of Krishna's "plays" or *līlās*. And in the classic *Rasikapriyā* of Keshavdas (1591), Krishna and Radha (his favorite among the *gopīs*) became themselves the hero and heroine, with Radha's moods receiving the great preponderance of attention.[6]

As this brief sketch suggests, it would be going too far to say that Indian love poetry, sacred or secular, always focuses on the longing of a woman for a man. In one lovely poem, for example, Surdas adopts the persona of a female go-between, a *sakhī*, who tries to persuade Radha to desist from her anger and rejoin Krishna. Here the wasted body is not hers but his:

> Ever since your name has entered Hari's ear
> It's been "Rādhā, oh Rādhā," only this mantra,
>   a formula chanted to a secret string of beads.
> Nightly he stays by the Jumna, in a grove
>   far from his friends and his happiness and home.
> He yearns for you. Like a great yogi
>   he is constantly wakeful through hours that are ages.
> Sometimes he spreads himself a bed of tender leaves;
>   sometimes he chants your treasurehouse of fames;
> Sometimes he closes his eyes in utter silence
>   and meditates on every pleasure of your frame –
> His eyes the libation, his heart the fire-oblation,
>   his mutterings and lapses, food for a Brahmin feast.
> So has Syām's whole body wasted away.
>   Says Sūr, let him see you. Fulfill his desire.[7]

It happens, then, that the male can also be a paradigm of longing – or at least, so it seems. Look closely. First, we do not actually know that Krishna is experiencing this mental torture. Yes, there is pleasure in contemplating it, but there is also pleasure in considering the possibility that this description of him may simply be an elaborate tactic on the part of the messenger girl; and Krishna himself may have given her the idea of saying what she says, with the purpose of drawing Radha to his side once again. I would not put it past him, and neither would many in the audiences who revel in this Brajbhasa poetry. Then too, it may be significant that Krishna's longing is not here represented as disease. There is weakness, yes, but it shows itself more characteristically as a heightened measure of (male) self-control – as yoga, or as the ritual manipulations of a priest. A mantra there is, as in Mira's poem (we translated that word as "spells"), but this is not a mantra of the sort that might be chanted over a body racked with disease.

Such things belong, rather, to women. And why? Because according to the pervasive views of Hindu males, at least, women are on the whole more vulnerable than men. There is also the competing view that in matters sexual, where men are in danger of losing control (particularly control of their preciously produced semen), women can be extraordinarily aggressive. But the preponderant emphasis is on a woman's vulnerability, her incompleteness – especially in relation to men – and this is what causes women often to be construed in the religious realm as natural devotees.[8] Obviously enough, this resonates to a structural imbalance in Indian society, where men are generally marked higher than women and the institutions of marriage by and large perpetuate the relative weakness and dependence of women. Such vulnerability may also be understood as a manifestation of female incompleteness. It is the absent y-chromosome all over again, most famously encountered in texts asserting that women's dharma can only be achieved in dependence on men in this life,[9] or that women must become men in a subsequent life before they can be candidates for release (*moksha*) from the bonds of this world.[10] Of course, there is a full range of texts and practices that challenge such views, both openly and implicitly,[11] but one cannot gainsay their existence. And they have been influential.

Yet one of the interesting things about the poem in which Sur as a woman laments her greedy eyes is that, unlike a host of other poems, the woman involved is a victim of her own hyperactivity, not her lethargy. Her very *agency* does her in – the insatiably restless probing of her eyes. Let's take this as a symbol of the poet's awareness that no single stereotype of female longing suffices to represent the disease with which human beings are afflicted in relation to the Divine.

We must recognize, moreover, that the *gopis*' state of dissipation, dishevelment, and disease is lauded as being far superior to the supposed health of spirit that is personified by the man who emerges as their opposite number. This is the urbane courtier Udho (in Sanskrit, Uddhava), who comes to the *gopis* as Krishna's messenger from Mathura with the advice that these distraught women can be cured by focusing on Krishna's invisible but nonetheless actual *presence* among them. They can do this by means of certain yogic techniques and a regimen of philosophical clarification. But this vision of divine pervasiveness comes across as just plain pallid, and the love-affliction of the female body shows just how vapid it is as a strategy of faith. The earlier *Bhāgavata Purāṇa*, in Sanskrit, may waffle on this point, but the sixteenth-century vernacular texts are very clear. Such male philosophizing stinks.[12]

All this gives a very positive conceptual spin to bodily, female affliction, but in real life one may wonder over whose dead body it gets spun. Does a woman contemplating this romantic paradigm of faith experience the same sense of amusement as might be expected in a man? Does she get the same sort of buzz that a man does from the idea that Krishna serves as a magnet for numberless, often rather faceless women?[13] The matter bears real research, and no one has yet quite done it, although Donna Wulff's current work on women's impressions of Radha comes close.[14]

I did once myself attempt a similar task on a literary level, and was struck by how poems attributed to Mirabai seemed to differ from poems attributed to Surdas. The poems signed Sur positively revelled in the gender disparity represented by this stand-off between Udho and the *gopīs*, while in poems attributed to Mira one found quite a different mindset to be characteristic. Her poems seemed often to build outward from "women's roles" rather than reinforcing a male/female disparity, although you would never know it on the basis of the poem we quoted here.[15] Similarly, in a group of poems attributed to Mira by lower-caste, peasant, and itinerant singers of both genders, we find a far more aggressive construction of her female embodiment, defined over against her upper-caste husband, than is typically found in the "authoritative" schoolbook collections edited by upper-caste Brahmin males.[16]

So it is striking how many registers are provided for the language of female suffering in Mirabai poems, and how active these tend to be. Poems attributed to Surdas are by no means less varied – in fact, he is the greater virtuoso – but the persona of the *virahiṇī*, helpless victim of separation, is far more prominent. Why? Why is it that men get off on the weakness – and specifically the sickness – of women?

THE UNSPOKEN MOTHER

This is a big question, and I would not wish to answer it in general terms – not yet, anyway. Instead, let me make a suggestion about the specific milieu in which a number of these cross-dressed lyrics emerged. I would draw attention to the fact that the separation of lovers (*viraha*) is understood to have a special, archetypally appropriate season in the liturgical year of

North Indian Hinduism. It is the rainy season, when the monsoon makes journeys hard and lovers are stranded far from one another. More than any other, this is the season for songs of estrangement. When women sing such songs, they often long for their brothers, hoping they will come soon to take them back to spend some time with the families into which they were born and from which they have been separated by marriage. But in the mouths of men, the songs of the monsoon are typically addressed not to family but to lovers, and above all to Krishna.[17]

To understand why this is so, we might well look around and see what else is happening in the monsoon season, which serves as culmination and release for the hottest weather of the year. When the rains come, the earth turns green overnight. Waters rush dark with life, and thousands of microbes have their day. Whether from sheer heat or from microbe-mania, this is the season of disease, and the gendered language of religion is available to recognize that fact. The hot season and the monsoon are often felt to belong especially to the Goddess.[18] Feverish or pustular diseases like smallpox tend to be seen as goddesses whose visitation is experienced simultaneously as affliction and grace. These are real sufferings, but to contemplate them as divine holds a special promise. As Edward Dimock writes of Sitala – that is, smallpox:

> By hearing of suffering, by realizing the extent of human frailty, one with the eyes to see may be spared the necessity of more particular pain. Śītalā allows us cognition of our position in the universe, and recognition of herself as Mother.[19]

I would stress two aspects. First, diseases such as smallpox bring bodily suffering in a real, obviously physical way. Second, their agency is understood as female, and not only female but maternal. And now the intriguing point: this massively present Mother – the Goddess with many names and forms – is eerily absent from the narrative world of Krishna. Her place has been taken by her shadow. The divine Woman who is massively, threateningly present is replaced by a human woman who suffers massive absence – the absence of Krishna.

The metaphor of disease shows the connection between these two, suggesting that we have a displacement here, a displacement whose purpose is to project the illusion of control. Men who stand in danger of being afflicted by the all-too-present Goddess generate a world in which women are afflicted by the absence of an irresistible God. These men project themselves into such a world through poetry, art, music, performance, and ritual and thereby have the fantasy of experiencing themselves – that is, the male Krishna-self, as invincible. Faced with the danger of real suffering, they play in the suffering of imagination. Faced with the danger of real disease, they play at imagined disease. Their keyboard, their dress, their role is a woman in love.

But why is the Goddess experienced as so threatening that her image bifurcates in this way? Why is this sleight-of-hand so particularly successful with men? There is no way of providing a definitive answer to questions such as these, but my own urge is to venture into the realm of psychogenesis, guided by thinkers such as Dorothy Dinnerstein, Nancy Chodorow, and Karen McCarthy Brown; or in an Indian milieu, by Sudhir Kakar, Stanley Kurtz, and Jeffrey Kripal.[20] I would want to ask about the problem that boys face especially, the need to achieve a double separation from their mothers – separation by virtue of maturity and separation by virtue of sex. In a girl, I imagine, the power of mimesis holds out the prospect of healing that first tear of separation: in some sense a daughter has the prospect of becoming her mother. But in a boy, the separation must be more fundamental if he is to climb into full adulthood. Hence the image of his mother is apt to remain at some level a threat of engulfment, and if he is a Hindu living in North India, that threat becomes aligned with the bodily realities of the season of heat and rains, and is perhaps accentuated by the fact that the boy may continue to live in his mother's physical presence even after marriage, as a member of the same extended family. No wonder he clings to his fascination with separation, while at the same time holding it at arm's length from his own ego.

He does this with a deft two-step that answers to both needs in his drama of psychic separation from his childhood and his mother (or mothers, as Stanley Kurtz has urged for extended families). As to the task of attaining a gender role that is contrary to his mother's, he reverses the genders in his own drama – his religious drama – so that the victim of separation becomes female, while the lover from whom she is parted is male. And to accomplish the task of attaining maturity, he imagines this male lover as omnipotent, eternally full of appetite and eternally fascinating to the women who surround him. Thus the young man disperses his mother everywhere, and he secures his victory by crippling the women who so desire him. He cripples them with the very desire he imagines them to have. By visiting upon these archetypes of womanly love a love that is disease, he controls the threatening Woman after all. For he represents himself – the ideal, projected self who is Krishna – as her only cure.[21]

FEMALE LONGING AS MALE PREGNANCY

The Indologist Martha Selby has recently been developing an exposition of sections of the most basic Indian medical text, the *Charaka Saṁhitā* (ca. first century CE), in which she focuses especially on the passages having to do with obstetrics.[22] Her work brings to the fore a number of unsuspected parallels to major motifs we have been considering here, just as the study of Galen throws light on various metaphors of gender that emerged in early Christian thinking.[23]

The first set of surprising parallels between the Indian medical literature and its theological/amatory counterpart are a series of direct contrasts between the condition of a pregnant woman and that of a *virahiṇī*. The one is full, the other empty. The one grows day by day; the other diminishes. The one nurses life inside; the other has lost her life. The one experiences heat in the good sense – the heat of the internal hearth, the heat of cooking; the other is assaulted by bad heat – a fever she cannot control. The one looks forward to separation, the good separation of birth; the other laments a separation she does not wish.

Yet there is another set of parallels that are not in the nature of oppositions and that seem in an almost excruciating way to show how closely the two archetypal women are bound together. Both are ultimately supine, for example. Both require medical help if they are to deliver or be delivered. And in both cases the chroniclers involved are primarily male, reporting on experiences that are understood to belong to women. True, a number of females hover about; in fact their presence is required. Charaka demands that in the advanced stages of pregnancy, "suitable women" who have given birth gather round the mother-to-be and urge her on. In *viraha*, meanwhile, the heroine's good friends are expected to comfort her, sometimes acting as messengers to Krishna, sometimes using their own suasion to try to draw her out of her deep depression. But behind these many women, or perhaps through them, the authoritative, authorial voice almost always remains male.

So does the ultimate subject, the agent who witnesses from within. In the poetry of love, of course, this is Krishna. With Charaka, however, it is the fetus, who is inevitably imagined as a boy. In part this derives from the well-known Indian preference for male progeny. Yet in this setting, I believe, it also stems from the desire of the author of the text to locate himself within the body he describes. This has huge epistemological advantages. It gives Charaka access, as a man, to a set of experiences that otherwise would come to him only second-hand. But if we think, as Charaka does, that the fetus is the real author of a woman's pregnancy, carrying forward the dynamism of the father's seed, and if that fetus too is understood as male, then the mother's own experience of her pregnancy becomes in some way second-hand. Her gender separates her from the prime mover of the pregnancy, who is, like Charaka, male. So Charaka, the outer "self" or author, can relish its desires and demands (sour food now, sweet food then) as cognate with his own. Even experiences so intrinsically female that Charaka can only have known them because women revealed this knowledge to men – for example, the sense of hot, vaguely itchy expansion that is said to feel like a bandage being peeled away from the skin[24] – are revalued through the agency of the male fetus.

Time and again, then, the woman is figured as the recipient of her own bodily experience, rather than as its true subject. The process is made male, and so is its *telos*, the much-desired birth of a son. Here too, in this quite unexpected place, we have *viraha* for the absent (or not yet present) male. It is he who will make her a real woman: a mother of sons.[25] Therefore her yearning is intense – both ideally, as in Charaka, and often in fact as well. It is widely reported that the most intense relationship in Indian societies, bar none, is felt to be the relationship between mother and son.

So far, so good. From a male point of view, it is the mother, the woman, who longs for the realization of that relationship. But it must be threatening when the son himself, the male, also longs for that same intimacy. Hence the literature of Krishna's childhood denies it. It drowns it out with the opposite fantasy: a host of would-be mothers, starting with Krishna's foster-mother and moving through all the other *gopīs*, who depend on him, who long for him to take their milk products or its distillate, their love.[26] God forbid that *he* should be emotionally dependent on *them*! So he steals their milk, rather than claiming or receiving it in a way that could imply any enduring connection.[27]

In a similar way much of the religious literature of estrangement and separation, though focused upon a woman's body, bears the mark of the male author. Here the agent who replaces the hidden male fetus is, of course, the absent male lover. Since he is the cause of her experience, he is its cure. He is, in fact, her deliverer – her delivery, just as the production of a male child at the moment of birth is for Charaka the true culmination of pregnancy. He, the lover, with his male presence, is her cure. Hence her love is best represented – retroactively, at least – as sickness.

Here in the world of erotic love, as in Krishna's childhood revels, the male author has a chance to play with an experience of separation that might be too threatening if experienced in "real life." As the doctor, the medical technician, Charaka can play with pregnancy and master it, without enduring its pain. As the poet, the verbal technician, Surdas can play with separation, feeling its threat but in a mediated, unthreatening way. His audience can do the same.[28]

And there is a final step. Much is gained by projecting this double fantasy of weakness and control, sickness and health – a fantasy that parallels pregnancy, the genesis of existence itself – onto the Big Screen. Much is gained by perceiving the primary actor as Krishna, that is, as God. We all come into the world as vulnerable babes, and we leave it for a future to which we are at least as vulnerable. But the power imbalance that men so anxiously establish between themselves and women is for men, at least, a major resource in this ultimate game of life. If one imagines God as male, then the threat of drowning that seems to be posed by women and by the sea of existence (*bhavasāgar*) that is life – these can in some measure be contained.

So *viraha* is a game. It is a man's game, a game of trying on women's clothes and women's feelings. It's a game of playing God, the way God (or Goddess!) plays with us men. This game gives a gender to longing.

NOTES

1. There is, of course, a huge range of interpretation concerning the Song of Songs, not all of which agrees in tone with that of Billings or turns to allegory. Even within the span of Christian allegorical interpretation, not all commentators accept that the terms of reference are Christ and the Church. I am indebted to Elizabeth Castelli for discussions on these matters, and to Marcia Falk, *The Song of Songs: A New Translation and Interpretation* (San Francisco: Harper, 1990).

2. I owe these details to the work of Gurinder Singh Mann, who has examined the manuscript carefully, and I translate from his transcription. The text differs in only two instances from the one found in the so-called Banno manuscript of Kanpur, dated 1642, which is published in W. M. Callewaert, "The 'Earliest' Song of Mira (1503–1546)," *Annali* 50: 4 of the Istituto Universitario Orientale, Naples (1990), pp. 365–366; also in *Orientalia Lovaniensia Periodica*, 22, 1991, p. 203. For further information and a different translation, see Nancy M. Martin(-Kershaw), "Dyed in the Color of Her Lord: Multiple Representations in the Mirabai Tradition," (Ph.D. dissertation, Graduate Theological Union, Berkeley, 1995), p. 115. Aspects of Gurinder Singh Mann's work on this poem appear in his

forthcoming *The Making of Sikh Scripture* (New York: Oxford University Press), chapter 6.

3. A heading-by-heading breakdown for a manuscript of Surdas's poems dated 1640 is given in J. S. Hawley, *Sūr Dās: Poet, Singer, Saint* (Seattle: University of Washington Press and Delhi: Oxford University Press, 1984), p. 48. A similar pattern is manifest in poems datable to the sixteenth century itself, as will be evident in Kenneth E. Bryant's critical edition (*The Poems of Sūrdās*) and my translation of and commentary on it (*Sūr's Ocean*), both forthcoming.

4. The Brajbhasha text upon which this translation is based has been established in the critical edition of Kenneth Bryant *et al.* (*Poems of Sūrdās*, forthcoming). The poem corresponds to number 3857 in the currently standard Nāgarīpracāriṇī Sabhā *Sūrsāgar* edited by Jaganāth Dās 'Ratnākar', Nanddulāre Vājpeyī *et al.* (2 vols., Varanasi, Kāśī Nāgarīpracāriṇī Sabhā, 1972 and 1976). In translating both Surdas poems presented in this essay, I have benefitted greatly from the comments and corrections of Vidyut Aklujkar in regard to accuracy, and Mark Juergensmeyer in regard to poetic style.

5. S. K. De, *History of Sanskrit Poetics*, 2nd rev. ed. (Calcutta: K. L. Mukhopadhyaya, 1960), vol. 2, p. 271.

6. This history is sketched with useful brevity in Barron Holland, "The *Satsaī* of Bihārī: Hindi Poetry of the Early Riti Period" (Ph.D. dissertation, University of California, Berkeley, 1969), pp. 82–87. See also Ronald Stuart McGregor, *Hindi Literature from its Beginning to the Nineteenth Century* (Wiesbaden: Otto Harrassowitz, 1984), pp. 118–129.

7. The Brajbhasha original is the Bryant version (*The Poems of Sūrdās*, forthcoming) that corresponds to Nāgarīpracāriṇī Sabhā 3399.

8. A frequently cited statement on women as natural devotees in the literature of Hindu *bhakti* (devotion) occurs at the end of A. K. Ramanujan's "On Women Saints," in *The Divine Consort: Rādhā and the Goddesses of India*, ed. J. S. Hawley and D. M. Wulff (Berkeley: Berkeley Religious Studies Series and Delhi: Motilal Banarsidass, 1982), p. 324. Ramanujan speaks of passivity rather than vulnerability. As to the "natural" analogue – female incompleteness in relation to men – Cynthia Humes (personal communication, April 2, 1998) points out that in the classic *Nāṭyaśāstra* of Bharata only one of the eight classical temperaments assigned to a hero, the *lalita guṇa* (light-heartedness), connects him intrinsically to a woman. Bharata's classification of a heroine is tellingly different. Here too Bharata employs an eightfold scheme, but in this case all eight of the "eight states" (*avasthāḥ*), as they were later to be called, situate the heroine in relation to a man. See Rākeśagupta, *Studies in Nāyaka-Nāyikā-Bheda* (Aligarh: Granthayan, 1967), pp. 49–51.

9. Especially *Manusmṛti* 5.147–151, 155, as in Wendy Doniger (with Brian K. Smith), trans., *The Laws of Manu* (New York: Penguin, 1991), p. 115;

but see also I. Julia Leslie, *The Perfect Wife: The Orthodox Hindu Woman according to the Strīdharmapaddhati of Tryambakayajvan* (Delhi: Oxford University Press, 1989), pp. 305–317.

10. We meet this conviction in a *bhakti* framework in the *Subodhinī* (10.14) of Vallabhacharya, where he insists that a woman must be reborn as a man before she is fit to worship the way the *gopīs* do. On Vallabha's further struggles with this point, see Mrudula I. Marfatia, *The Philosophy of Vallabhācārya* (New Delhi: Munshiram Manoharlal, 1967), p. 222.

11. See, for example, Mary McGee, "Desired Fruits: Motive and Intention in the Votive Rites of Hindu Women," in *Roles and Rituals for Hindu Women*, ed. Julia Leslie (Rutherford, NJ: Fairleigh Dickinson University Press, 1991), pp. 71–88; Gloria Goodwin Rehejia and Ann Grodzins Gold, *Listen to the Heron's Words: Reimagining Gender and Kinship in North India* (Berkeley: University of California Press, 1994), pp. 67–72, 121–148; and Velcheru Narayana Rao, "A Rāmāyaṇa of Their Own: Women's Oral Tradition in Telugu," in *Many Rāmāyanas: The Diversity of a Narrative Tradition in South Asia*, ed. Paula Richman (Berkeley: University of California Press, 1991), pp. 114–136.

12. I treat the theme in chapter 4 ("*Viraha*: Separation and Simple Religion") of *Sūr Dās: Poet, Singer, Saint*, pp. 93–118.

13. On the relative paucity of references to the names of individual *gopīs* (including Radha) in the early strata of the *Sūrsāgar*, for example, see Hawley, *Sūr Dās*, pp. 88–90.

14. D. M. Wulff, "Rādhā's Audacity in *Kirtan* Performances and Women's Status in Greater Bengal," in *Women and Goddess Traditions*, ed. Karen King and Karen Jo Torjesen (Minneapolis: Fortress Press, 1995), pp. 64–83.

15. J. S. Hawley, "Images of Gender in the Poetry of Krishna," in *Gender and Religion: On the Complexity of Symbols*, ed. Caroline Walker Bynum, Stevan Harrell, and Paula Richman (Boston: Beacon Press, 1986), pp. 231–256. In regard to issues relating to the signature that appears in poems attributed to Mira and Sur, see Hawley, "Author and Authority in the *Bhakti* Poetry of North India," *The Journal of Asian Studies* 47, 2 (1988), pp. 269–290.

16. We may view these contrasting corpuses in Parita Mukta, *Upholding the Common Life: The Community of Mirabai* (Delhi: Oxford University Press, 1994), especially pp. 90–105, on the one hand, and in Parsuram Chaturvedi, *Mirabai ki Padavali* (Allahabad: Hindi Sahitya Sammelan, 1973), on the other. A variety of related terrains are staked out by Nancy M. Martin(-Kershaw) in chapter 5 of "Dyed in the Color of Her Lord," pp. 254–337. Martin draws attention to a distinction between resistance and renunciation and emphasizes that sometimes "[t]he focus is not on Mira's transgression of gender roles from the perspective of upper-caste men; rather the view seems to be that of a woman trying to negotiate a

life of her own choosing within structures of power that subjugate her and in relation to other women who must do the same" (p. 317).

17. In a longer essay, this sweeping generalization would require massive qualification, for *viraha* is a theme so crucial to the literature of Krishna that we meet it virtually everywhere. Yet in the sixteenth-century *Sūrsāgar*, for example, all the poems dealing specifically with the rainy season (corresponding to Nāgarīpracāriṇī Sabhā 3918–3956) contain overtones of *viraha*, and the calendrical twelve-month (*bārahmāsā*) poems of *viraha* tend to begin with the hot or rainy season. A related genre, the four-month poem (*caumāsā*), focuses there entirely. On the latter two, see Charlotte Vaudeville, *Les Chansons des douze mois dans les litteratures Indoaryennes* (Pondicherry: Institut Français d'Indologie, 1965), translated as *Bārahmāsā in Indian Literatures* (Delhi: Motilal Banarsidass, 1986). As to qualifications, for example, one would quickly admit that in Rajasthan the desert climate yields a sort of year-round "culture of separation," as Friedhelm Hardy has observed in his *Viraha-Bhakti* (Delhi: Oxford University Press, 1983), p. 568.

18. Lawrence A. Babb, *The Divine Hierarchy: Popular Hinduism in Central India* (New York: Columbia University Press, 1975), pp. 128–153. In regard to connections between festivals for Krishna/Vishnu and the felt hegemony of the Goddess in the rainy season and somewhat thereafter, see Charlotte Vaudeville, "Krishna Gopāla, Rādhā, and the Great Goddess," in *The Divine Consort*, ed. Hawley and Wulff, pp. 2–5.

19. Edward C. Dimock, Jr., "A Theology of the Repulsive: The Myth of the Goddess Śītalā," in *The Divine Consort*, ed. Hawley and Wulff, p. 196. Dimock notes, however (p. 184), that Jvarāsura, the fever demon who is frequently said to accompany her, is male.

20. Dorothy Dinnerstein, *The Mermaid and the Minotaur: Sexual Arrangements and the Human Malaise* (New York: Harper & Row, 1976); Nancy Chodorow, "Family Structure and Feminine Personality," in *Women, Culture, and Society*, ed. Michelle Zimbalist Rosaldo and Louise Lamphere (Stanford: Stanford University Press, 1974), pp. 43–66; Karen McCarthy Brown, "Fundamentalism and the Control of Women," in *Fundamentalism and Gender*, ed. J. S. Hawley (New York: Oxford University Press, 1994), especially pp. 180–189; Sudhir Kakar and John M. Ross, "The Cloistered Passion of Radha and Krishna," in *Tales of Love, Sex and Danger*, Kakar and Ross (Delhi: Oxford University Press, 1986), especially pp. 99–103; Jeffrey J. Kripal, *Kali's Child: The Mystical and the Erotic in the Life and Teachings of Ramakrishna* (Chicago: University of Chicago Press, 1995), especially pp. 232–236; Stanley N. Kurtz, *All the Mothers are One: Hindu India and the Reshaping of Psychoanalysis* (New York: Columbia University Press, 1992), pp. 29–131.

21. I am sure this sounds reductionistic. One must recognize that whatever the narcissistic mood here – however strong the connection seems

between a male self and the self projected as male in Krishna – this does not make men's worship of Krishna the same as self-worship, any more than the projection of God or Allah as male makes that deity the same as his male worshipers. In all these cases, male devotees certainly experience themselves as quite different from the gods they worship; and the general contrast between the structures of Krishna's life and the life of domestic dharma, so fundamental to lives of most men, underscores the point. Still, as we currently see in the great debates about ordaining women and homosexuals to the clergy in modern Western Christianity, these resonances along gender lines between worshiper and worshiped are very important. Particularly in a theological universe where the analogy between self (*jīva*) and Self (*ātman*) is the subject of direct discussion, and in which (male) adepts learn to map out the world of Krishna on their bodies through practices of meditation and visualization, the significance of these connections is not to be minimized. In a longer exposition one would also want to consider the possibility that latent homosexuality is in the air. In doing so, one would have to give due weight to the fact that same-sex attractions between men were apparently understood rather differently in sixteenth-century India than they are in the modern West or in at least some parts of urban India today.

22.   Martha Ann Selby, "Like a Pot Brimming with Oil: The Care and Feeding of the Pregnant Body in Sanskrit Ayurvedic Texts," Dharam Hinduja Indic Research Center, Columbia University, March 12, 1998. On problems of dating and authorship associated with the *Caraka Saṃhitā*, see Kenneth G. Zysk, *Asceticism and Healing in Ancient India* (New York: Oxford University Press, 1991), p. 33. Charaka has continued to have a major effect on Indian medical knowledge – certainly through the sixteenth century and in some settings, today as well.

23.   Karen Jo Torjesen discusses Galen's medical writing and the effect of this single-sex theory of gender difference on early Christian thinking about salvation in detail in her chapter within this volume.

24.   This is Selby's favorite example among a set of similar experiences. The Sanskrit phrase is *vimukta-bandhanatvam-iva vakṣasaḥ*, found in *Carakasaṃhitā śarīrasthāna* 8.36. See Priyavrat Sharma, ed. and trans., *Caraka-Saṃhitā*, vol. 1 (Varanasi: Chaukhambha Orientalia, 1981), p. 476. A similar example – a Kerala text on the pains of childbirth – has been noticed by Sarah Caldwell in her "Waves of Beauty, Rivers of Blood: Constructing the Goddess's Body in Kerala," in *In Search of Mahadevi: Constructing the Identity of the Great Goddess,* ed. Tracy Pintchman (Albany: SUNY Press, forthcoming) and reported in Wendy Doniger, *The Implied Spider: Poetics and Theology in Myth* (New York: Columbia University Press, 1998), p. 114. Doniger's comment on the (un)translatability of language about women's experience from women to men (*Implied Spider*, p. 115) is worth noting in this context, and the entire chapter in

which it occurs (pp. 109–135) is an elegant exploration of "women's voices" in relation to questions of authorship, audience, cross-gender "gaze," and proximate and ultimate narration.

25. Hence the title of the popular book by Elisabeth Bumiller, *May You Be the Mother of a Hundred Sons* (New York: Random House, 1990). On ritual enactments of this theme in the *pumsavanā* and *chauk* rites, see Raj Bali Pandey, *Hindu Samskāras* (Delhi: Motilal Banarsidass, 1969), pp. 60–63; and Doranne Jacobson, "Golden Handprints and Red-painted Feet: Hindu Childbirth Rituals in Central India," in *Women in India: Two Perspectives*, Doranne Jacobson and Susan Wadley, 2nd enlarged ed. (Columbia, MO: South Asia Publications, 1992), pp. 148–153. Cf. also *Carakasamhitā śarīrasthāna* 8.18–19, as in *Caraka-Samhita*, ed. Sharma, pp. 466–467.

26. J. M. Masson, "The Childhood of Kṛṣṇa," *Journal of the American Oriental Society*, 94, 4 (1974), pp. 454–459.

27. This is the general subject of my *Krishna, the Butter Thief* (Princeton: Princeton University Press, 1983).

28. On *rasa*, aesthetic emotion, as shared, controlled experience, especially in the context of the performing arts, see Donna M. Wulff, *Drama as a Mode of Religious Realization* (Chico, CA: Scholars Press, 1984), pp. 25–44, and David L. Haberman, *Acting as a Way of Salvation* (New York: Oxford University Press, 1988), pp. 12–39. In relation to the male poet's access to the inner world of female experience, as in the case of Surdas, see the theological preamble that Hariray adds to the *Sūrdās kī Vārtā* attributed to Gokulnāth. An English translation appears in Richard Barz, *The Bhakti Sect of Vallabhācārya* (Faridabad: Thomson Press, 1976), pp. 106–107.

Part IV

SEXUAL LOVE AND RELIGION

Plate 13 An unusual indigenous fresco in the Roman Catholic tradition combining features of the Mexican apparition Our Lady of Guadalupe with more standard representations of the Virgin Mary holding the child Jesus. Here Mary is envisioned as a queen, much like a member of the Spanish royal family. Mission San Xavier del Bac, founded in 1700 and rebuilt in the late 1700s, lies on the present day Tohono O'odham Indian Reservation in southeastern Arizona, U.S.A. Photo: *Joseph Runzo*.

13

THE TARNISHED TEMPLE: SEX *and* DIFFERENCE *in* CHRISTIAN ETHICS

Karen Lebacqz

> Do you not know that your body is a temple of the holy spirit, who is in you, whom you have received from God? ... Therefore, honor God with your body.
>
> I Corinthians 6:19–20

The body as temple has been a recurring theme in Christian sexual ethics, both formal and informal. This passage from Paul's letter to the Corinthians has been used to chastise young Christians in hopes of keeping them from sexual activity. If the body is a temple, the thinking goes, then it must be respected and used carefully.

But in a pluralistic world, it is increasingly difficult to know what grounds can be found for any clear assertions about how the body is to be used or treated. Does it make a difference if the body is male or female? Can Christian ethics be separated from Jewish or Buddhist or Islamic ethics in a world where many Christians have dabbled in other religions?[1] What base can be found for a *Christian* sexual ethic in contemporary times?

Two recent books have tried to address these challenges: Lisa Cahill's *Sex, Gender, and Christian Ethics* and Marvin Ellison's *Erotic Justice: A Liberating Ethic of Sexuality.*[2] Both Cahill and Ellison push their readers to ask, "what is the *social* significance of sex?" How can we have a sexual ethic that takes seriously the *public, political* dimensions of sexuality? In a liberal culture that has largely confined sexual ethics to the private arena, both Cahill and Ellison reject that confinement and insist that a genuinely Christian ethic lifts sexuality out of the private arena and places it squarely in the public. As Cahill puts it, "Christian sexual ethics needs an analysis of the social ramifications of sex which is both critical and constructive."[3]

Cahill and Ellison are, of course, not the first voices to argue for a public dimension to sexuality; long ago Stanley Hauerwas sounded the call for "sex in public," as he called it.[4] But Cahill's and Ellison's voices are important because they place the problem of an adequate sexual ethics squarely within the complexities of a post-modern, pluralistic world in which attention to "differences" makes difficult any monolithic "Christian" view of sex.[5]

Yet Cahill and Ellison also diverge dramatically in their approaches to a contemporary Christian sexual ethic that has an adequate public dimension. Cahill turns to a neo-Aristotelian base, pushing us to consider whether there are values found universally in our sexual embodiment that might provide an adequate framework for a post-modern sexual ethic. Ellison turns not to our embodiment, per se, but rather to the social context in which that embodiment is found – to the social construction of sexuality, including the oppressive contexts of modern cultures. While Cahill might be said to look to the body as a "temple" adequate to ground a Christian sexual ethic, Ellison posits a "tarnished" temple that cannot be understood apart from oppressive cultural practices.

My task is to explore the challenges raised by each of these authors and the possibilities for rapprochement between these two divergent views of Christian sexual ethics. Is there any common ground? How can we take seriously our "embodiment," as Cahill would have us do, without falling into "essentialist" traps? How can we take seriously the social construction of sexuality, as Ellison would have us do, without falling into a post-modern relativism that leaves us little room for challenges to oppression? These are the questions that guide my thinking.

CAHILL'S MOVE

Cahill notes that our "post-modern" mindset challenges all norms and values, seeing them as the products of power arrangements in societies. While post-modernists want to make value judgments about such power arrangements, post-modern theory makes value judgments difficult to justify. Recognizing that "reason" takes a pluralist twist in contemporary society and that old modernist norms cannot simply be assumed, Cahill nonetheless is not content to say that ethics is relative or that we are simply bound to particular narratives or cultural configurations. To be so bound

would leave no grounds for assessing as wrong the social roles and treatment of women in our own or other cultures. To the extent that feminists
want to judge some social arrangements to be *wrong*, they must find a base
for value judgments. As a feminist, then, Cahill cannot rest content with
post-modernism. She thus searches for a ground that allows moral judgments that cut across cultures.

Cahill proposes to find that moral ground in a neo-Thomistic ethic that
derives norms inductively, from an examination of what many cultures see
as contributing to human flourishing. Turning to the work of Martha Nussbaum and others, she proposes that there are a number of values that must
be upheld in human life, including affiliation with others, religion, and
kinship. These are shared "framing" experiences that we find in and through
particularity but that transcend particularity. In other words, if all cultures
find that human flourishing requires certain support structures, such as
adequate child development, even though they express these structures in
particular forms, there is nonetheless embedded within those particulars the
grounds on which universal value judgments might be made.

Of special importance to Cahill in the list of framing experiences is
kinship. Sex gives us children – kin. It creates lineages and family structures.
Our liberal society has privatized sex. In its focus on pleasure and intimacy
as the "goods" of sexuality, it neglects the social meanings of sex and of the
body. In a privatized climate, mutual consent is presented as largely the
only behavior-guiding norm. This limiting of sexuality to its unitive, intimate, pleasurable dimensions ignores the fact that sexuality is also linked
with our capacity for reproduction. Is sex merely a question of "sex-drive"
or desire? Cahill posits that our embodiment is crucial. Our sexual bodies
have three intrinsic meanings, she asserts: pleasure, intimacy, and reproduction. Reproduction is an inherently social dimension, just as pleasure is
personal and intimacy interpersonal.

As embodied selves, then, our "good" or flourishing will be exemplified
when these three embodied meanings of sexuality are all affirmed. Trun-
cating or dividing them is deficient moral behavior.[6] Based on this
"embodied" understanding of sexuality, Cahill then proposes that monogamous heterosexual sex emerges as an ideal that holds together the three
meanings of our sexual embodiment. However, while monogamous heterosexual sex is the ideal, it does not function as a norm that would allow
us to reject or exclude those who fall outside the ideal. Cahill makes room
for the possibility of acceptable homosexual relationships, though such
relationships will not fully embody all the "goods" of our sexuality.

In sum, it seems that Cahill finds in our bodies – in our fundamental embodiment as sexual beings – a "temple" to be used in ways that honor God. While attentive to a variety of cultures and their particular practices, she proposes nonetheless that there is something universal to be drawn from those practices: in every time and place, it has been sex that yields children. This "kinship" function of our sexuality should not be overlooked in our post-modern haste to focus on personal pleasure and interpersonal intimacy. Only a use of the body that allows pleasure, intimacy, *and* reproduction will be fully an expression of the "goods" of this "temple."

ELLISON'S COUNTER-MOVE

> Just as each of us has one body with many members, and these members do not all have the same function, so in Christ we who are many form one body … We have different gifts, according to the grace given to us.
>
> Romans 12:4–6

Cahill's monogamous, heterosexual ideal is precisely what must come under attack from the perspective of Marvin Ellison. Christian sexual ethics, suggests Ellison, has often been *marriage* ethics, not *sexual* ethics. From the perspective of marriage ethics, "good sex is heterosexual, marital, monogamous, and reproductive."[7] Heterosexuality has been seen as natural and normal, and other forms of sexuality emerge as "unnatural."[8] However careful one may be (as Cahill is) to avoid discrimination against homosexual people, holding a heterosexual ideal drawn from traditional marriage ethics means that one has already adopted a kind of cultural hegemony and ideology that is inherently oppressive. Unwittingly, perhaps, this is precisely what Cahill appears to have done. Cahill's ethic presumes unity, while Ellison stresses difference.

Instead of establishing an ideal or "natural" or fully embodied sexuality that can be found in our physical bodies and their capabilities, Ellison argues that sexuality is not some immutable "essence" given by "nature," but is socially constituted. Its meaning and purpose cannot be grasped by biology alone, therefore. Drawing on Thomas Laqueur,[9] Ellison reminds us that several centuries ago, science operated on a "one-body" view of sex in which maleness was normative, and females were considered to be "inverted" or "inferior" males (the vagina was an inverted penis, for example.)[10] Today, we have a two-body model that largely assumes that men and women are inherently and fundamentally *different* (rather than assuming that they are the same, but with one of them inverted). Both of these views of the human body and sexuality, argues Ellison, are *social con-structions*.[11]

All views of sexuality – even all views of the body – are thus socially constructed.[12] "Our social relations are shaped," argues Ellison, "by a code of expectations we internalize and utilize daily..."[13] These "sexual scripts" are culturally dependent and hence variable. Sexual ethics must begin not by asking what our embodiment tells us, but by asking how these "scripts" are encoded into cultural practices and how they are shaped and framed by oppressive structures. Such an analysis will examine the ways in which our social constructions incorporate injustices such as racism, sexism, able-ism, and heterosexism. Very much to Ellison's credit, he begins by looking at disability (a much ignored subject) to show how our cultural preoccupation with bodily perfection oppresses disabled people. Similarly, he finds that racism and sexism frame sexuality in this culture by establishing and reinforcing patterns that eroticize dominance.

In short, Ellison proposes a new beginning place. He argues that the "crisis" around sexuality has been fundamentally misunderstood: the problem is not sex, but injustice. Human sexuality is distorted by oppression and unjust practices and structures. Ellison identifies three fundamental dimensions of sexual injustice: (1) a basic negativity toward sexuality and the body, (2) the eroticizing of non-mutual relations, and (3) "compulsory heterosexuality."[14] In his view, even our understanding of our bodies has been distorted, and thus an understanding of bodies or embodiment cannot make a good beginning place for a sexual ethic.

Proposing a dialectical relationship between past and present, Ellison argues that an adequate Christian sexual ethic will attempt to uncover the full range of voices and witnesses from the past, rather than depending on dominant constructions. The dominant tradition, he charges, has tended to obscure the centrality of justice in biblical faith. Once this centrality is recognized, all sources must be tested in terms of how they impact on the lives of marginalized people.[15] We will operate, he suggests, both out of a hermeneutic of suspicion that uncovers the injustices of the past and present and out of a hermeneutic of remembrance that uncovers and honors stories of resistance to that injustice.[16]

Ellison's goal is a liberating sexual ethic of erotic justice. Such an ethic will: (1) honor the goodness of human sexuality and embodiment, (2) show genuine gratitude for difference and diversity (rather than judging all differences against a single "ideal"), and (3) empower the moral agency of the sexually abused.[17] Erotic justice will be enhanced if, in addition, we: (4)

honor self-direction, (5) enable mutuality, and (6) establish fidelity.[18] Arguing that traditional Christian sexual ethics has focused on the form of relationship (e.g. whether it is marital or non-marital) rather than the substance of relationship (e.g. whether it is mutual or whether dominance is eroticized), Ellison argues that the basic norm is justice and that all sexual relations that deepen intimacy and love should be celebrated.[19]

In sum, Ellison sees in the body not a "temple" from which norms can be derived by examining the "natural" and universal meanings or uses of that temple, but rather a "tarnished," socially constructed temple whose meanings are shaped by oppressive practices and are therefore in need of liberation. His ethic, then, focuses on the modes of oppression that shape sexual constructions in our post-modern era and on the requirements of a justice adequate to overcome that oppression.

IMPASSE OR RAPPROCHEMENT?

We appear to have, then, two quite different approaches to the possibilities for a Christian sexual ethic in the post-modern world. One attempts to retrieve a universal, "true" meaning of our embodied sexual selves and to base an ethic upon that universal meaning, exemplified in particular practices but not limited to them. The other sees sexuality as a social construction always in need of liberative hermeneutics. Most particularly, Cahill attempts to find a universal ethic in our embodiment itself, while Ellison points us to the oppressive nature of all understandings of embodiment, and suggests that, in light of that oppression, an adequate sexual ethic must be oriented toward bringing about justice and must therefore begin by honoring the experiences and insights of the most sexually marginalized communities.[20] Although Cahill cannot be accused of being a simple essentialist, her apparent trust in an ability to discern through reason some universal "meanings" of the human body and its flourishing does not seem compatible with Ellison's strong social constructionist view. Have we simply reached an impasse?

I think not, though I confess that the differences in their views are striking and difficult to reconcile. Each offers an important critique to the other.

From his side, Ellison can offer a strong critique of Cahill. I have already indicated that precisely her positioning of monogamous heterosexual relationships as "ideal" would be problematic from Ellison's perspective. Underneath that critique is a more fundamental challenge: to posit that our embodiment itself gives norms is to assume either that our embodiment is free of cultural and social construction, or that we are able to discern in and through those social constructions some "essence" strong enough to be the base for a normative ethic. In fairness to Cahill, I must say that she makes every effort to recognize the social construction of family arrangements. It is precisely because of the impact of these arrangements on the flourishing (more accurately, the non-flourishing) of women that Cahill seeks for a universal ethics. Yet I think at root her argument fails because it depends on the idea that biology somehow sets the grounding for norms: because sex gives us children, sex ought to give us children.

There is a tension in Cahill's work. While her proclaimed method is inductive, in fact her ideal appears to be drawn not from examining a wide range of cultural practices but from a rather classic natural law identification of the "ends" of sexuality. Christian tradition has always held that there are two "ends" or purposes of sex: procreation and union. Roman Catholic tradition has tended to stress procreation, while Protestants have tended to stress union. Cahill emerges as a rather traditional Roman Catholic at this point. For all of the sophistication of her argument, I believe that she really does not derive norms from actual cultural practices but from an understanding of the fundamental capacities of our sex organs.[21] One of those capacities is generating new life, creating kin. Any use of our organs which does not incorporate this capacity must then emerge as somehow less than ideal: it does not fully embody the "ends" of our sexuality.

This is a modern version of a natural law ethic, and it is subject to the criticism that can be brought against all natural law ethics: either they derive "ought" from "is," or they depend on a particular cultural understanding of how reason operates. That is, why does the fact that sex gives us children automatically mean that heterosexual relationships are somehow "ideal"? Why does monogamous marriage emerge as part of that ideal? Since having children is only one of the functions of sex, by Cahill's own admission, it is not clear why it should emerge as a primary function. I believe that Cahill here falls back into a more traditional Roman Catholic argument than she wishes to do. Ellison is right to suggest that what we have here is a marriage ethic rather than a sexual ethic. Although Cahill claims to be drawing her ethic from cultural practices rather than from biology directly, I believe that she really draws more directly on biology than she admits.

However, precisely in doing so, Cahill raises a fundamental challenge to us: is there anything in our biology that sets limits on our behavior and that can provide grounds for a universal ethic in a post-modern world? Does our biology have *any* role in establishing sexual norms? Does the fact that children are first and foremost the product of sexual union set any limits on the proper use of our sex organs? Are we entirely socially constructed, or is there anything in our genes, chromosomes, and physical embodiment that matters for sexual ethics?

This question is particularly crucial in light of recent advances in genetic technologies. Cloning offers the possibility that children may some day be generated entirely without sexual intercourse. The development of human embryonic stem cells offers the possibility that we will someday understand how to take any human cell and give it the capacity to generate an entire human being. Without entering the specific debate about either of these discoveries, we must stop and ask whether there is anything wrong with a separation of sexuality and baby-creating. Cahill would say "yes." Whether her ethic is seen as emerging from various cultural practices or as reflecting a more traditional Roman Catholic stress on the "ends" of sexuality, it is clear that by holding up the link between sex and the public act of having children, Cahill provides grounds for a critique of contemporary and projected reproductive processes. Our genes do give us our fundamental physiology, including our hormones, our development as male or female or inter-sexual embodied persons, and possibly even our sexual orientation.[22] While the interpretation of the meaning of our embodiment may vary from culture to culture, there are certain biological bases that are universal. A thorough-going social constructionism may not work insofar as it ignores these biological bases.

And this brings us to the possible critique that Cahill might make of Ellison. Ellison's entire thesis rests on the presumption that oppression can be identified and that it is wrong. As a feminist, Cahill agrees that oppression is wrong. But how is it to be identified? If everything is socially constructed – if there is nothing in biology or cultural practices from which we can draw universals – then on what grounds can we identify practices as oppressive? Ellison's strong argument for justice is in need of a grounding for the norm of justice itself. While Ellison is correct, in my estimation, that current practices are oppressive, to argue so is to presume that some grounds can be found from which practices can be judged to be either oppressive or liberative. What are those grounds?

Ellison does a superb job of deconstructing the oppressions of our contemporary society and suggesting the shape of liberative practices, but he turns to a particular tradition to identify the nature of oppression and to establish the grounds from which one would identify practices as either liberative or oppressive. His call to listen to the voices of marginalized and oppressed people is compelling and resonates with the best of contemporary liberation theology, but it does not answer the problem of identifying what makes a practice oppressive. At crucial moments, Ellison – like Hauerwas before him – turns to Christian tradition to find the grounding for his central value. While he finds a different value from the one Hauerwas found (Hauerwas stressed hospitality to the stranger and trust in a future not secured by child-bearing, while Ellison stresses justice), the grounding is tradition-dependent. Thus, Ellison may give us an important contemporary ethic for Christians, but it is not clear that his ethic can speak across traditions. In a post-modern world, Ellison appears to be caught without resources for an ethic that can address oppressive practices across cultures. The benefit of a natural-law approach is the possibility that one will be able to find a universal ethic rather than a particular ethic grounded in and limited to a particular community and its history and story.

WHERE DO WE GO FROM HERE?

So where does this leave us? Where do we go from here? Is there any hope for rapprochement in two theories that seem so different? I believe so, though the following ideas are suggestive rather than definitive.

First, both Cahill and Ellison point to the *public* dimension of sex. To be sure, they point to different aspects of that public dimension: Ellison to the social and cultural framing of sexual experience, and especially to the institutional structures that oppress some groups of people in their sexual experience; Cahill to the public effects of sexual activity – the bearing of children, the begetting of kin. I suggest that any adequate sexual ethic must be able to account for both of these "public" dimensions: for the ways in which social constructions of sexuality are oppressive and for the ways in which sexuality itself is of necessity a "public" act in contrast to our liberal society that makes it "private."

Second, both Cahill and Ellison stress fidelity or stability of context. To be sure, Cahill finds the "ideal" expression of that in monogamous heterosexuality, whereas Ellison does not limit fidelity to this context. But both of them appear to hold that sexuality is best expressed and least oppressive in contexts that enable and encourage fidelity. For Cahill, fidelity would be important because of its role in providing a good environment for the rearing of children; for Ellison, fidelity might be centered more on the "unitive" aspects of sexuality. Whatever the grounding, they come together on an affirmation of fidelity as central to an adequate Christian social ethic.

Finally, both Cahill and Ellison stress the importance of non-oppression. It is precisely because of her concern for oppressive practices that Cahill searches for a universal sexual ethic that allows judgments to be made about oppressive practices. Ellison roots his entire sexual ethic in the demands of justice for liberation of the oppressed. While their methods and some of their conclusions may be strikingly different, they share a desire for a non-oppressive sexual context for both men and women.

Indeed, it might be that Cahill's method could be used to support Ellison's conclusion that justice is the primary norm. A cross-cultural inductive method might very well find that one of the dominant themes in all cultures is the stress on justice and the emergence of resistance to oppression. While this theme does not appear to be mentioned specifically by either John Finnis or Martha Nussbaum, on whom Cahill depends, it surely would emerge from a cross-cultural study attuned to issues of oppression and liberation. Recent theologies around the world stress liberation, the struggle against injustice, notions of resentment (*han*) toward ongoing oppression, and similar themes. That such similarities emerge from cultures as divergent as those of Asia, South America, and Africa suggests that the groaning against injustice is a universal and fundamental human experience. Such a finding suggests further that justice can be grounded not only in the specific traditions of the Jewish and Christian texts, as Ellison argues, but precisely in universal human experience.

We can have, then, a Christian ethic of sexuality that also provides a universal perspective. It will be a sexual ethics grounded in justice. It can transcend our differences not by positing an untarnished temple from which a timeless sexual ethics is derived, but precisely by attending to how tarnished the temple has become through our unjust structures and oppressive practices.

NOTES

1. I am firmly convinced that all religious traditions have something to teach us. This conviction is reflected in *Sexual Ethics: A Reader* (New York: Pilgrim Press, 1999), which draws on a variety of religious traditions to formulate reflections helpful to Christians thinking about sexual ethics.

2. Lisa Cahill, *Sex, Gender, and Christian Ethics* (Cambridge and New York: Cambridge University Press, 1996) and Marvin Ellison, *Erotic Justice: A Liberating Ethic of Sexuality* (Louisville, KY: Westminster/John Knox Press, 1996).

3. Cahill, *Sex, Gender, and Christian Ethics*, p. 10.

4. Stanley Hauerwas, "Sex in Public: Toward a Christian Ethic of Sex," in *A Community of Character: Toward a Constructive Christian Social Ethic* (Notre Dame: University of Notre Dame Press, 1981).

5. By contrast, Hauerwas' "narrative" approach to Christian sexual ethics was deliberately limited to and intended for the believing community of Christians and made no claims for relevance beyond that community.

6. Cahill, *Sex, Gender, and Christian Ethics*, pp. 111–113.

7. Ellison, *Erotic Justice*, p. 27.

8. Ibid., p. 33.

9. Thomas Laqueur, *Making Sex: Body and Gender from the Greeks to Freud* (Cambridge, MA: Harvard University Press, 1990).

10. This single-sex theory and its impact on early Christian theologies of salvation is discussed in detail by Karen Jo Torjesen in chapter 10 of this volume.

11. Ellison, *Erotic Justice*, p. 36.

12. See also Judith Butler, *Bodies That Matter: On the Discursive Limits of Sex* (New York: Routledge, 1993) for a strong feminist approach to the social construction of sex as well as gender.

13. Ellison, *Erotic Justice*, p. 39.

14. Ibid., pp. 24–26.

15. Ibid., pp. 62–68.

16. Ibid., p. 71.

17. Ibid., p. 28.

18. Ibid., p. 81.

19. Ibid., pp. 85–86.

20. This move is akin to the "epistemological privilege of the oppressed" of liberation ethics generally.

21. Thus, I believe that Cahill remains Thomistic, rather than Neo-Aristotelian in the tradition of Nussbaum.

22. See Dean Hamer and Peter Copeland, *The Science of Desire: The Search for the Gay Gene and the Biology of Behavior* (New York: Simon and Schuster, 1994).

Plate 14 Jain sculpture of ecstatic, erotic coupling bracketed by two celestial beauties on the exterior of the small ancient local Sas Bahu ("Mother-in-law and Daughter-in-law") temples in the Nagada temple complex in Rajasthan, paralleling the extensive erotic sculpture of the famous towers of Kandariya Mahadeva Temple in Khajuraho. This Indic interweaving of erotic and religious elements underlies both Hindu and Buddhist Tantra. Nagada, India. Photo: *Nancy M. Martin.*

14

REASON *and* ORGASM *in* TIBETAN BUDDHISM

Jeffrey Hopkins

INTRODUCTION

Much of world culture views reason and sexual pleasure to be antithetical and relegates the pleasure of orgasm to a baser level of the personality incompatible with the true and the good.[1] This has lent intellectual justification to exaggerated attempts by some males to assert control over the "baser" self: (1) by identifying women and, by extension, male homosexuals with these "base" passions, and (2) by committing violent acts (including sex) against these lowly creatures. They do this to foster the self-delusion that sexual impulses are under the control of their "higher" self. In Tibetan Buddhist systems, however, there are hints of a compatible relationship between reason and orgasmic bliss in that developed practitioners seek to utilize the blissful and powerful mind of orgasm to realize the truth and the all-good ground of consciousness. The practice is based on an experientially founded tenet that the most profound, subtle, and powerful level of consciousness, the mind of clear light, manifests in intense orgasm and that it can be used to realize the truth in an unusually powerful and effective way. The suggestion is that the sense of bifurcation between reason and orgasmic bliss is the result of not appreciating the basic nature of mind.

Tibetan teachings that present a series of related levels of consciousness in which conceptual reasoning and orgasmic bliss are viewed as parts of a continuum contrast with the sense of radical separation that is present in some situations of sexual violence. Many strands of modern society, especially in the United States, are almost pathologically concerned with controlling others' private lives. Why is this? It seems to me that a single, complex person is being divided into radically separate higher and lower selves such that the so-called higher self is exalted in status even to the point of becoming disembodied. This radical division lays the groundwork for projection of the lower self onto others, especially women and male homosexuals, and consequent even brutal attempts at control. The brutality ranges from outright physical violence to suppression of information about sex and sexual orientation such that our federal government even refuses to make information on sexual orientation available to teenagers who suffer a high rate of suicide due to conflicts related with sexual identity.

It is indeed an estranged society that fears knowledge of the actual practices of its members; the ludicrous perspective that is suggested by this situation is that of the "sodomy delusion," that is to say, if seemingly "straight" men tasted only once the joys of homosexual sex, they would be so enthralled that the halls of heterosexuality would be emptied, rather than a mere ten per cent defection. One gets the sense that the only way that the advocates of silence feel that heterosexual mores can be sustained is through the maintenance of ignorance, a state not of bliss but of pained projection of temptation onto others. Women and male homosexuals are viewed as tempting otherwise decent persons into their lower selves. Consider the fears that many have of gay teachers, who are seen as ready not only to convert but also to misuse their students; the fears, however, are ridiculous in the face of the statistics on sexual abuse by teachers, the overwhelming majority being by heterosexual men. It does not take much profundity to surmise that those who favor ignorance about sexual matters have separated themselves from aspects of their own sexual impulses and, like the paranoiac, are pursued by images of libidinous attackers who are actually manifestations of their own minds.

Our acculturation is often so much at odds with our inner selves that we seek somehow to separate from our own inner being. Also, the external demands to identify with the current presentation of what is socially acceptable are so great that the tendency toward separation becomes institutionalized through peer-group fortification such that the attempt to separate oneself from one's own inner being becomes even more encrusted and difficult to penetrate. It is helpful in such situations to be confronted with systems of therapy that undermine the sense of separation from one's own inner self by uncovering the mechanisms of projection. It is also helpful to reflect on systems of structural psychology that place seemingly unassociated and radically other states of mind in a coherent continuum of mind such that the intellectual justifications for projection are undermined. I find one such system in various teachings found in Tibetan Buddhism, which, although by no means a panacea, offers stimulating food for thought.

BACKGROUND

Buddhism began gradually to be introduced to Tibet in the seventh century CE, more than a thousand years after Shakyamuni Buddha's passing away (*circa* 483 BCE). The form Buddhism took in Tibet was greatly influenced by the highly developed systemization of the religion that was present in India through the twelfth century (and even later). The geographic proximity and relatively undeveloped culture of Tibet provided conditions for extensive transfer of scholastic commentaries and systems of practice, which came to have great influence throughout a vast region stretching from Kalmuck Mongolian areas in Europe where the Volga River empties into the Caspian Sea, Outer and Inner Mongolia, the Buriat Republic of Siberia, Bhutan, Sikkim, Nepal, and Ladakh. My sources are drawn primarily, but not exclusively, from one of the most scholastic orders of Tibetan Buddhism, the Ge-luk-ba[2] sect, founded by the polymath and yogi, Dzong-ka-ba[3] (1357–1419) who was born in the northeastern province of Tibet called Am-do.[4] This province was included by the occupying Chinese not in the Tibetan Autonomous Region but in the Ch'ing-hai Province. Dzong-ka-ba and his followers established a system of education centered in large universities, eventually in three areas of Tibet but primarily in Lhasa, the capital, which in some ways was as Rome is for the Catholic Church. For five centuries, young men (yes, women were, for the most part, excluded from the scholastic culture) came from all of the above-mentioned regions to these large Tibetan universities to study; until the Communist takeovers, they usually returned to their own countries after completing their degrees. My presentation will be largely from standard Ge-luk-ba perspectives[5] on the Tantra Vehicle, also called the Vajra Vehicle,[6] one of two basic forms of what Tibetan tradition accepts as Shakyamuni Buddha's teaching.

THE FUNDAMENTAL INNATE MIND OF CLEAR LIGHT IN HIGHEST YOGA TANTRA

In this Indo-Tibetan system it is said that during orgasm the mind of clear light – the basis of all consciousness and the most subtle and powerful form of consciousness – manifests, albeit only unconsciously, even to the untrained.[7] The *Guhyasamaja Tantra*, a Highest Yoga Tantra that is parallel in importance to the *Kalachakra Tantra*, divides consciousnesses into the gross, the subtle, and the very subtle.[8] We are all familiar with the grosser levels of mind – the eye consciousness that apprehends colors and shapes, the ear consciousness that apprehends sounds, the nose consciousness that apprehends odors, the tongue consciousness that apprehends tastes, and the body consciousness that apprehends tactile objects. To understand the perspective of this school of Buddhist thought, it is important that these five be considered not just as sensations known by another, separate consciousness, but as five individual consciousnesses that have specific spheres of activity – colors and shapes, sounds, odors, tastes, and tactile objects. These five sense consciousnesses are the grossest level of mind.

More subtle than the five sense consciousnesses but still within the gross level of mind is the usual, conceptual, mental consciousness. In Highest Yoga Tantra, these conceptions are detailed as of eighty types, divided into three classes. The first group of thirty-three is composed of emotions, feelings, and drives that involve a strong movement of energy[9] to their objects. Included in this group are fear, attachment, hunger, thirst, shame, compassion, acquisitiveness, and jealousy. The second group of forty conceptions involve a medium movement of energy to their objects; among them are joy, amazement, excitement, desiring to embrace, generosity, desiring to kiss, desiring to suck, pride, enthusiasm, vehemence, flirtation, wishing to donate, heroism, deceit, tightness, viciousness, nongentleness, and crookedness. The third group of seven conceptions involve a weak movement of energy to their objects – forgetfulness, error as in apprehending water in a mirage, catatonia, depression, laziness, doubt, and equal desire and hatred. Although the difference between the first two groups is not obvious (at least to me), it is clear that in the third group the mind is strongly withdrawn; the three represent, on the ordinary level of consciousness, increasingly less dualistic perception.

Either through meditative focusing on sensitive parts of the body or through undergoing uncontrolled processes as in orgasm or in dying,[10] the currents of energy that drive the various levels of gross consciousness are gradually withdrawn, resulting in a series of altered states. First, one has a visual experience of seeing an appearance like a mirage; then, as the withdrawal continues, one successively "sees" an appearance like billowing smoke, followed by an appearance like fireflies within smoke, then an appearance like a sputtering candle[11] when little wax is left, and then an appearance of a steady candle flame. This series of visions sets the stage for the withdrawal of all conceptual consciousnesses,[12] whereupon a more dramatic phase begins the manifestation of profound levels of consciousness that are at the core of all experience.

The first subtle level of consciousness to manifest is the mind of vivid white appearance. All of the eighty conceptions have ceased, and nothing appears except this slightly dualistic vivid white appearance; one's consciousness itself turns into an omnipresent, huge, vivid white vastness. It is described as like a clear sky filled with moonlight, not the moon shining in empty space but space filled with white light. All conceptuality has ceased, and nothing appears except this slightly dualistic vivid white appearance, which is one's consciousness itself.

When, through further withdrawal of the energy that supports this level of consciousness, it no longer can manifest, a more subtle mind of vivid red or orange appearance (called increase) dawns. One's consciousness itself has turned into this even less dualistic vivid red or orange appearance; nothing else appears. It is compared to a clear sky filled with sunlight, again not the sun shining in the sky but space filled with red or orange light.

One's consciousness remains in this state for a period, and then when this mind loses its support through further withdrawal of the energy that is its foundation, a still more subtle mind of vivid black appearance dawns; it is called "near-attainment" because one is close to manifesting the mind of clear light. One's consciousness itself has turned into this still less dualistic, vivid black appearance; nothing else appears. The mind of black vastness is compared to a moonless, very dark sky just after dusk when no stars are seen. During the first part of this phase of utter blackness, one remains conscious but then, in a second phase, becomes unconscious in thick darkness.

Then, when the mind of black appearance ceases, the three "pollutants"[13] of the white, red/orange, and black appearances have been entirely cleared away, and the mind of clear light dawns. Called the fundamental innate mind of clear light,[14] it is the most subtle, profound, and powerful level of consciousness. It is compared to the sky's own natural cast – without the "pollutions" of moonlight, sunlight, or darkness – which can be seen at dawn before sunrise.

Because the more subtle levels of consciousness are considered to be more powerful and thus more effective in realizing the truth, the systems of Highest Yoga Tantra seek to manifest the mind of clear light by way of various techniques. One of these methods is blissful orgasm because, according to the psychology of Highest Yoga Tantra, orgasm involves the ceasing of the grosser levels of consciousness and manifestation of the more subtle, as do dying, going to sleep, ending a dream, sneezing, and fainting. The intent in using a blissful, orgasmic mind in the spiritual path is to manifest the most subtle level of consciousness, the mind of clear light, and use its greater power and hence effectiveness to realize the truth of the emptiness of inherent existence. The theory is that the apprehension that phenomena exist inherently or from their own side is the root of suffering because it induces the plethora of counter-productive emotions that produce suffering. In orgasm, phenomena that are over-concretized such that they seem to have their own independent existence melt into the expanse of the reality behind appearances. The pleasure of orgasm is so intense that the mind becomes totally withdrawn and fascinated such that both the usual conceptual mind and the appearances that accompany it melt away, leaving basic reality.

Through consciously experiencing this process, one can realize that ordinary conceptions and appearances are over-concretized. Sex, therefore, can become a practice through which this exaggeration of the status of appearance and mind is identified and subsumed in the source state. The fundamental state – which dawns in conscious orgasm – is not a dimming of the mind into an emotional state that is opposed to the truth, although it is often experienced as such because all of the usual conceptual minds are withdrawn during it. Rather, it is the basis of phenomena – that into which all appearances dissolve and thus the foundation of appearance. It is the reality behind appearances. Our unfamiliarity with it causes its implications to be missed in unconsciousness. Through developing realization of the emptiness of inherent existence by recognizing the interrelatedness of persons and phenomena and through developing great compassion by recognizing relatedness over the continuum of lifetimes, one can become closer to this state and thereby more capable of appreciating its significance.

By utilizing this subtle level of mind, the power of the wisdom-consciousness realizing the truth is enhanced such that it is more effective in overcoming what prevents liberation from the round of rebirth and all its suffering. Such a wisdom consciousness is also more effective in overcoming what prevents knowledge of others' dispositions and of the techniques that can benefit them and thus serves to further the altruistic goals that are behind the quest for wisdom.

Sexual expression, therefore, can be used as an avenue for exploring the profound nature of consciousness which eventually brings release from craving from the root. Using an ancient example, the process is compared to a worm's being born from moist wood and then eating the wood. In this example (formed at a time when it was assumed that a worm or bug was generated only from wood and heat), the wood is desire; the worm is the blissful consciousness; and the consumption of the wood is the blissful consciousness's destruction of desire through realizing emptiness. As the First Pan-chen Lama, Lo-sang-cho-gyi-gyel-tsen,[15] says:

> A wood-engendered insect is born from wood but consumes it completely. In the same way, a great bliss is generated in dependence on a causal motivation that is the desire of gazing, smiling, holding hands or embracing, or union of the two organs. The wisdom of undifferentiable bliss and emptiness, which is this great bliss generated undifferentiably with a mind cognizing emptiness at the same time, consumes completely the afflictive emotions – desire, ignorance, and so forth.[16]

Through desirous activities such as gazing at a loved one, or smiling, holding hands, embracing, or engaging in sexual union, a pleasurable consciousness is produced; it is used to realize the truth of the emptiness of inherent existence, whereby desire itself is undermined. The pleasurable consciousness is generated simultaneously with a wisdom consciousness, and thus the two are indivisibly fused. Without desire, the involvement in the bliss consciousness would be minimal, and thus Highest Yoga Tantra makes use of the arts of love-making to enhance the process.

In Ge-luk-ba texts, the undifferentiability of bliss and realization of emptiness is explained conceptually in terms of subject and object even though it is beyond all dualism. The bliss consciousness is the subject that realizes emptiness as its object. The reason for making this distinction is to emphasize that the bliss consciousness is used to realize the profound nature of reality, the emptiness of inherent existence – the emptiness of over-concretization – and thus is not a mere unconscious mind of orgasm. The aim of the sexual yoga is, therefore, not mere repetition of an attractive state but revelation of the basic reality underlying appearances. Nevertheless, to experience the union of bliss and emptiness, sexual pleasure has to be developed in fullness, and to do this it is necessary to implement techniques for avoiding premature ejaculation and extending the experience of pleasure; otherwise, a valuable opportunity is lost in the ephemerality of orgasm.

The twentieth-century Tibetan intellectual, Gedun Chopel,[17] who traveled to India and wrote his own *Treatise on Passion*[18] based on the *Kama*

Sutra, advocates the usage of sexual pleasure to open oneself to the profound, fundamental state at the core of all consciousness. As he says:

> The small child of intelligence swoons
>   in the deep sphere of passion.
> The busy mind falls into the hole of a worm.
> By drawing the imaginations of attachment downwards
> Beings should observe the suchness of pleasure.
>
> Wishing to mix in the ocean of the bliss
>   of the peaceful expanse
> This wave of magician's illusions separated off
> By perceiving the non-dual as dual, subject and object,
> Does one not feel the movement and igniting
>   of the coalesced!

Phenomena that are over-concretized such that they seem to have their own independent existence are burnt away in the expanse of the reality behind appearances:

> If one really considers the fact that the one billion worlds
>   of this world system
> Are suddenly swallowed into a gigantic asteroid devoid
>   of perception or feeling,
> One understands that the realm of great bliss
> Is that in which all appearances dissolve.

Gedun Chopel also speaks of deities that are present in the body during sex:

> At the time of pleasure the god and goddess giving rise to bliss actually
> dwell in the bodies of the male and the female. Therefore, it is said that what
> would be obstacles to one's life if done [under usual circumstances] are
> conquered, and power, brilliance, and youth blaze forth. The perception of
> ugliness and dirtiness is stopped, and one is freed from conceptions of fear
> and shame. The deeds of body, speech, and mind become pure, and it is said
> that one arrives in a place of extreme pleasure.

The question is *how* to sustain sexual pleasure so that its spiritual value is not lost and the experience turns into an unconscious dimming of mind. He proposes forgoing cultural prohibitions so that sexual pleasure can be deepened and extended such that it penetrates the entire physical structure. With lyric beauty he advises that inhibitions be cast aside:

> Smear honey on each other and taste.
> Or taste the natural fluids.

> Suck the slender and bulbous tube.
> Intoxicated and confusing the memory, do everything.

As a technique to lengthen the experience of sexual pleasure, he suggests pausing in the midst of intense feeling and letting the feeling of bliss pervade the body:

> If one does not know the techniques of holding and spreading the bliss that has arrived at the tip of the jewel [i.e., the head of the phallus], immediately upon seeing it for a moment it fades and disappears, like picking up a snowflake in the hand. Therefore when, upon churning about, bliss is generated, cease movement, and again and again spread [the sense of bliss throughout the body]. Then, by again doing it with the former methods, bliss will be sustained for a long time.

Through techniques of strengthening and lengthening sexual pleasure, both mind and body become bathed in bliss, opening the possibility of realizing the nature of the fundamental state.

The practice of sexual yoga is, to my knowledge, always explained in terms of heterosexual sex, in which a consort of the opposite sex[19] is used. The reason given concerns the structure of channels or nerves in the respective sexual organs, and thus insertion refers not just to insertion in the vagina but to contact with special nerve centers in the vagina that are lacking in the anus. Thus, colorful drawings of male and female deities in sexual union decorate the walls of temples – not those of same-sex couples. However, the type of sexual yoga that Gedun Chopel describes has its foundations in the doctrine – found in the Old Translation School of Nying-ma[20] – that the blissful mind of clear light pervades all experience and is accessible within any state. This is the theoretical underpinning of his advice to extend the intense state of sexual bliss in order to explore the fundamental state of bliss. It seems to me that this *can* be done with same-sex or other-sex partners and *should* be done with whatever type is more evocative of intense feeling on all levels.

The ultimate goal is not just to experience this basal state into which phenomena have dissolved but also to perceive all the various phenomena of the world *within* the mind of clear light, without exaggerating their status into being independent. One is seeking to perceive interdependence without an overlay of divisive concretization. Emptiness does not negate phenomena; it negates only the exaggerated status of inherent existence and hence is compatible with love and compassion, which are enhanced through recognizing the connectedness of persons and of other phenomena. It is said that, with such a perspective, truly effective altruism is possible since the faculty of judgment is not clouded by afflictive emotions such as anger. The final state is not abstracted away from phenomena but is an appreciation of connectedness and embodiment. All phenomena are seen as manifestations of the mind of clear light, still having individuality but not exaggerated into being autonomous. Viewed in this perspective, the mind of orgasm as experienced in this type of sexual yoga is a means of linking to others, promoting intimacy and relationality, and is not an abstraction of oneself away from others into an auto-hypnotic withdrawal, although it might seem so at first.

To summarize: the innermost level of consciousness is the fundamental innate mind of clear light, which is identified as the eighth in a series of increasingly subtle experiences that occur frequently but unconsciously in ordinary life. These deeper levels of mind manifest during the process of dying, going to sleep, ending a dream, fainting, sneezing, and orgasm in forward order:

1.   mirage,
2.   smoke,
3.   fireflies,
4.   flame of a lamp,
5.   vivid white mind-sky,
6.   vivid red or orange mind-sky,
7.   vivid black mind-sky,
8.   clear light.

These eight also manifest in reverse order when taking rebirth, waking, starting to dream, ending a fainting spell, ending a sneeze, and ending orgasm:

1.   clear light,
2.   vivid black mind-sky,
3.   vivid red or orange mind-sky,
4.   vivid white mind-sky,
5.   flame of a lamp,
6.   fireflies,
7.   smoke,
8.   mirage.

These states of increasing subtlety during death, orgasm, going to sleep, ending a dream, and so forth and of increasing grossness during rebirth, post-orgasm, awakening, beginning a dream, and so forth indicate levels of mind on which every conscious moment is built. From the perspective of this system of psychology, we spend our lives in the midst of thousands of small deaths and rebirths.

Conceptual over-concretization of objects prevents realization of the most profound and ecstatic state by generating attachment to superficial, unreal exaggerations. This attachment, in turn, fosters an inability to sustain the basic, blissful state that undermines emotionally imbedded self-deceptions. The suggestion is that ordinary conscious life is concerned with only the gross or superficial, without heed of more subtle states that are the foundation of both consciousness and appearance. We know neither the origin of consciousness nor the basis into which it returns.

It is said that ordinary beings are so identified with superficial states that the transition to the deeper involves even fear of annihilation; when the deeper states begin to manifest and the superficial levels collapse, we panic, fearing that we will be wiped out and, due to this fear, swoon unconsciously. As the late-eighteenth- and early-nineteenth-century Mongolian scholar Nga-wang-kay-drup[21] says in his *Presentation of Death, Intermediate State, and Rebirth*,[22] at the time of the clear light of death ordinary beings generate the fright that they will be annihilated.[23] Similarly, the emergence of the foundational state in orgasm is so drastically different from ordinary consciousness that it is usually experienced as a dimming of the mind.

The fact that the mind of clear light – which is so awesome when it newly manifests – is one's own final nature suggests that the otherness and fear associated with its manifestation are not part of *its* nature but are due to the shallowness of untrained beings. The strangeness of our own nature is a function of misconception, specifically our mistaken sense that what are actually distortions of mind subsist in the nature of mind. We identify with these distortions such that when basic consciousness starts to manifest either in orgasm or in dying, we are unable to remain with the experience. The more we identify with distorted attitudes, the greater the fear of the foundational state, which to those who are trained has within it a source of sustenance beyond the dualism of subject and object. The systems of religious education found in the Tibetan cultural region can be viewed as aimed at overcoming this fear of one's most basic nature.

REASON AND ORGASM

Although all consciousnesses arise from and return to the mind of clear light, the conceptualization that these grosser levels have their own independent existence causes these states to be alienated from their own source. In this Buddhist system, reason is a form of consciousness that in ordinary life is estranged from its own nature. Far from further fortifying the seeming separateness of reason through theorizing that such estrangement is a virtue, practitioners are called to try to perceive the inner nature of all states of mind, harmonious with the ground-state that can, through yogic training, be experienced consciously in orgasm. Not only the doctrines of structural psychology in Tibetan Buddhism but also the paintings and statues of male and female in sexual union and of ithyphallic males that abound in Tibetan temples convey the message that the state of the all-good is harmonious with orgasm.

From this point of view, reason is gross in relation to orgasmic bliss, and when reason is considered a disembodied phenomenon, it is arrogant in its sense of distance from its own source-state. Under such circumstances the continuity between orgasm and conceptual consciousnesses such as reason is not being realized. It is my contention that this Indo-Tibetan perspective of continuity could help to alleviate the sense of loathing that some males experience with respect to the power that sexual pleasure has over them, when the surface personality is collapsed in orgasm and the panic of annihilation sets in. Fearing the destruction of the seemingly controlled self, they project their sexual impulses onto others, especially women and gay men – because they seem to wallow in sex and tempt them into their lower selves. Male homosexuals are threatening also because they are seen as males who approach sex, not from an overweening need for control but out of intimacy. Little do these people know that homophobic attitudes that block intimacy are also rampant among gays. As all of us, gay and non-gay, have seen, there is a strong tendency in some males to hate the sexual recipient, whether this be a woman or a man, as the source of their degeneration into an uncontrollable state. They attempt to assert control and dominion over the collapse and annihilation of their usual ego through hating the source of their sexual desire which they project onto others – these others being persons who are attracted to males. They seek domination both of their own sexual craving and also of the process of dissolution – in orgasm – of what is actually their superficial self. Panicking at their own disappearance in orgasm, they look for someone else to blame and to control even in brutal ways in order to distance themselves from their own craving for orgasm. At once attracted to and repelled by their own inner nature, they lash out in distorted disgust, attempting to claim a privileged position over a process that does indeed undermine their identification with superficial states. What is actually an exaggeration of a superficial state tries to pretend control over its profound source.

It seems to me that gay-bashing often arises from the tension of such persons' being faced (sometimes in fact but mostly in their imagination) with males who have not adopted this ridiculous projection. The Indo-Tibetan perspective that conceptual thought and orgasmic bliss have the same inner nature and that, in fact, the state of orgasmic bliss is more subtle than conceptual thought might help to undermine the warped need to attack homosexuals out of fear that they have not assumed the "proper" male perspective of dominance.

I do not mean to suggest that in these Indo-Tibetan systems reason is discarded, for it is highly valued as a means to open oneself to greater compassion and increased wisdom and, thereby, to break down the barriers to the conscious manifestation of the mind of clear light. However, the usefulness of reason becomes impossible when it exaggerates its own status into that of an independent, disembodied faculty, a process which promotes projection of other aspects of the personality onto others. Once reason is separated out as an autonomous entity and once persons identify mainly with this disembodied faculty, it is all too easy to view states and impulses that are actually part and parcel of one's own mind as threateningly impinging from the outside. Fear and rejection of sexuality lead to projection of sexuality onto women and homosexuals and result in fear, rejection, and abuse of women and homosexuals. Conversely, the elevation, exaltation, glorification, and deification of women (though seldom of homosexuals) has the same root in denial of sexual passion.

The perspective of Tibetan systems may be useful in counteracting this tendency of self-created separation, for it presents reason as compatible with orgasmic bliss not only because the mind of clear light that manifests in orgasm is the inner nature of all consciousnesses but also because reason can reveal the conflict between appearance and reality and a mind of orgasm can realize this same truth with even more impact. In this way, the veil of the exaggerated concreteness that is superimposed on phenomena is lifted, and the all-good ground of consciousness can manifest. This system of spiritual development that places such a high value on orgasm, viewed as harmonious with reason, beckons us to recognize the inner continuity of

these seemingly separate states, thereby helping to undermine the perni-
cious processes of projection.

Let me be clear that I am not holding up Tibetan culture as a problem-
less model, a Shangri-La of sexual and social harmony and tolerance. Rather,
I am suggesting that the model of consciousness found in Tibetan systems
may be helpful in alleviating the estrangement of levels of the personality.
Such a revolution in perspective requires recognition of vulnerability and
thus is not easy. Perhaps, reflection on this Tibetan presentation of the connection between conceptual, reasoned levels of consciousness and the
powerful state of orgasm may be useful for *both* non-homosexuals and
homosexuals since the intellectual justifications that support homophobia
are not limited to those who identify themselves as heterosexual.

NOTES

1. For more about the topics of this paper, see Jeffrey Hopkins, *Sex, Orgasm,
   and the Mind of Clear Light: The Sixty-Four Arts of Gay Male Love* (Berkeley: North Atlantic, 1998). This essay was previously published under the
   title "The Compatibility of Reason and Orgasm in Tibetan Buddhism:
   Reflections on Sexual Violence and Homophobia," in *Gay Affirmative
   Ethics*, Gay Men's Issues in Religious Studies, vol. 4, ed. Michael L. Stem-
   meler and J. Michael Clark (Las Colinas: Monument Press, 1993); in
   Que(e)rying Religion: A Critical Anthology, ed. Gary David Comstock and
   Susan E. Henking (New York: Continuum, 1997); and in *Queer Dharma:
   Voices of Gay Buddhists*, ed. Winston Leyland (San Francisco: Gay Sun-
   shine Press, 1997). It appears here by permission of the author who holds
   the copyright.
2. *dge lugs pa.*
3. *tsong kha pa blo bzang grags pa.*
4. *a mdo.*
5. Given the emphasis within the Ge-luk-ba sect not just on separate
   monastic universities but even more so on individual colleges and given
   the general provincialism of the culture, it might seem impossible to
   speak of "standard" postures of the sect, but my meaning here points to
   generally recognizable, or at least representative, explanations.
6. *rdo rje theg pa, vajrayana.*
7. The section on the fundamental innate mind of clear light is adapted
   from my "A Tibetan Perspective on the Nature of Spiritual Experience",
   in *Paths to Liberation*, ed. Robert Buswell and Robert Gimello (Honolulu:
   University of Hawaii Press, 1992).
8. The material on the levels of consciousness is drawn from Lati Rinbochay's and my translation of a text by A-gya-yong-dzin (*a kya yongs
   'dzin*), alias Yang-jen-ga-way-Io-dro (*dbyangs can dga' ba'i blo gros*); see

our *Death, Intermediate State, and Rebirth in Tibetan Buddhism* (London: Rider and Co., 1979; rpt. Ithaca: Snow Lion Publications, 1980).

9. Literally, wind or air (*rlung, prana*).
10. The similarity between orgasm and death in terms of seeming self-extinction is frequently noticed in "Western" literature, Shakespeare being the most prominent.
11. Literally, a butter-lamp.
12. The three sets of conceptions correspond to the three subtle minds that appear serially after conceptions cease, but it is not that the three sets of conceptions cease serially; rather, they disappear together, resulting in the gradual dawning of the three subtler levels of mind.
13. *bslod byed.*
14. *gnyug ma lhan cig skyes pa'i 'od gsal gyi sems.*
15. *blo bzang chos kyi rgyal mtshan.*
16. *Presentation of the General Teaching and the Four Tantra Sets* (*bstan pa spyi dang rgyud sde bzhi'i rnam par gzhag pa'i zin bris*), Collected Works of Blo-bzang-chos-kyi-rgyal-mtshan, the First Pan-chen Bla-ma of Bkra-Shis-lhun-po, vol. IV (New Delhi: Guru Deva, 1973), 17b.5–18a.1.
17. *dge 'dun chos 'phel*; 1905–1951.
18. See Gedun Chopel, *Tibetan Arts of Passion*, translated and introduced by Jeffrey Hopkins (Ithaca: Snow Lion Publications, 1992), from which I have drawn some of the material in this article.
19. The female is called "mother" (*yum*), and the male is called "father" (*yab*). The terms are rich with suggestions (never made explicit in the tradition) of copulating with one's parent; it would seem that for heterosexuals this would be with the parent of the opposite sex, and for homosexuals, with the parent of the same sex.
20. *rnying ma.*
21. *ngag dbang mkhas grub*; 1779–1838. Also known as *kyai rdo mkhan po.*
22. *skye shi bar do'i rnam bzhag*, Collected Works (Leh: S. Tashigangpa, 1973), vol. 1, 466.2. Cited in Rinbochay and Hopkins, *Death, Intermediate State, and Rebirth in Tibetan Buddhism*, p. 47.
23. The fear-inspiring aspect of its manifestation accords with the often described awesomeness and sense of otherness that much of world culture associates with types of profound religious experience.

Plate 15 Contemporary Rajasthani miniature painting in Mughal style, depicting the languorous joys of food, drink, and erotic love (*kama*), an ideal affirmed within both Hindu and Muslim traditions. Private Collection. Photo: *Nancy M. Martin and Joseph Runzo.*

15

THE EROTIC AS POWER *and the* LOVE OF GOD

Carter Heyward

I begin with a poem I wrote ten years ago as prologue to a book on erotic power and the love of God:

> I had to prepare for this and
> not just by reading Lorde and Weeks and Raymond
> or my own stuff.
> I had to do more than think
> about "sexuality" "theology" "ethics."
> In order to come to this
>
> I had to connect with you
> through memories fantasies humor
> and struggle
> sometimes touching
> often amazing
> always worthy of respect.
> In order to come
>
> I had to get myself some daffodils
> and wait for them to open,
> and I had to lie down beside my old dog Teraph
> and rub some comfort into his worn out legs
> and make myself some Mocha Java decaf
> with just enough milk to cut the acid,
> and then I had to sit for the longest time
> and remember

Denise   ANC   Black Sash
South Africa
and I had to ask myself how
we are connected to these movements
for joy and survival
and I had to believe that we are.
In order to come,

I had to write a poem
about hiding some sisters and their cats from the fascists,
a love poem it was,
and then hold in my heart an image of my month old
niece, my namesake
whom I love and have not seen,
and spend some painstaking time
with friends and playful
time as well
and I had to be alone for a good long while
for my roots to secure.
In order to come,

I had to make love,
and if I had not had a precious woman
to caress my lusty flesh
and bring me open not only to her
but to myself and you
I still would have had to find a way
to enter more fully
the warm dark moisture
of One in whose hunger
for survival and passion
for friends   and movement
for justice   and yearning
for touch and pleasure
we are becoming
Ourselves.[1]

EROTIC POWER AS LOVE OF GOD — HOW DARE A CHRISTIAN MAKE THIS CLAIM?

What on earth does a good Christian think she is saying, and doing, here? Surely this is not Christian theology or Christian ethics, Christian biblical faith or Christian life!

It is almost routine among academics in these post-modern times to speak in the plural of those "locations" in our lives which we once assumed to be singular and unified – to speak in this case not of one Christianity but of many Christianities, including those in which good Christians not only often enjoy sex but also understand this intense enjoyment as right and good. There are some Christians who would go even further and suggest not only that sexual pleasure can be right and good, but moreover that it can be – and indeed often is – sacred, literally an experience of the Holy, of "godding,"[2] as much a doorway or passage into the heights and depths of God as any fully human experience can be.

Ten years ago I wrote *Touching Our Strength: The Erotic as Power and the Love of God*. In order to make a case for erotic power's *being* the love of God, I drew appreciatively from African Caribbean lesbian feminist Audre Lorde's essay "Uses of the Erotic: The Erotic as Power," which has become a classic among feminists, womanists, and others with a passion for justice for women.[3] Lorde was not attempting to present the erotic as a *religious* construct in her work, and she most certainly was not interested, in this essay at least, in the Christian God. Lorde was interested in "creative energy,"[4] what she named "the life force of women."[5]

Prior to engaging Lorde's work, I had begun to understand that this power which is the fuel of our creativity and liberation in their many dimensions, public and private, collective and individual, *is* in fact coterminous with "God" as understood by those Christians who see the Sacred as being close to the heart of creation rather than at a distance from us, in the midst of human and other creaturely life – with us, embodied – rather than primarily over and against us. What Lorde termed "the nurturer or nursemaid of all our deepest knowledge,"[6] I had begun to speak of as "our power in relation," more exactly I would come to realize – our relational power for making right, mutual relation, in which all parties are empowered, quickened, to be more fully who we can be in right, mutual relation.[7] There is nothing static or fixed in mutual relation; it is, in the most radical sense, ec-static. Moreover, the experience of sacred power is not only relational; it is transformative.[8]

It seemed evident to me, on the basis of my familiarity with Audre Lorde's writings and politics, that what she called our "creative energy" was what I believed to be our "relational power," a source of spiritual faith and transformative life energy I had begun to experience in fresh new ways through my own processes of coming out as a lesbian in the late 1970s. So it was not surprising to me (or many other lesbians) to hear Lorde daring to name this life-energy "erotic." I found Lorde's bold affirmation heartening and inspiring, specifically her affirmation of women's life energy – I would say, our sacred energy, our God-root. This is perhaps not so far philosophically from what Paul Tillich understood to be the Ground of our Being, but it is wonderfully and wildly more embodied, bloodier and juicier, than what Tillich and most other Christian theologians have either had in mind or conveyed.

With this fresh – erotic – image of God, I continued along in my own life, becoming increasingly attentive to the task of being as public and as good-humored a lesbian feminist theologian of liberation as I could be during the 1980s and the grim reapings of the Reagan era. By 1989 I was delighted to be able to put my own mind to the task of presenting the erotic not only as our creative power but moreover – from a Christian perspective – as the love of God.

Having hinted here at the possibility not only that Christian theology can be sex-affirming and "erotically-empowering" but moreover that sex can be a source and resource for Christian faith and theology, I want to do some theological reflection that may clarify this possibility. This theologizing will involve, first, our noticing the split between justice and love in Christianity. We will explore the violence generated in this split and how the feminist movement has tried to address the violence without addressing the split. We will then loop back to the notion of erotic power being a primary resource for that love-making which *is* justice-making – especially in the context of sexual violence and gender abuse.

THE SPLIT BETWEEN JUSTICE AND LOVE

We would be here a very long time indeed if, as a Christian council, we were trying to sort out the roots of the split between *justice* as a public, collective aim and *love* as a private, almost sentimental, attachment. In one way or another, the tension between the well-being of society and of the person, of the group and of the individual, has been a basic and central issue for Christian ethics from the earliest Christian community disputes (in which Paul was a primary player) to the present-day interests in matters of reproduction and sexuality. Karen Lebacqz and Marvin Ellison are right that good sexual ethics are public ethics, with roots in the social and communal contexts of our lives. But the Christian churches – Protestant, Roman Catholic, and Orthodox – have tried hard historically to prevent sex and gender from becoming matters open to serious public debate.[9]

There is not a major Protestant denomination in the United States today that is not embroiled in disputes around the issue of sexual activity between men and between women and whether or not the church, in order to help "make justice roll down like waters" (Amos) should affirm that gay/lesbian sex can be "right" and "good." One of the reasons that this debate is so confounding among most white Protestants in the U.S. is that, except in the arena of sex and gender, "justice" matters historically have been perceived as belonging outside the church. Justice has meant social justice, public justice, and the well-being of the public; social order has been relegated for the most part to the state.

Many white Protestant churches, for example, customarily have had "social action" committees, which has been a means of recognizing, but also marginalizing, a special interest. In this case, it has almost always been an indication that justice has not been seen as indispensable to the church's very identity as Christian. In the arena of race and racism, for example, most white Protestant churches – if they ever made it onto the very public Civil Rights train – had to run to catch up with it, and then leap onto the caboose as it moved out of sight.

If justice-making has been viewed as the world's responsibility, which is simple-minded but still true for most white Protestants, it is equally the case that love-making has been claimed by the church as its own private business. And whereas the Roman Catholic Church in the West often has been less inclined than most Protestant churches to view justice-making in matters of economic exploitation as belonging to the world and not the church, the Roman church has been even more inclined than mainstream Protestants to insist that, in the realm of sexual justice and gender justice, the only justice that counts is in the hands and opinions of church fathers. Thus, in the ethical realm of love-making, Protestants and Catholics have been undivided in their claim that it is the church's business primarily, not the business of "secular humanists," "radical feminists," "liberal politicians," theological neophytes, and others caricatured either as not belonging to the church, not caring a whit about matters of right and wrong, or not being good, right-thinking Christians.

For Christians, the split between justice-making and love-making is, at root, a split between public and private realms of accountability. This slicing of matters of love, sex, and gender from the realm of public account-ability is tantamount to setting Christianity outside, and above, all requirements for justice for women, gay men, lesbians, bisexual and trans-gendered people. Attitudes of Christian leaders toward all sexual deviants (including feminist women) is a bit like the attitude of U.S. leaders toward the so-called two-thirds world – either play by the rules set for you by those who know better, or be punished.

While the spiritual arrogance and tyranny of the Christian church in relation to its own members, especially in the realms of gender and sex, reaches back to its earliest beginnings as yet another patriarchal religious movement, its preoccupation with sex as one of its central, even defining, problems originated in the fourth-century settlement with the Roman state, according to historian Samuel Laeuchli.[10] The church having lost its central mission of political resistance to the state, Laeuchli contends, Christian prelates and priests in the West had to find a new central purpose and identity – which they did at the Council of Elvira (Spain) in 381 CE, through drawing up a series of laws regulating the sexual behavior of Christian leaders.

It often is hard for many white, theo-politically progressive Christians who are appalled by the church's misogyny and homophobia to grasp the extent to which for most of Christian history, the church has been preoccupied, at times obsessed, with making sure that the state legislates and enforces the church's own judgments about what is right and good in the realm of gender relations and sexual behavior. In predominantly Christian cultures, such as the United States, from the colonial period on down to this day, white ruling-class Christians have insisted that, in matters of love, sex, and gender, the state should either actively enforce the church's rules (for example, its anti-sodomy and anti-abortion teachings, and more recently, in 1996, the Defense of Marriage Act) or stand passively in the wings as Christian customs are lived out. In other words, how husbands treat wives, how parents treat children, how gender is interpreted, how children are educated especially about sex, what resources are available to children, and so forth, should be primarily the business of Christian parents, not public schools or other publicly funded resources.

THE FEMINIST EFFORT TO BRING JUSTICE TO LOVE-MAKING

The feminist movement of the last thirty years has been, perhaps more than anything else, a major, brave, and often effective effort to bring some public accountability into the realms of gender and sex. Our differences and disagreements notwithstanding, feminists have pushed consistently and forcefully for justice for women in the public and private realms of our lives. The old slogan from the early 70s "the personal is political" was a way of saying that nothing is outside the realm of justice for women – not the workplace, not religion, not sports, not the military, and most certainly not the bedroom.

In raising our voices in this way, feminists have raised up the great moral necessity for sexual and gender justice in our historical period, and we would hope for ever more. It is not uncommon to hear feminists celebrate the small gains of the movement as victories that someday our daughters and sons, our nieces and nephews, will be able to harvest more fully than we ourselves.

Amidst this larger social movement for justice for women, Christian feminists have been working to make the church more fully accountable for ways in which its own doctrines, discipline, and worship have been hammered out on the bodies of women and of all queer people (those who do not conform to the church's standard of what Jewish feminist Adrienne Rich has named as "compulsory heterosexuality").[11] Christian feminists have also struggled to show how often the church colludes with the state in shaping sexist, heterosexist, racist, and classist institutions and social policies that do violence to women, children, many men, and other creatures as well. The criminal justice system and various welfare-reforms are contemporary examples in the United States of the egregious systemic violence being waged against poor people and racial/ethnic minorities in general – and against poor women and racial/ethnic women in particular ways.

Perhaps the most effective effort among feminists in these last decades has been the movement against sexual violence – a movement, if you will, to bring justice to the heretofore private arena of gender relations and sexual activity. Here, as in the larger society, Christian feminists have been outspoken and have made some progress toward making the church as well as the state more accountable, legally as well as morally, for violence done to women and children.

Regardless of who we are and how "safe" we personally may feel in this moment, women are to some degree aware, unless we live with our heads in the sand, that our life together is being shaped constantly by rape, threat of rape, beating of women, intimidation by sexual threat, and the misogynist privileging of patriarchal religious and cultural traditions as a means of keeping women and sex under the control of men.

And that means us – us women, us men, and whatever sex we may desire with whomever. As a people – *we*, not just you and I as random individuals – are "contained" and organized in ways that promote patriarchal social relations via such institutions as marriage, tax structures, health care, and education. Moreover, in this period of world history, a global political economy is spinning our lives into realms of profit for the few and loss for the many far beyond most of our wildest dreams about what a "free economy" or "private enterprise" is or ought to be. As Christian feminist, social ethicist Beverly W. Harrison has noted, "Karl Marx may have overestimated communist workers' abilities to break the chains of alienation, but he was right about the *intrinsically* non-democratic, exploitative nature of capitalism."[12]

In this global context, misogyny (together with racism in its various tribal and ethnic forms, but especially white racism) provides much content to the violence that keeps the world in the hands of ruling-tribe males. We need to be clear that rape, wife-beating, and child-abuse are not social anomalies, not done primarily by wicked individuals who are out of social control and out of step with the rest of the world. In fact, men who rape and beat people, and women who act in similar ways, are very much in control of the world. The perpetuation of a culture of sexual violence, intimidation, and fear is a glue holding the world together at the turn of another millennium.

This point has been made repeatedly by feminists in religion and elsewhere: sexual violence is a staple of patriarchal capitalism throughout the world.[13] And whereas the extent of this problem cannot be over-stated – the problem is as pervasive, cross-cultural, and bad as women say it is; the Beijing conference of 1996 testified vividly to this – the solutions to this problem can be more or less creative, more or less liberating for greater or fewer numbers of women, men, and children. I believe that, while most Christian feminists have gotten the problem more or less right, we have gotten the solutions more or less wrong.

Christian feminists realize how deeply sexual violence has been rooted in the misogyny and homophobia of Christian life and teachings. Moreover, we see that the churches for too long have tried to govern gender relations and sexual activity as private "spiritual" matters, thereby keeping them out of the realm of public accountability. What we feminists on the whole have failed to realize, however, is that the long-term solution to the problem of abusive and violent gender relations will not be in tightening up and securing the rules that govern patriarchal power relations – in which social power is unequal, static, systemically diminishing of women (and others on the bottom of the power relation), and often actually violent to those on the bottom who try to rise up to share power.

The solution to this massive problem of sexual violence and abusive gender relations can be only through a thoroughgoing transformation of patriarchal power relations, including relational power in matters sexual. It is the urgent business of feminists, womanists, mujeristas, and other women-affirming religious leaders to be acting together as agents of this radical transformation. And it is this sense of mission that grounds this chapter.

RIGHT PROBLEM — SEXUAL VIOLENCE; WRONG SOLUTION — KEEPING THE SPLIT BETWEEN LOVE AND JUSTICE

In the context of endemic sexual violence, most feminists – many Christians and others – have concluded that, at least in a patriarchal world, which is the only one we have, men's sexual power is largely dangerous. These feminists have come to believe that, whether it is in the genes, learned through socialization, and/or bestowed as "privilege," men's sexual power can best be understood as the energy of sexism which drives lots of men to use their penises to subdue women, sometimes men, and sometimes children.

Think about it. The word "f—" doesn't really mean intercourse or sex; the energy and feel of this word makes it clear that, as a verb (and nowadays it is used as all figures of speech!), "f—!" means "submit!" It is an aggressive expression of domination, conquering, and subjugation, which conveys strong sexual meanings and the multiple, often conflicting, sexual feelings which are probably experienced by most people. Gay, lesbian, bisexual, heterosexual, one-gendered or transgendered, men or women, celibate or sexually active – we are all sexual, gendered beings in a heterosexist, patriarchal social world, and we are all schooled by life to respond in our bodies to strong messages of domination and submission.

This is why pornography, the intermingling of sex with violence, is fun for so many folks, including often – but by no means only – people who act in sexually violent and abusive ways. It is also why certain religions – Christianity chief among them in the United States – can become such powerful symbolic carriers of pornographic sexual fantasies, in which the Power of Love can so easily get twisted into a Violent Master. It is also why, generation upon generation, many Christians are more turned on by spiritualities of domination and submission rather than friendship and mutuality. How then does this state of affairs fuel, and deepen, the split between justice and love?

Many feminists in these times have come to understand the exercise of "sexual power" much like Western Christianity, especially since Augustine, has presented it. The experience of sexual power – lust, or concupiscence – is bad, dangerous, and to be avoided except in the most tightly constricted social relationships. Of course, for the church, the problem of sexual desire historically has been located in women. Refuting this misogynist and sexist claim, feminists such as Mary Daly, Andrea Dworkin, and John Stoltenburg, and Christians such as Marie Fortune have insisted that the problem with sexual power is that it has been shaped by patriarchal social relations. Because males carry the power in patriarchy, many of these feminists have located the problem of sexual power in men's social power. (Some feminists would probably suggest that sexually aggressive "butch" women share this problem.)

Thus, for most Christians, including many Christian feminists, sexual power is assumed to be potentially dangerous, often violent emotionally, if not physically, and in need of tight regulation. In these schemas, sex becomes almost a synonym for violence; justice requires the tight regulation of sex; and love is idealized as "something" (some commitment, affection, hope – or, for Christians, "God") that often has nothing to do with sex or violence and little to do with justice.

By equating most sex with violence and most sexual safety with regulation and constriction, many of the very feminists – secular and religious – who courageously called attention to the real problem of sexual violence in our time have seemed not to understand that sexual power is not always violent, even when it flings far outside boundaries set by Miss Manners. However nervous it may make us, sexual power-play between adults who *say* they are consensual is usually not a problem of violence with which we need to be concerned unless it is happening in our own beds and we do not like it.

For example, consider these situations: sex between an older man or woman and a younger man or woman, or sex between a person with institutional clout and someone "under" him or her, or sexual liaisons, gay or straight, that are energized by feelings and fantasies of control and submission. These situations can be lustful, playful, and intensely enjoyable rather than violent and abusive. When they are not violent or abusive, they are not problems to be solved by laws and litigation but rather are windows into the multiple psycho-spiritual and moral complexities of human being.

Just look at what was happening in the United States in the late 1990s as Americans (and the world) bore witness to the efforts of Grand

Inquisitor Kenneth Starr to rile folks up about the sexual mischief of President Bill Clinton. Responding to this state of affairs in an editorial opinion piece in the *New York Times*, Gloria Steinem suggested what I believe to be a fair line between that sexual activity which does not usually belong in courts of law or in professional codes of ethics, on the one hand, and acts of sexual violence, on the other. Steinem's point was brief: no means no; yes means yes.

Some of the clearest feminist voices on issues of sexual harassment have not been as commonsensical as Steinem's. For that reason – and despite the ongoing need still today for laws and sanctions against sexual violence and sexist public policy – we feminists and other justice-advocates in the U.S. took a strange detour somewhere in the last two decades of the twentieth century, and we stepped through a looking-glass onto a minefield, in which everything remotely sexy now threatened to blow up under us. In the realm of sexual harassment, feminists like Catherine McKinnon, Andrea Dworkin, and Marie Fortune began to equate all sex where there is even a hint of what McKinnon calls "unequal institutional power" with violent or abusive sex. This seems to me a doomed equation not because there may not often be some truth in it, but because it does not reflect the actual psychological, social, biological, political, or spiritual moorings of many (perhaps even most) peoples' experiences and patterns of sexual desire.

Until the Clinton scandal began to push us toward the ledge of this unreal and unworkable equation, I had feared that we were all in danger of being blown apart by the equations of sex, sexiness, rumors of sex, fears of sex, sex play, and sexual power with sexual violence and abuse. Some days I woke up thinking that we were heading back through history to an Inquisition in which, once more, church and state would be joining forces to blame sex and sexy people for the very evils being generated by the patriarchal and economic powerbrokers of church and state.

In locating abusive power relations so much in sexual activity and sexiness, we have been losing sight of the magnitude of the non-sexual abusive power in gender, race, and class relations in workplaces, schools, and other institutions. We have confused sexual behavior and gender discrimination in institutional situations. And whereas an unwelcome sexual proposition may be disgusting, all women and men have both a right and a responsibility to say yes or no or maybe. Sexual behavior may be sleazy, but should we be trying to judge legally or stop sexual interactions between adults who say they are mutually consenting in situations where job performance and the ambience of a healthy work-place are not being adversely affected? I think not.

The crisis in Washington reminded us of an even deeper spiritual malaise than even foolish sexual activity between consenting adults. It reminded us that in these times we are not as likely to be destroyed by unwanted sexual advances or sleazy sexual attitudes as we are by fear-based, mean-spirited, punitive public policies that cut no slack for human vulner-abilities or imperfections, questions or complexities, our own or those of others.

The Washington fiasco suggested that those who would tighten up our sex lives would set us against one another in order to save us from our own and others' frayed and ragged ways of being human. To me as a relational, sensual character, this is a contemporary image of Hell. As real and nasty as anything Dante dreamt up, it is a clean and orderly, neat and regulated way of occupying public space in which there is neither desire nor permission to make mistakes and learn from them, make amends or receive them, seek forgiveness or offer it in realms of intimacy, longing, and desire – the very stuff not only of sexuality but also of spirituality.

As I hurried through Harvard Square to and from meetings in Cam-bridge and Boston in these times, I could not help glancing occasionally at the wall around Harvard Yard and thinking of Canadian novelist Margaret Atwood's chilling futuristic vision in *The Handmaid's Tale*, in which social deviants like feminists and queers were hung from this very wall in order to build a right-thinking, right-acting society on the basis of strict gender conformity and zero-tolerance sex rules.

But I want to put the implications of this discussion beyond the arenas of consensual sex between adults and simply boorish sex into the realm of sexual abuse. By "abuse," I mean *violence*: coercion, intimidation, rape. We ought not to overlook or deny the pervasiveness of sexual violence in the warp and woof of patriarchal cultures and religion. I am suggesting that we will not get very far in either justice-making or love-making, even in the realm of sexual abuse, if we constrict ourselves tightly with rigid rules, expectations of sexual conformity, fear of litigation, and threat of punish-ment. We certainly can and – within reason and good common sense – ought to bring our criminal and civil justice systems to bear on abusive gender relations and violent sexual activity. But more than this, more than anything else, we need to be struggling to transform our system of justice and to radicalize the meanings of justice, including gender and sexual justice, at all levels of our life together. But how are we to do this? How can we actually live as agents of such radical social and personal transformation? The rest of this chapter is an exploration of this question.

THE EROTIC AS POWER AND THE LOVE OF GOD: BEYOND "JUSTICE" AND "LOVE" — HEALING THE SPLIT

On this question, we Christians, who have contributed so much to the split between "justice" and "love" in the West, have a particular responsibility for its healing. From a Christian religious perspective, I believe we need to root our understandings of both "justice" and "love" in an understanding of the love of God, however we may name this Sacred Power.

As a Christian priest and lesbian feminist theologian, I increasingly have come to understand and name the love of God as our "erotic power," and to believe that this naming of *eros* as sacred is a theologically creative, and theo-politically challenging, mode of participation in the processes of social change, healing, and liberation – and specifically of a sexually violent social order.

Let me summarize the problem and set some terms for a theological response. The convergence in our time of feminist claims of justice with an ideology crafted out of an equation of unequal sexual power relations with violence has generated a conundrum for those who hate violence, love justice and sex, and who often experience our most creative sexual energy through the struggle for mutuality in the context of unequal power relations – between, for example, men and women, older and younger adults, people of different tribes, cultures, abilities, or professional "locations." And these relations may be intensely sexual. I believe that the solution to this problem is for us to bring justice and love together so radically and so inextricably that the two are in fact one – and neither is what we ordinarily assume it to be in a post-modern world! Our popular, super-rational understanding of justice (the imposition of law and order) and our idealized notions of love (an act which "does no harm"[14]) must be transformed if we are to make justice that is loving and make love that is just.

What then are we talking about if, in the context of sexual behavior and gender relations, "justice" does not refer primarily to the redressing of relational wrongs through law and courts nor "love" to "danger-free" relational acts which embody both intimacy and a guarantee that harm will not be done?

Here is what the 1991 Report of the Presbyterian Church's Special Committee on Human Sexuality had to say about "justice-love or right-relation with self and others":[15]

We intentionally connect justice and love to emphasize that genuine caring for concrete human well-being is never content with a privatized, sentimentalized kind of loving, but rather demonstrates a devotion that enables persons and institutions to flourish in all their rich complexity. Such love, such justice, such passion for right-relatedness seeks to correct distorted relations between persons and groups and to generate relations of shared respect, shared power, and shared responsibility.[16]

Justice-love or right relation is *mutuality* in which both or all parties are called forth to come out into the fullness of their potential as friends and lovers of the world, of one another, and of the Spirit that moves through them, connecting each to all. But it is important that this justice-love not be idealized simply as a vision. We need rather to recognize it as the warp and woof of our lives insofar as we are involved in the struggle for right, mutual relation.

Concretely, this means that love-making, if it is just, requires more than deep personal attachment and even commitment. Love-making that is just is an embodied energy for relational *struggle* toward more mutuality with our lovers. Whether in the smaller or larger arenas of our lives, such struggle puts us in the midst of the relational ambiguities and complexities inherent in all power relations, from the most systemic to the very personal. No relationship in the real world is danger-free. Every real connection, like every real person, is at times broken, wounded, hurt, and even occasionally, I imagine, harmed by those whom we love and those who love us.

In a sexist, patriarchal society, those who harm others often are acting in violent ways – battering, raping, emotionally "torching" those whom they love. But just as often, I suspect, those who cause pain and bring harm to a relationship are not so much "abusing" or "violating" those whom they love. They are rather simply stumbling along, messing up, acting in confused and confusing, stupid or irresponsible ways, and generating relational crises.

The only way through these real life crises is to struggle with one another toward more fully mutual dynamics in which all parties can experience ourselves as more fully empowered – healed, if you will, to "pick up our beds and walk" (to cite an old Christian image of healing). Love-making that is just does not come with a promise to "do no harm," but lovers can promise to struggle toward this utopic possibility in a spirit of humility in which we hold ourselves and one another accountable for whatever hurt and damage may be generated by our own frayed sensibilities and flawed behavior. None of us can do this without adequate community support – something that most people in this society do not have and which, therefore, we need to be building as foundational to the work of justice-love.

It is true that justice-making, if it is loving, requires more than redressing wrong relation where there has been wounding or betrayal. Justice-making that is rooted in love is never simply about litigation and punishment. Whether in the realm of social justice and political revolution or in the more personal realms of intimacy, justice-making involves struggling systemically for right mutual relation, in which every party in the transaction can be empowered in some way – those redressing the wrongs they have done, those making amends, as well as those who have been victimized, wronged. Such advocacy is a basis of strong community.

The justice system in our society is fastened in the assumption that we no longer have community and, thus, that we can no longer give one another much common space or permission for such love, mutuality, or humility. Wrongdoers are advised by lawyers not to apologize to those whom they have wronged, since an apology can be taken legally as an admission of guilt. Victims of violence seldom are encouraged to imagine, much less seek, any sort of shared healing with those who have violated them. In matters of sexual violence and gender abuse, there is a widespread assumption these days among victims and their advocates that the less contact people have with their abusers, the healthier they can become; and the more the abuser is punished, the greater the justice will be.

I am not suggesting that violent men and women should not be held accountable and punished for the harm they do. Most often they should be, and we need to see to it that they are. This is something the justice system, because it is sexist and because most victims of abuse are women and children, does not do consistently or effectively. I am suggesting that the reason the justice system is failing everybody – victims and perpetrators alike – is because it is founded on adversarial rather than mutual relation. Whereas adversarial dynamics make us enemies and teach us to hate each other, mutual relation is rooted in an assumption that we human beings are basically good and that, spiritually, our purpose in life is to struggle with each other toward sparking this goodness among, between, and within us all.

Of course this is not easy. In fact, it is a daunting possibility, and all the more so because mutuality is radically counter-cultural. It flies smack in the face of the dominant political and economic culture in which, with every breath, we learn fear and, with it, greed, competition, and adversarial social relations. What then can we do about this state of affairs? Because the crisis I have been describing – sexual violence and our failure to address it creatively – is a spiritual crisis, one of our primary responsibilities as religious leaders is to generate creative, liberating spiritual responses to it.

When *Touching Our Strength* was published in 1989, some of my students were upset with me. "How can you make these strong affirmations of erotic power in the context of such a sexually violent social order as ours?" they asked me. As always, I learned much from my students, including ways that I might have been clearer in what I wrote. More than anything, these students and others have led me over the last decade to see more clearly that, precisely because the world we know *is* so terribly and pervasively violent, we must find responses that are themselves more radically transformative of our lives, and our life together, than what we have come up with so far. Otherwise, the sexual violence and gender abuse fastened in the patriarchal split between love and justice will grow only deeper, and our lives will be ever more split between idealized notions of "love" and harsh, adversarial images of "justice."

I like the concept of "erotic power" as the sacred energy of justice-love for several reasons. First, it shocks our feminist sensibilities in a sexually violent social order to think of *eros* as a sacred, liberating, healing resource. For many of us, the experience of erotic power as sacred gives us not only a shock but, in Sallie McFague's words, a "shock of recognition," suggesting that we have been here before. Somehow we know where we are.[17] The very notion of *eros* as a good, creative energy pushes us beyond where most of us are comfortable going. Ethics and theology should not, of course, make us comfortable but rather should challenge us to wrestle with complexity.

Second, the image of erotic power as the love of God denotes the deep truth that our sacred power is our yearning for connection in the cosmos, in our communities, in our work and love; and that this yearning, this *eros*, is sacred, an image of the Divine. Christians and others who historically have divided love into different kinds – *agape, philia, eros* – have done exactly what most contemporary feminists in religion have done: perpetuated a false split between an idealized "love" (*agape*, the love of God, if you will) that does no harm and the "love" (*eros*, or sexual love) that messes up badly! I believe it is important that we who would challenge this split help each other learn to see, experience, believe in, and understand the love of God as the very heart and essence of *eros* rather than its foil.

Third, a non-idealized understanding of erotic power as a positive, creative energy for healing may help us begin to envision and try ways of building a more fully just world than we will ever accomplish through the courts of law as they currently function. A non-idealized understanding of *eros*, love, and sexuality might help transform the justice system in several ways. By demystifying sex and sexual abuse and bringing it into the non-idealized realm of regular old human interaction, transgression, and violation, we would take some of the steam out of the litigation business and relieve lots of lawyers of their need to build their lives on the bodies of victims and perpetrators of sexual sins and crimes. More fundamentally, by pulling the rug out from under the adversarial system of justice, we in the United States would be reconstructing a foundation of our national heritage, in which "liberty and justice for all" might begin to represent more images of friendship, hope, and cooperation than of autonomy and animosity.

Fourth, the experience of erotic power as the love of God, as we take it in and feel it and know it in our bones and genitals and skin and hearts, becomes our mightiest weapon in defending ourselves and others against the fear which is our deadliest foe in the struggle against sexual violence and abusive gender relations. Like the mythological Amazon warriors, we can indeed draw strength and courage from the ground we share, from one another's well-being, from our own and others' passion for justice, and from knowing deeply in our bodyselves that we are not alone but rather are spiritual heirs of an ongoing struggle which is never lost – and which, in fact, is won again and again in every "moment" in which our love-making is just and our justice-making rich with compassion. In such knowledge, our fear can and does give way.

Fifth, our erotic power is the root of our capacity both to envision community and to build it as a life-project. We need to realize that while white Christians talk about "community" all the time, it seems the more we talk about it, the less we have it or even know what we are talking about. What we do know, we white Christians and many others in the United States today, is that we miss community. We may never have known it really, community, but we know we are missing out on a primary resource not only for survival but moreover for what womanist theologian Delores Williams calls "a quality of life,"[18] the enjoyment of life that makes it worthwhile.

But how do we go about building community? I offer only a few suggestions here. First, community building requires making time in a world in which our time is being gobbled up curiously by gadgets that we thought would save time. Second, it means finding or creating and sharing projects that are important to us and "do-able" in terms of size and time. Such a project can be as simple as learning to drum or as complex as taking on the death penalty or managed care, but it means coming together regularly and spending time with one another.

Third, community building often means making solidarity with diverse people around projects or political work. It means navigating differences of opinion, perspective, and personality. It means loosening up our own control needs – a mightily erotic project for many of us – since being together with others means having less control over our own time, space, and agendas than when we are alone. A durable, good-humored patience is vital to community-building. I do not think we can be patient with ourselves or each other unless we are making solidarity with one another – learning to listen, "hearing one another to speech,"[19] and experiencing a shared energy for healing social and personal wounds, whether we are six or eighty-six.

And fourth, community building is steeped in relational spirituality, whether or not we use spiritual language. By "relational spirituality," I refer to the assumption that coming together not only is good for us and others but, in some way, empowers each of us to be "more" than we are alone. Many people today yearn for this depth of connectedness, to know that we are not alone, not only to take on various projects but moreover to share our strength, hope, and experience with others. This, I believe, more than even the massive problem of addiction in our society, is what the proliferation of "Twelve Step" programs has been about.

STAYING POWER[20]

Finally, I want to say a little about how we "keep on keepin' on" – our staying power. This puts another spin on the image of erotic power as a creative energy that reinvents itself, a bottomless pool of resourcefulness precisely because it belongs to no one. When I am tired or spent, I can rest, and you can step forward, because the power belongs to no one of us. It is no one's possession. It is an energy we generate together or not at all, and because it is shared, it is sacred. "In the beginning is the relation,"[21] and in the relation is the power, now and for ever.

And in the relation, in the power, in the justice-love, there is no room for posturing or getting stuck either in self-righteousness or victimization, which is why we must help one another learn how to struggle toward making mutual relation even in the context of sexual violence – *especially* in the context of sexual violence. But please be clear that this does *not* mean now or ever that women should stay in abusive relationships. For a woman to do this is dangerous, it is usually damaging, and, more often than many realize, it is deadly for women. Where there are other options – and we should all be helping create them – for a woman to remain in a violent relationship is the wrong thing to do. We ought never to stay where we are likely to be slaughtered unless we are reasonably clear that we can protect one another and others who are vulnerable.

And yet the struggle for mutual relation, which is fueled by erotic power, requires us to hold the larger picture in view – and to stay in it. This does *not* mean staying in the particular relationship in which our lives (bodies or souls) are in danger but rather staying in the larger picture – in life and in the struggle for justice for all raped, battered, and other violated women, children, and men.

Staying in life, in struggle, and for some of us women, staying in patriarchal religion, we act as agents of transformation – reimagining God as Mother, priest as woman, earth as sacred, and so forth. And we ourselves are transformed through our engagement with the sexism, heterosexism, racism, and other structures of violence and evil that tear at us. For some Christian and post-christian women, to stay in the church is to make peace with the oppressor, to be trapped in an abusive relation. It is too high a price to pay. For others of us, to stay in the church is to refuse to make peace with the oppressor and to resist the violence of patriarchal religion. The latter choice, like all justice-making, requires community.

In or out of patriarchal religion, our staying power in life and struggle enables us to redeem ourselves and one another from even the most terribly violent moments of our common life and individual journeys. Our power to stay in the struggle makes us more trustworthy advocates of children, the earth, the animals, one another, and ourselves. For it deepens and secures our roots in the struggle for an uncompromised justice. The more deeply rooted we become in this radical struggle – which truly is our hope – the better able we are to accompany violent men and women on the hard pilgrimage through the repentance and conversion that involves changed behavior and yearns toward transformed lives. And more than many of us dare admit, even to ourselves, we sometimes *are* these people who violate the possibilities for mutual relation in larger and smaller ways.

As broken, difficult, sometimes violent, people and as agents of liberation, we can invite one another to share the creative work of social and personal healing. Always flawed and often confused, we can keep searching for ways to embody the erotic power which fuels our liberation from such captors as the consumerist greed for more and more of whatever we may enjoy, be it booze or beauty, money or food, fancy clothes or status, control or sex.

Embodying *eros* as friends, companions, colleagues, and sometimes sexual lovers, we can participate in the ongoing redemption of creation – and of the Creator as well – from the powers of evil which thrive in unchanging power relations of domination and control. We make justice not simply as the courts may provide but as we sisters and brothers can generate through our erotic yearning for mutual relation and our commitments to it as both destination and journey.

NOTES

1. Carter Heyward, *Touching Our Strength: The Erotic as Power and the Love of God* (San Francisco: Harper, 1989), pp. 1–2.

2. In addition to *Touching Our Strength,* see my earlier book, *The Redemption of God: A Theology of Mutual Relation* (Lanham, MD: University Press of America, 1982); Virginia Ramey Mollenkott, *Godding: Human Responsibility and the Bible* (New York: Crossroad, 1987); James B. Nelson and Sandra Longfellow, ed., *Sexuality and the Sacred: Sources for Theological Reflection* (London: Mowbrays, 1994); Anne Bathurst Gilson, *Eros Breaking Free: Interpreting Sexual Theo-Ethics* (Cleveland: Pilgrim, 1995); Marvin M. Ellison, *Sexual Justice* (Louisville: Westminster/John Knox, 1996); Daniel T. Spencer, *Gay and Gaia: Ethics, Ecology, and the Erotic* (Cleveland: Pilgrim, 1996); and Melanie S. Morrison, *The Politics of Sin: Practical Theological Issues in Lesbian Feminist Perspective* (Groningen, Netherlands: Rijksuniversiteit Groningen, 1998).

3. Audre Lorde, "Uses of the Erotic: The Erotic as Power," in *Sister Outsider* (Trumansburg, NY: Crossing, 1984), pp. 53–59.

4. Ibid., p. 55.

5. Ibid.

6. Ibid., p. 56.

7. The theme "power in relation" runs through several of my books, in particular: *The Redemption of God: A Theology of Mutual Relation* (1982); *Our Passion for Justice: Images of Power, Sexuality, and Liberation* (New York: Pilgrim, 1984); *Touching Our Strength: The Erotic as Power and the Love of God* (1989); *When Boundaries Betray Us: Beyond Illusions of What Is Ethical in Therapy and Life* (1993), 2nd edition (Cleveland: Pilgrim, forthcoming); and *Staying Power: Reflections on Gender, Justice, and Compassion* (Cleveland: Pilgrim, 1995). While I have used this exact term, "power in relation," as a way of speaking of God, a number of theologians from whom I learn so much have similar understandings of God, power, and relation. I am thinking of such theologians as Dorothee Soelle, Tom

F. Driver, Delores S. Williams, Rita Nakashima Brock, Anne Bathurst Gilson, and Kwok Pui-lan.

8. Joseph Runzo makes this point in the opening chapter of this volume.

9. Crediting Ellison in his book *Sexual Justice* (1996), Karen Lebacqz has emphasized this in her chapter.

10. Samuel Laeuchli, *Power and Sexuality* (Philadelphia: Temple University Press, 1970).

11. Adrienne Rich, "Compulsory Heterosexuality and Lesbian Existence," *Signs* 5, 4 (1980), pp. 631–660.

12. In conversation with me. Beverly W. Harrison, the Carolyn Williams Beaird Professor of Christian Ethics at Union Theological Seminary in New York City, is a renowned feminist social ethicist and critic of "capitalist spirituality." Her writings include *Our Right to Choose: A New Ethic of Abortion* (Boston: Beacon, 1983), which will soon be published in second edition with a new introduction; and *Making the Connections: Essays in Feminist Social Ethics* (Boston: Beacon, 1985), in which she addresses issues of sex, power, and God.

13. Christian and other feminist theologians who have addressed the problem of sexual violence in its massive proportions include Joanne Carlson Brown and Carole Bohn, ed., *Christianity, Patriarchy, and Abuse* (Cleveland: Pilgrim, 1989); Marie M. Fortune, *Sexual Violence: The Unmentionable Sin* (New York: Pilgrim, 1983); Delores S. Williams, *Sisters in the Wilderness: The Challenge of Womanist God-Talk* (Maryknoll, NY: Orbis, 1993); Marjorie Suchocki, *The Fall to Violence: Original Sin in Relational Theology* (New York: Continuum, 1994); Carol J. Adams and Marie M. Fortune, ed., *Violence Against Women and Children: A Theological Sourcebook in the Christian Tradition* (New York: Continuum, 1995); and Rita Nakashima Brock and Susan Brooks Thistlethwaite, *Casting Stones: Prostitution and Liberation in Asia and the United States* (Minneapolis: Fortress, 1996).

14. Marie M. Fortune, *Love Does No Harm: Sexual Ethics for the Rest of Us* (New York: Continuum, 1995).

15. "Presbyterians and Human Sexuality, the 203rd General Assembly (1991) Response to the Report of the Special Committee on Human Sexuality, Including a Minority Report" (Louisville, KY: Office of the General Assembly, 1991), p. 7.

16. Ibid.

17. See Sallie McFague, *The Body of God: An Ecological Theology* (Minneapolis: Fortress, 1993) [a portion of which also appears in Joseph Runzo and Nancy M. Martin, ed., *The Meaning of Life in the World Religions* (Oxford: Oneworld, 1999) by permission of Fortress/Augsburg Press], and *Super, Natural Christians: How We Should Love Nature* (Minneapolis: Fortress, 1997).

18. Williams, *Sisters in the Wilderness*.

19.   Nelle Morton, *The Journey is Home* (Boston: Beacon, 1985).
20.   Heyward, *Staying Power: Reflections on Gender, Justice, and Compassion*.
21.   Martin Buber, *I and Thou* (NewYork: Scribner's, 1958).

SUGGESTED FURTHER READING

PART I: LOVE AND SEX IN THE CONTEXT OF RELIGION

Beck, C. J. *Everyday Zen: Love and Work*. San Francisco, Harper San Francisco, 1989

Black, J. and Green, A. *Gods, Demons and Symbols of Ancient Mesopotamia*. Austin, University of Texas Press, 1995

Bloch, A. and Bloch, C. *The Song of Songs: A New Translation*. Berkeley, University of California Press, 1995

Boyarin, D. *Carnal Israel: Reading Sex in Talmudic Culture*. Berkeley, University of California Press, 1993

Chopel, G. and Hopkins, J. *Tibetan Arts of Love*. Ithaca, Snow Lion Publications, 1992

Eilberg-Schwartz, H., ed. *People of the Body: Jews and Judaism from an Embodied Perspective*. Albany, State University of New York Press, 1992

Halperin, D. M., Winkler, J. J. and Zeitlin, F. I., ed. *Before Sexuality: The Construction of Erotic Experience in the Ancient Greek World*. Princeton, Princeton University Press, 1990

Jantzen, G. *God's World. God's Body*. Philadelphia, Westminster Press, 1984

Keuls, E.C. *The Reign of the Phallus: Sexual Politics in Ancient Athens*. Berkeley, University of California Press, 1993

Kinsley, D. *The Goddesses' Mirror: Visions of the Divine from East to West*. Albany, State University of New York, 1989

LaFleur, W. R. *Freaks and Philosophers: Minding the Body in Medieval Japan*. New York, Zone Books, 1999

— *The Karma of Words: Buddhism and the Literary Arts in Medieval Japan*. Berkeley, University of California Press, 1983

— *Liquid Life: Abortion and Buddhism in Japan*. Princeton, Princeton University Press, 1992

Lucie-Smith, E. *Sexuality in Western Art*. New York, Thames and Hudson, 1991

Lynch, O. M., ed. *Divine Passions: The Social Construction of Emotion in India*. Delhi, Oxford University Press, 1990

McFague, S. *Models of God: Theology for an Ecological, Nuclear Age*. Philadelphia, Fortress Press, 1987

Parratt, S., N., and Parratt, J. *The Pleasing of the Gods*. New Delhi, Vikas Publishing House, 1997

Parrinder, G. *Avatar and Incarnation*. Oxford, Oneworld, 1997

Posner, R. A. *Sex and Reason*. Cambridge, Harvard University Press, 1992

Quirke, S. *Ancient Egyptian Religion*. New York, Dover Publications, 1992

Rawson, P. *The Art of Tantra*. London, Thames and Hudson, 1993

Roberts, A. *Hathor Rising*. Rochester, Inner Traditions International, 1995

Runzo, J. "Eros and Meaning in Life and Religion," in *The Meaning of Life in the World Religions*, ed. J. Runzo and N. M. Martin. Oxford, Oneworld, 1999

Scott, K. and Warren, M., ed. *Perspectives on Marriage: A Reader*. New York, Oxford University Press, 1993

Solomon, R. C. and Higgins, K. M., ed. *The Philosophy of (Erotic) Love*. Lawrence, University Press of Kansas, 1991

Stewart, R. M., ed. *Philosophical Perspectives on Sex and Love*. New York, Oxford University Press, 1995

Tannahill, R. *Sex in History*. Scarborough House, 1992

Westheimer, R. K. and Mark, J. *Heavenly Sex: Sexuality in the Jewish Tradition*. New York, Continuum Publishing Company, 1996

PART II: LOVE AND RELIGION

Barks, C., trans. *The Essential Rumi*. San Francisco, HarperSanFrancisco, 1995

Biale, D. *Eros and the Jews: From Biblical Israel to Contemporary America*. Berkeley, University of California Press, 1997

Brummer, V. *The Model of Love*. Cambridge, Cambridge University Press, 1993

Danielou, Alain. *Gods of Love and Ecstasy: The Traditions of Shiva and Dionysus*. Rochester, Inner Traditions International, 1984

St. Francis de Sales. *Introduction to the Devout Life*. Trans. J. K. Ryan, Garden City, New York. Image Books, 1966

Hanh, T. N. *Cultivating the Mind of Love: The Practice of Looking Deeply in the Mahayana Buddhist Tradition*. Berkeley, Parallax Press, 1996

Hawley, J. S. and Juergensmeyer, M. *Songs of the Saints of India*. Oxford, Oxford University Press, 1988

— and Wulff, D. M., ed. *The Divine Consort: Radha and the Goddesses of India*. Boston: Beacon Press, 1986

Hopkins, J. *The Tantric Distinction: a Buddhist's Reflections on Compassion and Emptiness*. Rev. ed. Boston, Wisdom Publications, 1999

St. John of the Cross. *Living Flame of Love*. Trans. E. A. Peers. Garden City, New York, Image Books, 1962

Martin, N. M. *"Love and Longing in Devotional Hinduism"* in *The Meaning of Life in the World Religions*, ed. J. Runzo and N. M. Martin. Oxford, Oneworld, 1999

Moyne, J. and Barks, C. *Unseen Rain: Quatrains of Rumi*. Putney, Threshold Books, 1986

Nicholson, R. A. *Rumi: Poet and Mystic*. Oxford, Oneworld, 1996

Ramanujan, A. K. *Hymns for the Drowning: Poems for Visnu by Nammalvar*. New Delhi, Penguin Books, 1993

— *Speaking of Śiva*. London, Penguin Books, 1973

Scholem, G. *Major Trends in Jewish Mysticism*. New York, Schocken Press, 1941

— ed. *Zohar: The Book of Splendor*. New York: Schocken Press, 1963

Siegel, L. *Fires of Love – Waters of Peace*. Honolulu, University of Hawaii Press, 1983

Smedes, L. B. *Love Within Limits: A Realist's View of I Corinthians 13*. Grand Rapids, Wm. B. Eerdmans, 1978

Steegmann, M. G., trans. *The Book of Divine Consolation of the Blessed Angela of Foligno*. New York, Cooper Square Publishers, 1966

St. Theresa of Avila. *The Autobiography of St. Theresa of Avila*. Trans. E. A. Peers. Garden City, New York, Image Books, 1960

— *Interior Castle*. Trans. E.A. Peers. Garden City, New York, Image Books, 1961

Werner, K., ed. *Love Divine: Studies in Bhakti and Devotional Mysticism*. Richmond, Surrey, Curzon Press, 1993

Zaehner, R.C. *Hindu and Muslim Mysticism*. Oxford, Oneworld, 1960/1994

PART III: GENDER AND RELIGION

Ahmed, L. *Women and Gender in Islam*. New Haven and London, Yale University Press, 1992

Brown, K. M. *Mama Lola: A Vodou Priestess in Brooklyn*. Berkeley, University of California Press, 1991

Bynum, C. W. *Holy Feast and Holy Fast: The Religious Significance of Food to Medieval Women*. Berkeley, University of California Press, 1987

Cabezon, J. I., ed. *Buddhism, Sexuality, and Gender*. Albany, State University of New York Press, 1992

Cahill, S. E. *Transcendence and Divine Passion: The Queen Mother of the West in Medieval China*. Stanford, Stanford University Press, 1993

Christ, C. and Plaskow, J., ed. *Womanspirit Rising: A Feminist Reader in Religion*. New York, Harper & Row, 1979

Cooey, P. M., Eakin, W. R., and McDaniel, J.B., ed. *After Patriarchy: Feminist Transformations of the World Religions*. New York, Orbis Books, 1991

Daly, M. *The Church and the Second Sex*. New York, Harper & Row, 1964

Dinnerstein, D. *The Mermaid and the Minotaur: Sexual Arrangements and the Human Malaise*. New York, Harper & Row, 1977

Erndl, K. M. *Victory to the Mother: The Hindu Goddess of Northwest India in Myth, Ritual, and Symbol*. New York and Oxford, Oxford University Press, 1993

Fiorenza, E. S. *In Memory of Her: A Feminist Theological Reconstruction of Christian Origins*. New York, Crossroad, 1989

Gilligan, C. *In a Different Voice*. Cambridge, Harvard University Press, 1982

Haddad, Y. Y. and Findly, E. B., ed. *Women, Religion, and Social Change*. New York, State University of New York Press, 1985

— and Esposito, J., ed. *Islam, Gender, and Social Change*. New York, Oxford University Press, 1998

Hawley, J. S. "Images of Gender in the Poetry of Krishna," in *Gender and Religion*, ed. C. W. Bynum, S. Harrell, and P. Richman. Boston, Beacon Press, 1986

— *Krishna, the Butter Thief*. Princeton, Princeton University Press, 1983

— and Wulff, D. M., ed. *Devi: Goddesses of India*. Berkeley, University of California Press, 1994

Jaini, P. S. *Gender and Salvation: Jaina Debates on the Spiritual Liberation of Women*. Berkeley, University of California Press, 1991

King, K., ed. *Images of the Feminine in Gnosticism*. Philadelphia, Fortress Press, 1988

— ed. *Women and Goddess Traditions in Antiquity and Today*. Minneapolis, Fortress Press, 1997

King, U. *Women and Spirituality, Voices of Protest and Promise*. London, Macmillan Education, 1989

Laqueur, T. *Making Sex: Body and Gender from the Greeks to Freud*. Cambridge, Harvard University Press, 1990

Lerner, G. *The Creation of Patriarchy*. New York, Oxford University Press, 1986

Mahowald, M. B., ed. *Philosophy of Women*. Indianapolis, Hackett, 1978

Mookerjee, A. *Kali: The Feminine Force*. London, Thames and Hudson, 1995

Mukta, P. *Upholding the Common Life: The Community of Mirabai*. Delhi, Oxford University Press, 1994

Ochs, C. *Women and Spirituality*, second edition. Lantham, Rowman and Littlefield, 1997

O'Flaherty, W. D. *Women, Androgynes, and other Mythical Beasts*. Chicago and London, University of Chicago Press, 1980

O'Neill, M. *Women Speaking, Women Listening: Women in Interreligious Dialogue*. New York, Orbis Books, 1990

Rosen, S. J., ed. *Vaiṣṇavi: Women and the Worship of Krishna*. Delhi, Motilal Banarsidass, 1996

Ruether, R. R *Sexism and God-Talk: Toward a Feminist Theology*. Boston, Beacon Press, 1983

Schimmel, A. *My Soul is a Woman: The Feminine in Islam*. New York, Continuum, 1997

Sered, S. S. *Priestess, Mother, Sacred Sister*. New York and Oxford, Oxford University Press, 1994

Sharma, A., ed. *Religion and Women*. Albany, State University of New York Press, 1994

— ed. *Today's Woman in World Religions*. Albany, State University of New York Press, 1994

— ed. *Women in World Religions*. Albany, State University of New York Press, 1987

— and Young, K., ed. *The Annual Review of Women in World Religions*, volumes 1–4. Albany, State University of New York Press, 1990–1996

— and Young, K., ed. *Feminism and World Religions*. Albany, State University of New York Press, 1999

Smith, M. *Rabi'a: The Life and Work of Rabi'a and other Women Mystics in Islam*. Oxford, Oneworld, 1994

Spretnak, C., ed. *The Politics of Women's Spirituality: Essays on the Rise of Spiritual Power Within the Feminist Movement*. New York, Anchor/Doubleday, 1982

Stowasser, B. F. *Women in the Qur'an, Traditions, and Interpretation*. New York, Oxford University Press, 1994

Torjesen, K. J. *When Women Were Priests*. San Francisco, Harper San Francisco, 1993

Tsomo, K. L. *Sisters in Solitude: Two Traditions of Buddhist Monastic Ethics for Women*. Albany, State University of New York Press, 1996

Wire, A. *The Corinthian Women Prophets: A Reconstruction Through Paul's Rhetoric*. Minneapolis, Fortress Press, 1990

Young, K. and Sharma, A. *Images of the Feminine – Mythic, Philosophical and Human – in the Buddhist, Hindu, and Islamic Traditions: a Bibliography of Women in India*. Chico, New Horizons Press, 1974

Young, S. *Encyclopedia of Women and World Religion*. New York, Macmillan Reference, 1999

Zimbalist, R. M. and Lamphere, L., ed. *Women, Culture, and Society*. Stanford, Stanford University Press, 1974

PART IV: SEXUAL LOVE, ETHICS AND RELIGION

Belliotti, R. A. *Good Sex: Perspectives on Sexual Ethics*. Lawrence, University Press of Kansas, 1993

Cahill, L. *Sex, Gender and Christian Ethics*. Cambridge and New York, Cambridge University Press, 1996

Ellison, M. *Erotic Justice: A Liberating Ethic of Sexuality*. Louisville, Westminster/John Knox Press, 1996

Gudorf, C. E. *Body, Sex, and Pleasure: Reconstructing Christian Sexual Ethics.* Cleveland, Pilgrim Press, 1995

Hawley, J. S., ed. *Fundamentalism and Gender.* New York, Oxford University Press, 1994

Heyward, C. *Our Passion for Justice: Images of Power, Sexuality, and Liberation.* Cleveland, Pilgrim Press, 1984

— *Touching Our Strength: The Erotic as Power and the Love of God.* San Francisco, HarperSanFrancisco, 1989

Hopkins, J. *Sex, Orgasm, and the Mind of Clear Light: The Sixty-Four Arts of Gay Male Love.* Berkeley, North Atlantic, 1998

Kellenberger, J. *Relationship Morality.* University Park, Pennsylvania State University Press, 1995

Klein, A. C. *Meeting the Great Bliss Queen: Buddhists, Feminists, and the Art of the Self.* Boston, Beacon Press, 1995

Lebacqz, K. and Barton, R. G. *Sex in the Parish.* Louisville, Westminster, 1991

Leupp, G. P. *Male Colors: The Construction of Homosexuality in Tokugawa Japan.* Berkeley, University of California Press, 1997

May, L., Strikwerda, R., and Hopkins, P. D., ed. *Rethinking Masculinity: Philosophical Explorations in Light of Feminism.* Lantham, Rowman and Littlefield, 1996

Nelson, J. B. *Body Theology.* Louisville, Westminster, 1992

— *The Intimate Connection: Male Sexuality, Masculine Spirituality.* Louisville, Westminster, 1988.

— and Longfellow, S. P., ed. *Sexuality and the Sacred: Sources for Theological Reflection.* Louisville, Westminster/John Knox Press, 1994

Nye, R. A., ed. *Sexuality.* Oxford, Oxford University Press, 1999.

Parrinder, G. *Sexual Morality in the World's Religions.* Oxford, Oneworld, 1996

Seow, C-L., ed. *Homosexuality and Christian Community.* Louisville, Westminster/John Knox Press, 1996

Shaw, M. *Passionate Enlightenment.* Princeton, Princeton University Press, 1994

Steinberg, L. *The Sexuality of Christ in Renaissance Art and in Modern Oblivion.* Chicago, University of Chicago Press, 1996

Stevens, J. *Lust For Enlightenment: Buddhism and Sex.* Boston, Shambhala, 1990

Thatcher, A. and Stuart, E., ed. *Christian Perspectives on Sexuality and Gender.* Grand Rapids, Eerdmans, 1996

Wojtyla, K. (Pope John Paul II). *Love and Responsibility.* New York, Farrar, Straus and Giroux, 1981

INDEX

Page numbers in *italics* refer to plates